GERMAN PROTESTANTISM SINCE LUTHER

The Church Architecture of Protestantism: An Historical and Constructive Study. One hundred illustrations. (T. and T. Clark, Edinburgh; Scribners, New York, 1934.)

Edward Irving and His Circle, including some Consideration of 'Tongues' Movement in the Light of Modern Psychology. Illustrated. (Jas. Clarke, London, 1937.)

The Churches Pictured by Punch: Side-lights on Modern Church History, 1844-1944. Illustrated. (Epworth Press, London, 1947.)

Story of American Protestantism. Three Centuries of Christian Work and Witness. (Oliver and Boyd, Edinburgh; The Beacon Press, Boston, Mass., 1950.)

The Churches in English Fiction. A survey of the social scene in its religious aspects, from Jane Austen to Compton Mackenzie. (Edgar Backus, Leicester, 1949.)

GERMAN PROTESTANTISM SINCE LUTHER

BY

ANDREW LANDALE DRUMMOND

Ph.D., B.D.(Edin.), S.T.M.(Hartford Theological
Seminary, U.S.A.)

The historian is a prophet with his face turned backwards.
—FRIEDRICH VON SCHLEGEL.

Great men condemn the world to the task of explaining them.
—G. W. F. HEGEL.

LONDON : THE EPWORTH PRESS

PUBLISHED BY

THE EPWORTH PRESS
(FRANK H. CUMBERS)
25–35 CITY ROAD, LONDON, E.C.1

*

New York . *Toronto*
Melbourne . *Capetown*

*

SET IN MONOTYPE BASKERVILLE AND PRINTED IN
GREAT BRITAIN BY THE CAMELOT PRESS LTD.
LONDON AND SOUTHAMPTON

CONTENTS

Part One

CHURCH AND RELIGION

PREFACE

DURING the spring of 1928 I had the privilege of visiting Reformation shrines—Eisenach, Wittenberg, Augsburg. As a student of the late Professor James Mackinnon, the greatest British authority on Luther, I was well prepared for this pilgrimage. At Marburg I was shown the signature of Patrick Hamilton, the Scottish martyr who was present at the opening of this Evangelical University in 1527. The historic *Schloss* on the heights, which recalls Stirling Castle, was the scene of the memorable eucharistic debate between Luther and Zwingli. Four centuries have elapsed since then, but even Protestant Christendom is still divided by different views of the Lord's Supper.

'Now that you are in a Lutheran country', wrote Lord Chesterfield to his son in 1774, 'go to their churches, observe the manner of their public worship, attend to their preaching. Inform yourself of their Church government, whether it resides in the Sovereign, or in Consistories and Synods. Whence arises the maintenance of their Clergy, whether from tithes, as in England, or from voluntary contributions, or from pensions from the State. Do the same when you are in Roman Catholic countries. . . .'

Chesterfield's assignment seemed relevant to a post-graduate theological student and blended with artistic interests. One day I stood in the great square at Dresden and surveyed the Baroque splendour of Bähn's octagonal *Frauenkirche*—that 'religious opera house' seating seven thousand persons, so massive externally, so gay internally with its tiers of swelling balconies in white-and-gold, its wedding-cake altar backed by towering organ-pipes. Historic imagination visualized the *Frauenkirche* as it was two centuries ago when Canaletto painted Dresden; that church was a perfect symbol of the social splendour which seemed so permanent. 'Alas!' commented Wesley on a visit to Dresden in 1738; 'where will all these things appear, when "the earth and the works thereof shall be burned up"?' Young Goethe ascended the dome of the *Frauenkirche* to view the city devastated by war; the sexton assured him that the fabric was bomb-proof. In 1928 the colossal Baroque edifice remained, but only as the monument of a vanished social order. Who could foresee that twenty years later even the outer shell of past grandeur would be reduced to rubble, with Russians occupying the ruins of Dresden? But in front of the church the name Luther still stands out clearly on the base of his blitzed statue—a symbol of hope.

On my return from Germany I often wished that someone would bridge the gulf that separated Luther (in the minds of British and American readers) from the Lutheranism of the Fatherland after the First World War. Dr. Henry Grey Graham's 'St. Giles Lecture' on the Lutheran Church (1884) indicated that the history of German Protestantism was much more interesting than was generally supposed. My mind turned to the possibility of writing a book on the subject. The more I read, the more formidable appeared the obstacles. I received much kindly encouragement, however, from Professor Lang of Halle, Dr. Keller of Zurich, and the late Dr. J. R. Fleming, the Church historian of modern Scotland. Then came the Second World War. The struggles of the Confessing Church demonstrated the vitality of the German Evangelicals; the Reformation was, after all, not in vain. Post-war interest in the future of Germany and social history suggested that a number of general readers might welcome such a book as *German Protestantism Since Luther*.

My cordial thanks are due to the Scottish National Library, Edinburgh; to Professor G. H. C. Macgregor, Glasgow; to Dr. Mitchell Hunter, Miss E. R. Leslie, M.A., and the Rev. J. B. Primrose, M.A., of New College Library, Edinburgh; to Mr. W. R. Aitken, M.A., F.L.A., of the County Library, Perthshire; to Mr. G. F. Cunningham, B.A., Alva; to the Scottish Central Library, Dunfermline, and the Central Library, London, for going out of their way to procure for me German books difficult to obtain in this country. I recall with pleasure illuminating discussions with fellow-students at Marburg, particularly the Rev. E. A. Payne, B.D., B.Litt., now Tutor at Regent's Park College, Oxford. And I am indebted to my friend, Dr. T. Crouther Gordon, D.F.C., Clackmannan, President of the St. Serf's Ministerial Club, for encouraging me to share my reflexions on German Protestantism with a wider circle.

A. L. DRUMMOND

EADIE MANSE
  ALVA
    SCOTLAND

Reformation Day 1949

INTRODUCTION

THE name of Martin Luther is the hall-mark of German Protestantism. His translation of Scripture, like our Authorized Version, made the Bible a true *Volksbuch*.[1] His *Little Catechism* ranks with *The Shorter Catechism* as a rational guide to Man's chief end. 'It was his intention to make German Psalms for the people . . . so that God could speak directly to them in his word and they might in their songs directly answer Him.'[2] His vernacular Mass, infused with the free spirit of the Gospel, was the point of departure for the liturgical development of German Protestantism. His name was stamped on the title-deeds of a 'Confession' as distinctively as Wesley's on a denomination, though, like the founder of Methodism, he disclaimed any intention of founding a sect. 'I pray you leave my name alone, and do not call yourselves Lutherans but Christians.' The Union of Lutherans and Calvinists, which took place in 1817 in Prussia and certain other States, caused the disappearance of the name 'Lutheran' in most areas of Germany; the dominant confession surrendered its title in favour of 'Evangelical', just as 'Wesleyan' was replaced in England by the larger title of 'Methodist' to facilitate the Union of 1932.

Nevertheless, the prestige of Luther's personality has persisted. His black gown, worn with bands or ruff, is still the customary garb of the German pastor, who has mercifully escaped the 'Vestiarian controversy' that seems to haunt the Anglican clergyman through the echoing centuries. Churches are still dedicated in Luther's honour; statues, pictures, and stained glass keep alive his memory. Divinity students are indoctrinated *De vocatione Lutheri*. Spangenberg, a contemporary, hailed him as 'the third Elijah, the second St. Paul, and the Angel of Revelation'. Even Calixtus, the most level-headed Lutheran of the seventeenth century, spoke of him as inspired (ὁ Θεόπνευστος Lutherus). The Pietists loved to dwell on

---

[1] 'Where was your religion before Luther?' Roman Catholics still ask Evangelicals. And they receive the forthright answer that their fathers got: 'Where yours never was—in the Bible!' (Sometimes the retort is the homely counter-question: 'Where was your face before you washed it?')

[2] Luther's *Ein feste Burg* has been called 'the German Te Deum' and the German *Marseillaise*. Up till 1897 it went into eighty translations in fifty-three languages.

his simple heart-religion. Their successors, the Rationalists, viewed him as the enlightener of humanity. Romanticists hailed him as an artist in temperament, a hero of the glamorous past. Democrats recognized in this sturdy product of mining and peasant stock a true son of the people. As the Tercentenary of the Reformation approached, Goethe spoke up for him as a patriot. 'What God says in the Koran is true—"We have sent no nation a prophet who does not speak directly to the people!" Thus the Germans were no nation till the time of Luther.' His appeal to his fellow-countrymen still outweighs any popular interest in Calvin at Geneva or Knox at Edinburgh. This concentration on one man is not altogether healthy (has not Barth remarked that the cult of Reformed saints and heroes did not attract devotees 'till the people were no longer certain of the Reformed idea'?).

Luther's name is revered in the outposts of Scandinavia and Finland. When his stock fell in England owing to Tractarian dislike of 'that burly Schismatic' he gained new friends in Carlyle and Browning, who extolled 'grand, rough old Martin Luther'. Many a conservative Anglican, clinging to tradition, would still assent in resignation to the opinion of Erasmus: 'It hath pleased God to give us a drastic physician.'

The great Reformer has never lacked detractors. John Wesley wished that he had 'a faithful friend, who would at all hazards rebuke him plainly for his rough, intractable spirit, and bitter zeal for opinions' (1749). Most of Luther's opponents, however, have been a motley array of 'debunkers'. Romanists have reviled him as heresiarch, psychopath, moral decadent. Socialists have abused him as the implacable persecutor of Anabaptists and insurgent peasants, martyrs of revolution. Liberals have noted that he translated 'barbarian' as *un-deutsch* and denounced the Jews in language reminiscent of Goebbels. Since the Second World War there has been another outburst of anti-Luther hysteria. Mr. A. J. P. Taylor has asserted that he 'turned with repugnance from all the values of Western civilization'.[3] Mr. Peter F. Wiener has even starred him as *Hitler's Spiritual Ancestor*.[4] There is no excuse for this campaign of slander. Years ago Dr. H. Böhmer dissolved prejudice by his careful study of the arch-Reformer in relation to his sixteenth-century background. Böhmer leaves the reader

---

[3] *The Course of German History . . . since 1815.* (London, 1945), p. 19.

[4] Reply by Gordon Rupp, *Martin Luther—Hitler's Cause or Cure?* (London, 1945).

with as clear a portrait as possible of the paradoxical personality
who is the fountain-head of Lutheranism.[5]

Leaving the fountain-head, we press on to follow the course
of the stream that has been so definitely coloured by his teaching and temperament. It would require the genius of a
Principal Lindsay to present a comprehensive and illuminating
panorama of the German religious scene. Some knowledge
of the political and economic background is essential. Social
historians like Johannes Scherr and Gustav Freitag reveal the
soul of the people as well as the setting of their life and work.
Autobiographies, novels, essays, and poetry often provide
illuminating sidelights that stir our imagination and correct
our perspective.

Over a century ago Pusey broke new ground for English
readers in his *Historical Inquiry into the Probable Causes of the
Rationalist Character of the Theology of Germany* (Oxford, 1828).
These two formidable volumes were competently written, but
the modern reader will find them jejune and unattractive in
style. The author refuted Hugh Rose and other controversialists by pointing out that rationalism was no longer
the predominant element in German religion; its main cause
was not the lack of Episcopacy or a uniform liturgy (as some of
his Oxford friends supposed). This one-sided development was
just the natural reaction that followed repeated overdoses of
'neat theology' during the later sixteenth and most of the
seventeenth centuries. For this exaggerated form of Lutheran
orthodoxy that cramped the movement of German divinity so
long, Pusey coined the term 'orthodoxism'. He had studied at
Göttingen, but did not make allowance for untravelled readers
who needed information about the conditions of Church life
in different parts of the Fatherland. Subsequent British
writers on German religion have concentrated on theology as
the distinctive Teutonic contribution to Christendom. This
has tended to produce an impression that there is little else to
record. Is there nothing to be said of the relations of Church
and State, ecclesiastical polity, 'social Christianity', worship,
and parish life?

It is a difficult task to present an account of Protestant
Germany that is interesting as well as adequate. Any attempt
to be copious would result in a desiccated encyclopedic summary.
There are accurate and well-proportioned modern Church

[5] *Luther . . . in the Light of Modern Research* (1904; E.T., London, 1930).

Histories in German which are useful for reference, but their numbered paragraphs and detailed analysis are hardly for us; we want to see the wood and not merely the separate trees. My endeavour is to sketch the general evolution of German Protestantism, and to fill in the outline with enough detail to give substance and vitality to the skeleton. Two main obstacles make a straightforward narrative history difficult—the fact that every German principality had its own State Church; and that the range of theological differences is so extensive (obvious to anyone who turns up standard doctrinal histories like Lichtenberger and Pfleiderer).

The following method of approach has been selected. Two main avenues, parallel to each other, have been opened up. The first takes the reader through the country of religious thought and experience. Much of this has been a *terra incognita* since Luther's death. The theological *terminus a quo* is the *Augsburg Confession*, the famous *Augustana* (1530) signed by the princes and free cities of Germany. This is the classic bond of all who call themselves Lutherans, whether liberal or conservative. The Anglican is not, temperamentally, a builder of dogmatic systems; he prefers to philosophize institutions. To the Lutheran, the question of Belief is paramount. Not for him the Anglican maxim: '*Lex orandi, lex credendi.*' *Credenda* has priority over *Addenda* which includes liturgy and such miscellaneous matters as are not decided by the authoritative theological formularies. The Lutheran thinks of himself as primarily an adherent of the *Augsburg Confession*: the Anglo-Saxon Protestant is less doctrine-conscious, but rather sensitive to the bearings of diverse theories of Church government and worship.

Assuming a general knowledge of the Reformation, we press on into the credal country of the later sixteenth and seventeenth centuries, when orthodoxy was considered the cardinal test of Christianity. Only a few voices are heard pleading for a more liberal outlook. As we weary of controversialist dust, we meet the Pietists, whose simple religion of the heart is comparable to that of the English Methodists. After some refreshment, we pass through arid country again; we see life in the cool light of reason. This brings us to the cross-roads where Schleiermacher stands with his face to the future. Different tracks branch out right and left. All we can do is to go ahead, keeping in view the diverse theological signposts and getting acquainted with such pivotal personalities as Tholuck and Harnack. While noting theological contours, we would not confine our survey to credal roads, but explore the highways and byways of the Spirit that traverse the land of hills and valleys, till they lead to the more familiar landscape of the twentieth century. Part One is therefore entitled 'Church and Religion' rather than 'Church and Doctrine'.

The second avenue takes us through the region of Church and State—which will prove, I think, more interesting than it sounds. We trace Lutheran polity to its source, explaining why no 'Church of Germany' was possible, and how the princes, instead of reforming the episcopal system, took over episcopal functions themselves and reorganized the Church as a State department. We shall trace the evolution of 'Territorialism' in Prussia, keeping other principalities in view. We will notice how the Lutheran tradition of subservience to the State weakened its witness and played into the hands of reaction and militarism. Fortunately, the Reformed (or Presbyterian) element in German Evangelicalism offered a rallying-centre for all who wanted to see the Church spiritually free and vital. The Reformed Church corrected some of the faults of Lutheranism and furnished the backbone of the 'Confessing Church' in its struggle against the Nazi State. The bad effects of Lutheran Territorialism are obvious; its good points call for elucidation.

I would like to have devoted more space to social life as influenced by religion since the Reformation. In compensation the reader will find an interpretation of the 'Social Gospel' in the nineteenth century. The Industrial Revolution came late in Germany, but it was a rapid process, producing economic problems that clamoured for solution. It says much for the vision and resourcefulness of German Evangelicals, that despite the crippling restrictions that made it hard for a multitude of regional State Churches to act together, voluntary effort built up a splendid network of philanthropic institutions and agencies known as the 'Inner Mission'. The growth of materialism and Socialism proceeded apace after the German Empire was established in 1871. The alienation of the masses from the Evangelical Churches, due mainly to their servile attitude to the State, increased during the industrial era. 'Christian Socialists' eventually appeared on the scene, but unlike Maurice, Kingsley, and Westcott, often went off at a tangent and led their followers into the wasteland of anti-Semitism and fanatical nationalism. The 'Social Gospel' was easily perverted by 'crackpots' who prepared the way for National Socialism.

Economic and religious problems were complicated by the presence of a substantial minority of Roman Catholics, mostly in the south and west. During the static eighteenth century they had learned to live on fairly good terms with their Protestant neighbours. This relationship worsened unfortunately in the nineteenth century, when the revival of Jesuit activity provoked Bismarck's relentless *Kulturkampf*. The challenge of Rome brought into existence a number of associations which aimed at bridging the hiatus between the isolated State Churches and so presenting a united Protestant front. The disappearance of all the German princes in 1918 implied the collapse of the Territorial *Summepiskpat*; the crisis called into being a new system that combined the advantages of Establishment with those of a Free Church, and provided for the federation of the various *Landeskirchen*.

At this point nomenclature calls for clarification. Luther and his immediate successors had no intention of conceding the historic name of 'Catholic' to the *Papisten*. According to O. Ritschl, Hunnius (1585-1643) was the first Lutheran divine to apply *Katholisch* to Roman Catholics exclusively. This is the present usage on the Continent as well as in the United States; a 'Catholic' is an adherent of Rome (whatever 'Anglo-Catholics' may say). Ecumenically, no doubt, it is a pity to allow one brand of Christendom to monopolize an historic title. Nevertheless, clarity is vindicated in the German Evangelical version of the Apostles' Creed, which substitutes 'Christian' for 'Catholic' (following Luther's *Little Catechism*, *eine heilige christliche Kirche*). Germans prefer the name 'Evangelical' to 'Protestant' (coined when the Reformers protested against the 'Recess' of the Diet of Spires, 1529). In spite of historic associations, 'Protestant' was rarely used after the first phase of the Reformation. It was considered negative and colourless, but still survives, to denote Lutheran rather than Reformed usage.[6] It is interesting to compare the use of these terms in England. Till the Oxford Movement

[6] Bishop Knox, conducting English Church services in a Continental hotel, bespoke a lounge for worship. To his horror he found it furnished with altar, crucifix, and candles. When he expostulated, the Manager replied: 'But you said—for a *Protestant* service!' [He should have said, *Reformed*].

English Churchmen gloried in the name 'Protestant', which they have now abandoned to definitely Low Churchmen. 'Evangelical', on the other hand, which had once a wide connotation, has tended to shrink to a level denoting a particular brand of theology based on a literal view of Scripture. In this work we shall use 'Evangelical' as the equivalent of 'Protestant', to cover all Christian Churches in Germany that are not Roman Catholic.

I have ventured to round off Part One with a brief account of the revolution in theology under Barth between the Wars, and Part Two with a record of the reorganization of the Churches in 1919 leading to the impact of Nazi aggression, met by the heroic 'Confessing Church'.

I intended to include chapters on the evolution of public worship from Luther till the liturgical experiments of Otto and Heiler, including the development of the *Chorale*; but this was obviously too big an order—could one mention Church music without an adequate account of Bach, surely a product of Protestant devotion—and much else? Changes of taste in the history of preaching is another aspect of the German Church that some readers might have found interesting, even entertaining. And what of the overseas activities of German Evangelicals? I would like to have said something of the transplanting of Lutheranism to the United States and of Foreign Mission enterprise. It has only been possible to touch on these vital questions incidentally, mentioning a few relevant books for the benefit of anyone who desires to pursue these lines of study.

Goethe was attracted as a youth by the relationship between Church and State, the Community and the Individual. It is reassuring to know that this man of universal genius confessed: 'Church history was almost better known to me than secular history . . . and always highly interested me.' Goethe's interpreter, Thomas Carlyle, remarked in his essay on Werner: 'The religion of Germany is a subject not for slight but for deep study, and, if we mistake not, may in some degree reward the deepest.' It is hoped that this general survey may encourage specialists to make a more intensive study of particular aspects of German Protestantism.

The land of Luther is in a desperate plight, but a faithful remnant has passed through the fire of Nazi tyranny; *Nec tamen consumebatur*. The 'Confessing Church' may sink its identity as an administrative body, but its spirit is essential if

B

the German people are to be won for Christ. Never more than about a tenth of the combined German Protestant population, it is the only leaven that is capable of raising mass apathy and dull traditionalism in the Churches, the only salt that is qualified to act as a preservative against the corruption of political power that has perverted Lutheranism in the past. This 'sacramental host' is ready, in the words of Montgomery's great hymn, to bring release to 'slaves and rebels'. The scene is a setting of apocalyptic devastation, but the Cross of Christ is uplifted, and shines resplendent, 'towering o'er the wrecks of time'. Living waters issue from the temple of God and flow with healing power into this waste land. In the course of time there is sure to be growth and a harvest. 'Everything shall live whithersoever the river cometh.'

Part One

CHURCH AND RELIGION

CHAPTER ONE

SCHOLASTIC LUTHERANISM
AND ITS CRITICS

T HE reader who explores for the first time the *terra incognita* of German Protestantism since Luther must be prepared for initial disappointment. He starts with a vision of the world regenerated by the glorious Gospel. Presently, however, he finds himself wandering in an arid theological wilderness, his nostrils assailed by the acrid smoke of harsh polemics; no unifying pillar of fire directs his steps with radiant glow; discordant guides speaking unintelligible jargon compete in offering their services. It would almost seem as if Luther's Promised Land were a mirage. No wonder many pilgrims looked back with nostalgia at the solid comforts of Egyptian bondage—the certainties and benefits of the pre-Reformation Church. The desert seems to stretch ahead indefinitely. We must wander for nearly one hundred and fifty years till we reach the fresh streams of Pietism, toward the close of the seventeenth century. Yet there are a few oases to cheer us by the way. The open-hearted Calixtus welcomes pilgrims like Gaius of old and we catch a gleam of the fair domes of Andreae's 'Christiano-polis' on the horizon.

Luther, the Moses of the German Reformation, died in 1546 without leaving a Joshua. To change the metaphor, the great Reformer in his later years had failed to guide the stormy course of the Pilgrim Ship, and no gifted pilot of genius could be found to take his place. The Reformation was no longer riding on the crest of the wave, but was cast on the ebb-tide; the buoyant confidence of conquest had abated. Luther's prestige was still considerable, and his views carried authority. Unfortunately, ideas that he threw off in the heat of strife became primary articles of faith with his successors. Luther was scarcely buried before Lutherans started to whiten his sepulchre, attributing to him authority that he never claimed on all manner of questions. The Children of Israel 'took the bones of Joseph with them' when they crossed the wilderness, but had the sense to bury them honourably when they reached the Promised Land. Lutherans were not so wise; they preserved the bones of Luther's ideas like a fetish, and built them into an artificial skeleton. a closely articulated doctrinal system.

'Luther was not abreast of the knowledge accessible even in his own time,' observed Harnack.[1] In some ways the father of the Reformation was capable of considerable penetration and sound judgement. 'I would fain see all the arts, especially music, serving Him who hath given them to us.' To Luther's love of beauty we owe the preservation of the medieval heritage in Lutheran churches enriched with stained glass and statuary, pictures, and wood and metal. If he avoided the iconoclasm of the Puritan, he also avoided the narrowly liturgical conservatism of the Anglican. 'If God's Word is not preached it would be better neither to sing nor read, nor to assemble at all. . . . We must be masters of ceremonies and not let them be masters of us.' Here is balance and insight, such as we do not find in Luther's utterances on the right relation of Germans to foreigners, Jews, and social reformers.[2] He was essentially a preacher. He did not have the time nor the patience, to relate 'Gospel' to 'doctrine' with the constructive genius of Calvin.

Some nations have managed their theology to their own satisfaction without architectonic system-builders, e.g. the English. Not so the Germans, with their urge to analysing, defining, comparing, and concluding; to them subtle doctrinal distinctions were the breath of life. The Reformation was far from being a finished product. There was no Protestant Pope, no bench of bishops, to formulate and fulminate. There was no single German State capable of bringing into existence a National Church and nurturing it into maturity. Into the void came a new order of scribes charged with distinguishing between the husk and the kernel of essential Lutheranism. The confusion and uncertainty of the times played into the hands of men who were confident that they could interpret the Word infallibly against the claims of Rome, Calvin, and the sects.

A new scholasticism arose that presented the laymen with a complete and detailed chart of belief. The emphasis was all on unadulterated doctrine (*reine Lehre*). The intellect was under strict control and the emotions had less outlet than in the Roman Church. The fatal flaw in the method of these system-

---

[1] Such assertions are corrected by Philip S. Watson's study of Luther's theology, *Let God Be God* (London, 1947).

[2] For his opinion on various subjects see H. T. Kerr, *A Compend of Luther's Theology* (London, 1945). Dr. Kerr has also a convenient 'compend' of Calvin.

builders was inability to realize that the relationship between dogma and religion implies a distinction. Sometimes this blindness was so extreme as to indicate *furor theologicus*. The experts who expounded Luther-lore, like the Scribes and Pharisees, expected the uninitiated to hear and obey. When persuasion failed, coercion was readily applied.

'An original impulse weakens as it spreads; the living passion petrifies in codes or creeds; the revelation becomes a commonplace; and so the religion that began in vision ends in orthodoxy.' This pathological process is exemplified by the course of German Lutheranism, although ascendant authoritarianism was not able to enforce complete uniformity.

At Luther's death the shades of German Protestant theology were almost as varied as the kaleidoscopic colours of the French Chamber of Deputies, ranging from Right to Left. To make this analogy strictly logical, however, it would have been necessary to rescind repressive measures against the revolutionary peasants and Anabaptists, so drastically applied as early as the 1520's. Their outlawry meant that the 'Extreme Left' was as effectively eliminated as in a modern Fascist state. The controversies that agitated Lutheranism were mostly the academic disputes of theologians rather than soul-shaking questions that concerned the layman. There was one exception, the Antinomian issue—the only major dispute among Lutherans in Luther's life.

Ever since the days of the Apostle Paul the question had been raised from time to time: 'Are Christians entirely free from the law of Moses, to which the unregenerate are still subject?' Johannes Agricola said 'Yes', stressing the Gospel-given knowledge of the love of God as the producer of penitence. He restated the antithesis between the law and the Gospel in a one-sided way; public morals would have suffered had his views been countenanced. He did not claim, like certain extreme 'enthusiasts' of Cromwell's era, that what the world called sin was permitted to 'the saints'. He did say that, if he sinned, it did not affect his election by God. The immanence of God within him turned poison to health. As for others, no amount of unselfish living could save a man from hell, if he was not among the elect. Luther denounced Agricola as an Antinomian in the literal sense of the word; he was 'against the law' (ἀντι νομος). The charge of 'Antinomianism' has sometimes been made against Calvinists who disparaged 'deadly doing' and 'legal preaching'. It is worth noting, surely, that the first adherent of the Reformation to advocate the Antinomian heresy was not a Calvinist, but a prominent Lutheran. Agricola (whose real name was prosaic Schneider) was a fellow-townsman of Luther, a native of Eisleben. Soon after his appointment to a Chair at Wittenberg in 1536, the sparks flew. So great was the conflagration that Agricola thought it prudent to leave the Lutheran Mecca for Berlin. His *Hegira* was hurried but he was not pursued. At Berlin he found a protector in Joachim the Second, Elector of Brandenburg; and in that obscure capital he served as court preacher and general superintendent till his death in the plague of 1566. Writing to the Elector of Saxony soon after his departure to Berlin, Agricola recanted his Antinomianism, but this did not reassure Luther. With the legitimate exaggeration of a poet, Browning pictures 'Johannes Agricola in Meditation'. It is a soliloquy superb in spiritual audacity and imaginative power.

If Luther's temper was roused by heretics like Agricola, his equanimity was restored by his friend, Philip Melanchthon, who survived him for fourteen years. He recognized in him a stabilizing and constructive genius, correcting and completing what he lacked. 'I hew the trees,' said Martin, 'Philip planes them.' The man of action was followed by a thinker. Luther's words were 'half battles'. 'There lay their strength while he lived and uttered them; their weakness too, when exposed to the static silence of the printed page.'[3] 'Dr. Martinus' was in some respects medieval in outlook: the 'Protestant Preceptor of Germany'[4] transmitted to his followers the Humanist strain of Erasmus.

These 'Philippists' constituted the nucleus of a Lutheran 'Left Wing'. Without any intense desire for the rigid discipline of Geneva, they found there a cosmopolitan attitude that seemed to correct the national limitations of German Lutheranism. They were attracted by the ideal of a highly educated ministry, of a Church in connexion with the State but not its creature, of an ecclesiastical polity that associated elected laymen and clergymen in representative Councils. They further admired Geneva's zeal for realizing the Kingdom of God in human relationships. The *Testimonium Spiritus Sancti*,

[3] Quartercentenary of Luther's death, *Times Literary Supplement* (23rd February 1946).
[4] J. W. Richard, *Melanchthon the Protestant Preceptor of Germany* (Heroes of the Reformation Series, 1899).

on which Calvinist (Reformed) theologians relied and to which they appealed, offered a solution to the difficult problems that were raised by the Doctrine of the Infallible Bible; if unanimity could not be secured on every minor issue, would it not be wiser to leave something to the inner workings of the Holy Spirit?

When we consider that the German mind is specially addicted to order and system, we can understand that there was much support for a modified Calvinism. What one Confession lacked, the other often supplied. Lutherans were *anti-Judaic* in protesting against the legalism of Rome—were not Calvinists inclined to re-establish a new legalism, 'good works' consisting in the avoidance of amusements and ceremonial, besides the performance of arduous religious exercises? The Reformed were *anti-pagan* in protesting against the superstitious element in the Romish cultus—were not Lutherans illogical in holding on to shreds of medieval ritual, which had lost their point since the abolition of the Mass[5] and for which there was no warrant in Scripture? The Marburg Colloquy of 1529 cast into classic form the opposition between traditional Lutheranism and the radical Protestant view of the Lord's Supper. Luther, the irascible supernaturalist, refused to shake hands with Zwingli the cool rationalist, in token of their essential agreement on all other points. 'You are of a different spirit,' he objected. The spirit of schism had certainly entered the Reformation movement. The rock of offence was the rite that Christ intended to be the bond of fellowship. Neither Luther nor Zwingli did justice to the Lord's Supper. One insisted on a medieval interpretation that seemed sheer superstition to many Evangelicals. The other denuded the sacrament of its mystic symbolism and reduced it to a mere memorial. A convincing *via media* was offered by Calvin's solution. In the Communion Christ's presence was 'real'—not because it was material, but because it was spiritual. Indeed, Melanchthon considered that Luther, in later life, was much impressed by the Calvinist interpretation of the Lord's Supper as a *via media* between his own 'consubstantiation' and Zwingli's bare 'memorial' theory.

---

[5] Luther's *Deutsche Messe* (1526) is described by Professor R. Will of Strasbourg as 'a roughly pruned Mass full of contradictions, but offering a framework for traditional ceremonial'. Romanists compare it to a mere torso. It is more like a sponge filled with the Water of Life, valuable as a container not easily replaced: but only Divine grace (intensely experienced) can give it power. After Luther, it became singularly barren. His successors used liturgy as a means of indoctrination. 'A directly didactic aim dries up real devotion' (Moffatt).

James Howell, in his *Familiar Letters* (1645-55) described Calvinism as 'this Geneva bird'. It flew hence to France 'and hatched the Huguenots. . . . It took wing also to Bohemia, Holland, and Germany, high and low'. This cosmopolitan flight of the 'Geneva bird' did not appeal to German Lutherans. The mere fact that Calvin was French furnished his enemies with an effectual weapon. Despotic princes, self-indulgent in private life, could not bear his principles of government by consultation, the autonomy of the Church, and the ideal of an austere, unselfish life. Conservative theologians therefore received considerable support from vested interests when they proclaimed that their aim was to preserve the *status religionis in Germania per Lutherum instauratus*. To accuse their brethren of 'Crypto-Calvinism' was an effective *argumentum ad hominem*.[6]

Discussions fanned by quartos of querulous Latin merely made animosity blaze the fiercer. Jena and Leipzig were the headquarters of the conservative Lutherans. Among these, Matthias Flacius Illyricus (1520-75) was a leading light. It would be more appropriate perhaps to call him a 'stormy petrel'. A native of Illyria (Dalmatia) he had aspired to the monastic vocation as a youth. Attracted after a time to Melanchthon, he reacted violently against his gentle teacher, who remarked sadly: 'We have nurtured a serpent in our bosom.' Flacius then proceeded to Wittenberg, Magdeburg, Jena, and Antwerp. His scholarship was admired, his ultra-orthodox views approved, but other men found him difficult —too opinionative and temperamental for team-work. *Persona non grata*, he died an exile in Frankfurt, accused of arrogance, obstinacy, and even malice. Kawerau charitably explains these defects as due to a slightly unbalanced mind (cf. article in *New Schaff-Herzog Cyclopedia*). That is not surprising in view of the neurotic atmosphere of Lutheran Scholasticism. Bitter controversialist though he was, Flacius proved to be a pioneer in some respects. He compiled a Scripture Dictionary, indicating that the Bible was a sacred library rather than an arsenal of texts (*Clavis Scripturae Sacrae*, 1567). He initiated a celebrated chronicle, the *Magdeburg Centuries*. This composite work was an attempt to write Church History from an Evangelical point of view, proceeding century by century from the Apostolic Age to the thirteenth century (the first volume appeared in 1559,

---

[6] cf. H. Leube, *Calvinismus u. Luthertum im Zeitalter der Orthodoxie* (Leipzig, 1928); Krauth, *The Conservative Reformation and its Theology* (Philadelphia, 1872).

the last in 1574). The *Magdeburg Centuries* had a wide circulation; it was much in demand among preachers as a storehouse
of controversial material, for it was replete with vivid anecdote,
in which the Pope figured as 'Incarnate anti-Christ'. Foxe's
Booke of Martyrs drew much of its lurid material from the
Centuries. Romanists had good reason to complain of this
'*pestilentissimum opus*' and Baronius answered it in his *Annals*.[7]
In spite of a polemical purpose, the *Magdeburg Centuries* has
generally been recognized as a landmark in the free study of
Church history. Flacius enunciated principles better understood
now than in his day, such as, 'History is the foundation of
doctrine'.

'The ever memorable' John Hales of Eton in 1618 compared
the two parties in the Lutheran Church. The 'softer' section
(*molliores*) were fairly open-minded, ready to admit that some
doctrines were essential and others of marginal importance;
the 'hard-shell' section (*rigidi*) were intransigent. 'We may well
despair of the latter,' was the opinion of Hales, 'for they so bear
themselves, as if . . . they would rather agree with the Church
of Rome than with the Calvinists. He that is conversant with
the writings of Hunnius and Grawerus will quickly think as I
do. The first of which hath so bitterly written against Calvin
that Parsons the Jesuit furnisht himself by compiling Hunnius
his book. If the whole lump be leavened, as those two pieces
which I but now named, they are certainly too sour for the
moderate man to deal with.'

Fortunately, there was a leaven of humanism that prevented
the spirit of freedom from utterly perishing in Germany. Marburg, Heidelberg, and Helmstädt, were centres of 'Philippist'
liberalism. They followed in the footsteps of Philip Melanchthon, the peace-maker. Melanchthon's historical instinct
reverted to the original unity of the Christian Church; subsequent divergences he viewed as excrescences rather than as
proofs of incorrigible heresy. He confessed that he was quite
unable to pronounce the word 'Shibboleth'.[8] Consequently,
he was bitterly attacked by ultra-Lutherans for his conciliatory
attitude toward Roman Catholics and Evangelicals who did
not believe that Luther was infallible. In the sixteenth century
'Euodias and Syntyche' were very far from being 'of the same
mind in the Lord'. Melanchthon was only thirty-three when

---

[7] cf. Mark Pattison's *Casaubon*, Chapter 6 (1875).
[8] cf. Franz Hildebrandt, *Melanchthon: Alien or Ally?* (Cambridge, 1946).

he prepared the seventeen articles of the *Augsburg Confession*.
He designed it as a spacious canopy to shelter several parties
with honour.[9] It had even been drafted in alternate forms, the
variata and *invariata*, differing slightly about the Lord's Supper;
the *variata* edition was indeed signed by Calvin, in the meaning,
he said, of its author.

The *Augsburg Confession* in the twentieth century appears like
a generous blanket to cover many diverse bodies that claim the
name of Lutheran today, whether in Europe, America, or
elsewhere. But the sixteenth century had an unnatural craving
for the discomfort of rigidity. 'The bed is shorter than that a
man can stretch himself on it; and the covering narrower than
that he can wrap himself in it' (Isaiah 28[20]). The *Augsburg
Confession* did not suit those who sought austerity rather than
ease in Zion.

The infallible Book called for an infallible interpreter. The
Romanists had two pillars of authority—the Bible and the
Church. The Lutherans, having made the Church the thrall of
the State, were compelled to lean heavily on the other pillar,
the Bible. An authoritative Confession of Faith was their
substitute for an infallible Church. Compelled by conscience
and reason to present a united front to Rome, Lutherans sought
defence in a coherent, cogent Confession capable of enforcing
uniformity. The Faith of the Catholic Church had been
definitely expanded and confirmed at the Council of Trent
(1545-63). In the picturesque Alpine capital of the Southern
Tyrol (significantly fortified) two books lay open on the altar
of the Council church—the Bible and the *Summa Theologiae*
of St. Thomas Aquinas. Lutheranism sought an authoritative
Confession to lay alongside of the Bible on the altar of symbolic
belief—something more massive and elaborate than the
Augustana.

A series of conferences resulted in the compilation of a new
formulary which would settle all diverse interpretations. It
bore the promising title of *The Formula of Concord* (1577).
Unfortunately, it brought not peace but the sword. One of the
theologians responsible was Martin Chemnitz (1522-86) who,
after dabbling in astrology, took the straight and narrow way of
Lutheran orthodoxy. Against Crypto-Calvinism he thundered

---

[9] Unfortunately, he unwittingly forged a chain which his enemies adopted—
the system of *Loci Communes* that linked proof-texts, like beads on a thread, the
connexion being external and artificial.

in his *Repetitio Sanae Doctrinae de Vera Praesentia*:[10] against Romanism of the new Counter-Reformation model he brought his biggest ordnance to bear in his *Examen Concilii Tridentini*. Even Chemnitz had weak links in his armour, however; did not that seventeenth-century pioneer of Modernism, Chillingworth, point out that this German defender of the faith declared the following New Testament books were apocryphal —*2 Peter, James, Hebrews,* and *Revelation?*

The *Formula Concordiae* of 1577 was designed to settle ambiguity in Lutheran doctrine, so that all Lutherans could present a solid front to their adversaries. The followers of Luther and Melanchthon had hitherto differed as to what was 'indifferent' and 'essential' to salvation and Church fellowship (the 'Adiaphoristic Controversy'). The issue came to a head in the Leipzig Interim of 1548. This was a compromise with the Catholics, negotiated by Melanchthon, which allowed the jurisdiction of bishops and certain medieval rites; Justification by Faith was affirmed, but the important qualification 'alone' (*solo*) was relegated to things 'indifferent' (*adiaphora*). Matthias Flacius objected that the Emperor was no fit judge of *adiaphora,* and feared that the scheme was a plot to bring back Popery, step by step. He fled from Wittenberg to Magdeburg (converting the latter into a centre of rigid Lutheranism). By his vigilance, Flacius has been credited with having saved the Reformation. The Religious Peace of Augsburg (1555) secured the dominance of Lutheran doctrine in Lutheran states. Strict Lutherans were now in a position to obtain a final settlement of outstanding points, reducing as far as possible what was still debatable as 'non-essential'.

The *Formula Concordiae* (1577) was adopted by a majority of the German states by 1580, largely through the pressure of the ultra-Lutheran leader, Augustus Elector of Saxony. It was first received and then rejected by Brandenburg, Brunswick, and the Palatinate. Among the Free Cities, it was approved by Hamburg and Lübeck, condemned by Bremen and Frankfurt. Sweden and Denmark eventually accepted it (the latter having previously made its very publication a crime punishable by death!). The States which rejected the *Formula* were mostly Reformed, adhering to the more liberal Heidelberg

[10] The anti-Calvinist fulminations of Chemnitz are charitably overlooked by the spiritual descendants of Calvin at Mansfield College, Oxford. There he is represented in stained glass and in strange company—Melanchthon, Zwingli, Beza, Grotius, and Böhme.

Catechism of 1563. When the University of Helmstädt was formally opened by Duke Julius of Brunswick, a noble youth bore on a damask cushion the Bible and the *Corpus Doctrinae*—a conciliatory Confession drawn up by the ducal theologians.

The *Formula Concordiae*, palladium of hyper-orthodoxy, became an engine for putting down differences of opinion, rather than an irenicon for reconciling them. It never took into account the fact that 'a man convinced against his will, is of the same opinion still'. The *Formula* was the vehicle of Scholastic Lutheranism. Lacking in doctrinal proportions, it was laboured in its minute elaboration, exhausting as well as exhaustive, never rising above the limitations of its period. Centuries later, when most of Germany looked on these Confessions as little more than historic landmarks, German immigrants in America echoed the ancient controversies. Thus, while the 'General Synod of North America' (1820) was content to accept the *Augsburg Confession*, the 'Synodical Conference' of 1872 enforced subscription to all the creeds epitomized in the *Formula Concordiae* of 1577. Even on a new continent hereditary dogmatism triumphed.

Germany of the later sixteenth century revelled in doctrinal discord. The Antinomian and Adiaphoristic controversies were not the only ones. The Synergist issue turned on the share of human liberty allowed by divine grace in conversion. Flacius maintained that 'man was composed of nothing but sin'; Major insisted on good works as necessary and useful to holiness. Osiander declared that man was justified by an infusion of Christ's divine nature; Stancarus argued that he was justified by Christ's human nature—a heresy so damnable that in some principalities his adherents were denied Communion and even decent burial. The theologians remembered every jot and tittle of 'sound doctrine'; they forgot Christ's new commandment 'that ye love one another'. Even worship became a vehicle of hatred rather than a means of grace. Lynx eyes were swift to note any pastor who omitted to exorcise the devil before Baptism; vulpine ears were quick to hear whether he reversed the Lord's Prayer and said (like the Calvinists) *Vater unser* instead of *unser Vater*. In 1592 you could actually hear people singing in church the polemical hymn:

> Guard Thou Thy saints with Thy Word, O Lord,
> And smite the Calvinists with Thy sword!

The sword was wielded in no metaphorical sense by the civil arm, with the approval of zealous religionists who wanted *their* cause to prevail at all costs. 'Godly princes' were often sadistic as well as coarse, covetous, drunken,[11] and immoral. Though these champions of the faith were honoured with such titles as John the Steadfast, Ernest the Pious, and Augustus the Strong, we seldom read of any being acclaimed as the Virtuous. Augustus the Second, Elector of Saxony, far more than Butler's Puritan hero, Hudibras, sought 'by apostolic blows and knocks, to prove his doctrine orthodox'.[12] He imprisoned Strigil for three years for holding that man is not passive in the process of conversion. Having captured one of his enemies, Wilhelm von Grumbach, 'out of the native goodness of his heart' he modified the death sentence to that of being 'only quartered alive'. After a systematic, protracted heresy hunt for Crypto-Calvinists, he had himself represented in a medal as a victor in shining armour, holding a balance, the infant Saviour in one scale, and in the other the Devil with four Calvinists! Ultra-Lutheran vigilance did not cease after his death. The Chancellor of Saxony, after being imprisoned for heresy in a damp and verminous dungeon, was executed with a sword bearing the inscription: 'Beware, O Calvinist, Dr. Nicholas Krell!'

Such persecution, far from stabilizing Lutheran orthodoxy, drove many moderate Lutherans toward Calvinism. Melanchthon expired, utterly weary, repeating his frequent prayer: 'From the rage of the theologians, good Lord deliver us!'

The alleged intolerance of Calvinists is a commonplace of popular journalism in our own days. This charge is certainly not true of the Reformed Church in Germany, which has a good record for tolerance and magnanimity, judged by the standards of the sixteenth and seventeenth centuries. When Alva's victims streamed across the frontier from Holland into the duchies of the Lower Rhine in 1567, they showed no signs of the fanaticism that persecution usually breeds in the perse-

[11] One jovial prince habitually closed letters to friends with the greeting: *Valete et inebriamini!* Landgrave of Hesse formed a Temperance Society but the first president died of drink. Lewis 'the Pious' of Württemberg indulged freely in drinking-bouts, but was usually sober enough to send his boon-companions home in a cart, in company with a pig.

[12] Nathaniel Ward, an outstanding New England Calvinist who had lived in Germany, actually defended Lutheran intolerance: 'Frederick of Saxony spake not one foot beyond the mark when he said he had rather the Earth should swallow him up quick, than he should give a toleration to any opinion against any truth of God' (*The Simple Cobbler of Agawam*, 1647).

cuted. They settled down amicably among their Lutheran neighbours, who were attracted by their vital spiritual experience and Presbyterian ways.

In different parts of Germany there were princes whose patience was exhausted by the bigotry of Lutheran ecclesiastics. Conspicuous among these rulers was Frederick the Third, Elector Palatine of the Rhine. 'Luther is no Apostle,' he declared, 'he also can err.' He liked the Lutherans still less. Tradition says that the limit was reached when in his presence Heshusius, the Lutheran Court chaplain, seized the chalice from his Zwinglian colleague, Klebitz, at the holy table— surely sacrilege on the part of one who held High views of the Eucharist! Both Heshusius and Klebitz were dismissed— one for magnifying sacramentalism, the other for minimizing it. 'Frederick the Pious' then referred the issue to Melanchthon, who gave too guarded a verdict. Whereupon the Elector, on his own authority, entrusted two young men, Zacharias Ursinus and Caspar Olevianus, with the task of composing a Confession of Faith. As a first step each of them submitted his own suggestions. When a fusion of the drafts was effected, it was found that the two authors had contributed to a remarkable harmony, for the scholarship of Ursinus blended perfectly with the fervent grace of Olevianus.

This *Heidelberg Catechism* was published by authority in 1563. It differs from other Reformation Standards by its moderation, its organic form, and its devotional spirit. It has been described as 'the product of the best qualities of head and heart, and its prose is frequently marked by all the beauty of a lyric'. Frederick's enemies summoned him before the Emperor Maximilian the Second for infringing the 'Peace of Augsburg' (1555) which accorded recognition only to Catholics and Lutherans. A sturdy Lutheran, Augustus of Saxony, tapped the Elector Palatine on the shoulder: 'Fritz, thou hast indeed more piety than us all.' These words of a persecutor in his better moments secured Frederick immunity. But his son Lewis was a Lutheran of the Lutherans. During his reign the *Heidelberg Catechism* was eclipsed in the land of its birth from 1576 to 1583. However, it was subsequently adopted in Hesse, Anhalt, Bremen, etc. Abroad, it was acknowledged by the Reformed Churches of Holland, Hungary, Transylvania, and Poland. It was read in Britain and France, 'and probably shares with the *De Imitatione Christi* and *Pilgrim's Progress* the honour of coming next to the Bible in the number of tongues into which it has been translated'. Dr. Alexander Smellie, who edited the German text with an English translation (1900) has commended the *Heidelberg Catechism*[13] as far in advance of the harsh spirit of its age.[14] It appealed to warm-hearted Christians all over Europe who found other Confessions too grimly dogmatic, and yet it was sufficiently Calvinistic to be endorsed by the Council of Dort.

In 1618 the Dutch invited distinguished foreign divines to the pleasant town of Dort (Dordrecht) to clarify the Arminian-Calvinist controversy. Two-thirds of the foreign delegates were Germans; their influence did much to mould the famous 'Decrees' of the Synod which vindicated Calvinism. John Hales of Eton gave a graphic, human account of the conference,[15] while his fellow-countryman, Bishop Hall, exclaimed: 'There is no place on earth as like heaven as the Synod of Dort!' Abraham Schulz (Scultetus), Court Preacher to Frederick, Elector Palatine, compared it to the Council of Trent: '*Here*, God's grace and judgements were heard; *there*, men's statutes and papist decrees.'[16]

The prospects of Calvinistic Europe were bright. The continued use of Latin by scholars facilitated official correspondence between the Churches and the interchange of professors of many lands. Pareus of Heidelberg attracted students from all over Europe, and, by stressing points of agreement rather than of difference, won for Reformed Germany an ecumenical reputation.[17] Unfortunately, this growing confidence in the future of Protestantism was inflated by political miscalculation. Scultetus urged his sovereign, Frederick the Fifth, Elector Palatine of the Rhine, to accept the throne of Bohemia in 1618—the immediate cause of the Thirty Years War. He counted on the Elector's father-in-law, James the Sixth, sending substantial aid to 'the hope of

---

[13] *The Reformation in its Literature* (London, 1925).

[14] In Lower Lusatia, Pastor Kolkwitz was suspended in 1660 for using Luther's *Catechism* for the Lutheran section of his flock and the *Heidelberg Catechism* for his Reformed parishioners. In the eighteenth century this attitude would have been generally commended.

[15] *Letters from the Synod of Dort* (publ. Glasgow, 1765). As late as 1694 *Ursin's Catechism* was prescribed reading at Edinburgh University.

[16] James Moffatt, *The Thrill of Tradition* (London, 1944), Chapter 4, the 'New Trent Religion'.

[17] German theologians rank high in the Calvinist procession marshalled by Professor Heppe. See his *Reformed Dogmatics* (E.T., G. T. Thomson, London, 1950).

C

Reformed Christendom'; he ought to have known that pusill-animous monarch better.   Considering that 'Crypto-Calvin-ism' was such a bugbear to most Lutherans, it is surprising that they rallied to the defence of Frederick. The German princes chose sides and changed them to suit their interests; and this was one determining factor in the prolongation of hostilities. The Elector of Brandenburg, Calvinist though he was, found himself hampered by the fanatical Lutheranism of his people as well as by geographical isolation; still, he had no need to appoint a Romanist as his Chancellor—Count Adam Schwart-zenburg, who was in the Emperor's pay.

Western Germany, where the Reformed Church was in-fluential, had to bear the brunt of the Thirty Years War. The Palatinate of the Rhine was reduced by Tilly's hordes from a garden to a wilderness; the famous Palatine Library was removed to Rome; Frederick and Elizabeth trod their *via dolorosa*.[18] Nassau experienced the rod through being the Emperor's favourite region for quartering his troops. Hesse-Cassel lost a quarter of its population; the celebrated University of Marburg was a major casualty; but the Landgrave refused to sign the compromise Peace of Prague (1635) and fought till the rights of the Reformed were recognized. Central and eastern Germany also suffered. Leipzig was burnt five times and Magdeburg six times sacked with horrors 'for which history has no speech and poetry no pencil' (Schiller). The Burgo-master of Schweidnitz, Silesia, confronted with the formidable demands by the occupying forces, sent back the requisition list with a prayer written on the back—the only possible com-ment.[19] The Protestant Swedes were as merciless as the Catholic Imperialists; many a brutal persecutor of the Coven-anters learnt his trade as a mercenary in 'high Germanie'. The horrors of these years are graphically depicted in Grimmels-hausen's popular novel, *Simplicissimus*, a vagabond's tale written in 1668.[20]

---

[18] See *The Winter Queen* by 'Marie Hay' (Baroness Herbert von Hindenburg) (Constable, 1910). This novel, excellent for background and character, is biased, like so many books on the Stuarts. The Reformed are 'sour Puritans'; Scultetus resembles a caricature of Knox; the fanaticism of Lutherans and Papists is ignored. The balance is redressed by several Reformed romances. S. Sturm's *Einer is euer Meister* (Bronner, Frankfurt) describes the origin of Palatinate Calvinism. 'George Taylor' (Professor Hausrath) describes the strife between Lutheran and Calvinist in *Clytia* (E.T., Low, 1883).

[19] C. V. Wedgwood, *The Thirty Years War* (London, 1938), p. 256.

[20] E.T. by Goodrick (London and New York, 1912).

Churches were closed, bells melted, pastors and people impoverished.[21] Yet the faithful still assembled to worship God. They sang songs in the night of tribulation; Dr. Millar Patrick has related many a touching incident associated with the *Chorales* of J. M. Altenburg, G. Neumark, Matthäus von Löwenstern, and Martin Rinkart.[22] There were few religious books for laymen, but all over Germany Johann Arndt's *True Christianity* was read in pious homes. Arndt ranged beyond Lutheran orthodoxy; he breathed the practical mysticism of Tauler and Thomas à Kempis; he pleaded for warmhearted discipleship and fellowship of the Spirit. Pure life came before the 'pure doctrine' so esteemed by the doctrinal experts. *Vom Wahres Christentums* (1605) was translated into nearly every European language (despite clerical opposition). During the weary years of war it was read by Calvinists from Bohemia, Lutherans from Sweden, and even by Catholic soldiers from Spain. In Germany it heralded the Pietist Movement (as we shall soon see). It was essentially a book for the heart, proclaiming doctrinal disarmament and unity of the spirit.

When the Treaty of Westphalia at last terminated the Thirty Years War in 1648, a favourite *Te Deum* (tells tradition) was Rinkhart's hymn: 'Now thank we all our God'. There was little cause for jubilation. Germany was ruined agriculturally, industrially, intellectually—even if there is exaggeration in the claim that the population was reduced from 17,000,000 to 5,000,000. Among the universities, only Königsberg kept its organization intact; liberal Helmstädt mustered a handful of 625 students enrolled in 1625; the Reformed Universities of Marburg and Heidelberg were shattered.

The Treaty of 1648 recognized the Reformed Church, but did not guarantee its survival. Indeed, 'the chastisement of our peace was laid upon' the Palatinate. All looked well when the Elector Charles Lewis returned from exile in England, determined to make the wilderness blossom like the rose. He welcomed foreigners and offered cultivators twenty years'

---

[21] The brutality bred by war was reflected even in parish life. Tholuck cites a pastor's declaration of 1644: 'J. Volkwartsen tried to kill me with my own spade. He was afterwards killed by his own brother. . . . P. Jensen tried to stab me in the sexton's house. He went to sea and during a storm they threw him overboard. He tried to hold on with his hands but they cut them off. A. Frese, who committed adultery with my wife, went after me with a loaded gun. D. Momsen broke two of my ribs. He has done penance for it. . . . I have forgiven him.' Tholuck (a Lutheran historian) cites many such instances in *Das kirchliche Leben des 17ten. Jahr hunderts* (1861; unfortunately no E.T.)

[22] *The Story of the Church's Song* (Edinburgh, 1927).

exemption from taxes. As a former member of the Westminster Assembly, he had learnt by experience the folly of coercion. Calvinists, Lutherans, and Roman Catholics were encouraged to live together amicably. Distinguished foreigners were imported to fill chairs at Heidelberg: Hottinger from Zurich and Spanheim from Holland.

The Palatinate had still to undergo its second baptism by fire. The Elector Charles, in promoting the marriage of his daughter 'Lise-Lotte' to the Duke of Orleans, did not foresee the consequences. On the extinction of his line, Louis the Fourteenth claimed the Electorate for his brother and sent General Melac, a modern Attila, to make the land a desert. Twice he sacked Heidelberg with revolting excesses.[23] The 1680's were terrible years. When Louis was compelled to renounce the Palatinate in 1697, the Jesuits remained to carry on his work.[24] The most prosperous German principality that professed the Reformed faith was utterly ruined.

After 1648 the Lutheran Churches had the opportunity of profiting from the mistakes of the past. The common people were sick of theological controversy. What cared they whether Calovius was right or Weigelius past redemption? For many years churches had been closed, children untaught, and homes undisciplined. In all walks of life a low moral level prevailed. 'My people have committed two evils; they have forsaken me, the fountain of living waters, and hewed them out cisterns, broken cisterns, that can hold no water.'

These broken cisterns were overgrown with the clinging moss of outworn theology. Barren orthodoxy choked the fresh flow of living water. Few comforters were ready 'to speak a word in season to him that is weary'. The stones of dogma were offered the hungry. Lutheran theologians, like the Bourbons, 'had forgotten nothing and learnt nothing' during the prolonged ordeal of total war. Blind to the need for regeneration, they loaded the exhausted Germans with dogmatic burdens. Scholasticism continued to be as cumbersome and pedantic as ever. Gerhard's *Loci Theologici*, written before the war of 1610-20 was distinguished by a candour all too rare among men who traverse the hot ashes of controversy: whereas Calovius' many-tomed *Systema* (1655-77) was deplorably heavy. Morning

[23] See Robiano's novel, *Die Rose von Heidelberg*, for an account of the destruction wrought and the persecution of Protestants that followed.

[24] See p. 76, *infra*.

and evening Abraham Calovius used to pray: 'Fill me, O God, with hatred of the heretics!'[25]

As late as 1685 Quenstedt declared that the Divine authority of Scripture would be imperilled by the admission that it contained any human element whatever. This went farther than even Chemnitz, the guardian of orthodoxy a century earlier. Could Luther have returned from the grave, he would have been execrated as a heresiarch. The Epistle of James 'a right strawy epistle'? Why, every jot and tittle was derived from Adam in Paradise! To correct the Lutheran translation was to commit the crime of 'Bible-murder'. Had not the University of Wittenberg declared in 1638 that it was blasphemy against the Holy Ghost to admit that there was any bad Greek in the Epistles?[26]

'Thank God there is peace, for the wandering scholars have come back!' cried the resin-gatherers of the Black Forest on meeting the vagabond hero in Grimmelshausen's *Simplicissimus*. Alas! they did not come back to stay after the Thirty Years War. The universities suffered like the Churches. They lost their international reputation. The 'wandering scholars' of the new era were the noblemen who signed their name in the matriculation album for a small fee, and then proceeded on 'the Grand Tour'. For a long time scholarship retired from the university to the scholar's study. One thinks of Leibniz. Yet it was the same in other lands, as Mr. G. N. Clarke has pointed out; men like Hobbes and Bayle owed little to colleges but depended on princes, patrons, and the public.[27]

In German universities the conditions were unfavourable for literature and science; theology, which ought to have helped men in their quest for truth, threw a protecting cloud of obscurantism over pedantry and prejudice.[28] Had a man of genius arisen in academic cloisters, the buds of his fancy would soon have faded for want of light and air. In Luther's day German religion was in touch with life and literature. The vernacular drama, in the hands of Hans Sach, meistersinger

[25] Yet he was not entirely immersed in theology. He buried five wives and begot thirteen children. Four months after the death of his fifth wife, in his seventy-second year, he married the daughter of his colleague, Quenstedt.

[26] Tholuck, *Der Geist der lutherischen Theologen Wittenbergs . . . des 17 Jahrhunderts* (Hamburg, 1852).

[27] *The Seventeenth Century* (Oxford, 1929), Chapter 17.

[28] Undergraduate spirits erupted periodically in 'town and gown riots'. The townsmen were known in academic circles as 'Philistines' (Matthew Arnold borrowed this term to denote the uncultured middle class). At Jena in 1689 the university preacher took as his text: 'The Philistines be upon thee.'

and shoemaker (1494-1576) gave promise of future brilliance, unretarded by academic restraint as in France, or by Puritan prejudice as in England. This hope was damped by the theological preoccupations of Lutheranism, which became more marked after the Thirty Years War. The German divines produced heavy tomes, but none of them were stamped with the imprint of individuality. Nor did they excel in their own sphere from a literary point of view. They produced no classics—no Hooker, no Donne, no Andrews, no George Herbert, no Jeremy Taylor, no *Prayer Book*.[29] After Luther's time theology was largely written in Latin till the eighteenth century and could aspire to no niche in the national literature. Indeed, the German tongue was generally considered as beneath the dignity of 'the Queen of Science'. Latin was also the language of law and philosophy—represented by Pufendorf (*d.* 1694) and Leibniz (*d.* 1706). The vernacular was despised by most educated men; it was garishly decorated with an incredible number of words borrowed from French, Spanish, and Italian. 'The unkempt literature of the Reformation age undoubtedly stood in need of guidance and discipline,' conceded Professor J. G. Robertson; 'but the seventeenth century made the fatal mistake of trying to impose the laws and rules of romance literature on a people of purely Germanic stock.'[30]

Unlike the English divines, German Protestant leaders did little to encourage Literature. The Lutheran Church produced *Chorales* of fine quality (Gerhardt, Nicolai, Neumeister, etc.); these blended the masculine strength of Luther with the feminine tenderness of the Pietists. There was no *Pilgrim's Progress*, no *Paradise Lost* (Klopstock wrote his *Messias* in the eighteenth century, but he was, as Coleridge remarked, 'a very German Milton'). The orthodox Lutheran clergy were unconcerned with the task of preventing literature from losing touch with the people. Their eyes were holden with theology. Balthasar Schupp, the satirical preacher and moralist of Hamburg was one of the few ministers to express scorn of the

[29] Within twenty years of Luther's death, no fewer than 132 Lutheran liturgies appeared, mostly variations of his German Mass. Almost without exception these *Agende* were pedantic and petrified. The clergy were even compelled to take their texts from the Lessons for the day—the 'Pericopic system', which some preachers described as a 'tight-laced corset for the soul'. Lutheran Liturgies, however, tended to become less elaborate and were not cumbered by compulsory psalms and canticles, like the Church of England *Prayer Book*; they followed the Western eucharistic tradition, not the monastic offices.

[30] *A History of German Literature* (Edinburgh, 1931).

'Baroque' poets and a keen desire for vernacular realism. Von Logau, the epigrammatist, praised Opitz as 'a German Virgil', but ridiculed the copying of French customs that flourished after 1648. The German Courts, far from scorning the artificial culture of Louis the Fourteenth (whose troops ravaged the Palatinate and other principalities), welcomed everything *alamodisch* that aped the fashions of Versailles. In the early eighteenth century Gottsched, a pastor's son, made French classicism the literary standard of the Fatherland. It was many years before Herder and Lessing arose to stimulate genuine German culture and relate literature afresh to religion and life.

The advance of science in seventeenth-century Germany was as suspect in Lutheranism as in Romanism. Kepler (1571-1630) was an old-fashioned Lutheran, to be sure; but the fact that he disputed the dominant view of the Eucharist was enough to debar him from a Science Chair in Württemberg. The people of Nürnberg, that Evangelical stronghold, caused a medal to be struck, ridiculing Copernicus as an 'upstart philosopher',[31] challenging the authority of Scripture. At Wittenberg, the authorities were not satisfied with the outward conformity of Professor Reinhold, who, convinced that the 'new astronomy' was true, was nevertheless prepared to go on teaching the old; they entrusted the subject to Peucer, who was 'sound enough' to denounce the Copernican theory in his lectures as 'absurd and not fit to be introduced into the schools'.

In Restoration England, educated Churchmen in general welcomed the new scientific spirit promoted by the research of the Royal Society. In Germany the orthodox held tenaciously to the opinion that all who preferred natural explanations of the Wonders of Nature were supporters of 'science falsely so called'.[32] Büttner, a Leipzig lawyer, compiled exhaustive tables on a basis of eighty-six Bible texts, proving that God uses the heavenly bodies to instruct men as to the shape of things to come; his *Comet Hour-Book* had a wide circulation. The great comet of 1680 was greeted as a divine warning against 'godless philosophy' by a host of preachers, who echoed the

---

[31] They would be surprised to hear modern Lutheran scholars speak of Luther's achievement as 'a Copernican revolution'. Philip S. Watson has summarized the argument: 'Just as Copernicus started with a geocentric, but reached a heliocentric conception of the physical world, Luther began with an . . . egocentric conception of religion, but came to a theocentric conception. In this sense, Luther is a Copernicus in the realm of religion' (*Let God be God*, p. 34).

[32] cf. A. D. White, *History of the Warfare of Science with Theology* (2 vols., New York, 1897).

opinions of a famous printed sermon, delivered at Ulm by Superintendent Dieterich sixty years earlier.

More serious was an obscurantist attitude to witchcraft. Luther in his *Table Talk* asserted: 'Satan produces all the maladies that afflict mankind.' Lutheran scholastics, instead of ridiculing or ignoring *diablerie* as a medieval superstition, gave it a new lease of life. Pastor Gast (*d.* 1572) was the first to credit a certain character, Dr. Faust, with genuine super- natural powers. When the first Faust *Folksbuch* (anonymous) was published at Frankfurt in 1587 it was a best-seller—and good orthodox propaganda, a 'cautionary tale' for heretics who wanted to know 'all things in heaven and earth'. Faust was damned for his love of antique beauty ('pagan') and his interest in secular science ('magic'). Not till the eighteenth century did the humanist spirit awaken to the imaginative point of the story. The didactic literalist attitude of the sixteenth and seventeenth centuries was never blinder than in its grotesque misuse of folk-lore. Luther's own ideas of the devil were medieval.[33] He insisted that the purpose of Christ's descent into 'hell' was to engage in a hand-to-hand struggle with Satan, while Melanchthon the humanist thought that his intention was to meet Socrates and Plato. Just opposite the pulpit in the town church of Wittenberg, a very spirited imp is represented as peering out upon the congregation; Luther would doubtless find this suggestive as he preached. He eman- cipated the Germans from the fear of the Pope, but not from the fear of the devil, working with the support of his hierarchy and satellites in co-operation with human beings who had sold themselves to be his instruments.

Scholastic Lutheranism, entrenched in Church and State, instead of minimizing the superstition of witchcraft, stimulated popular hysteria (medieval Germany had a black record for anti-Semitism). Confessions extorted by torture had slight basis save in carousals in lonely places of debauched *Landsknechts*, wild students, and loose women; drink and narcotic herbs accounted for many a weird experience of 'Witches' Sabbaths'. Witch-burning started at Brandenburg in 1545 and by the end of the century Protestants rivalled Romanists in credulity

---

[33] A version of the Faust legend makes him Luther's anti-type. L. marries, F.'s love is lawless. Both visit Rome; L. is shocked, F. is amused. Both lecture at Wittenberg; L. on Scripture, F. on forbidden lore; L. shies his inkpot at the devil, F. makes friends with him (Calvin Thomas, Introduction to Goethe's *Faust*, London, 1912, Part I).

and ferocity. Torture, employed for reasons of state or for heresy in some European countries, was applied in Germany in all kinds of criminal cases after the Reformation, disregarding the limitations of Charles the Fifth's Imperial code. In Protestant and Catholic Germany alike, torture became a science and an art. ('There are more varieties of torture than parts of the human body,' remarked Gravius of Cleves in 1631.) Engravings reproduced in *Kulturgeschichten* indicate a turn for sadism that culminated in Nazi concentration camps. In Scotland and New England witch-trials were few and the ordeals mild compared to those practised in Germany. Penalties were ferocious 'for Satan would give supernatural power to his devotees'.[34]

The first Protestant to protest against witch-baiting was Johann Weyer, or Wier, a physician of Cleves. In his *De Praestigiis Daemonum* (1563) he admitted that witchcraft existed (thus satisfying orthodoxy); but the charges of raising storms, producing diseases, and bearing children to Satan were delusions suggested and propagated by Satan himself. His human victims were not to be persecuted but liberated (Lutheran liturgies provided for exorcism). Nevertheless, it was seven centuries before the theory of diabolic agency was altogether surrendered, and its manifestations ascribed to an unsound mind. Weyer's irony was not understood by his own generation. When he explained that in the hierarchy of hell there were 'seventy-six princes and 7,405,926 demons, errors excepted', they were positive that such precise information could only have been procured from Satan himself.[35]

It is to the credit of an otherwise harsh sovereign, Frederick William the First, who bullied his son, afterwards Frederick the Great, that in Prussia demoniac possession ceased to be a crime; but he had to use his absolute authority against the persecuting zeal of clergy and jurists. Professor Thomasius of Halle, the enlightened Pietist, was a pioneer of common sense and humanity, who was followed by the rationalists.

Anti-Semitic hysteria also abated in the eighteenth century. Luther had done much to inflame it, even in cold print, e.g. his *Address to the Christian Nobility of the German Nation*. The University of Giessen republished his fulminations in 1612, and

---

[34] See Meinhold's *Amber Witch* (E.T., World's Classics). This vivid tale of a pastor's daughter and mass hysteria reproduces the seventeenth-century atmosphere with unvarnished realism.

[35] A. D. White, op. cit., Vol. II, Chapters 15, 16.

denounced all Christians who befriended the unhappy race. Churchmen as mild as Bucer of Strasbourg, spoke against the Jews. The Reformed, as well as the Lutherans, called for strong measures against 'the enemies of our Lord'; they were not even satisfied by the fact that these poor creatures suffered legal, commercial, and social ostracism in the ghetto. If some German rulers restrained the hand of persecuting preachers and jurists, the reason was seldom creditable; spendthrift princes had good cause to keep on good terms with wealthy Hebrews. One thinks of Oppenheimer ('Jew Suss' of Feucht-wanger's novel) plotting with his master, Charles Alexander of Württemberg, to suppress the Diet and replace Protestantism by Romanism, in his principality. The plot failed with the Duke's death and the execution of the execrated Jew in 1737. The prosperity of a 'protected Jew' did not often mean relief for his poorer co-religionists, but was apt to provoke fresh outbursts of anti-Semitic hysteria. The *Aufklärung* did some-thing to ameliorate the position of Jews among the educated classes of Germany, but prejudice and dark superstition persisted. Lessing was a brave man to select a Jew as the hero of his masterpiece, *Nathan the Wise*, as late as 1779.[36]

Returning to Lutheran orthodoxy, we may note that humanists found the new scholasticism no more congenial than the old; what Erasmus had dreaded had come to pass. The very teaching of the classics in schools was threatened. It was seriously suggested that boys be taught Latin from the works of Buchanan and Greek (not too much of it) from Nonnus (fifth century A.D.). The opinion was even expressed that in the interests of orthodox belief and morals it would be as well if the knowledge of Greek was to be confined to theologians.

The sole sign of mental activity was a ceaseless anti-heresy campaign. Old and young were drilled in the *Catechism* relent-lessly. There was a steady drip of indoctrination from the pulpit. Catechetical sermons were printed as well as preached, e.g. the *Katechismusmilch* of Professor Dannhauer, published in five quarto volumes at Strasbourg in 1657-8. This type of religious instruction is evidently not yet obsolete, for in the same city Pastor Stricker celebrated the four hundredth anniversary of Luther's *Catechism* by preaching no less than fifty-seven sermons on the same theme! One university library catalogues no less than 1,590 catechetical sermons for children; these

[36] See. p. 90, *infra*.

abounded in preservatives from Calvinistic error, warnings against antichrist, and scholastic definitions of predestination. Even in the middle of the eighteenth century this method of indoctrination lingered in schools and training-colleges for teachers. Thus Carl Philipp Moritz, in *Anton Reiser*,[37] describes the 'Inspector's' early morning lectures on Dogmatics, based on Gesenius's interpretation of Luther's *Smaller Catechism*:

This filled Anton's head with a good deal of learned lumber, but he learnt how to make divisions and sub-divisions, and to go to work systematically.[38] His note-books grew bigger and bigger and in less than a year he possessed a complete system, with passages from the Bible to prove it, and a complete polemic against heathen, Turks, Jews, Greeks, Papists, Calvinists. He was able to talk like a book about transubstantiation, the five steps of the exaltation and humiliation of Christ, etc.

It was the practice of the Institute where Anton was taught that the adults, who were being educated as schoolmasters, had to distribute themselves among all the churches and take notes of the sermons, which they then submitted to the inspector. Anton now found his pleasure in taking notes of sermons doubled because he saw that in this way he shared the occupation of his teachers, and those to whom he showed the sermons showed him increasing respect and met him almost as an equal. He finally collected a thick volume of reported sermons, which he regarded as a precious possession.[39]

Pulpiteers of the sixteenth and seventeenth centuries were not content with demolishing living heresies: they turned their attention to dead ones—Patripassianism, Valentinianism, and the rest. These excesses were not confined to obscure polemists. In 1658 a preacher with a reputation, Jacob Andreae, published a volume of sermons divided into parts corresponding to the four quarters of the year; each quarter was assigned to smiting in turn Papists, Zwinglians, Schwenkfeldians, and Anabaptists. *Odium theologicum victor!*

Court-Chaplain König declared on his death-bed in 1664: 'Dear father confessor, since I perceive that God is about to

---

[37] E.T. by P. E. Matheson, 'World's Classics', pp. 98ff.

[38] Such mental discipline, exercised generation after generation, no doubt contributed to the German tradition of writing books all cut and dried, with excessive divisions and numbered paragraphs.

[39] Convention prescribed wearisome elaboration in sermon-building. Preachers tried to clothe these 'homiletic skeletons' with fables, conceits, and strained comparisons. Paradoxical titles were in favour to flavour heavy discourses, e.g. 'Bitter Oranges and Sour Lemons'; 'Pale Fear and Green Hope in Sleepless Nights'; 'Splendid Poverty'; 'Salted Sugar', and 'Heaven in Hell'.

take me out of this world, I wish it understood that I remain faithful only to the unchangeable Augsburg Confession: I die the avowed enemy of all innovations and syncretistic error.' One of the few instances in which divines showed the slightest independence of princes was their insistence on the use of the *nominal elenchus*—a scholarly euphemism for the practice of naming persons in the pulpit and abusing them relentlessly in public. When Frederick of Brandenburg ('the Great Elector') enjoined all Lutherans to refrain from preaching against Calvinists, Paul Gerhardt, the saintly hymnologist, preferred to resign his Berlin parish rather than keep silence. He has been described as 'a divine sifted in Satan's sieve', but an enormous amount of sectarian chaff must have remained unsifted in spite of his sincere and fervent piety—how otherwise can we account for his obstinate fanaticism? In spite of all this cult of theology it is recorded in Tholuck that one year at Leipzig, the book-fair of all Germany, not a single Bible could be found. As late as 1720 two pastors in East Prussia had no Bible and had never possessed one.

'The seventeenth-century Lutheran Church exhibited some of the characteristics of the English Puritan movement,' remarked the late Professor W. P. Paterson, 'but it had more in common with the doctrinal hair-splitting of the Puritans than with their religious and moral aspirations.' Those of us who shrink from the controversies of the Puritans and Covenanters and look across the 'German Ocean' for a sea-change will find the atmosphere much more heavily laden with sulphur; the thunder of controversy is louder among the Lutheran host, the dust and smoke thicker, the courtesies between embattled foes fewer. When Protestantism finally won the right of survival at the end of the Thirty Years War, its remaining vitality was dissipated by a renewal of argument 'in Babylonish dialects which learned pedants much affect'. We read in Moffatt's translation of Acts 19[9] that Paul 'continued his argument every day from eleven to four in the lecture-room of Tyrannus'. In Germany the Church became a veritable 'lecture-room of Tyrannus'. The ecclesiastics forgot the great Apostle's timeless counsel about 'speaking the truth in love'.[40] No wonder the mass of the people lost interest in organized religion, confused by

---

[40] N. Paul interpreted *Protestantismus U. Toleranz* in the sixteenth century from a Romanist viewpoint (1911). K. Völker replied, as an Evangelical, in his *Toleranz U. Intoleranz* (1912).

rival beacons in the gloom and contradictory voices crying in
the wilderness. A. K. H. Boyd's parody of a famous hymn could
be literally applied to Scholastic Lutheranism although the
experts of the sixteenth and seventeenth centuries would be
mortified by the charge that they were 'small in doctrine'.

> We are all divided, several bodies we,
> Small in hope and doctrine, less in charity.

CHAPTER TWO

LIBERAL LUTHERANISM

ONE figure stands out in shining relief against the dark background of scholastic Lutheranism. This is Calixtus of Helmstädt, who developed the relatively liberal tradition of Melanchthon. Principal Tulloch has praised him as 'the only *living* theological thinker between Luther and Bengel'. Dr. W. C. Dowding[1] has given a graphic picture of his times, based on Hencke's biography (1853). The Thirty Years War forms the grim background of his illustrious career.

Georg Callisön or Calixtus (1586-1656) was the son of a country pastor in Holstein. He entered the 'Julian University' of Helmstädt, founded by the Duke of Brunswick in 1576 to promote Melanchthonian Lutheranism. After graduation Calixtus decided 'to know his age and his place in it'. His first tour took him to Jena, Giessen, Marburg, and Heidelberg (1609). After seeing the Lutheran and Reformed universities, he ventured to Cologne—so Catholic that it was known as 'the German Rome'. In England he met that distinguished Humanist, Isaac Casaubon, who had just settled in a more congenial environment after occupying Chairs at Geneva and Montpellier; Henry the Fourth had honoured him in Paris, and now it was the turn of James the First. The English bishops were delighted to find in Casaubon an Anglican ready-made, a Huguenot, who, by independent study, had learnt to appreciate the benefits of their *Via Media*. Calixtus also was interested in the Church of England. We do not know whether he met such men as George Herbert and Bishop Andrewes, but he visited Oxford and admired the colleges. His contemporary, Balthasar Schupp, thought that 'it was not so much his teachers in Germany who led Calixtus to the reading of the Fathers and of Church history, as the Bishops in England, who possess most splendid libraries'. His followers were afterwards accused of Anglican tendencies; but the sympathies of Calixtus were not with Laud's school. He would have agreed with Chillingworth and Jeremy Taylor that the Apostles' Creed contained adequate doctrine. If men were only content to be 'plain and honest

[1] *Life and Correspondence of Calixtus* (Oxford, 1863).

Christians' instead of 'zealous Papists, earnest Calvinists, and rigid Lutherans . . . heresy and schism would be banished the world'. Bishop Stillingfleet, the latitudinarian, considered that the writings of Calixtus would be useful in England, if reprinted *en masse*.

Re-crossing the Channel, the young German post-graduate proceeded to Paris. There he presented a letter of introduction from Casaubon to De Thou, a liberal Catholic historian, Roman only (as Grotius said) 'with thirty exceptions'. The *Edict of Nantes* was partly his work and the Pope had placed his *History* on the 'Index', as heterodox. With an unusually broadened outlook and a quickened imagination, Calixtus returned to the restricted world of German theology. How was he to mediate the fruits of his *Wanderjahre* to his suspicious fellow-Lutherans?

Although never ordained, he was appointed 'Abbot' of the secularized monastery of Königslütter and Professor of Theology at Helmstädt (1616). Helmstädt was as liberal a University as could then be found in Germany and was much frequented by the upper classes from all over the Fatherland; here was a favourable opportunity of influencing a cultured community in a genial spiritual climate. Calixtus saw the dangers of unphilosophical religiosity as well as the dangers of unreligious philosophy. He had a sense of historical perspective rare in those days. He pointed out that the first five centuries, as the Age of the Creeds, were of supreme importance; indeed the *consensus quinquesecularis* offered the only sure basis of agreement in theology. Protestants should realize that they had a share in the heritage of the undivided Church till the sixteenth century; 'Catholicism' should not be confused with the 'Romanism' of the Council of Trent.

To his Catholic critics Calixtus appeared to cancel ten centuries of Christian thought: to his Protestant critics he seemed to offer a loophole for the return of Romanist practices. This new theology was branded with the name of 'Syncretism'[2] —an attempt to blend inharmonious elements artificially. His novel emphasis on Christian Ethics seemed to detract from the pre-eminence of theology as 'Queen of Sciences'. The condemnation of unchastity, drunkenness, and other sins of the times appeared to undermine 'Justification by Faith'—a faded

---

[2] A term as old as Plutarch, who used it politically to denote the policy of Cretan cities to forget dissensions in the face of common danger.

banner often employed to cover moral failure. Calixtus incurred the charge of Judaism by teaching that the Trinity was not as clearly revealed in the Old Testament as in the New. His friendly attitude to the Reformed and his interest in the 'Federal Theology' of Johannes Cocceius[3] provided apparent proof that he was a 'Crypto-Calvinist'. It is not surprising that a man so advanced in his opinions and so inclusive in his sympathies should have caused perplexity and irritation even to his friends: but the degree of petty persecution which he had to endure surprises the modern reader. He was accused of making a hotch-potch of religion, so that in the words of the proverb, 'one could not tell the cook from the waiter'. He was attacked for being a non-smoker. A man was actually fined for calling him 'a great and venerable theologian'!

The fact that Calixtus continued to be 'Primarius Professor of Theology' at Helmstädt for most of his life did not tire the persistence of his adversaries, even during the horrors of the Thirty Years War; he never succeeded in 'living down' his reputation of being an unsound 'Syncretist'. One of his implacable opponents was a Hanoverian pastor, Statius Buscher, who described Philosophy and Reason as the women who are 'enjoined to keep silence in the churches' (both being feminine in German). His *Abomination of Desolation in the Holy Place* was a venomous personal insult. The victim only deigned to reply (in Latin) 'by princely order'.

In 1646 Wittenberg, Leipzig, and Jena, joined forces against the heresy of Helmstädt. The spearhead of the attack was Electoral Saxony, whose claim to be the arbiter of orthodoxy suggested a kind of Lutheran primacy. Calixtus was sick of 'Censures', 'Appeals', and 'Refutations', but with grave courtesy rejected these claims. 'Why do you press upon us so many times the *Book of Concord*? Do you wish it to have the force of a symbolical book, to which we should be bound, as we are to the *Augsburg Confession*? What none of our Serene Masters require of us, and what has never formed part of our professorial oath—how can we permit you to prescribe?'

Calixtus tried to show his contemporaries that the outpouring of the Spirit upon all flesh would be but meagre if the Church's faith was limited to the formularies of stringent

---

[3] Cocceius (Koch) was a native of Bremen, although he taught in Dutch universities. The fact that he drew his inspiration direct from Scripture rather than from Confessions gave a touch of freshness to the Reformed theology, which prevented it from petrifying like Lutheran dogmatism.

Lutherans. He derived a melancholy satisfaction in watching the feuds of his ultra orthodox foes. Deadly strife broke out at holy Wittenberg in 1653. 'Could one drop of Christ's blood have saved the world? Or was the effusion of much blood necessary?'

Writing to Chancellor Schwartzkopff, his brother-in-law, in 1650, Calixtus expressed fear for the future of the Evangelical faith. 'If things are to go on according to the intentions of Electoral Saxony . . . we shall have a new papacy and a new religion. The thoughtful will either go over to Rome, or take a course of their own.' This was just what happened. Occult sects like the Rosicrucians and the Behmenists[4] made converts. Johann Scheffler (1624-77), a Breslau physician, better known as the poet 'Angelus Silesius', faced the indignation of his family and fellow-citizens by becoming a Roman Catholic in 1653, finding in that communion room for traditional German mysticism which scholastic Lutheranism had squeezed out of existence.

Calixtus had personal experience of several cases of defection. Young noblemen like Ludolf von Klenke were flattered when they made the 'Grand Tour' to Rome, separated by Papal authorities from their tutors and subjected to high-pressure propaganda, returning to the Fatherland as apostates from Protestantism. When the immature Duke of Brunswick, John Frederick, was attracted by the brilliance of southern Catholicism, Professor Blume of Helmstädt, dispatched to counsel him in Italy, was himself drawn into the vortex; asked to account for his own perversion, he explained that he could see no future for German Evangelicalism, dominated by the grim fanaticism of Lutheran Saxony. Queen Christina of Sweden and the Landgrave Ernest of Hesse were also perplexed and appealed to Calixtus as the most judicious divine in Christendom. Neither of them were dissuaded from going over to Rome ultimately.

A final case may be mentioned. Bartold Neuhaus, a Helmstädt acquaintance of Calixtus, had been appointed tutor to the princes at Weimar. The courtiers did not take him seriously when he expressed doubt as to whether the Pope was really antichrist. He disappeared in 1622, and returned north in 1627 as a Romanist (Canon of Hildesheim, Provost of a monastery and Imperial Agent for the district). Complacent and supercilious, he called on his old friend's at Helmstädt, who

---

[4] See p. 53f., *infra*.

D

received him courteously. In spite of this, the renegade issued scurrilous pamphlets such as *Calixtus castigatus*. Calixtus did not deign to reply, but thought it advisable to address an irenicon to the Catholic universities of Germany (1632).

We do not fanatically reject everything which the Pope has; for if so, we would reject Christianity. But this we complain of, that the Pope will not abide by what he has inherited from the Apostles. . . . Antichrist indeed sits in the temple of God, and yet it remains the temple of God, by the sustaining power of Christ, Luther did not intend to introduce innovations: he held to the Creeds of the first five centuries. If there was no Luther before the sixteenth century, neither was there a Council of Trent to make new dogmas.

The appeal closed on a high note. Let Catholics and Protestants labour after the things that make for peace. The author would do his utmost to settle the schism of the Church, for which all Christians must share responsibility.

This irenicon did not have any marked effect. Roman controversialists continued their attacks. Some ultra-Lutherans accused Calixtus of secret leanings toward Rome, while others followed Calovius in the conviction that he was secretly attached to Calvinism. In South Germany the much-maligned Helmstädt professor received welcome support from old imperial cities like Nürnberg, where the mild influence of Melanchthon still lingered. The idea of Christian reunion was probably suggested by the *Irenicum de Unione* (1614), a well-known manifesto written by David Pareus, whom he had met at Heidelberg. Calixtus was influenced by impressions received later in England. He found a kindred spirit in John Durie (or Dury), Apostle of Christian Unity.

Durie was the son of a Presbyterian minister banished by James the Sixth. He became pastor to an English congregation at Elbing, East Prussia[5] (the sole emporium of the Eastland Company in the Baltic).[6] 'Duraeus' interviewed King Gustavus Adolphus when he occupied Elbing. He declared that he had Archbishop Abbot's permission and the support of twenty

---

[5] Scots merchants built kirks in strongly Lutheran Baltic ports, e.g. Dantzig, Memel, Königsberg, and Tilsit (before 1660). Each of these became the nucleus of a German Reformed congregation, when the descendants of the founders were eventually assimilated (T. A. Fischer, *The Scot in Germany*).

[6] Piquant to note that another pastor at Elbing, Nathaniel Ward, was Durie's very antithesis although Pareus, liberal Calvinist professor at Heidelberg, persuaded him to enter the ministry. 'I lived in a city where a Papist preached in one church, a Lutheran in another, a Calvinist in a third. . . . The Religion of that place was but meagre, their affections Leopard like.' Ward afterwards achieved notoriety as an intolerant New-England Calvinist.

English theologians, to promote 'ecclesiastical union between us (the Reformed) and the Lutherans'. He hoped 'to sett the divines of Germany, as many as are fitt upon this work'.[7] The Swedish king died soon afterwards, so there was no 'Lion of the North' to champion his cause; but 'Duraeus' engaged the attention of the English Ambassador, Sir Thomas Roe, thereby meeting such pivotal personalities as Oxenstierna, Elizabeth of Bohemia, Comenius, and Andreae. He was mindful of the English Reformers' brotherly attitude to Continental Protestants. He even 'accepted reordination from Archbishop Laud, but failed to secure thereby his unequivocal support'.[8]

When Durie arrived in Germany his zeal for Education, Foreign Missions, and Christian Ethics brought him into touch with many kindred spirits, but his wide interests were subordinated to his passion for Christian Unity.[9] The University of Helmstädt was impressed by his emphasis on essentials, his readiness to 'relegate by-questions to the Schools'. In 1639 he met Calixtus in the ducal palace at Brunswick. They found much in common—were they not both 'voices crying in the wilderness'? Crusaders seeking the liberation of Zion? The establishment of the Commonwealth threw open to Durie a new door of opportunity; England could now overcome her insular isolation from Continental Protestantism. Not even the Restoration of 1660 discouraged his efforts. Ignored by Charles the Second, he gained the patronage of the Landgrave of Hesse, though 'the Great Elector' rejected his plans. An incorrigible idealist, he persisted in 'rowing against the current of the times'. After an incessant round of journeyings, colloquies, and correspondence, prosecuted for fifty-two years (mainly in Germany) Durie died at Cassel in 1680. William Penn met him ('unseren Landsmann') when he was seventy-seven and expressed appreciation of 'his approaches to an inward principle'. Like St. Paul, Durie could declare with complete conviction: 'This one thing I do.' He became latterly a man of one-track mind, at odds with his era. History will sustain his claim to be a 'single-minded peacemaker', acquitting him from the charge of being a 'Proteus' or an 'ambidextrous divine'. The tragedy is that his field of action was seventeenth-century Germany.

Durie extended his reunion projects to include the Roman

---

[7] *The Purpose and Platform of My Journey into Germany* (1631).
[8] J. T. McNeill, *Unitive Protestantism* (Chicago, 1930), p. 278.
[9] See J. M. Batten, *John Dury, Advocate of Christian Reunion* (Chicago, 1944).

Catholics.[10] His central thought is the Communion of Saints interpreted as spiritual co-partnership. H. Leube finds here the main motive of his endeavours.[11] Calixtus shared this hope of a wider Christian reunion, and the opportunity for definite action seemed to have arrived in 1645 from an unexpected quarter.

In that year Vladislaus the Fourth, the enlightened King of Poland, summoned a conference at Thorn, to explore avenues leading to the reunion of Roman Catholics, Lutherans, and Reformed. The Polish Primate, Lubiensky, summoned 'the Dissidents' in a tone of ecclesiastical arrogance, but the King issued an invitation more happily phrased, and a number of eminent foreigners were included. 'The Great Elector', as Duke of Prussia, owed allegiance to Poland. He therefore suggested that Calixtus should join his own Lutheran representative: this invitation was accepted with alacrity.

In August 1645 the Polish nobility assembled to welcome the conference, in whose honour troops lined the streets of Thorn, 'Queen of the Vistula'. The *Colloquium* opened with due pomp. It was solemnly declared that the word 'controversy' should be banished from the proceedings—auspicious omen! In spite of this attempt to secure a measure of unity by verbal methods, the right spirit was wanting from the very beginning. Sharp disputes arose over precedence, titles, and such questions as whether or not the sessions should be opened with prayer. It was commonly said that what took three months could have been done in three days. The Protestants of Thorn were anxious to make use of Calixtus, but they were thwarted by the circumstance that he was a foreigner; worse than that, his arch-enemy was the formidable Dr. Abraham Calovius of Königsberg. Calovius was polite when they met, but most violent when it was suggested that Lutherans and Reformed should co-operate, so far as they agreed in their opposition to Rome. Calixtus, despite his old age and lengthy journey, found himself excluded from the Conference and had to content himself with unofficial contacts.

The Reformed had a private room, and there I used to go when invited and fetched. . . . Is it possible that hatred has risen to such a pitch amongst us, that the Reformed are not fit for a man to walk across the street with? The Jesuits, on one occasion appointed a solemn academical Act in their Church; they invited me and I went. The Bishop of Samogitien invited me

[10] In his last work, *The True Christian* (written in French).
[11] *Calvinismus u. Luthertums*, pp. 240ff.

to dine. I went and returned to my lodgings in his carriage. It cannot surely have come to pass that all the offices of kindness and humanity must cease between us, especially at a conference called together by a Christian king, *ut animi conciliarentur?*

It was a sign of the times that so eminent a man as Calixtus, who had already been slighted, should have considered it necessary before leaving Thorn to protect himself against detraction and spite by a formal *testamur* from the leading Lutherans there. The Conference broke up with little to show for its wasted energy—in spite of the fact that one of its members was Comenius, that truly ecumenical Czech who had made 'irenic study' his life-long occupation. What had already been said of the Synod of Dort was repeated and applied to Thorn:

Quid synodus? nodus. Patrum chorus integer? aeger. Conventus? ventus. Gloria? stramen. Amen.'[12]

A Conference between Lutherans and Reformed had previously been held at Leipzig (1631). Much more successful was the Colloquy convened at Cassel in 1661. On this occasion the Lutheran representatives came from the University of Rinteln and were of the mild school of Calixtus. The Reformed divines were Swiss, appointed to fill vacancies at Marburg University after the disorder of the Thirty Years War. Both sides showed a reasonable spirit, but Lutheran views on the Lord's Supper and Reformed views on Predestination prevented complete agreement. Gradually, however, the sharp differences between 'Syncretists' and Orthodox Lutherans were modified by the emergence of a new movement, Pietism.

If the seventeenth century was a 'contentious, dividing age' as Richard Baxter declared, it was also an era abounding in theories of 'Universal Concord' (to quote the title of a work by Baxter dating from the fateful year 1660). Sully, Comenius, and Grotius, propounded schemes of world federation, and these were often linked up with schemes of Christian Reunion. The English Civil War was marked by appeals for spiritual fellowship, from Davenant (1641) to Stillingfleet (1661). William Forbes, a fellow-countryman of Durie wrote *Considerationes modestae et pacificae controversiarum* (London 1658). The fact that a second edition was published at Helmstädt in 1704 reminds us that the irenic influence of Georg Calixtus still lingered there. German advocates of Christian Unity had

[12] 'What kind of a Synod? A knot. A sound chorus of fathers? Sick. A conference? Wind. Renown? Straw.'

been early in the field; the year 1614 witnessed the publication of J. V. Andreae's *Fama Fraternitatis* and of David Pareus' better known *Irenicum*.

The position of the ecumenical movement was changed at the close of the Thirty Years War, when political forces ousted religion; henceforth the balance of power became the accepted basis of international relations. In the words of Treitschke: 'The Peace of Westphalia came to be looked upon like a *ratio scripta* of international law; everyone uttered thanksgiving that some sort of *status quo* had now been established. People began to feel themselves part of an organized European society, and all the sovereign states began, as it were, to form one great family.' Even before 1648 political and religious motives had been intertwined in the policy of Gustavus Adolphus, who had intervened in the Thirty Years War to deliver Lutherans and Reformed from their Romanist enemies—but also to safeguard Sweden's position as a European power. His premature death brought to an end a rare opportunity of Lutheran and Calvinist conciliation.

The thorough-going Erastianism of German princes, however, permitted experiment within their principalities. Thus in Brandenburg 'the Great Elector' placed Lutherans and Reformed on an equal footing, though he found it hard to impress on them his own spirit of tolerance; they were too preoccupied with theological controversy to be interested in education and public morals. His successors on the throne of Prussia made the psychological blunder of deliberately disregarding doctrinal differences and taking the eighteenth-century layman's short cut, indifference to theology. Both in domestic affairs and as regards schemes of union with the Church of England, the Prussian kings approached ecclesiastical problems too often from the profitable avenue of dynastic interests. This is a cogent illustration of Professor J. M. Batten's statement that 'the church unity projects sponsored by princes chiefly for political grounds far outnumbered those occasioned by the fervent arguments of irenic advocates, who were pleading for a unity that was in accord with the essential character of the Christian faith'.

One of the most interesting projects was that of Leibniz, which aimed at no less than the reunion of Protestantism and the Roman Catholic Church.[13] The religion of Leibniz seems

---

[13] See G. J. Jordan, *The Reunion of the Churches, a Study of G. W. Leibnitz and His Great Attempt* (London, 1927).

to have been even more 'basic' than his philosophy. Pioneer of
the Enlightenment as he was, he devoured the controversial
literature of the seventeenth century (Lutheran, Syncretist,
Calvinist, Jesuit,[14] and Jansenist). He made himself familiar
with the 'Conciliar Movement' in Church History as well as
with reunion proposals among Protestants. It was a great joy
for him to find on the Roman Catholic side an enthusiast for
reunion as zealous as Durie. This was Royas de Spinola, a
Spanish Franciscan who became Bishop of Neustadt in 1636.
Spinola obtained the Pope's consent to his negotiations in
Germany. He recalled the early Protestant demand for a free
Council of Christendom, and proposed admitting Protestants to
membership in it 'as visible members of the Catholic Church'.
Leibniz secured the support of liberal Lutherans such as F. U.
Calixtus (son of the great Calixtus) and G. W. Molanus. In
1683 Molanus presented Spinola with a memorandum praised
by Jordan as 'the most liberal offer to the Church of Rome in
the history of Irenics'. Modified by Calixtus, Jr., it was published in 1691. This scheme, analysed by Jordan, provided for a
General Council, to whose decisions assent was to be pledged
in advance. Clerical marriage and Communion in both kinds
for the laity were to be allowed: nor would recantation of
former errors be required. Rome approved of the proposition
in theory, but in practice continued to encourage Louis the
Fourteenth to persecute the Huguenots.

In 1691 Molanus wrote his *Private Thoughts on the Method of
Reuniting the Protestant with the Roman Catholic Church*, which
Leibniz sent to Bossuet on condition that its contents should
not be made public. Bossuet was first approached indirectly by
the Electress Sophia of Hanover, mother of our George the First.
She had a sister, Louisa, who had been converted in France to
Romanism. On hearing of the negotiations between Spinola
and Molanus, she persuaded her sister to admit Bossuet (with
whom she was on intimate terms) to the discussion. Bossuet
was willing to make the concessions required by Molanus as to
Communion, clerical marriage, and no recantation. Would
Protestants have to accept the whole body of Catholic dogma?

[14] Leibniz met Jesuit missionaries from China in Rome. Immensely impressed,
he published *Novissima Sinica* as a suggestion to Lutherans, embodying his ideas in
a memorandum to the Berlin Academy of Sciences (1700). He characteristically
linked Foreign Missions with ecumenical ideals. He visualized a 'universal
seminary' for training missionaries, linked with an 'oriental college' for reviving
the ancient Churches of the East.

The great Bishop of Meaux was a good Gallican, who believed in the infallibility of Councils, but not of the Pope. Leibniz made much of the fact that France had not accepted the Decrees of the Council of Trent. His hopes were shattered when Bossuet exclaimed: 'Show me the French Catholic who does not accept the creed of Trent!' Dr. Moffatt considered that this Tridentine appeal was a sort of Maginot line hurriedly thrown up for defence; the German philosopher 'knew too much about tradition and the sacraments for his opponent'.

Bossuet, historian of *The Variations of the Protestant Churches* (1688) asked the obvious question: 'Have you any sound method of preventing the Church from becoming eternally variable, on the supposition that it is possible for her to err?' Leibniz replied: 'We prefer, my lord, to be members of such a Church, always moving and eternally variable.' The correspondence was closed in February 1702.

Leibniz was long suspected of being a Roman Catholic at heart, but this was definitely disproved by his letters and *Systema Theologicum*, written in 1686 but not published till 1819. His mentality was completely different from that of his famous antagonist.[15]

On Bossuet's side the fundamental conception is that of a static body of belief fixed by infallible councils; and Trent was sanctioned by him on this basis of infallibility. For the progressive mind of Leibniz, all conciliar decisions were reformable in the light of larger truth and changing conditions; for he was at once a Conciliarist of the Gerson type and the chief founder of the *Aufklärung*.[16]

In assessing the value of seventeenth-century efforts at Christian reunion we find that the attempts of individual idealists failed because they were in advance of their age, while the politically motivated experiments of Protestant princes came to naught because they lacked a genuine spiritual impulse. The coercive uniformity of certain Romanist rulers in Germany was only successful superficially. Admittedly the discussions broadened men's minds by relating Christianity to ethics and international peace. But the utilitarianism of the *Aufklärung* and the crass erastianism of *Kleinstaaterei* combined with other factors to destroy the spirit of true Churchmanship. Nor did this irenic spirit reach the ordinary pastor and his parishioners.

Against the dark background of the seventeenth century shine the luminous personalities of Leibniz, Calixtus, and Durie.

[15] H. W. Carr, *Leibniz, His Life, Times, Doctrine, Influence* (London, 1929).
[16] J. T. McNeill, *Unitive Protestantism*, p. 282.

To these we must add the illustrious names of Comenius and Andreae. Comenius, like Durie, was a foreigner. Born in 1592, an obscure native of Bohemia, John Amos Comenius (Komenski) took advantage of the welcome extended by the German universities to foreigners who did not enjoy adequate educational opportunities in their own land. At the Reformed universities of Heidelberg and Herborn he laid the foundations of his encyclopedic learning, fused with evangelical fervour. In some respects Comenius was a child of his age. With the Book of Revelation as his basis he promised the millennium in 1672; he guaranteed miraculous assistance to all who would undertake the destruction of the Papacy and the House of Austria; he even wrote to Louis the Fourteenth offering him world dominion if he would overthrow the enemies of God. On the other hand, the name of Comenius is honoured by the historians of Education as a pioneer, a forerunner of Rousseau and Pestalozzi. Anxious that Protestant education should attain the efficient level of the Jesuits, he surpassed these efficient pedagogues. In teaching he shifted the emphasis from the material to the child. He appealed to imagination through 'ear-gate' and 'eye-gate'. His confidence in human nature irradiated a world theologically darkened by exaggerated dogmas of 'the Fall'.

Although Comenius lived in an age of hard-hitting controversy he had an international reputation in the widest sense; he was an advocate of world peace and Christian reunion, a promoter of the co-operation of science and learning. In losing his own country as a result of the Thirty Years War, he became a citizen of the world. He reorganized the educational system of Sweden; he was invited to Transylvania and England, was even offered the Presidency of Harvard College. He was a humanist in a deeper sense than his eminent contemporary and correspondent, Milton; he was devoted to both scientific research and evangelical religion. When driven from Bohemia in 1624, this last and greatest Bishop of the Moravian Brethren settled at Lissa. Thirty years later he lost nearly all his manuscripts when the city was burnt by the Poles. He finally settled in Amsterdam, where he died in 1671.

Comenius was an incorrigible optimist. The Protestant Powers betrayed his country at the Treaty of Westphalia in 1648—a foretaste of 'Munich 1938'. The Czech people were given no guarantees to safeguard their civil and religious liberty, which they had lost by the Thirty Years War. They were turned over to the systematic cruelty of the House of Austria, whose one aim was to destroy Czech culture, just as their Jesuit allies sought to destroy all freedom of faith and thought. None of these calamities deprived Comenius of his ideals. Fully merited was the praise of Leibniz: 'May the time come when multitudes of men of good will shall pay homage to thee, thy deeds, thy hopes, and thine aspirations.' His personality and achievements have been attractively presented to the modern reader by Professor Matthew Spinka, a fellow countryman.[17]

Comenius had a German friend named Johann Valentine Andreae,[18] one of the most remarkable men of the seventeenth century. He was the grandson of Jacob Andreae, an enlightened divine who endeavoured to mediate between ultra-Lutherans and liberal Melanchthonians. As Superintendent of Calw in Württemberg, J. V. Andreae had to face the hard realities of the Thirty Years War. Temperamentally a student he was forced to 'hang his pen on the willows of Babylon'. Calw was sacked in 1634, and so desperate was the situation that he was compelled to act as physician and grave-digger. Growing reputation resulted in his appointment as Court Preacher at Stuttgart in 1639, with a seat in the Consistory. There he endeavoured to incorporate in the Württemberg Church the main features of Genevan polity. His administrative reforms were thwarted by stubborn officials, just as his educational endeavours to replace 'indoctrination' by Christian Nurture were resisted, almost nullified, by pedants and ecclesiastics. His enemies accused him of heresy. The very sketches he wrote to ridicule the Rosicrucians were produced to prove that he was an upholder of their specious claims to esoteric knowledge. He described himself as 'a fighter against wild beasts'. The calamities of the Thirty Years War were not readily repaired after the peace of 1648. Church and State had already been demoralized. So slow was the process of recuperation and so inadequate were the forces of Christian reconstruction that Andreae lamented: 'Woe is me that I dwell in Meshech.' Yet he was not as unsuccessful as he thought; the Church of Württemberg never lost the impress of his ideals.

---

[17] *John Amos Comenius, that Incomparable Moravian* (Chicago, 1943).
[18] His *Autobiography* (in Latin) edited by Reinwald (1849), is 'an important monument of the period' (Janssen). J. V. Andreae has had numerous biographers, e.g. Hossbach (1819), Glocher (Stuttgart, 1886), Landberger (Barmen, 1886), Wurm (Calw, 1887).

Progressive educationalists remembered Andreae. Spener, the Church reformer, 'would fain have recalled him from the dead'; Herder, the enlightened, described him as 'a rare, beautiful soul' who 'blossomed as a rose among thorns'. These floral tributes would not be sufficient to give him a distinguished place in the German Hall of Fame. His reputation rests upon the fact that his churchmanship was wrought out against a broad background of citizenship—inclusive, progressive, and far in advance of his era. Only in recent years has the study of Utopias recalled from the limbo of obsolete political tractates Andreae's *Christianopolis*. It was published in 1619, as Germany was plunging into the Thirty Years War. The author was no armchair theorist, but a man of God who had actually tried to apply, in his own parish, some of the ideals which he threw on the screen of romance as 'the shape of things to come'. Andreae's social vision far outstripped Luther's. His citizens of 'Christianopolis' had no objections to the *Augsburg Confession*, but did not idolize it: 'They disapproved our morals, not our religion.' The author saw that the Lutheran Church of his own day had become a preaching and teaching institution confined to Sunday; he wanted a Church that would transform the life of the community on weekdays. True religion was brotherhood, not arid polemics. 'Justification by faith alone' had led to unbridled selfishness, as Roman Catholics were quick to observe. Christians needed to be reminded that they were 'members of one another, their brother's keeper'. The author was no mere humanist in hoping that his fellow men would readily put his ideals into action. He dedicated his Utopia to Arndt, the famous evangelical author of *True Christianity*. *Christianopolis* had its source 'in that Jerusalem which thou, Arndt, didst build with mighty spirit against the wishes of the sophists.'

(J. V. Andreae was born in 1586 and died in 1654. Educated at Tübingen, he made a special study of languages and history (modern as well as ancient). He travelled widely in Europe, observing men, manners, and institutions. He was much impressed with Geneva. Indeed, his very idea of a Utopia was inspired by a visit to the city of Calvin in 1610. His emphasis on institutions was corrected by a growing interest in education and science, stimulated by Bacon, Comenius, and Hartlib.[19] That suggested the provision of a college for research in

[19] G. H. Turnbull, *Hartlib, Dury, and Comenius* (London, 1947).

Christianopolis, the bond of union in intellectual co-operation being Christianity, because it alone 'reconciles God with men and unites men together'.)

Mr. Lewis Mumford in his *Story of Utopias* assesses *Christianopolis* highly and vindicates its originality. It was not fantastic like Campanella's *City of the Sun* and Bacon's *New Atlantis*. 'There was nothing of the snob or dilettante about Andreae. His eye fastens upon essentials and he never leaves them except when he turns his gaze piously to heaven.' *Reipublicae Christianopolitanae Descriptio* was published in Latin at Strassbourg in 1619. An English translation with an historical Introduction by F. E. Held is now available.[20] One hundred short chapters cover every aspect of communal life.

'Christianopolis' was a moated, walled, and bastioned German city of the seventeenth century, but the streets were spaciously disposed according to a consistent plan. The modern principle of 'zoning' was applied by the separation of 'heavy' and 'light' industries, workshops being conveniently and hygienically located. A sociologist like the late Professor Patrick Geddes would have approved of the co-operation of Heart, Head, and Hand, along with the author's criticism of the theory of the leisured class (they shrink from contact with earth, water, coal, etc., but think it grand to possess 'horses, dogs, harlots, and similar creatures'). A married couple in Christianopolis could count on having a three-roomed house with their own bathroom and kitchen-garden, while the furniture was simple so as to save the housewife's time. There was adequate sanitation, research laboratories, and supply depots for domestic tools and medicines. The schools were run as miniature republics, to encourage self-government. There was a Natural History Museum and provision for teaching arts and crafts. The law was far more lenient to transgressors than was usual in the seventeenth century; nevertheless, lawyers were excluded from 'Christianopolis' and books were censored in the interests of morality.

Public spirit, stimulated by enlightened leadership, was not considered an adequate incentive to the good and full life, which the community aimed at providing. A circular Temple was set significantly at the very heart of the city. Andreae had probably Geneva in mind when he warned the people against 'those who, under the pretext of religion, make the churches

[20] Oxford (1916).

look mean, but do not fail to provide for their own domestic luxury'. No image could be seen 'except that of the crucified Christ'. The Temple was designed not only for worship but for 'music, sacred drama, and discussions'. Religion was meant to integrate, not to isolate.

Andreae's Utopia has appealed to men of the most varied temperaments. He gloried in St. Paul's claim to be 'a citizen of no mean city'. But like the great Apostle, he was sorely thwarted by circumstances. The walls of 'Christianopolis' gleam fair against the stormy background of the Thirty Years War, which was starting when the book first appeared. 'Here religion, justice, and learning have their abode and theirs is the control of the city.' After three centuries this ideal seems as far off as it did by the end of the Thirty Years War. Yet in the perspective of history the outline of this city of God stands firm and its fabric rises in harmonious proportions. Compare it with the fantastic dream-scenery of some Utopias and the grim, factory-like features of other ideal communities! Seldom have the scientific, humanist, and religious aspects of a social ideal been better synthesized, avoiding on the one hand, the fanciful features of the Renascence, and on the other, the mechanistic, materialist fallacies of the nineteenth and twentieth centuries.

This study of Liberal Lutherans gives some idea of what they might have achieved in promoting social Christianity, humane and constructive, had they not laboured against terrific odds as a minority in a land reeking of war and *furor theologicus*. One recalls the kindling words of another seventeenth-century reformer, Pastor Robinson, who warned the Pilgrim Fathers of the besetting sin of their era. In his farewell address he lamented that the Evangelical Churches had 'come to a period in religion. . . . The Lutherans cannot be drawn to go beyond what Luther saw. And the Calvinists stick where Calvin left them. . . . Luther and Calvin were precious shining lights in their times, yet God did not reveal His whole will to them. I am very confident that the Lord hath more truth and light yet to break forth out of His Holy Word.'

CHAPTER THREE

THE PIETIST LEAVEN

As the seventeenth century grew old, the winds of the Spirit blew into the close class-rooms where the theologians had tried to settle religion by argument and definition. In spite of men of goodwill like Calixtus, the party of unadulterated dogma (*reine Lehre*) maintained the ascendancy. Aberrations from the norm of orthodoxy were to be answered by instruments of logic alone. Stiff formalism carried into the pulpit learned disputes far above the understanding of ordinary men. The religious experts forgot a deep, wise saying of Luther: 'The heart of religion lies in its personal pronouns.' No attempt was made to meet the real needs of the layman or to supply an outlet for his emotions. He existed just to be indoctrinated! The University of Wittenberg went so far as to claim that the symbolic books of Lutheranism 'possessed the force of divinely revealed and binding truth, not only in matters of doctrine, but in *all* affairs'. The effect of this rigid severity was well expressed by Herder: 'Every leaf of the tree of life was so dissected that the dryads wept for mercy.'

Fresh blood flowed into the body ecclesiastic when the 'Great Elector' of Brandenburg welcomed the Huguenot exiles, driven from France by Louis the Fourteenth in 1685. Then there were the German pioneers of 'Pietism'. The living spirit of the Lutheran faith had been kept alive by popular books like Arndt's *True Christianity*, the hymns of orthodox Paul Gerhardt, and the vivid, realistic preaching of such men as Balthasar Schupp and Theophilus Grossgebauer.

'Schuppius' preferred the 'university of life' to academic groves. As a young man, he wandered on foot through North Europe, gaining a shrewd knowledge of the world and its ways. He actually resigned the Chair of History at Marburg in order to preach. At Hamburg he became known as a pulpiteer who had no use for homiletic pedantry; he preferred to look at life straight and interpret its meaning with caustic wit. Like Latimer, he told humorous anecdotes to enforce Bible teaching and to improve the moral and social position of the people, so much neglected by the orthodox. His salty satire was wholesome.

On the shores of the Baltic Grossgebauer raised 'the alarm cry of the watchman in Zion'; Rostock was his Zion, and there he held forth as educational reformer and orator for God.

Nor must we overlook the contribution of the mystics, the quiet seekers after God. We think of Jakob Böhme, immortalized for English readers by Dr. Rufus M. Jones in his *Spiritual Reformers of the Sixteenth and Seventeenth Centuries.*

Böhme of Görlitz (1575-1624) was the greatest of the German mystics since Meister Eckhart in the thirteenth century. The son of a well-to-do peasant, he became a shoemaker. His craft kept him in touch with humanity; unlike Swedenborg, he had no angel visitors. Yet he shrank from the coldness and formality of organized religion, and thirsted for a more immediate experience of the divine love and power. He experienced phases of 'illumation', which he recorded in books. *Aurora* (1612) gained him the support of Karl von Ender and other men of liberal mind and mystical temperament. In spite of his patrons' influence he was accused of heresy by Pastor Richter of Görlitz, and ordered by the Town Council 'not to meddle with such matters'. The publication of his *Weg zur Christo* (1624) resulted in his being summoned to Dresden. Humble though he was toward God, Böhme naturally offended the ecclesiastical authorities by denouncing Churches as the offspring of the Great Harlot of the Apocalypse; their fate was destruction—a consummation that he hoped to advance by means of his books. He died shortly after being officially condemned, the last rites of the Church being grudgingly permitted. His last words have never been forgotten in the literature of devotion: 'Open the door and let in more of that music!'

Böhme had aristocratic supporters; he was a layman whose mystical books appealed to a limited circle. This probably accounts for the fact that he was not more harried by the authorities of Church and State. He had a crude, occult strain of nature-mysticism which links him with speculative persons like Paracelsus. On the other hand he was a 'spiritual genius, humanly untutored but God-taught'. Whenever he broke away from his fancies, he struck out sayings of profound insight such as: 'External reason supposes that hell is far from us. But it is near us. Everyone carries it in himself.'

Böhme was influenced by two earlier German mystics, Schwenckfeld and Weigel. Caspar Schwenckfeld (*d.* 1561) was a remarkable thinker, whose views on the person of Christ, considered wildly heterodox in the sixteenth century, anticipated modern Christological speculation at many points. As a man of affairs at the Court of Liegnitz, he knew the outer as well as the inner world. A group of thoughtful, earnest disciples grew up in Silesia. Some Schwenckfeldians settled in Pennsylvania in 1734. Their descendants still cherish unparalleled loyalty to the founder's teaching, exemplified by Professor E. E. S. Johnson's labour of love—editing the voluminous *Corpus Schwenckfeldianorum*. Valentin Weigel (*d.* 1588) tended toward a more pantheistic mysticism. Indeed he exalted 'the spirit' over 'the letter' to such an extent as to endanger the historicity of Scripture as a record of facts.

Böhme became much better known abroad than either Schwenckfeld or Weigel, in spite of the vagueness of his teaching and the weirdness of his terminology. His message appealed irresistibly to people of a mystical temperament. 'Böhmenist' societies appeared in England, which afterwards merged into the Quaker movement. 'Jacob Böhme has found a place among us,' said Carlyle, 'and this not as a dead letter but as a living apostle.' William Law was influenced by Böhme's views about 1734. Law's style was as clear and perspicuous as Böhme's was obscure and prolix. He therefore popularized the teaching of the German mystic more successfully than his predecessors (the first English translation came out in 1652). On the Continent, Böhme's sayings were often quoted.[1] Thus Angelus Silesius, the mystical poet, recognized the secret of his attraction in his verses. The Fish lives only in water, the Plant in earth, the Bird in air, the Salamander in fire—'and God's Heart is Jacob Böhme's Element'.

By the close of the seventeenth century these varied constituents—evangelical, mystical, and speculative—blended to form the revival movement generally known as 'Pietism'. The word originated in 1689 as a term of ridicule (like 'Methodists'), but was soon accepted as the usual designation for the followers of Spener and Francke. In seeking to deepen devotional life and to reform the Church according to the spirit and pattern of the Gospel, they anticipated the English Methodists: 'They made a regular business of *Pietas*.' Werner Mahrholz defines Pietism as 'an energetic reaction against the mechanization and

---

[1] Bishop Martensen, the Danish theologian, wrote *The Life and Teaching of Böhme* (E.T., London 1949).

intellectualization of the Evangelical Church and a reversion to the Eckhart tradition of German mysticism, a tradition that was never completely broken off'.[2]

Pietism has often been harshly criticized as purely negative, sectarian, ultra-Puritan, seeking to fly from the world (*Weltflucht*) rather than aiming at its redemption. There are pictures of Pietism that certainly bear out this idea. One thinks of the Quietist community at Pyrmont, so vividly described by Moritz in *Anton Reiser*. About 1760 these devotees lived a segregated existence on the estate of Herr von Fleischbein, according to the strict principles of Madame de Guyon, the famous Quietist. They considered that it was man's chief end to 'kill all the passions and eradicate all individuality'—not a healthy or a happy home for a growing boy. In such extreme circles the Elect, despairing of the salvability of the world, sought refuge with the aim of saving their souls in fellowship.

It is fairer, however, to let the Pietists speak for themselves. They have a rich 'literature of self-revelation' that is attractively arranged for the modern reader in Mahrholz's anthology, *Der deutsche Pietismus, 1600-1800*.[3]

Recent research has revealed interesting aspects of Pietism, indicating more cross-fertilization of German life than appears on the surface. It was less isolated than was formerly supposed. A psychological and sociological approach throws light on complex phenomena.

Broadly speaking, we may divide Pietists into four main groups: (i) Those who were Church reformers, but realized that regeneration would depend on a minority of laity and clergy; they would act *negatively* like salt, to preserve the Church from further decay, and *positively* like leaven, to raise the standard of devotional life and discipleship. (ii) Those who had little interest or hope in the Church, but hesitated for secular reasons to cut themselves off as dissenters; they were nominal Churchmen, finding their real spiritual home in the fellowship of the 'twice-born', who formed societies for mutual inspiration and uplift. (iii) The more thorough-going groups hived off from the official churches altogether; they prized close fellowship and in some cases formed communities where they engaged in business and agriculture. (iv) At the outskirts of Pietism and Mysticism there was a tangled undergrowth of uncouth,

---

[2] *Deutsche Selbstkenntnisse . . . von der Mystik bis zum Pietismus* (Berlin, 1919), p. 143.
[3] Berlin, 1921.

E

heretical sects, that flourished rankly in the early eighteenth
century. In the Wetterau area of Hesse the Counts of Witgen-
stein offered refuge to sectarians on condition of obedience to
civil authority and good behaviour. The second condition was
not always observed, as in the case of the 'Buttler Gang' in
Wetterau. Eva von Buttler and her two lovers declared that
they were Mary, Joseph and Jesus. They soon gained supporters, but engaged in such immoral practices that even the
tolerant Count felt constrained to expel them. They lacked
the ascetic note characteristic of Anglo-American 'fancy'
religions like Shakerism, which exalted Ann Lee as 'Mother of
God'.

The normal characteristics of Pietism were as follows: an
eager desire to preach a simple religion of the heart, the expression of immediate feeling rather than the result of study
and reflexion; emphasis on the 'Second Birth' and the fellowship created between all who shared this experience; the
distinction between the quality of life produced by 'the converted' and 'the worldly' (whether members of the Church or
not). Pietists stressed the devotional reading of the Bible.
Where religion was a matter of rote, they called for spiritual
intelligence (even in the Reformed Palatinate the ignorant
prayed 'deliver us from the Kingdom' and in the Creed declared
that Christ was 'ponsified under Pilate'). Pietists sought to
bridge the gulf between clergy and laity by dwelling on the
'priesthood of all believers' as originally preached by Luther.
They urged that Christian discipleship was more than formal
acceptance of dogma: it called for holiness, philanthropy, and
evangelism.

The Pietist leaders were men of varied temperaments.
Spener may be compared to Luther, as the man who gave the
movement its impetus. Francke resembles Melanchthon, in so
far as he systematized ideas that had been already set going in
the experience of believers. Bengel adapted Pietism to the
parochial system. Thomasius registered the humanitarian
impulse of Pietism in better laws. Arnold's faith was tinged
with a gleam of rationalism even more marked than that of
Thomasius. Zinzendorf was inspired by strong emotionalism
and a gift for leadership, which impelled him to found a Church

---

4 Children still suffer from adult mumbling, even in New York. Recent instances: 'Harold be Thy Name', 'Give us this day our jellied bread'; 'Lead us not
into Penn Station' (*Reader's Digest*, June 1949).

whose members were all active missionaries. These men, each in their own way, 'digged again the wells of their fathers that the Philistines had stopped'.

Philipp Jakob Spener, the founder of Pietism, was a native of Alsace (1635-1705). He was the son of a princely *Hofmeister*, but was strictly brought up. He studied at Strasbourg, then one of the most enlightened German universities. He cultivated history and philosophy, Hebrew and Greek, as well as theology; and he won his master's degree by a critique of Hobbes (1653). After acting as tutor at the Court of the Palatinate, he visited the universities of Tübingen, Basel, and Geneva. At Geneva he was impressed by the active part taken by laymen in Church life, and was influenced by the mysticism of Labadie. Jean de Labadie (1610-74) was a French Jesuit who studied Calvin's *Institutes* and was converted to the Reformed Church. He became a professor at Montauban in 1650 and a pastor at Geneva in 1659. Spener felt the influence of this distinguished convert before he developed the extremely Puritanical views that brought him into conflict with orthodox Protestants in later life.[5]

On Spener's return to Germany he was appointed principal pastor of Frankfurt-on-Main. There he published the book which launched Pietism as a definite movement—*Pia Desideria* (1675). This was a plea for a renewal of real personal religion on a basis of Luther's principles. It owed much to Arndt's *True Christianity* and Baxter's *Saints' Everlasting Rest*.

Spener determined to redeem public worship from the taunt that 'in the Lutheran temple there were four dumb idols—the font, the altar, the pulpit, and the confessional'. He determined to diminish the 'medieval residuum'—Latin Vespers, vestments, intoning, etc. He aimed at bringing freshness and reality into the sanctuary. Travellers noticed this. So we find Bishop Burnet, at Strasbourg and Frankfurt, approving of the 'considerable interval of silence, at the end of the prayers, for private devotions'.

Spener realized that personal religion must be enriched by corporate discipleship, if it was to cure those evils that a century

[5] Head of a separatist community at Amsterdam, Labadie fell out with the magistrates. Princess Elizabeth, granddaughter of James the First, allowed the hard-pressed exiles to settle in her principality of Herford, Westphalia. As 'abbess' of a secularized ecclesiastical principality of 7,000 inhabitants, this gifted lady made her court a 'city of refuge' as well as a 'court of the muses'. Ecstatic sectaries of every kind foregathered, including William Penn, who failed to win her from the Reformed Church to Quakerism, though he gained her sympathy.

of official Lutheranism had failed to remedy.[6] The theologians had been partly responsible for laying exclusive stress upon right opinion; true orthodoxy (*Lehre-Reinheit*) involved 'true living' (*Lebens-Heiligkeit*). Good works and faith, far from being separate, were as closely related as rays to the sun. Christianity was an experience to be shared and practised by the laity— not a mere doctrine to be preached by the clergy and passively accepted by their hearers.

Spener was not content with publishing these 'pious wishes' (*Pia Desideria*): he demonstrated their practical value. He abandoned the stilted diction of the pulpit and preached Christ in simple, direct words; he appealed for conversion and eschewed controversy. The typical sermon of scholastic Lutheranism was a soporific, but although Spener was a lengthy and by no means eloquent preacher, there was no complaint of chronic *Kirchenschlaf* ('sleeping in church') when he held forth; his earnestness and sincerity won him eager hearers.[7] Converts and inquirers he formed into *Collegia Pietatis*, where men and women met regularly to study the Bible, share their experience, and seek a corporate growth in grace. The ideal was 'a band of men, whose hearts God had touched'. While allowing for this release of lay energy (too long pent-up), Spener believed that the Ministry was of divine appointment; but pastors must be sympathetic soul-winners, not penal officials, deferential to the well-born and disciplinarians to the poor. They must remember that 'pastor' means shepherd, and not simply preacher. Pastoral oversight would convert audiences into real congregations. Had this programme been fully carried out, the gulf between the Lutheran Church and the people would have been bridged by fellowship.

Spener's name soon became known throughout Germany. In 1686 he was appointed Court Chaplain at Dresden, where High Lutheranism was in complete control. His fearless fidelity to what he considered his duty made the Elector of Saxony uncomfortable, but he refused to resign. In 1691 he

[6] Hence his sympathy with the Reformed Church, as more progressive in outlook. One of his friends was Joachim Neander of Bremen (*d.* 1680), who wrote hymns and was a pioneer in introducing them into Reformed worship as companions to the metrical psalms. After experiencing hermit life and separatism, Neander promoted the fusion of Pietist experience and Reformed order, which is still a characteristic of the lower Rhine.

[7] Spener found an ally in improved acoustics. When the Thirty Years War devastated Germany, many new churches were built. Elaborate Gothic was replaced by a simple *Gotteshaus*—related to the peasants' home by its flat ceiling, white-washed walls, and coloured woodwork.

was promoted to St. Nicholas, Berlin, where the atmosphere was more congenial. He now held the important position of Head of the Consistory. He seldom appeared in public; he was immersed in writing books and pamphlets, besides answering countless letters asking for spiritual guidance. His innovations were marked by a change of emphasis rather than of doctrine. Like the Apostle Paul, he was accused of 'turning the world upside down' because he preached conversion—the urgent need of the second birth.

Spener's Christ-inspired achievements had the success that they deserved,[8] but his critics were as waspish as he had feared. He was embarassed by the opinions and practices of followers who tended to be one-sided. He gave no encouragement to zealots who over-emphasized the breach between sacred and secular; some things that were 'worldly' could be hallowed (heraldry was Spener's hobby). He stressed conversion, but did not insist on its being immediate. There was a note of eschatological urgency in his preaching, but he was not obsessed, like some Pietists, with the imminent end of the world.

This moderation failed to conciliate orthodox Lutheranism, though Ritschl has maintained that Spener 'was not himself a Pietist'.[9] In 1695 the University of Wittenberg charged him with no less than 264 errors! The previous year, however, witnessed the foundation of a new university, as favourable to Pietism as Wittenberg had been hostile. This was Halle. The patron was the Elector Frederick William the Third of Brandenburg, who became the first King of Prussia in 1701.

Spener's friend, August Hermann Francke (1663-1727),[10] was appointed the first Professor of Greek and Oriental languages at Halle. This gave a tremendous impetus to Pietism, as Halle was destined not only to be the seed-plot of future Pietist pastors, but also to be the training-ground of a new generation of Prussian officials. Francke, a native of Lübeck, had the good fortune to be nurtured under the influence of Ernest the Pious, who reigned at Gotha between 1640 and 1674. This enlightened Duke, much in advance of his age, has been called 'the pedagogue among the princes and the prince

---

[8] P. Grünberg, *P. J. Spener* (3 vols., 1893-1906). Wildenhahn, *Life of Spener* (E.T.), Philadelphia, 1881).

[9] Ritschl was too anti-Pietist to do justice to the movement (*Geschichte des Pietismus*, 1880-6). Tholuck, a generation earlier, was much fairer.

[10] Guericke's *Life of Francke* (1827) (E.T., London, 1837).

of pedagogues'.[11] His *Schulordnung* (1642) provided that children over five years of age should be sent to school and kept there till they knew German, arithmetic, singing, and catechism. Corporal punishment was abolished, humane methods of teaching were introduced, and adequate arrangements made for the training of elementary teachers.

Francke thus had the privilege of being brought up in a tradition of enlightened pedagogy. But personal experience convinced him that education was not enough for the renewal of spiritual personality. On a certain red-letter day he was busy preparing a sermon. He suddenly felt conscious of a terrible emptiness; he had received no Divine commission for Christian work. The whole of his past rose before him in the void of inner darkness. It was 'as if he were standing on the high tower of Lüneberg and looking down on all the houses'. He prayed in anguish—was there no God and Saviour? Peace came: 'Henceforth I was in earnest for God, and willing to suffer all for his sake.' His conversion led to the formation of a Bible-study group among the students of Leipzig—the renowned *Collegium Philobiblicum*. Francke's name was now coupled with that of Spener and became unpopular with the authorities. Driven from Leipzig, he attracted large congregations at Erfurt (including Roman Catholics). His successful preaching resulted in an order to leave the city within forty-eight hours. Spener left Dresden the same year (1691).

Francke's work at Halle was a conspicuous success. There he preached and lectured from 1694 to 1727. Between 800 and 1,200 divinity students passed through his hands annually— the record for the universities of Germany. The clergy of Prussia, compelled to study at royal Halle, were steadily leavened with a spirit that was Biblical rather than Confessional. Francke valued 'a drop of true love more than a sea of knowledge. . . . Our aim must be not to build up *scientia*, but rather *conscientia*.' He believed that if the Bible was widely read by the laity, Luther's dreams would come true. He therefore founded the Canstein Institute (1712), which distributed three million Bibles by the end of the century. Belief in the power of Scripture to renew mind and heart inspired his educational programme—schools for the nobility, burghers (various grades), artisans, ragged children, and girls (hitherto neglected). Education led to philanthropy. His orphanage at

[11] J. T. Phillips, *History of Ernest the Pious* (London, 1740).

Halle, started with a slender capital of one pound, grew into a chain of charitable institutions that spread throughout Germany —hospitals, dispensaries, almhouses, and 'homes' of every kind. The '*Francke'sche Stiftungen*' still exist, to remind us that the founder revived the philanthropic side of pre-Reformation religion, which was destined to flower afresh in the 'Inner Mission' of the nineteenth century.

Several of Francke's collaborators at Halle deserve mention. For twenty-eight years he was assisted in the Orphanage by Carl von Bogatzky (1690-1774). Bogatzky was the son of a Silesian nobleman; disowned for refusing to enter the army and for Pietist views, he was successful in converting not a few of the nobility. But for his hymns and a devotional manual, his name would probably have passed into oblivion. The *Guldenes Schatzkästlein der Kinder Gottes* (1718) went into at least sixty editions. Recast by John Berridge, Wesley's friend, it became a household word in England as the *Golden Treasury*, being widely used far into the Victorian period. Bogatzky carried the warm spirit of Pietism into a sceptical age. He had much to do with the *Cöthen Hymns*—a German parallel to the *Olney Hymns*.

Francke's successor at the Paedagogium and orphanage, as well as in the pulpit of St. Ulrich's, was his son-in-law, J. A. Freylinghausen (1670-1739). Francke used to say that Frey- linghausen's sermons were like continuous, gentle rain that sinks deep, while his own were like heavy showers whose effect soon dries up. Refreshment for the soul was provided in music as well as preaching. Freylinghausen was the Charles Wesley of Halle. He also composed melodies. His *Geist-reiches Gesang- bung* (1704) went into many editions, claiming to include 'hymns ancient and modern'. The tunes were inspired by a warmer, more personal feeling than the *Chorales* of the Reforma- tion and scholastic Lutheran types, but this was not carried to such 'lively' lengths as was common later among the Moravians. The Gospel set to music by Freylinghausen was destined to be wafted far beyond Germany.

Francke's outlook was extra-mural. From his 'lighthouse' (as he called the University of Halle) he looked to the ends of the earth and considered the opportunities that had been seized by Roman Catholics, but neglected by Protestants. The official Lutheran Churches were not merely apathetic but hostile to Foreign Missions. Their scholastic leaders argued that the command to 'preach the Gospel to the whole world' applied exclusively to the Apostles, for only they were qualified by *Vocatio Immediata*;[12] then there was Luther's doctrine *De Vocatione* for the ordinary man: 'Let the cobbler stick to his last.' (If this unimaginative precept had been obeyed in England, Carey the cobbler would never have become the Apostle of India.) Francke was inspired by Leibniz's 'Latest News from China' and adopted many of his ideas. He encouraged Callenberg to found an *Institutum Judaicum* for training missionaries to the Jews. Then he transmitted the missionary impulse to his friend the King of Denmark; the Halle-Danish Mission started in South India and began to issue its famous reports in 1710. Francke's broad-mindedness in adopting the scientific methods of an advanced thinker like Leibniz did not appease the prejudices of orthodox Lutheranism. The Divinity Faculty of Wittenberg denounced missionary advocates as false prophets. In 1722 the hymnologist Neumeister of Hamburg, closed his Ascensiontide sermon by giving out the hymn:

> 'Go out into the world', the Lord of old did say;
> But now: 'Where God has placed thee,
> *There* he would have thee stay!'

At Halle they preferred to sing Bogatzky's pioneer missionary hymn: 'Awake, thou spirit of the first witnesses!' Considering the dead-weight of Lutheran prejudices, and the fact that Missions were launched by voluntary effort in a poor country and put into effect without the advantage of starting in a German colony, Francke's pioneer campaign deserves the utmost credit. A door of outlet for heroism was opened, and Luther's doctrine of 'loyalty to vocation' was redeemed from its pedestrian application. German Pietism blazed the trail of Protestant Missions.

Francke looked west and saw the German colonists unshepherded in Pennsylvania. Francis Pastorius, a young jurist and a convert of Spener, had founded the Frankfurt Land Company, and built Germantown in 1685, but the settlers were at the mercy of a motley array of cranky sectarians.[13] It was Francke who sent out H. M. Muhlenberg to organize

[12] Warneck gives an entertaining (and pathetic) account of the objections to Missions alleged by scholastic Lutherans (*History of Protestant Missions*, Edinburgh 1901).

[13] The more peculiar sects—Mennonites, Amish, etc.—furnished material for the 'Pennsylvania Dutch' (*Deutsch*) still 'encysted in the body of the Quaker colony'. They speak a barbarous jargon, refuse modern amenities in defence to the letter of Scripture, and 'keep themselves to themselves'.

the Lutheran Church in America on the best Pietist lines.[14]

Francke's colleague, Professor Thomasius (1655-1728) was one of the founders of the Pietist University of Halle. He was also a herald of Rationalism.[15] He realized that despotism in Church and State could only be broken by the combined operations of Heart and Head. If the German soul could be freed from the bonds of rigid dogma, politics and jurisprudence would also be released from theological control. As a young man, Thomasius was influenced by the enlightened theories of Pufendorf and Grotius. Appointed Professor of Natural Law in his native town of Leipzig (1684) he started to attack traditional prejudices of every kind. For instance, he declared that the use of Latin in the universities was mere pedantry, and in 1687 he made the daring innovation of lecturing in German. Soon afterwards he reached a wider public by his monthly magazine which corrected undue religious and moral intensity by claiming a place for the lighter side of life. He defended the Pietists from unjust charges, he argued for mixed marriages between Lutherans and Calvinists, he ridiculed the pretensions of the learned, he satirized the superstition of witchcraft and the legal use of torture. This was treason to the authorities of ultra-Lutheran Saxony. Thomasius was forbidden in 1690 to write or lecture. He only evaded arrest by flight to Berlin. The Elector of Brandenburg offered him a refuge at Halle, where he became the first Professor of Law and took a leading part in the organization of the University, which he served for the rest of his life. Christian Thomasius was too liberal to be classified as a hundred-per-cent Pietist, but his rationalism was certainly tinged with pietism. It was a common saying in the eighteenth century that 'he who goes to Halle returns either a Pietist or a Rationalist'. To a certain extent the two traditions blended. Had this fusion been general throughout Germany, the chilly winds of 'Enlightenment', following the hot-house warmth of Pietism, might not have had such adverse effects. Three universities register a changing mental and spiritual climate. Wittenberg was the sepulchre of seventeenth-century scholasticism, Halle the living home of eighteenth-century Pietism, and Berlin the brain-centre of nineteenth-century eclecticism.

[14] A. L. Drummond, *Story of American Protestantism* (Edinburgh, 1949), Chapter 1.

[15] The two movements have been sympathetically related by Tholuck, *Vorgeschichte des Rationalismus* (Halle, 1853-62).

Even more rationalistic than Thomasius (and yet a Pietist) was that remarkable but neglected pioneer of modern thought, Gottfried Arnold (1666-1714). Also a native of Saxony, and a teacher's son, Arnold studied at Wittenberg and found that citadel of orthodoxy uncongenial, as he soon developed heretical leanings. In 1689 he became acquainted with Spener at Dresden, while acting as tutor in the household of General Wirkholz. He attended private meetings conducted by 'the father of Pietism', and found some outlet for his turbulent soul at these conventicles. But though he had a high regard for Spener he did not consider that his proposals for regenerating Protestantism went far enough. Spener reciprocated Arnold's friendliness, but was doubtful of his radicalism. He afterwards made the comment that Arnold's voluminous works were 'like a net filled with many good as well as foul fish and will have to be read separately'. In 1693 Arnold retired to the old-world town of Quedlinburg, which was a centre of the Separatist movement. There he wrote his first important book, *Die Erste Liebe*, dealing with the life and faith of the early Christians. This was a 'sure fire' subject, for Pietists were ardently eager to rekindle the zeal of the Apostolic Age. Arnold was called to a Chair of Church History; he astonished the learned by resigning from the University of Giessen after a year. His disgust with the 'bombastic, glory-seeking rationalism of academic life grew daily'. He again retired to Quedlinburg (1698) where he came under the influence of Gichtel, the ardent mystic (who unlike his master, Böhme, became a Separatist). Arnold's Separatist phase did not last long. The antagonism to wedlock which he shared with the ascetic community broke down when he married in 1701, and shortly afterwards he returned to the fold of the Church, holding several charges. Antagonism, however, had been aroused by his radical views, and even the protection of the King of Prussia (who appointed him his first historiographer) failed to shield him.

The work that provoked bitter opposition and even persecution was his *Unpartheyische Kirchen und Ketzer Historie*.[16] In this first Church History written in German, Arnold traced the development of Christianity from New Testament times till 1688, with 'unbiased' attention to heretics, as the title indicates. Tolstoy came across this book and praised it as 'remarkable though little known'. Pfleiderer considered that he was more

[16] 1699; new ed., *Schaffenhausen*, 1740-2.

impartial to heresy than toward the Church. What was truly remarkable was the fact that a Church historian (and a Pietist) should champion in print those who had been branded down the centuries. The ultra-orthodox often fall into opposite heresies from their opponents; the two extremes correct each other; saintly men have often been reviled as heretics by ecclesiastical councils seeking strife and self-aggrandisement; minorities have often represented the true Church. These facts are fairly generally admitted today, but they were bitterly resented in 1700. Thomasius was one of Arnold's few defenders. Like some other radicals, he was an intolerant advocate of tolerance, an unconciliatory controversialist. Lord Selborne observed: 'His hymns, like those of Toplady, whom in these respects he resembled, unite with considerable strength more gentleness and breadth of sympathy than might be expected from a man of such a character.' Arnold believed that the love of Christ extends to the mistaken as well as to the godless. Hence the significance of the *Kirchen und Ketzer Historie*, which interested Goethe as a young man; it would have been much less attractive if it had been merely a rationalist's plea for toleration, actuated by indifference to Christian truth.

Passing from Arnold, we come to Johann Albrecht Bengel (1687-1752), singled out by Principal Tulloch as the only religious thinker of note between Calixtus and Schleiermacher. Bengel, as a commentator, worked out in practice Chillingworth's thesis that 'the Bible, the Bible only, is the religion of Protestants' (1637). He admitted that the *Augsburg Confession* was a great work, 'considering the times in which it was drawn up', but deprecated the misuse of a Confession as a dam to block the gladdening stream of divine truth. As a stimulus to Bible study Bengel published his famous *Gnomon* in 1742. This Index to the New Testament was used by John Wesley in compiling his *Notes*. Professor John Ker considered that it had done more for the study of the Bible than any book since *The Commentaries of Calvin*.

In some respects Bengel was a pioneer in Biblical Criticism. He was the first to attempt to separate the 'families' into which the various manuscripts of the New Testament are grouped. He was open-hearted and open-minded. His only weakness was an irrepressible urge to prognosticate; 1836 was to be the fatal year of world catastrophe. Yet men as able and spiritual, who lived a century later, were as rash—with much less excuse, considering the advance of science and philosophy.

During Bengel's boyhood Pietism had radiated from Halle to over thirty cities, but did not find entrance so readily in country districts, unless a pastor or landowner offered hospitality. Bengel took the significant step of inviting the Pietist leaders to visit his native Church of Württemberg. He wanted to absorb the best in Pietism, excluding its idiosyncrasies. The preaching of Francke was welcomed by nobles and peasants, as well as by the University of Tübingen. It was obvious, however, that Pietism had its faults as well as its virtues.

Spener himself complained that in reality Halle Pietism fell far short of his *Pia Desideria*. As a Church reformer he had encouraged the formation of what we would now call 'cells', i.e. group meetings of ardent souls, nuclei of spiritual life, a leaven to quicken the lifeless mass of the official Church. In actual practice, however, the *ecclesiola* often became the rival of the *Ecclesia*. Zeal often degenerated into fanaticism (*Schwärmerei*). A rigid distinction was apt to be drawn between 'the once-born and the twice-born', 'the regenerated and the worldly'. Leaders of Pietist circles even kept weekly registers of the sequence of emotions experienced by the devout; they made strict inquiries as to whether the weaker brethren had been guilty of dancing, attending the playhouse, or playing cards. A new form of 'justification by works' was in danger of emerging in a country that had hitherto been spared the rigours of Puritanism. 'Thou must be filled with the Spirit,' urged Grossgebauer, 'as the drunkard is full of wine.' The ecstatic mistook their own fancies for the inspiration of the Holy Ghost and found in apocalyptic writings their congenial pasture; they would decide their doubts by turning up the Bible at random. Such was 'charismatic Christianity'. The *Stillen im Lande* were as temperamental as the converts of Corinth, but they dressed in sad coloured garments. Some would withdraw as far as possible from all intercourse with 'the world': others, in the guise of pedlars, would wander from place to place, extolling the 'pearl of great price'.

Bengel considered that 'the pietistic character, which took its form at Halle, is rather too contracted for the times we live in'. Members of prayer groups were apt to show too narrow and sectarian a spirit. He reminded them that 'Conversion is the finger-hand of the clock—very important, but we must remember also the round dial-plate—all duties in their turn'.

The devout should look over the walls of their little meetings, meet 'the world' on their own ground and evangelize boldly. 'Many a flake of snow may be absorbed by the moisture on the ground; but at length, as it continues to fall, the whitening fields show that it is gaining the ascendant, *Sparge, sparge, quam potes!*' With dry humour Bengel dealt with the charge that the Church's corruption was responsible for Dissent: 'Our separatists consider themselves "experienced"—and we must put up with it.' Sects are a useful corrective to ecclesiastical laxity, but no sect can take the place of the Church, the *vivum corpus*, the undying body of Christ. Bengel's high position as a Bishop and member of the Supreme Church Council of Württemberg enabled him to take over the best in Pietism and adapt it to the parochial system of his principality.[17] Rigid division of worshippers into 'regenerated' and 'unregenerated' was discouraged; the Gospel should be infused into the Church service rather than be merely allowed to effervesce in the conventicle. The kindly people of Southern Germany responded to Gospel preaching that was warm without being fanatical. To a considerable extent the conflict of Pietism and the Enlightenment was avoided by a blending of the best in each. The comparatively free institutions of the principality had a healthy reaction on religion. Everyone in old Württemberg recalled with complacency the saying of Fox: 'There are in Europe only two constitutions worthy of the name, that of England and that of Württemberg.' There were high standards of public life in Bengel's country. In his own words: 'Worldly honour (like one's own shadow) flees from us if we pursue it, but pursues us if we run away from it.' Piety, learning, and sagacity were finely integrated in Church and State. Pfaff, Oetinger, and the Mosers carried the tradition of Bengel down to the close of the eighteenth century.

Returning to the subject of Pietism in general, it should be born in mind that the nobility contributed more support to the movement in Germany than in England, where few great ladies resembled the Countess of Huntingdon in patronizing a sect. The close fellowship of German aristocrat, burgher, and artisan was one of the few factors that modified rigid class segregation. Sometimes, however, religiosity was stimulated by fraternization rather than by the Word. For instance, the Duke of Saalfeld would accompany his Pietist friends to their

[17] cf. *Memoir of J. A. Bengel, Prelate in Württemberg*, by J. C. F. Burk (E.T., 1837).

prayer-meetings in the forest, by day and moonlight. He not only provided refreshments, but gave his largest coach for the purpose: 'He even played the coachman himself . . . to bestow public honour upon the pious wives of certain shoe-makers.' So says Semler in his autobiography, adding: 'Instead of exaggerating, I do not say all that might be said.'

It was a Saxon nobleman, Nicholaus von Zinzendorf (1700-60), who dominated the last great outburst of Pietism. Zinzendorf's[18] temperament was warmly sentimental. Even in childhood he would write little love letters to his Saviour and throw them out of the window in the hope that they would be wafted to their destination. As a youth he recorded: 'All my wishes were directed toward the bridegroom of my soul.' This deeply emotional attitude toward Jesus often found expression in erotic terms—which has provided material for a modern psychoanalyst.[19] A disappointment in love he interpreted as a call to do special work for God. He kept looking for an opportunity. He was certainly well prepared to be a burning and a shining light, for he was nurtured in Pietism. Spener was his godfather and Francke was his schoolmaster. To please his family he left the congenial atmosphere of Halle for arid Wittenberg, where he studied law to fit himself for a diplomatic career. 'The Grand Tour' was the next phase, his object being not to see other lands but to seek out good men in every Church. In Paris he met eminent Jansenists. This made him much more sympathetic toward Roman Catholicism than Francke and Spener, who regarded the Papacy as the arch-enemy of Pietism. Gottfried Arnold had been prepared to admit good elements in the Latin Church, but Zinzendorf eagerly appreciated the emotional colouring given by symbolism to the Christ-child. He was convinced that a child-like faith was the key to Christianity. Such a faith was rooted not in the mind at all—'it is a light in the heart'. This belief was carried to an irrational degree, much farther than Spener and Francke would have gone. 'He who wished to comprehend God with his mind becomes an atheist.' The one essential was to believe in the blood and merits of the Lamb of God. 'All the essential theology can be written with large characters on one octavo sheet.'

[18] A. G. Spangenberg, *Count Zinzendorf* (1772; E.T., London, 1838) p. 3. F. Bovet, *The Banished Count* (London, 1865).

[19] O. Pfister, *Die Frömmigkeit des Grafen von Zinzendorf* (2nd ed., Vienna, 1925).

After a short time in the State service of Saxony, Count Zinzendorf settled down on his estate at Bethelsdorf, determined to use every opportunity of advancing the Gospel as a Christian landowner. He tried to reach the outside world by issuing tracts and hymns. Though still a Lutheran, he thought that true Christianity might be better served by a free association rather than by a State Church. These thoughts took a practical turn in 1722 when he offered a retreat to a band of persecuted Protestants from Moravia, a remnant of the 'Hidden Seed' which Comenius had nurtured, when the Thirty Years War crushed the ancient and indigenous Evangelical Church of Bohemia. Might not that Seed produce rich fruit of the Spirit, if sown in the more tolerant soil of Protestant Germany? Persecution had made these exiles cling to small peculiarities of creed, organization, and worship. They could hardly get on with one another, but love and patience might yet work wonders. So Zinzendorf and his good lady built for them on their estate the village of Herrnhut ('the Lord's Watch'). The exiles were not always grateful to their benefactors; on one occasion they even denounced him in his own manor house as one of the 'Beasts of Revelation'. In spite of difficulties an orderly social life revolved around the Count as presiding genius. The community was grouped in 'Choirs'— bachelors and spinsters, married couples, widows and widowers. There were also small 'bands' which allowed a greater intimacy. Emphasis was laid on personal religious experience, but individualism was corrected by brotherhood. Everyone was expected to attend morning and evening prayers. The *militia Christi* was founded on a family rather than a monastic basis. 'No Christianity without community,' said Zinzendorf, just as Schleiermacher told a later generation that 'all religion is social'.

At first the new 'Moravians' worshipped in the Lutheran church at Bethelsdorf, but felt more at home in their own meetings. Gradually, they crystallized into a separate denomination. 13th August 1727 is reckoned as the birthday of the renewed 'Church of the Brethren' (*Erneuerte Brüderkirche*). As the influence of Zinzendorf spread throughout Germany, Moravian groups (usually fairly small) were formed wherever support was forthcoming; they were led by elders, the 'Unity of Brethren' being under control of a representative conference. It took some years for the *ecclesiolá* to separate entirely from the *ecclesia*; the same process was to occur on a larger scale in England when the Methodists hived off from the National Church.

The missionary character of Moravianism is illustrated by the meeting of August Spangenberg and John Wesley in Georgia on 7th February 1736. Wesley had been much impressed by the heroism of the Brethren during a fierce storm on the voyage and was glad to meet the young German pastor. Spangenburg suddenly asked: 'Do you know yourself? Does the Spirit of God bear witness with your spirit that you are a child of God? Do you know Jesus Christ?' 'I know that He is the Saviour of the world,' replied Wesley, after a moment of painful hesitation. 'True,' said Spangenburg, 'but do you know that He has saved *you*?' This interview did not save Wesley from the mistake of forcing asceticism and High Anglicanism on the settlers of distant Georgia. But on his return to England, he came under the influence of Peter Böhler, another disciple of Zinzendorf; and was finally converted in London at a Moravian prayer-meeting, while someone was reading Luther's *Preface to Romans*—that memorable 24th May 1738.[20]

'Methodist', like 'Pietist', was a nickname that stuck. Without going into any detailed account of how the English movement diverged from the German group to which it owed its very soul, we might note some parallels. The Wesleys were men of good birth like Francke and Spener, who sought to reform the Church from within. Zinzendorf may be compared to English Evangelicals like Lady Huntingdon who, without attacking the Established Church, did not view with aversion the formation of a new sect that would be more mobile. The Moravians taught John Wesley to say: 'The world is my parish.' Both Pietists and Methodists laboured under the disadvantage of having a good many enthusiastic but ill-balanced followers, whose ideas ran directly counter to the good sense so characteristic of the eighteenth century, needlessly offending people of education and culture. Both Pietism and Methodism were movements that sought to release the lay forces of Christianity by stimulating the *Ecclesia* through countless *Ecclesiolae*. The Methodist 'Class Meeting' resembled the Pietist groups that met regularly for Bible study and mutual edification; the very name 'Class Leader' was a translation of *Stundenhalter*. This

[20] For impressions of Lutherans and Moravians see Wesley's *Journal* (Vol. I., Everyman Ed.).

warm devotion flowed into the rhythm of sacred song with this difference—the hymns of Wesley looked to Christ, 'lost in wonder, love, and praise', while the hymns of Zinzendorf too often concentrated on the feelings of the individual. Finally, there was a common tendency to asceticism; the German Pietist would say Amen to Wesley's dictum: 'Friendship with the world is spiritual adultery.'

In one respect Pietism and Methodism differed radically. The former reacted against extreme scholastic dogmatism, while taking for granted the general background of Lutheranism; Zinzendorf minimized all *Kopfwissenschaft* ('head-knowledge'); only one thing was needful, a surrendered heart. Methodism, on the other hand, was an instinctive recoil from the rationalism so prevalent in Wesley's England. The traditional Evangelical doctrines of the Fall of Man, the 'verbal inspiration' of Scripture, and the preaching of hell—all were revived in full vigour, involving the rejection of modern science and its conclusions. The Bible was the greatest of devotional books to the Pietist: it was an inflexible standard of orthodoxy to the Methodist.

In 1749 the British Parliament recognized the Moravian Brethren as 'an ancient Protestant Episcopal Church'. Zinzendorf himself had been consecrated a bishop in 1737. That was of some consequence. It gave his missionaries a recognized status in the British Colonies; and it improved their standing in Germany, for the House of Hanover was affiliated with so many princely families. In Prussia, Mennonites, Quakers, and even Socinians, already enjoyed freedom of worship; but in ultra-Lutheran Saxony other Protestant Churches were barely tolerated. British approval was definitely an asset to the Moravians. The Lutheran clergy grew less bitter when they noticed that Zinzendorf was not attempting to organize schism on a large scale (like the later English Methodists). In most parts of Germany the Moravians were content with small conventicles, settlements on the estates of friendly noblemen, charitable foundations and quasi-monastic institutions for the Sisters and Brethren.

The influence of Bengel on Zinzendorf must be borne in mind. These two men of God 'show in what different moulds Christianity may be cast,' said Dr. John Ker, 'the one full of thought and regulated feeling; the other full of impulse, demonstrative expression, and action.' Bengel met Zinzendorf

F

in 1733 and hailed him as 'the prophet of the age'. He agreed with the Count that there had been 'a sad falling off' in the spiritual atmosphere of Halle, but would not admit that 'the Lutheran Church was beyond recovery'; no sect, however Christ-inspired, could supersede the Historic Church, even if the sect was 'a Philadelphia' and the official Church 'a Laodicaea'.

Zinzendorf's suggestions for the incorporation of the Church of Württemberg and the Church of the Brethren did not, however, appeal to Bengel, who was too Catholic in his sympathies to see how the 'garden culture' of the Church could be blended with the 'hothouse culture' of the sect. Among the Brethren, hymns of a tasteless, even offensive kind, were only too popular; morbid imagery about the wounds of Jesus infected devotion. God the Father was virtually deposed in favour of God the Son. Slowly the Moravians outgrew the excesses of what their own historians call 'the time of sifting'.

Burk, in his *Life of Bengel* explained how union negotiations failed, but amicable relations were maintained between the Moravians and the Church of Württemberg. At last in 1778 Spangenberg published what Bengel had long wanted, a Confession of Faith (*Idea Fidei Fratrum*). Alongside of reluctance to formulate belief, there lingered strange survivals of Biblical usage, e.g. the casting of lots to ascertain the will of God. It was only gradually that the Moravians crystallized into a denomination; for many years the members of each congregation were divided into groups according to their origin (Lutheran, Reformed, etc.). Not till 1750 did the Brethren establish a central board of finance; before that, Zinzendorf had to raise funds as best he could.

The Moravians form a 'Bridge Church'. The Bible is their rule of faith and life, but they claim that their principles are in keeping with the ancient creeds, the *Augsburg Confession*, the *Westminster Standards*, and the *Thirty-nine Articles*. Each congregation has its elders. Their bishops ordain ministers, but are assigned to no particular diocese. Four Provincial Synods regulate affairs in Germany, England, and the United States (North and South), subject to a General Synod meeting at Herrnhut about every ten years.

Had the Moravians sought to become a numerous denomination in Germany, they would probably have attained this aim; but they deliberately limited their work at home in favour of expansion abroad.[21] They were content to minister to 'the scattered' (*Diaspora*) without drawing them into their own fold. They rejoiced in being a leaven, 'Hidden Seed', to use their own ancient phrase; it would be difficult to estimate in statistics their pervasive, fruitful influence in Europe. Their world membership is only about 60,000, and of that, only a tenth are to be found in Germany. The glory of the Moravians is the fact that their Church is practically a missionary society.[22]

10th February 1728 was a memorable 'Day of Prayer and Fellowship' at Herrnhut. Distant lands were named—Turkey, Morocco, Greenland, Lapland. 'But it is quite impossible to reach them!' was the general objection. 'The Lord can and will give us strength and grace for that,' replied Zinzendorf. Twenty-six unmarried brethren then declared that they were ready to be trained as missionaries. In 1731 the Count went to Copenhagen for the coronation of his friend, Christian the Sixth. Having secured royal support from Denmark (like Francke) he gave orders for missionaries to sail for the West Indies, Greenland, and later, South Africa. In spite of their idiosyncrasies, the Moravians were pioneers in understanding the psychology of native races. They anticipated Wesley in claiming the world as their parish. Their universalism was a striking contrast to the 'particularism' of contemporary Germany. The Epic of Herrnhut is one of the most outstanding contributions of Germany to Christendom.

Zinzendorf's personality was remarkably picturesque and arresting. He was certainly the greatest German Evangelical since Luther. Like Luther, he was enthusiastic, temperamental. His personality was attractive in spite of minor oddities and concern about his authority. His courtly training did not prevent him from being 'all things to all men'. His dress was simple, but his personal appearance was distinctive. Although eager to lead men in the straight and narrow way and usually impatient of the intellectual approach to the Christian Faith, he was ready to discuss religion in a fair-minded spirit with seekers after truth. Count Zinzendorf[23] devoted his fortune and his gifts to Christ's cause. He resembled Wesley in that his

[21] J. T. Hamilton, *History of the Moravian Church* (1900); W. G. Addison, *The Renewed Church of the United Brethren, 1722-1930* (London, 1932).

[22] J. E. Hutton, *A History of the Moravian Missions* (1922).

[23] Various aspects of his life have been treated by O. Uttendörfer in *Alt-Herrnhut* (Herrnhut, 1924); *Die Brüder* (3rd ed., Herrnhut, 1922); *Zinzendorf u. die Jugend* (Berlin, 1923); and *Zinzendorf's Weltbetrachtung* (Berlin, 1929).

zeal for preaching did not prevent him from being a most successful organizer.

Spener, Francke, and Zinzendorf, were 'repairers of the breach, restorers of paths to dwell in'. In spite of their zeal, sincerity, and organizing ability Pietism petered out by the middle of the eighteenth century and ceased to be a dominating influence in German Protestantism. It was overshadowed by a rapid growth of rationalism. The defects of Pietism were not apparent in the life and work of Spener and Francke, whose methods seemed adapted to their times. But the smaller men who followed them were timid intellectually, apt to neglect the revelation of God in nature and history, besides being distrustful of contemporary thought in science and philosophy. Like Zinzendorf, they were preoccupied with the moods and motives of the heart, absorbed by the mystery of Conversion. They were drawn into isolated coteries of 'regenerated' people, who talked 'a language of Canaan' and practised a way of life that seemed narrow, ascetic, even bigoted, to the average good-natured German. These groups, for the most part, were neither integrated adequately within the life of official Churches nor entirely separated and so invigorated by independence (the conservative 'Evangelical' wing of the Church of England has a similar position as an 'ecclesiola'—in Anglicanism, but not quite of it). In German Pietism the note of renunciation was too pronounced; 'meekness' and 'separation' were too often presented in the letter rather than in the spirit of the New Testament. This faith was not set forth in a stirring, militant manner, nor was it regularly organized as a movement likely to stir the nation as a whole. Its achievements were therefore less widespread and less permanent than those of English Puritanism and Methodism.

In some respects Pietism delayed the growth of rationalism: but in other ways it sowed the seeds of the *Aufklärung*. Traits of Pietism played a subtle but significant part in modifying and enlarging the national character during the eighteenth century. It was a pervasive leaven in education, language, and literature. This is the thesis of Dr. Koppel S. Pinson, who has knit together many diverse strands in German psychology and sociology. His *Pietism as a Factor in the Rise of German Nationalism* (Columbia Press, 1934) takes the reader up to the time of Schleiermacher; it does not deal with the perverted form of nationalism which emerged in the later nineteenth century.

Pietism helped to thaw the ice that had frozen the German spirit after the warmth of Luther had given place to the glacial climate of Lutheran scholasticism. Pietism was one of the chief springs of imaginative and spiritual life that gushed up in the renascence of the later eighteenth century. It blended with rationalism so far as both were in favour of Individualism, previously crushed by Lutheran orthodoxy. On the ethical side, both Pietism and Rationalism appreciated the individual conscience and discounted moralizing that was merely traditional. Consider the views of Zinzendorf. Evangelical though he was, his individualistic approach paved the way to the *Aufklärung* attitude. He emphasized the human side of Jesus ('I believe he spoke broad dialect'). He denied that dogma was essential in large quantity. In his hymns he struck the chord of subjective feeling instead of merely setting Church doctrine to music. He looked over the wall of that cultivated garden, the Church, and surveyed non-Christian faiths, observing that 'every religion contains a divine thought'. Even Zinzendorf the zealot prepared the way for the individualism, humanism and universalism of the *Aufklärung*.

Individuality was farther advanced by a fresh recognition of the value of the Common Man, whom Church and State had hitherto taught to remember his low station. The princely Courts had fostered false standards of sycophancy. A new conviction was stirring men's hearts—that rank does not always have right on its side. This salutary tendency was typified by J. J. Moser, an enlightened Pietist who took an important part in the public life of eighteenth-century Württemberg. 'I sing the song of him whose bread I eat; but right is always right with me and wrong is wrong. . . . I never allowed myself, in my service of God or land, to be intimidated . . . or to defend anything that I considered unjust or exaggerated'.[24]

Pietism did more to bridge class divisions than rationalism, with its emphasis on the superiority of the educated (*Gebildete*). Gottfried Arnold went so far as to declare that 'the most forlorn beggar boy . . . is just as precious to God as a prince' (a sentiment that shocked orthodoxy in Church and State). On the positive side Pietism awakened the self-esteem of the plain man by practical emphasis on the 'priesthood of believers'. Clerical arrogance was arraigned and condemned. People of the humblest occupations held office in Pietist groups, notably

[24] cf. his *Lebensgeschichte* (3rd ed., Frankfurt, 1777).

among the Moravians. 'Self-revelation' was valued at its spiritual worth. Formerly, only the life of a man of noble birth or genius would have been found interesting by the public: now the autobiographies of ordinary men and women were written and read (this was also the case with the lay preachers of early Methodism in England). These narratives described the religious experience of people in all walks of life—peasants, soldiers, merchants, housewives, and servant girls. Conversion stories had a wide circulation and were collected in book form. J. J. Moser, the Württemberg statesman, did not consider it beneath his dignity to compile such an anthology.[25]

Pietism was also on the side of the plain man in criticizing slavish adherence to foreign customs, e.g. the wearing of wigs, which in France survived as a class distinction till the Revolution. French fashions were fostered by the stylish *Ritterakadamien* that came into vogue in the seventeenth century for the education of young noblemen; French influence was paramount from the age of Louis the Fourteenth onward, reflected in 'gallant' literature and '*alamodisch*' display. Frederick the Great could hardly express himself in good German. As late as 1785 a writer complained that 'all edicts and ordinances are sent to the German peasant in the French language and he must often run miles to have a lawyer translate these'.

Learning, like Fashion, was defended from the mob by a linguistic barrier: '*Lingua latina potissimum docti ab indoctis discriminantur.*' This perversion of Humanism had been accentuated at the Reformation, when 'the most humble village preacher, scribe, or magistrate' followed the example of those at the top of the tree by contorting their name into classical form—so Kochoff became Chytraeus; Hausleuchter, Oecolampadius; Buchman, Bibliander, etc. As late as 1726 Mosheim wrote his *Ecclesiastical History* in Latin. (In Hungary it was still used in State administration a century later.)

Nor was Latin emphasized merely in learned literature and in the universities. The Pomeranian *Kirchenordnung* of 1535, renewed in 1690, forbade teachers to speak German, while the pupils were to speak only Latin in school, church, and even at play. The Brunswick *Kirchenordnung* of 1543 branded reformers who wanted to eliminate Latin in the Liturgy as 'ignoramuses and fanatics'. The Frankfurt School Ordinance of 1654 decreed heavy penalties for contravention of similar regulations;

---

[25] *Altes u. Neues aus dem Reich Gottes* (Frankfurt, 1733-5).

as late as 1703 Oldenburg renewed earlier laws of the same type.
Even that progressive divine, Calixtus, praised a prince for
having lisped Latin soon after he was weaned! German was
taught from Latin text-books. As late as Carl Moritz's time,
well on in the eighteenth century, it was 'the only subject in
which anyone could win honour or approval . . . in fact Anton
expressed himself more correctly in Latin than in German'.
A few social reformers protested against the pedantic use of the
classics. Grimmelshausen, in his seventeenth-century novel,
Simplicissimus, writes of a German hero conquering the world,
and bringing with other blessings the speaking of German only.
The survival of Latin as a *lingua franca*, however, was a blessing
to John Wesley, for it enabled him to converse with the
Moravians. But for the survival of the common language of
Christendom, Methodism might have taken shape differently.

Francke emphasized the teaching of Latin at Halle, but the
Pietists realized that only through the mother-tongue could the
masses be reached. It was Arndt who created a genuine
vernacular literature. Previous books, professedly popular,
were far above the heads of the people, with such formidable
titles as *Praxis devotionis*, *Meditationes eucharisticae*, etc. The
Pietists produced booklets with a genuine folk-flavour, e.g. the
Frauenzimmers Gebetbuch, the *Brandopfer der Glaubigen*, etc.
Vernacular tracts addressed to the housewife, the peasant, and
the craftsman were effective in maintaining the spiritual glow
of Reformation piety, along with the hymns of Gerhardt and
Zinzendorf. This Pietist stirring of the emotions and imagination kept the German soul alive during the arid years of the
Aufklärung, stimulating the upsurge of a genuinely German
literature in the later eighteenth century. It was the enlightened
Pietist, J. J. Moser,[26] scholar, historian, and legal reformer,
who declared: 'Since I write for Germans, I therefore prepared
my book in the German language.' Moser developed the ideal
of patriotism on a Christian as well as a cultural basis. This
ideal was destined to flower in the life of Schleiermacher.

To Pietism Germany owes its system of elementary education. Frederick William the First of Prussia enacted that all
children between the age of five and twelve should go to school.
He was convinced that this was as necessary for the young as
education at Halle for intending clergymen. He realized the

[26] cf. M. Fröhlich, *J. J. Moser in seinem Verhältnis zum Rationalismus u. Pietismus*
(Vienna, 1925).

value of the Pietist conviction that the heart of the pupil, as well as his mind, must be thoroughly trained (military efficiency was admittedly an end in view). Apart from the Hohenzollerns, the followers of Francke and Spener gave a fresh impulse to elementary education from Württemberg to Holstein, and from the Rhineland to East Prussia. Moreover, they were eager to extend to poor folk the advantages of secondary education, so far as facilities were available. Their Pietist record compares favourably with the utilitarian standards of the *Aufklärung*, expressed by Frederick the Great: '*Le vulgaire ne mérite pas d'être éclairé.*' The Romantic Movement became conscious of the debt they owed to the common people in preserving national traits and folklore, which the 'enlightened' classes despised. This heritage was partly transmitted through a living conception of *Volk*. 'The development of true nationalism is but the growth of individual freedom writ large.' It was only in the nineteenth century that false nationalism triumphed.

Rudolf Sohm has described Pietism as 'the last great surge of the waves of the ecclesiastical movement begun by the Reformation. . . . Then came a time when another intellectual movement took possession of the minds of men.' Rationalism submerged Pietism for a time, but owed something to it— notably an interest in Bible study. It is true that cold analysis was apt to displace warm devotional reading, but some of the most active Pietists were not without scholarly interests. For instance, Francke went out of his way to study under a Rabbi and used to say: 'Hebrew and Greek are the two eyes of Bible knowledge,' and 'Theology is the richer culture of Christianity.' 'Enlightenened Pietism' bridged the gulf between crude, ecstatic Pietism and 'flat rationalism'. As we shall see, the waters of life flowed underground during the eighteenth century, a trickle here and there, to reach flood-tide in the early nineteenth century.

In the past century, unfortunately, it has sometimes withdrawn to the narrow channel of Biblical literalism, as in the case of Hengstenberg.[27] Sometimes it has merged with the stream of revived Lutheran orthodoxy. Sometimes it has been too content in the backwaters of the *Gemeinschaften*.[28] It has often suffered from the group emotionalism of credulous people, easily impressed by fluent exhorters. When Pearsall Smith, the plausible American evangelist, preached 'Perfect Holiness

[27] See p. 133f., *infra*.　　　　　　　[28] See p. 253f., *infra*.

NOW!', Pietists flocked after him in Germany, even more than in England. 'All Europe lies at my feet!' he declared in 1875. Another revival movement, different but akin in emotional intensity and keen on 'sharing experience', has in recent later years made headway in certain German circles. The Oxford Group has undoubtedly made a strong appeal to sections of the upper class whose ancestors were responsive to Pietism. Such movements, however, have been confined to coteries. Karl Barth, in spite of his hearty dislike of tepid religion, roundly declared: 'Better with the Church in hell than with pietists, of higher or lower type—in a heaven which does not exist.'

Considering the permanent contribution of Pietism to German religion, Ebrard, Goebel, and other historians of the Reformed Church have claimed that it only became dangerous when the State insisted on controlling preaching and liturgy so as to throttle all spontaneity. In the Reformed Churches of the lower Rhine laymen were allowed to take part in informal meetings for prayer, Bible-study, and hymn-singing. Individualism, over-excitement, and ultra-puritanical ethics were corrected by the regular preaching of the Word, catechizing, and the democratic operation of Church courts.

Pietism tinged the stream of Schleiermacher's life and thought; it sparkled clear in the soul of Tholuck; it filled the old wells of mysticism in the Rhineland and Württemberg; it released the spirit of warm Evangelical piety from doctrinal and ritual formalism; it made the Bible live as it had never done since Luther's day in the consciousness of the German people. How true are the words of Dr. John Ker: 'No work of faith or labour of love is ever wasted. Though, like the old fountain of the Greeks, it sinks below the sea and seems lost in sand and bitter waters, it rises in another land, as a streamlet of the river of life, which makes glad in after years the City of our God.'[29]

[29] *History of Preaching* (London, 1888), p. 238.

CHAPTER FOUR

THE REIGN OF RATIONALISM

IN Germany the Age of Reason is known as the *Aufklärung* (elucidation, clarification). Rationalism was not slow in spreading from one country to another in the cosmopolitan eighteenth century. In the age of Louis the Fourteenth every German prince aimed at making his *Residenz* a miniature Versailles. Under Louis the Fifteenth, *Illuminisme* was the prevailing fashion. Frederick the Great's patronage of Voltaire involved the relaxation of theological rigour ('let every man go to heaven his own way'). 'Enlightened circles' would have approved of Bridges' estimate of the Reformers as *avant couriers* of Voltaire:

> Luther and Calvin, who, whate'er they taught,
> Led folk from superstition to free thought.

Frederick the Second established 'a colony of French infidels' in Berlin. He also imported the works of English Deists. Deism attracted attention in England when Toland published *Christianity Not Mysterious* (1695). It petered out in Middleton's *Free Enquiry* (1748), if we allow that Butler's *Analogy* (1736) was not such a mortal blow as Mr. Gladstone affirmed. It was not difficult to confute writers who knew little Latin and less Greek, were defective in historic sense, and did a good deal of reckless guesswork in the fields of Biblical Criticism and Comparative Religion. The Deists merely rippled the smooth surface of English life: among the Teutons they caused a lively stir as they proceeded to 'throw out the baby with the bath-water' (to apply Luther's homely expression). In 1738 Shaftesbury's *Characteristics* appeared in German translation; Tindal's *Christianity as Old as Creation* followed in 1741. To such writers rationalism was 'the residuum left in man's higher mental life when you have purged out everything derived from Christianity'. Across the Rhine a large middle class, not sophisticated enough to appreciate French *Illuminisme*, lapped up with avidity Deism that had been rejected by the English public. In these circles the *Freidenker* (Free-thinker) flourished. As Wesley remarked: 'Freethinkers, so called, are seldom close thinkers.'

In view of subsequent Anglo-Saxon complaints about 'German rationalism' (too readily identified with German theology in general), we are apt to forget that the English Deists and Hume started it.[1] The 'German critics' of the nineteenth century simply repaid with interest the debt that their eighteenth-century forebears had too recklessly incurred. What had already been made in England (and discredited there) became so popular as an imported article that it changed the whole course of mental taste in Germany for generations. The Deists raised questions about the verbal inspiration of Scripture, etc., which others were more competent to answer. The Teutons had a native skill in marshalling arguments, a patience in constructing theories as well as in demolishing traditions, which Anglo-Saxons somehow lacked.

It is curious that the sequence of Rationalism and Pietism was reversed in the two countries. In Great Britain various shades of Deism flourished in the first half of the eighteenth century: by 1748 the movement had passed away, leaving hardly a trace on the national consciousness, save certain deposits at the time of the French Revolution which were more political than religious. Bolingbroke and Hume gave way to Wesley and Whitefield.

In Germany the first half of the century was the Age of Pietism, represented by Francke and Spener. But Pietism was past its best by 1740, when Frederick the Great became king of Prussia and renounced the Evangelical convictions of his ancestors. Lessing and Semler presided over the destiny of German Protestantism in the second half of the eighteenth century, and secured the triumph of rationalism on a scale unthought-of in England.[2] At the close of the century Kant proposed Reason (*Vernunft*) as religious criterion—so far as the 'practical reason' restored to the soul that certainty of God and its own immortality which the processes of 'pure reason' refused to sanction.[3] In the early nineteenth century Schleiermacher was to substitute sentiment (*Gefühl*) for dogma and Hegel the Idea (*Begriff*). Thus German speculation advanced up the path opened by Deist pioneers.

[1] cf. H. L. Stewart, *Modernism Past and Present* (London, 1932), Chapter 8.

[2] Besides standard German works, e.g. Tholuck's *Gesch. des Rationalismus* and Kohn's *Aufklärungsperiode*, several are in E.T., e.g. Hagenbach's *German Rationalism* (Edinburgh, 1865) and *History of the Church in the Eighteenth Century* (New York, 1869).

[3] cf. F. Paulsen, *Kant der Philosoph des Protestantismus* (Berlin, 1899).

Pietism, with its vigorous assertion of the necessity of individual conviction in religion, and its consequent disparagement of Church authority, naturally contained within itself the germs of rebellion. From Pietist circles there emerged strange figures like Dippel and Edelmann. Johann Conrad Dippel (1673-1734) studied theology, quarrelled with the Church and became a physician. Like other adventurers of his age, lured by alchemy, he stumbled into the more promising sphere of chemistry; he is credited with the discovery of Prussian blue and 'Dippel's animal oil'. His scientific interest turned him against historic Christianity, and he assailed the faith in such works as *Papismus Vapulans Protestantium* (1698). Love was all that God required of man, said Dippel; all else was due to human fraud or misunderstanding. Jews, Turks, infidels, and heretics could be members of the true Church of God if they only became aware of 'the light that lighteth every man'.

This crude interpretation of St. John was also taken up by Johann Christian Edelmann (1698-1767). Edelmann had been a follower of Zinzendorf, but afterwards explained that he had been one of the fools misled by Brother Ludwig. 'The Word was God' only in the sense that God was Pure Reason—an adequate guide to all problems of religion and life. His *Autobiography*[4] published by C. W. Klose (Berlin, 1840) reveals a strange life. He attracted sufficient attention to cause his writings to be publicly burnt at the Emperor's command, but found protection at Berlin under Frederick the Great. Edelmann died in abject poverty, but was more fortunate than his fellow-adventurer, Dippel, who wandered over Germany, Holland, and Scandinavia, frequently getting himself into trouble with the authorities.

It was not through these rebels from orthodoxy and pietism that the most powerful impulse toward rationalism was derived. The master-mind was essentially that of a great European, Gottfried Wilhelm Leibniz (1646-1715). Leibniz had won fame as mathematician, diplomatist, and man of affairs. We have already been introduced to him as a pioneer of Christian reunion and of Foreign Missions. He never ceased to be a loyal Lutheran, yet his teaching, as popularized, diverged far from the historic Christian Faith. 'All is for the best in the best of all possible worlds.' That was clearly contradicted by the facts

---

[4] Selection in Mahrholz, *Der deutsche Pietismus* (Berlin, 1921), pp. 389-422.

of life and satirized for all time in Voltaire's *Candide*: but it appealed to those who were satisfied with the world as it was and also to those who gloried in the advance of science and education. 'Evil is simply the necessary limitation of every created thing, something metaphysical, not moral.' Here was a welcome change from the traditional emphasis on sin, whether stated theologically by the orthodox or experimentally by the pietists. 'The course of events is regulated by a pre-established harmony.' This left little room for the human will, and promoted a Deistic attitude even among ordinary laymen.

The theories of Leibniz were popularized by Christian Wolff (1679-1754). Wolff planted rationalism, not in the arid acres of Lutheran orthodoxy (where men's minds had no material to work upon save stale dogma), but in the well-weeded soil of Halle which had hitherto produced nothing but the sensitive plant of Pietism. Appointed to the Chair of Mathematics and Natural Philosophy in 1706, he assumed an attitude of 'candour' and opposed special claims for Christianity as a unique religion. In 1721 he caused consternation by his academic treatise on '*The Practical Philosophy of the Chinese*'. The principles of Confucius witnessed to the sufficiency of human reason and moral principle. There was nothing altogether new in this notion as far as Germany was concerned, but it fell like a bomb on the devout academy of Francke and Spener. For ten years Wolff was subjected to persistent attack. He was so exasperated that he unwisely appealed to Frederick William the First of Prussia. His enemies had already gained the King's ear, and knew how to put their case to a military monarch. If Wolff's 'Determinism' were recognized, they reasoned, no soldier who deserted could be punished, since he acted by necessity! The argument was conclusive. Wolff was ordered to leave the realm within forty-eight hours on pain of a halter. He was welcomed, however, by the Landgrave of Hesse and installed in a Chair at Marburg, whence his influence spread throughout western Germany. One of the first acts of Frederick the Great was to recall him to Halle. His return in 1740 was a popular triumph. He soon lost his old power of attracting students, but his prestige was immense with the public. Men said that he taught philosophy to speak German. The pulpits resounded with the praise of 'pre-established Harmony' and 'sufficient Reason'.

Wolff's successor at Halle, J. S. Semler (1725-91) was no

philosopher, but a pioneer in Biblical Criticism. Spinoza had been expelled from the synagogue at Amsterdam for holding destructive views of the Old Testament as early as 1656. But in Holland freedom of thought was more widespread than in Germany. It was daring of Semler to deny the equal value of both Testaments, to reject the Divine authority of the traditional canon, and to question the accuracy of the text. He revived previous doubts as to the authorship of certain books, notably *Hebrews*. He called attention to the fact that there were different types of theology even in the New Testament. He pointed out that the Nicene Creed marked a divergence from the original deposit of the Apostolic Age; it was the product of three centuries of speculation. Semler outgrew his narrow upbringing, but not the Christian faith. Indeed, his interesting *Autobiography*[5] (1781-2) makes it clear that he was saddened by the rationalistic excesses of his followers. 'He had kindled a flame which spread altogether beyond his control, and consumed some things which were dear to him.'

Two notable radicals carried Semler's principles too far. Reimarus and Bahrdt. Hermann Reimarus (1694-1768) was unquestionably an able man. As Hebrew Professor at Hamburg he made his home a centre of the highest culture. His abundant leisure was so engrossed that he did not have time to finish his *Apology for the Reasonable Worshippers of God*, which he kept revising till his death. These essays defended the active use of the human reason, criticized the miraculous element in both Testaments, and almost rejected revealed religion. Fraud and delusion were frequently shown lurking at the roots of the supernatural. Reimarus was too extreme for even the tolerant taste of the age. It is not surprising that when Lessing published this work after his death (1774-8) he entitled the book *Fragments of an Anonymous Author*, said to have been discovered in the Grand Ducal Library at Wolfenbüttel. There was nothing mysterious about these '*Wolfenbüttel Fragments*'; they were just deistical tracts. The manner in which they were issued guaranteed good publicity, but the ensuing controversy did not add to Lessing's reputation. It is worth noting that the Reverend C. Voysey, the Anglican founder of the 'Theistic Church', translated Strauss's *Life of Reimarus* (London, 1879).

Karl Friedrich Bahrdt (1741-92) followed Reimarus as a pioneer of New Testament Criticism. Coarse and truculent,

[5] Selection in Mahrholz, op. cit.

he lacked the polish that made his predecessor *persona grata* to the educated classes. Learning he certainly possessed, but reverence and imagination he lacked. As the son of a General Superintendent at Leipzig, he enjoyed social advantages; but even as a boy he was somewhat unbalanced. The scandals of his private life drove him from one university to another, as professor and preacher. In 1773 he published a 'model version' of the New Testament, accommodated to the principles and prejudices of the 'Enlightenment'. This was so heretical that the High Court of the Empire actually intervened and suspended him from his functions as General Superintendent of Dürkheim (1778). Poverty-stricken, he retired to Halle, in spite of academic opposition; there he was permitted to lecture on non-theological subjects, thanks to friends at court. Many were the pamphlets he wrote in a rough and ready style that reached the common people. He may be described as a kind of German Tom Paine.[6] Bahrdt settled as an inn-keeper near Halle, with his daughters and mistress (he had repudiated his wife). His aim was to produce a 'moral system' capable of replacing supernatural Christianity. With incredible egotism he announced: 'I looked upon Moses and Jesus, Confucius, Socinus, Luther, and myself, as the instruments of Providence through which he is working for the welfare of men'! Bahrdt's freedom terminated with the death of his fellow-sceptic, Frederick the Great. A new Pharaoh ascended the throne who knew not Joseph. Religious reaction was at work in Prussia.[7] Bahrdt wrote a lampoon on the *Edict* of 1788, which ordered a general return to orthodoxy. Unlike Semler, he had the courage of his convictions in days when rationalism had ceased to be fashionable. He was sentenced to a year's imprisonment. There he wrote an *Autobiography*, which has been described as 'a mixture of lies, hypocrisy, and self-prostitution'.

Albrecht Schweitzer, in his classic *Quest of the Historical Jesus (from Reimarus to Wrede)*, has pointed out the supreme service rendered by the German Enlightenment—namely, the stirring of a new critical interest in the Founder of Christianity. Creeds and Confessions had only been interested in Christology as one section of an elaborate blue-print of belief. English Latitudinarians and Scottish Moderates were not lured by

---

[6] J. M. Robertson, in his *Short History of Free Thought*, gives as favourable an account of him as facts permit.

[7] See p. 192f., *infra*.

the quest of the historic Jesus. We may be thankful that the Germans *were*, in spite of their shortcomings. Eighteenth-century investigators like Reimarus suffered from lack of historic perspective. They were quite unaware of the need for Wonder in religion. They sought to recover Jesus from the dogma-laden dust of libraries, but they merely reduced Him to the level of a purveyor of enlightenment and edification. They paraphrased His wonderful words of life in chilly, urbane eighteenth-century diction. They explained that the angels over Bethlehem were the *aurora borealis*, misunderstood by the shepherds' fancy; Christ's cures were effected by animal magnetism; His Resurrection was accounted for by the supposition that he was not dead, or else his disciples were under a hallucination. Anything supernatural in His teaching was 'an accommodation' to the mental limitations of His hearers. So the 'enlighteners' worked through the Bible and measured it by the yardstick of their own common sense. A later generation complained that it required more faith to accept their rationalistic explanations than to accept the Bible as it stood.

Not all the pioneers of critical Bible study were rationalistic. J. A. Ernesti (1707-81) did not surrender Lutheran dogma, when he claimed, as a good classical scholar, that Scripture should be interpreted by the same methods as Livy or Thucydides, without undue theological bias. J. D. Michaelis (1717-91) was brought up on conservative lines. Strangely enough, 'a visit to England in 1741-2 lifted him out of the narrow groove of his earlier education'. He translated part of Richardson's *Clarissa* into German and studied English literature, secular as well as sacred. Despite his conservatism in proclaiming the antiquity and divine authority of the Hebrew vowel-points, he broadened the scope of Bible study by linking it up with history, geography, and science.[8]

The real father of the Higher Criticism, however, was a student of Michaelis at Göttingen, J. G. Eichhorn (1752-1827). Eichhorn realized that the Reformers had been less fettered by literalist theories of Verbal Inspiration than their successors. Luther was indifferent as to whether or no Moses wrote the Pentateuch; he considered *Chronicles* of less historical value than *Kings*; and he thought that *Isaiah* owed its present form to later hands. But to orthodox Lutherans such investigations were taboo. Eichhorn did not allow himself to be biased by either

[8] cf. his *Autobiography* (ed. Hassencamp, 1793).

tradition or radical theories. 'The Higher Criticism', he remarked, 'is not a new name to any humanist.' But when he published his *Introduction to the Old Testament* in 1783 he was 'presenting the produce of a hitherto unworked field'. In this first comprehensive attempt to apply critical methods to the sacred books, he had few implements of research save Astruc's *Conjectures as to the Composite Structure of the Pentateuch* and Bishop Lowth's *Lectures on Hebrew Poetry* (both published in 1753). When young Pusey studied at Göttingen in 1825, he sat under Eichhorn with zest, although the sage was completing fifty years of productive work and was nearing the end of his course. Pusey was impressed by his outstanding ability as a critic, but was struck with 'his total insensibility to the real religious import of the Old Testament narrative'. That was the weak point of subsequent German scholarship (a limitation which Cheyne noted in his *Founders of Old Testament Criticism*). At Göttingen Pusey learnt a humility and patience not common at Oxford in his day. Years later he would remark: 'A German professor would think nothing of doing so and so'—meaning Eichhorn. He realized that his own countrymen in England were utterly unprepared for a deluge of new knowledge about the Bible; might he not become a channel of communication, cautiously regulating the flowing current? For a time Pusey revelled in the role of interpreter but did not relish a reputation for heresy; as one of the Tractarian triumvirate, he soon closed his eyes to new light and relapsed into more congenial Anglican attitude—insular conservatism.

During the eighteenth century English theologians were not quite so suspicious of German 'Neology' as they afterwards became,[9] but there was little attempt to keep in touch with German scholarship even among the Latitudinarians. For instance, Ernesti had criticized the accepted tradition that the New Testament was not written in pure Greek; he had solid grounds for his theory that ought to have interested Englishmen who made much of the Classics. Yet his *Institutio Interpretis Novi Testamenti* was not translated till 1833. Herbert Marsh was one of the few English divines to study in Germany; he proceeded from Cambridge to Leipzig. In 1801 he completed his translation of Michaelis's *New Testament Introduction*, but the first edition of the original had appeared in 1750. Crabb Robinson, who travelled in Germany between 1801 and 1805

[9] See p. 138f., *infra*.

G

mentioned Marsh's work with pride to a certain Lutheran pastor in Saxony. Herr Hildebrandt replied: 'Michaelis's book is already forgotten here; we have a more learned commentary in the work of Paulus.'[10]

H. E. G. Paulus (1761-1851) had the privilege of enjoying the friendship of Goethe and Schiller when he was a professor at Jena. Even this stimulating intercourse failed to awaken in him the sense of wonder. When transferred from the Chair of Hebrew to that of Theology in 1793 he had to swear by the Confessional Standards. This oath he justified by his own definition of orthodoxy, not as 'right opinion' but as 'upright conduct in inquiring after truth'. His exegesis reduced prophecy to the barest human limits—to prophesy (*weissagen*) was equivalent to saying something wise (*weisses sagen*). He continued to lecture and write in the flat, banal style of his predecessors; only occasionally did the drip of verbiage sparkle in a rare remark of insight, such as: 'The truly miraculous thing about Jesus is Jesus Himself.'

Paulus might have learnt much from his friend J. G. von Herder, the Court Preacher at Weimar, about the need for historic perspective, the relationship of religion to the arts, and particularly the place of poetry in the Bible. To Herder, as to his friend Eichhorn, the Old Testament was 'the mirror of the folk soul of Israel'. Many of the 'Enlighteners' would gladly have obliterated every trace of oriental imagery; some of them would readily have reduced Luther's Bible to the stilted diction of a licentiate's 'trial-sermon'. Herder appreciated the poetic sentiment of the East, not indeed directly by travel in the Levant, but in the course of a voyage from Riga to Nantes, where he experienced the varied moods of Nature as never before. He was influenced by Rousseau—but never became a temperamental Romanticist. In his *Letters to Theophron* Herder observed: 'As a child listens to his father's voice, and as a man to that of his betrothed, so do we hear God's voice in the Scriptures, and thereby learn the music of eternity which sounds through them.... If God's Word is presented to me in the hand of criticism as a squeezed lemon, God be praised that it becomes once more a fruit to me, growing as it does upon the tree of life.' As a Christian humanist, Herder sought to recover the

---

[10] Robinson heard Paulus lecture, also Fichte, Hegel, Schlegel, Schiller, and Schelling. He gives an entertaining account of student life at Jena. cf. Edith Morley, *Crabb Robinson in Germany* (Oxford, 1929).

unity of life, which orthodox and rationalist had neglected.
Poetry, philosophy, and history were 'a holy triangle' for the
inspiration, illumination, and guidance of mankind. Orthodox
formulation and rationalist abstraction were both inadequate;
the true watchword of Christianity must be: 'No one for
himself alone, but every one for all.' Religion must not be
identified with knowledge imparted from without, 'for it is an
inward conviction, an awareness of the divine operating in our
hearts'. As educator, writer, and preacher, Herder took every
opportunity of moulding the ideals of his age.

> What we love, others will love,
> And we will teach them how.

Another influence of great importance in German eighteenth-century thought was G. E. Lessing (1729-81). Lessing
was not merely a dramatist and man of letters with a sympathetic outlook. Despite the fact that he 'edited' the *Wolfenbüttel
Fragments*[11] he was no superficial rationalist. He arrived at
Berlin in 1750, the same year that Frederick the Great invited
Voltaire to Potsdam. But it was not till 1780 that he published
his epoch-making *Education of the Human Race*. In this pregnant
essay, 'Lessing set forth a way of thinking which was indeed
original . . . pursued by the ablest Modernists ever since, with
scant acknowledgement of the thinker who first pointed it
out'.[12] The key to the right understanding of religion and
civilization was the sense of progress, development. 'What
education is to the individual, Revelation is to the whole human
race.' Primitive man could only understand religion in crude
terms, rudimentary picture-language indicating rewards and
punishments. The Old Testament was a primer advancing
from what was elementary to what was more mature. Only
gradually did men realize that Virtue was its own reward, that
Conscience was an inner voice, and Immortality the inevitable
result of the infinite value of the soul. The 'chosen' race were
elect to a duty rather than to a privilege. Moreover, 'for this
purpose God selected the most uncivilized people, that He
might begin with them at the very beginning'. Another
fruitful idea, helpful at a time when the Higher Criticism was
in its infancy, was insistence on the fact that Christianity
preceded the New Testament; it was therefore greater than its
own documents.

[11] See p. 84, *supra*.
[12] H. L. Stewart, *Modernism Past and Present* (London, 1932), p. 193.

In Lessing's own time, his drama, *Nathan the Wise* (1779), exercised a wider influence than *The Education of the Human Race*. It appealed directly to the 'humanity' and 'enlightenment' of the age. Jew and Moslem are boldly recognized as genuine seekers after God. Not only so. The playwright's ingenious use of Boccaccio's 'Parable of the Three Rings' rather goes to show how well a man may serve God in *any* religion, than how little he can place his faith in *one*. A man of the East bequeathed a marvellous opal ring to his family, to be handed always to the best-loved son. At last a father had three sons whom he loved equally well; he therefore caused two additional rings to be made, exact imitations; each son was given one secretly and was told he had been given the only one. After his death the sons quarrelled. The true ring was undiscoverable—'almost as undiscoverable as the true faith', added Nathan.

Nathan the Wise is essentially a '*Tendenzstück*'. There is no attempt to understand the psychology of the Jews, Moslems, and Crusaders; they are interpreted as though they were men of the eighteenth century. 'The young Templar comes to Palestine to fight for the Holy Sepulchre while disbelieving in the Divinity of Christ; he is prejudiced enough to hold aloof from the family of the Jew whose daughter he has rescued, and philosophical enough to be attracted by him when he finds him to be merely a Deist who goes to the synagogue because his fathers did.'[13] Lessing did well to depict true religion as love to man and love to God, showing what was common to the three world religions of the Middle East. But he did a dis-service to the Church Universal in refusing to acknowledge the unique features of Christianity. Smaller men than he carried universalism to an extent that reflected their own shallow complacency. To Dr. Teller, Provost of Berlin Cathedral, the Jews were 'true Christians', because they believed in God, Virtue, and Immortality (yet he sought, illogically, 'to purge the Bible of its oriental features'). At his death, admirers said that if the world had a few more such men as Jesus, Luther, and Teller, all would go well with it!

When Lessing engaged in controversy with Melchior Goeze, the Chief Pastor of Hamburg, for having published the heretical *Wolfenbüttel Fragments* he issued his *Anti-Goeze Letters*— These polemical epistles exposed obscurantist theology with vivacity and verve. Pastor Goeze appealed to his friends at

[13] T. W. Rolleston, *Gotthold Ephraim Lessing* (London, 1889), Chapter 16.

Court and the Brunswick government intervened. Whereupon
Lessing wrote to Elise Reimarus that 'perhaps they would let
him preach undisturbed from his old pulpit, the stage'.

It is significant that Lessing, who broadened the scope of
German theology, should also have been the renovator of the
German drama. The story of his attempt to found a German
National Theatre at Hamburg (1767-8), his recognition of
Shakespeare (hitherto not *hoffahig*—'unpresentable at Court'),
his own realistic plays of modern life (e.g. *Minna von Barnhelm*)
belong to the history of literature. But they are significant
when one considers the history of German Protestantism from
the broader point of view. There is hardly another country
where theology and drama could have worked together so
closely. In Britain and America Puritan prejudice against 'the
playhouse' lasted well into the Victorian period.

In eighteenth-century Germany, thanks to Lessing, the
stage came to be viewed not merely as neutral ground, but as
the ally of the pulpit. The drama, which had been fostered by
Humanism and the Reformation, was coming into its own after
being blighted by centuries of fruitless strife. Schiller, in a
lecture given at Mannheim when he was only twenty-five,
acclaimed the theatre as 'a living mirror of morals and a school
of practical wisdom, an infallible key to the secret passage of
the human soul; only there do men of the world hear the truth
and see man in his true character' (1784).

In the nineteenth century a number of German books were
written on the ethical nature of the theatre, its power to uplift
men from dissipation and stimulate their higher life. It would
not be difficult to collect passages from plays that did more good
than many a prosy sermon, such as Schiller's lines in the
Knights of St. John:

> Religion of the Cross, thou blendest as a single flower,
> The two-fold branches of the palm—
> Humility and Power!

Dramatic quotations in the pulpit undoubtedly appealed
more to the people than the latest rationalist theory, or Kant's
'categorical imperative'. But it was not altogether wholesome
that the theatre should be elevated into a school of morals at
the cost of reducing the church to a proscenium of oratory.
Confusion resulted when the preacher mimicked the high-
flown declamatory style of the actor, while the actor moralized
like a preacher on the stage. Even Schiller realized that this

could be overdone, and made sport of Iffland's way of settling accounts:

> When vice is paid off with shame,
> Virtue claims her reward.

Hans Sach, the cobbler-dramatist of Nürnberg, had sung in Reformation times of Luther as 'the Wittenberg nightingale'. Zacharias Werner the Romantic dramatist in the 'era of national regeneration', thought he could do better. Was his father not Professor of History and Eloquence at Königsberg, as well as dramatic censor? Zacharias wrote *Martin Luther, oder die Weihe der Kraft* ('the consecration of power') which was a popular success in 1807. The play opened realistically with miners being drawn up and down a shaft. Students greeted Luther's appearance with enthusiasm, 'The Reformer of the Stage!' The man of Wittenberg was presented, however, not as a prophet of progress, but almost as a medieval saint.[14] Werner had Romantic leanings toward Romanism; his conglomeration of history, mysticism, and sensationalism resulted in strange incongruities.[15] In 1811 he finally renounced Protestantism and wrote *Die Weihe der Unkraft* ('the consecration of powerlessness'). In 1814 he was ordained priest. 'During the famous Peace Congress of 1814 his eloquent but fanatical sermons were listened to by crowded congregations.'

If the influence of the stage was not altogether beneficial to preaching and worship it became a passion, sometimes an obsession to young men with a tendency to self-dramatization. There is a classic example of this in *Anton Reiser, a Psychological Novel*, by Carl Philipp Moritz.[16] It is practically an autobiography, for Moritz was a 'traveller' (German, *Reiser*) in more than one sense. The book is an interpretation of Life, a remarkable contribution to 'the Literature of Power'. The reader is transported to the '*Sturm und Drang*' period, when the soul of Germany was reawakening. We behold the unfolding of life from boyhood to youth—revolt against a narrow, pietist creed, and the limitations of an artisan's hard existence; a battle for education, self-expression, and religious convictions able to stand stress and strain; tense eagerness to go in for a theatrical career, causing unnecessary hardship and distress of mind.

---

[14] cf. Lessing's apostrophe: 'Luther! Thou hast freed us from the yoke of Tradition; but who is to free us from the more intolerable yoke of the letter?'

[15] cf. George Brandes, *Main Currents in Nineteenth-century Literature*, Vol. II, Chapter 15.

[16] 1785-90; E.T., World's Classics (1926).

Only when this ambition was finally thwarted did Anton Reiser find his vocation as pastor, educator, and professor.

The classical period of German Literature and Art was a veritable renascence. One has only to think of Kant, Fichte, Schelling, and Hegel in philosophy; of Klopstock, Winckelmann, Goethe, Schiller in prose and poetry; of Haydn, Mozart, and Beethoven in music.[17] 'But in religion and theology,' said Professor Schaff, 'that period, although a necessary transition from a lifeless, contracted orthodoxy to a deeper, broader, and more scientific conception of Christianity, was the most chilly and dreary in the history of Protestantism.' The fashionable world, the learned world, and the middle class generally were addicted to shallow rationalism, and the demand stimulated the supply.

The common people were not interested in 'isms. They retained a certain traditional piety, nourished by Luther's Bible, along with catechisms, hymns, and popular devotional books of the sixteenth and seventeenth centuries. There was enough salt to prevent the complete decay of religion. It was to be found mainly in country districts. There were also 'watchers in the night', as Dr. John Ker has reminded us in his illuminating chapter on 'Hidden Life in the *Aufklärung*',[18] These 'waiters for the morning' kept the lamp of faith burning during the weary night watches. They attracted few followers, but their influence went much farther than numbers indicated. There was Lavater, the Zurich pastor, Princess Galitzin, Hamann ('Wise Man of the North'), Novalis the aristocratic Romantic, Jung-Stilling ('spiritual adviser' to the Grand Duke at Karlsruhe), Oetinger ('Wise Man of the South'), and Claudius, the philosopher in home-spun. These 'seers' differed in opinion and personality but were at one in recoiling from the 'flat rationalism' of their age; they were in touch with contemporary life and literature, but thirsted for something deeper.[19] Despite their eccentricities they were wells of water to many around them through the arid exodus of the later eighteenth century.

Johann Kaspar Lavater (1741-1801), known in his day as 'The Prophet of Zurich', is now almost forgotten, remembered only for certain theories of physiognomy which had once a wide circulation, and as a literary influence, helping to free Germany from the bonds of classicism. Lavater's whole philosophy of

[17] See Gostwick's *German Culture and Christianity* (London, 1882).
[18] *History of Preaching* (1888). [19] For selections, see Mahrholz, op. cit.

life was based on intuition and feeling. He sought unity, but not uniformity. The cold abstract pattern of eighteenth-century universalism he found dead; he rejoiced in the vivid concrete. His favourite attitude was to view life as a symbolic garden full of differently coloured and scented flowers. 'The true poet,' he used to say, 'is a prophet. . . . The essence of poetry and prophecy is to speak out truth clearly and with enthusiasm, and to bring unseen things before the senses.' Lavater was surely in the Pietist succession, judged by his belief in enthusiasm—so disparaged in the eighteenth century. No Pietist in the orthodox sense, he was a genuine voice for God. His friend Goethe compared him to 'a dry plant to which the least feeling of God's own presence brought more joy than other men have in the possession of all the good things God can give with His hand'. The fact that he preached with zeal, *zelo ardentissimo*, did not prevent him from being in temperament an inquirer; indeed, his most characteristic book was called *Pontius Pilate* as it dealt with the timeless question—'What is Truth?' Lavater's love of truth and liberty made him a supporter of the French Revolution, but when a French army occupied Switzerland without justification in 1798, he wrote an open letter to the Directory denouncing their tyranny. When the French troops entered Zurich, a soldier demanded wine from him; and after receiving it, shot him through the breast. He refused to identify the assassin, and afterwards died from his wound. 'Blessed are the homesick,' he used to say, 'for they shall reach home.'

Lavater's patriotism and heroic death made a profound impression in Germany, for he had been received there with enthusiasm in his lifetime (Switzerland at that time being closely linked in culture with the North).[20] The ideal of 'the Christian Patriot' was thrown on the screen of German consciousness, and during the Napoleonic Wars Schleiermacher appeared to fill that role.

Lavater, like many kindred souls of his age, had no sympathy with ecclesiasticism and confessionalism. 'The true Church is the aggregate of all people possessed of Christ.' There are many paths to the presence of Christ. 'Thirteen cantons represent a firmer organism than all combined in one, and four gospels are better than one harmony.' He con-

[20] cf. P. Wernle, *Der Schweizerisch Protestantismus im 18 Jahrhundert* (Tübingen, 1923).

cluded that certain regions and temperaments were better adapted to Protestantism and others to Catholicism (an idea developed from Zinzendorf). Proselytism was therefore to be deprecated. There was something in the spirit of the age that responded to this irenic attitude. When the Emperor Joseph the Second issued his Edict of Toleration in 1781, the Jesuits fell into disfavour. Protestant churches were opened even in Vienna, and innovations invigorated the Catholic churches of the South. The shadow of the Counter-Reformation was apparently dispelled by the lucid *Aufklärung*.

A new generation, however, was growing up with no love for the Age of Reason. Young men were enthralled by the glamour and poetry of medievalism: they were repelled by Baroque Romanism, still more by frigid Protestantism. Early Romanticism was personified by Friedrich von Hardenburg ('*Novalis*', 1772-1801). The creed of Novalis was proclaimed in the opening sentences of his *Christenheit oder Europa*. He looked back to 'the happy, glorious, days when Europe was still Christian, the home of Catholicism one and indivisible'. That splendid unity was shattered by the Reformation—'a death-blow to Christendom'. The only hope was the recovery of out-ward unity, the revival of 'a visible Church without respect to political frontiers, drawing to its bosom all souls that thirst for the divine'. It was strange that the advocate of corporate reunion (necessarily on a basis of authority) was Novalis, a pilgrim who had set forth from a Pietist home in Saxony. It is true that the disciples of Zinzendorf had sometimes been drawn to the fellowship of Catholics by their warm-heartedness, so lacking in official Protestantism. But it was a sign of the times that men brought up in the Pietist fold should actually turn to the 'Mother Church', confessing their need of ampler nourishment. Had *Christenheit oder Europa* been actually published when written (1799) and not delayed till 1826, the cause of Catholicism in Germany would have been further advanced. The zeal of Novalis, however, was not helped by his pantheist sympathies for he was an ardent admirer of Spinoza, the 'God-intoxicated man'. Novalis outran the spirit of the age, which was the eighteenth century, slightly warmed by feeling, but cool toward anything in the direction of fanaticism. Carlyle introduced him to the British public as 'an anti-mechanist—a deep man'. Novalis was an enthusiast, a Romantic. George Brandes has compared him to a shaft let down into a deep mine, the German soul (*Gemüt*) whereby the searcher has access to treasures—and rubbish too—far beneath the level of consciousness.[21]

Romanticism tended toward Romanism in its emotional expression when it was not merely subjective and individualistic. In 1797 there appeared a beautifully printed volume with the title *Herzensergiessungen eines Kunstliebenden Klosterbruders* ('Heart-outpourings of an art-loving Friar'). This little book of Wackenroder's may be described as the primary cell of the German Romanticism—no product of genius, to be sure, but a germinating force that was destined to overthrow the classic temple that Goethe had wrought with matchless symmetry.[22] Sober standards of criticism were swept away. Bright colours effloresced; voluptuous music filled the air; religion was art, and art was religion. Men sought for the symbol of 'a blue blossom', 'a mystic word', and 'the magic of lonely woods'.

Romanticism, however, burst into flower only at the very end of the eighteenth century in Germany. It was preceded by a group of seekers after God who sought to find a place for feeling as well as reason in religion. We have already mentioned Lavater. Hamann, Jung-Stilling, and others are worth meeting, as real personalities and as men of God.

J. G. Hamann (1730-88) is usually remembered only as a minor literary 'influence' in Germany's 'storm and stress period' —the *Sturm und Drang* that ushered in the Age of Goethe and Schiller. From a spiritual point of view, however, his influence is more important, for he gave colour, shape, and direction to many ideas in circulation. He was born at Königsberg, his parents being humble Pietists. 'I have scarcely any desire to be a German; without much heralding I announce that I am an East Prussian.' He led a wandering, dissipated life and in 1758 found himself diseased and penniless in London. His distress led him to a thorough study of the Bible, which resulted in a remarkable conversion. The Pietist strain was only one element in his acquired character. Hamann was sophisticated as well

---

[21] op. cit., Vol. II, Chapter 12.

[22] Goethe went some way with the Romantics. He was fascinated by 'that remarkable man', the fawn-faced Werner. But when Werner, at a dinner-party, produced a sonnet comparing the moon to the Host, Goethe flamed forth; he 'hated perverted religiosity'. The poet turned pale and said not a word. 'Goethe quite literally turned his back upon the Romantic School' (Emil Ludwig's *Goethe*, Vol. II, pp. 156ff.).

as naïve, deeply religious though opposed to hard dogmatism. He reacted vigorously against the complacency of the *Aufklärung*. 'Was Reason given to make us wise?' he asked, 'just as little as the Law was given to the Jews to make them just: rather to convince us of the opposite, how irrational our reason is, and that our errors will be increased through reason, as sins were increased through the law.' The paradoxical nature of his teaching may be further illustrated by his saying (once attributed to Kierkegaard) that 'he would rather hear wisdom from Balaam's ass or from a philosopher against his will than from an angel or an Apostle'.

Hamann challenged the abstractions of the Rationalist and the asceticism of the Pietist with the assertion that passion alone gives to ideas and ideals—hands, wings, and feet. Only specialists are likely to read his books nowadays. 'He was the ferment that set the tough mass of our literature brewing once more,' explains a modern interpreter, 'like the true leaven he went up with the ferment and lives only in the consequences.' Born like Demosthenes with a speech defect, he was stimulated not only to speak correctly but to make a special study of language; and he found it to be a 'sacrament'—the expression of an individual's inner character, the perfect expression being the Word.[23] He was a seer who struck out brilliant epigrams and profound insights. Like William Blake, he distrusted closed systems and neat theories. He would have repudiated with spirit the charge sometimes levelled against him at the present day, that he had a part in creating the cult of the physical and the irrational, the sinister legend of blood and race that culminated and perished in the Nazi *Götterdammerung*. In spite of his individualism, he did not give way to egotism like some of his Romantic successors, nor did he surrender his independence to the claims of authoritarianism in Church and State. 'The Magus of the North' remained a convinced Protestant. That did not prevent him from shining in the circle of Princess Galitzin at Münster. She, a Catholic, enjoyed sharing his views on religion as well as literature, and often sought his guidance.

Another seer whose advice was much valued was F. C. Oetinger (1702-82), 'The Wise Man of the South'. Although tinctured with mysticism and theosophy, he was an enlightened Württemberg Pietist in the Bengel tradition. No philosophy was

[23] Article on Hamann by R. Gregor Smith (*Hibbert Journal*, April 1944).

profitable, he used to say, unless it fitted the Scriptures, as a key slipped into its lock. Oetinger was an unsystematic thinker, but he influenced many a Christian leader of the nineteenth century, notably Rothe.

Returning to North Germany, we must not forget Matthias Claudius, a patriarch who dwelt in an old-world village near Hamburg. Claudius liked to think of himself as the champion of the plain man as opposed to the philosopher and scholar. He could discuss music, literature, and religion shrewdly and with insight. Indeed, he talked to his own generation in the *Wandsbeck Messenger*, much as Addison addressed (more urbanely) the English Augustan Age in the *Spectator*. A happy picture of Claudius (1740-1815) is given in the *Life* of his son-in-law, Perthes the publisher, written by F. K. Perthes. Had Pietism been able to assimilate more of the geniality and kindly irony of Claudius, its influence in the later eighteenth century might have been more widespread and permanent. His harvest folk-song, 'We plough the fields and scatter', seems to be as popular in Britain as in Germany.

Another eighteenth-century personality remembered principally for his hymns was Gerhard Tersteegen (1697-1769). John Wesley's translation of 'Thou hidden love of God' has been acclaimed by Oliver Wendell Holmes as the greatest hymn in the English language. Tersteegen was not a Pietist; although nurtured in the Reformed Church, he was drawn to the mysticism that ran deep in the soil of Westphalia; it was 'the inner light', not the outward 'means of grace' that mattered; yet he never lost touch with the Communion of Saints, like some mystics. After being converted at the age of sixteen, he practised fasting, prayer, and almsgiving, supporting himself meagrely by weaving silk ribbons. When light and peace returned after much depression caused by these austerities, he made a new covenant with God, signed with his blood. 'I love most to be with the Father, but I am glad to be with the children.' Crowds would foregather round the Pilgrim's Cottage at Mulheim, mounting ladders to catch 'spiritual crumbs from the Master's Table'. Supported by the offerings of the faithful, he exercised an informal ministry. Although he was little concerned with contemporary problems, he attracted seekers, anxious about their souls, from all over Germany. Asked from what Churches these pilgrims came, he replied: 'I never ask—I only want to know where they are going to.'

Tersteegen was spiritual guide to a host of correspondents.[24]

Perhaps the most interesting of these 'watchers in the night' is Heinrich Jung-Stilling, whose autobiography reveals quaint glimpses of social and religious life.[25] He was born in 1740 in the Westphalian village of Grund. After his baptism, Pastor Stollbein was invited to a meal in celebration of the event. 'I hope that I am not to eat here among a swarm of peasants,' he remarked. The dignified grandfather, who had already put up with many affronts from this local clerical dictator, replied: 'No one dines here except myself, my wife, and my children—are they "a swarm of peasants"?' 'Aye, what else?' 'I must in that case remind you, sir, that you are anything else than a servant of Christ, you are a Pharisee. . . . Your Reverence, my grey hairs stand on end. Sit down or withdraw!' He then reminded the Pastor that one day the Prince had ridden past and gladly accepted his modest hospitality; 'Where cleanliness reigns, there anyone may eat'. The family refused to sit down to table with their clergyman—only the old man did so. The Pastor ate heartily, said nothing, and returned home to Florenburg. He took an active interest in the child he had christened, however. When he was still a small boy, he asked him one day: 'Dost thou know thy Catechism?' 'Not the whole of it.' 'That is the first thing children ought to know.' 'No, your reverence, not the first; children must first learn to pray that God may give them understanding to comprehend the Catechism.' After the boy had picked up a little Latin, the Pastor would test him with maxims, e.g. '*Medium tenuere beati*'. Heinrich replied: '*Plerique medium tenentes sunt damnati.*' ('Most of those are damned who kept the middle way'—'through being neither hot nor cold', he added). 'An excellent reply, boy,' said the pastor, who in course of time procured him a teacher's post.

Jung-Stilling was too original, too independent, to be a successful schoolmaster under eighteenth-century restrictions. To earn a living and find time for thought, he became a tailor. With 'half a French dollar' he went to study medicine at Strasbourg in 1768. There he met Goethe, who introduced him to Herder. At Kaiserslautern (a school afterwards incorporated in Heidelberg University) he lectured on 'agriculture, technology, commerce, and the veterinary art'. In 1787 he was

[24] Article by S. H. Moore on Tersteegen, *London Quarterly and Holborn Review* (April 1947). See also *The Quiet Way*. Letters of Tersteegen, Emily Chisholm (London, 1950).
[25] *Stillings Leben*; E.T., 3 vols. (1835).

appointed Professor of Economics at Heidelberg. His religious significance consists in the fact that to an unusual extent he thought deeply on the relation of body, mind, and soul. He was an occultist as well as an oculist, a 'seer' who predicted 1818 or 1819 as the date of the Millennium. He had correspondents all over Europe; distinguished visitors would seek him out. He found his niche in 1806, when the Grand Duke of Baden appointed him 'court counsellor' or spiritual adviser. There he remained till his death in 1817 ('Lord, cut the thread and give me rest').

A man of remarkable genius and insight, he was eccentric but not unduly so. He had no affinity with sectarian extremists, whom he characterized in a religious romance, *Theobald, or the Fanatic* (E.T., 1846); nor had he any sympathy with the glib assertions of noisy Rationalists, for 'a religion of head without heart is dead'. Despite his mysticism he had a simple faith in God's power and willingness to answer prayer. He believed in the reconciliation of the human and the divine; head, heart, and hand must combine to produce a balanced Christian character.

It is significant that young Goethe was the friend of Stilling[26] and Lavater; he even advocated their cause against the men of the *Aufklärung*. The dullness and insipidity of these 'enlighteners' irritated Goethe more than the vagaries of the pious. He aimed his keen shafts of satire at the *Allgemeine Deutsche Bibliothek*, an anti-Christian review published by Nicolai under the patronage of Frederick the Great. Goethe was usually sprightly and cheerful in the company of his religious friends; one thinks of that '*schöne Seele*', Susanne von Klettenberg, with whom he loved to discuss the Moravian Brethren.[27] He eventually quarrelled with Lavater, remarking in 1782: 'When a great man has a dark corner in him, he is terribly dark.' Actually the Prophet of Zurich was incurably Evangelical at heart. Perhaps Goethe had more in common with Basedow (1723-90), a follower of Rousseau, a pioneer in the understanding of the young,[28] who believed in Natural Religion to such an extent that he would have nothing taught in school which would offend

[26] Goethe enriched his vocabulary with such Pietist phrases as *Gefühl* (feeling), *dunkel* (gloomy, obscure). 'The sentimentality of the Werther period', said Gustav Freitag, 'is merely a step-daughter of the *Gefühlings-seligkeit* of the old Pietism' (*Bilder aus der deutschen Vergangenheit*, Vol. IV, Chapter '*Die Stillen im Lande*').

[27] *Autobiography* of Goethe, E.T., Moon, (London, 1932), pp. 560-3.

[28] R. H. Quick, *Educational Reformers* (1890).

Jew, Moslem, or Christian. The seeker after Light would enjoy listening to the disputation of the rough Rousseauist and the enlightened Pietist, till both were weary, and would sing in his peculiar way:

> Prophets right and prophets left,
> The world-child in the middle.

Men like Lavater and Jung-Stilling influenced a few elect souls, rather than public opinion. More leaven would have been necessary to make the bread of life palatable and nourishing for the German people as a whole. Religion, as it was generally presented to them, resembled Hosea's 'cake not turned'. One side was overdone, the other raw. Rationalism had certainly awakened Germany from her dogmatic slumbers after the dark night of Lutheran orthodoxy. But the clear light of the *Aufklärung* was too strong for a people that had spent nearly two centuries in a theological prison; they turned liberty into licence. The Bible, once an arsenal of texts against heretics, was now transformed into a repository of useful knowledge, where every man could find what he wanted and apply it as he liked. Reason, cut off from imagination and humour, soon lost touch with reality in vain abstractions and futile speculations.

There were exceptions of course. Bengel carried the warm devotional spirit of Southern German Pietism into Bible study, without being afraid of reason as an aid to reflection; he looked at the Scriptures directly, no longer through the distorting glasses of Confessional Theology.[29] There was Oberlin, the humble Alsatian pastor, who blended revelation and reason, evangelism and 'the Social Gospel'; Oberlin, 'the never-to-be-forgotten benefactor of the Steinthal' (as even Treitschke admitted), yet also a great European. His influence was considerable in Germany, and would have been even greater, but for the accident that some time before his birth, Alsace had been conquered by Louis the Fourteenth, and he was therefore technically a Frenchman.

In considering men of European influence, we must not forget 'rationalist supernaturalists' like Mosheim the Church Historian, who guarded the essentials of historic Christianity while speaking to men in the language of their own generation. Thus we find so orthodox a Calvinist as John Brown of Haddington, the self-taught theologian, in his *General History of the*

[29] cf. p. 65, *supra.*

Christian Church (1771) acknowledging his indebtedness to 'the celebrated Mosheim, Chancellor of the Hanoverian University of Göttingen'. Dr. Brown, we fear, would have classified Mosheim as 'a mere Moderate' had he heard him expatiating on tolerance, fortitude, diligence, and goodwill. He would approve still less of G. J. Zollikofer (1730-88), known to his generation as 'the Cicero of the pulpit'. His monument at Leipzig extols him as 'living on *here* by his teaching and *there* in the sphere of souls, where Jesus and Socrates live'.[30] This is not the spirit of the New Testament, but Zollikofer was an Enlightener with a Bible in his hand, a 'rational supernaturalist', after the school of Tillotson.[31] The 'flat rationalists' in many a German pulpit secularized preaching. They assumed that their hearers were interested in the latest phases of 'neology'. Or, determining to be practical, they dilated on 'the unspeakable Blessing of the Potato', 'The Advantages of Coffee as a Beverage', or 'The Ethical Significance of Hairdressing'. Not even the Christian Year recalled preachers to the Gospel. Here are some extreme examples—a Christmas sermon on the stall-feeding of cattle, a Palm Sunday sermon on the damaging of trees, an Easter sermon on 'The danger of being buried Alive', and a Pentecost sermon on drunkenness.[32]

The *Aufklärung* was more effective in modernizing worship and its setting than in modifying the archaism of social customs. Medieval remnants such as exorcism, auricular confession and absolution,[33] incense and chanting disappeared or survived only as local customs.[34] General Superintendents and Con-

---

[30] His successor in Dresden, Franz Reinhard (*d.* 1812) found that when he preached the free grace of God in 1800, some of his hearers were amazed, others were indignant (*Confessions*, E.T., Boston, Massachusetts, 1832).

[31] One recalls Dr. Thomas Chalmers' comparison of Scottish 'Moderate' sermons to a fine winter's day—short, clear, and cold. 'The brevity is good, and the clearness better, but the coldness is fatal. Moon-light preaching ripens no harvests.'

[32] Herder's *Provincial Letters to Preachers* (1773) was an impassioned protest against secularization of the sermon.

[33] In Goethe's youth Absolution fees formed part of the pastor's stipend (*Autobiography*). Johanna Schopenhauer gives a vivid description of Confession at Dantzig (late eighteenth century), in her *Jugendleben* (1839). Her family arrived at the 'comfort-room' (*Trostkammer*) with the requisite fee, while a queue of the lower orders waited outside. A bottle of wine suggested spirituous rather than spiritual comfort. 'Kneeling before our spiritual guide, enthroned in full canonicals, we made our confession. I, a very short one, out of Gellert's odes. My father, out of pity for the poor people waiting, cut short the polite conversation that followed Absolution.' He slipped the divine a fee, who, glancing to make sure that it included the daughter's, with an unctuous smile, nodded thanks to her parents.

[34] Wesley was surprised to find the pastor at Meissen arrayed in a chasuble of 'gold and scarlet, a vast cross both behind and before' (1738). Lutheran Saxony is still very Catholic in ceremonial.

sistories re-cast liturgies and hymnaries to eradicate non-rational elements; Baptismal and Communion formulas, as well as the ancient responses, were altered to suit 'the enlightened taste of this age'. The introduction of salon etiquette within the sanctuary was more popular with the polite classes than with the poor. Gellert's hymns, elegant and didactic, became fashionable. The old *Chorales* were ruthlessly adapted. Gerhardt's evening hymn, 'How peaceful all the forests rest', is an example. Frederick the Great dismissed it as 'stupid stuff'. The experts substituted: 'The whole world is now asleep.' In the interests of geographical accuracy it was ultimately altered to: 'Half the world is now asleep.' Reason also ousted sentiment in the planning of churches as 'auditories' (to use Wren's phrase) rather than shrines. The cruciform plan gave way to the square, the octagon, or the oval, so that hearers should be grouped conveniently near the preacher; the pulpit was placed immediately behind the altar, with the organ pipes as a background. This arrangement is one of the more permanent results of the *Aufklärung*.

In spite of the achievement of emancipating the human mind from purely traditional thinking, the general drift of the *Aufklärung* was disappointingly negative from a Christian point of view. Its sterility was largely due to over-belief in human reason. There must have been many an intelligent man of the eighteenth century who would have admitted that the experience of FitzGerald's 'Omar' was his:

> Myself when young did eagerly frequent
> Doctor and Saint, and heard great argument
>   About it and about: but evermore
> Came out by the same door as in I went.

H

CHAPTER FIVE

FROM SCHLEIERMACHER TO HEGEL

THE condition of religion was most unsatisfactory at the end of the eighteenth century, in spite of a small company of 'enlightened Pietists'.

The traditional creeds had been undermined and their defenders had propped them up with very shaky supports. Deism was itself dying of inanity. In the light of Kant's *Critique* the great speculative systems now appeared as castles in the air. Kant's own attempt to save belief in the three essentials of rational theology by making them postulates of the practical reason had subordinated religion to morality. . . . Theology was discredited both as to content and as to method.[1]

One-sidedness had been the bane of German scholarship, whether dogmatist, Pietist, Rationalist, or Moralist. There was a want of balance in the German mentality, which Luther had noted under the coarse symbolism of a drunken peasant: 'He no sooner gets up on one side of his horse than he falls over the other.'

The scattered rays of theology were destined to be absorbed by one who was uniquely qualified to rehabilitate the Christian Faith, in an age obsessed by rationalistic culture, commercial expansion, and military glory. Friedrich Ernst Daniel Schleiermacher (1768-1834) well deserves the title of 'renovator of German theology' and 'the only great Protestant theologian since Calvin'.[2] So biased an historian as Treitschke had to admit: 'Even yet, no theologian arrives at inward liberty who has not settled accounts with Schleiermacher.' Whether we agree with his subjective conception of Christianity or not, we cannot afford to ignore him any more than biologists can ignore Darwin. His interpreters are legion,[3] though the human interest of his life has often been ignored in English-speaking lands.[4]

[1] G. Cross, *The Theology of Schleiermacher* (Chicago, 1911), p. 105.

[2] He is depicted in stained glass as one of an international company of Christian leaders in Mansfield College Chapel ('the most Catholic place in Oxford', said Friedrich Heiler).

[3] See H. R. Mackintosh, *Types of Modern Theology—Schleiermacher to Barth* (London, 1937); W. B. Selbie, *Schleiermacher, a Critical and Historical Study* (London, 1913).

[4] Notable *Lives* by Schenkel (1868) and Dilthey (1870; new ed., 1922). Dilthey's ranks high among German biographies. Neither, unfortunately, are in E.T. Troeltsch, Naumann, and others, contributed to *Schleiermacher, der Philosoph des Glaubens* (Leipzig, 1910)—a valuable study of his work as Churchman, educator, etc. A selection from his *Letters* was translated by Miss Rowan (2 vols., London, 1860).

Who could delineate the system of a genius or narrate his fascinating biography within the limits of a few pages? All that we can attempt in this short study is to point out his place in the procession of Christian witness, to see what he owed to diverse sources in the Germany of his time, and observe how he drew from this treasure things new and old, like the wise scribe of the Gospels, borrowing in order to create what was more excellent.

Schleiermacher's parents contributed complementary traits. From his mother, he inherited a steady intellect of a rather dry type; her relatives (Stubenrauch, Spalding, and Sack) occupied high positions in the Reformed Church, their temperament approximating to that of contemporary English Latitudinarians or Scottish Moderates. From his father he inherited an uneasy orthodoxy which was the result of a conflict between the rationalistic spirit of the age and ancestral Pietism.[5] Gottlieb Schleiermacher was determined to protect his children from the assaults of scepticism. He therefore planted them in Moravian schools, where their souls would be safe from the freezing winds of free thought. Barby was like a walled garden, and every secular plant was treated as though it were a weed. That merely whetted the appetite of Friedrich and his companions for stolen fruit; Goethe's *Werther* and heavier philosophy were smuggled into the school. The authorities broke up the reading circle and the ringleader's name was put on the black list. Then followed a period of tension between the fond but rigorous father (a military chaplain) and the rebellious son, sick of the hot-house atmosphere of the seminary, longing for the freedom of the university. This strife, reminiscent of Gosse's *Father and Son*, was fortunately terminated by the intervention of Uncle Stubenrauch. Friedrich was allowed to study at Halle, though pestered by paternal admonitions. Looking back on Barby, he afterwards acknowledged his debt to Pietism. He declared himself 'Moravian of a higher order'. While admitting the shortcomings of the Zinzendorf tradition, he rejoiced in their conviction that Christianity was essentially 'the faith of the heart', and only in a secondary sense was it

[5] Elias Eller, an Elberfeld ribbon-weaver, wove a fantastic sect out of his personal experience. He declared that a certain Anna, whom he seduced and later married, was the Apocalyptic 'Woman clothed with the sun'. Eller, driven from Elberfeld, founded a new Zion and a flourishing factory at Ronsdorf. The Elector Palatine gave legal sanction to this settlement (1741). Daniel Schleiermacher, grandfather of Friedrich, was appointed *Prediger* of the community. An 'enthusiast', he was one of the last in Germany to be charged with sorcery.

dogma to be accepted or criticized. Religion was something to be accepted and shared, 'caught as well as taught'. Like Wesley, he learnt to maintain the spiritual glow and to own all as brethren whose hearts were likewise touched and warmed by God.

Schleiermacher found Halle arid, although it had once been the fountain of Pietism. The Enlightenment had little to offer to seekers who sought to penetrate the surface of life and find the deep wells of speculation and feeling. Schleiermacher found refuge in 'the holy and repudiated Spinoza', and afterwards delighted in Plato (whose works he translated). He was not sorry to leave Halle and accompany his uncle, Professor Stubenrauch, who had retired to a country parish. Like Moses, Paul, and Mohammed, the young man was the better for withdrawal to the wilderness. 'In quiet solitude I watched the great ferments of the inner and the outer world' (Kant's philosophy and the French Revolution). He passed through a sceptical phase. Lucien, Montaigne, and Wieland neutralized the fresh colours of his youthful enthusiasm; but 'flat rationalism' was not to have the last word. A tutorship in East Prussia brought him into 'a little world of humanizing graces'; it taught him the value of persons as well as ideas.

Then came a complete change of scene. Schleiermacher became chaplain of the Charité Hospital, Berlin, which was situated opposite the Veterinary Hospital (in one institution, he noted, 'they treated men like beasts—and in the other, beasts like men'). Out of personal experience he reflected: 'In order to have religion, man must first have found humanity.'

It was his leisure hours in Berlin that were most formative. Rationalism had done little to elevate the moral life of the capital ('the modern Venusberg'). Romanticism did not achieve much better results from an ethical point of view, but was alive with enthusiasm and fresh ideas. German Romanticism was not merely a protest against cold classicism and a discovery of medieval art and literature. It was an ambitious attempt to blend religion, patriotism, philosophy, and letters. In Friedrich Schlegel's words: 'Mythology and Poetry, symbolic Legend and Art are one and indivisible.' 'We sought to rear an intellectual tower of Babel', explained Schleiermacher's friend, Steffens, 'that all might behold.' This 'cloud-capp'd tower' could count on little more than a common enthusiasm among its builders. Imagination could only etherealize the naturally sensuous, of which already Berlin knew too much. 'Self-expression' might emancipate, but it was not constructive. If God was *feeling*, then the *generation* of feeling was the *regeneration* of man! Years later, Alexander von Humboldt looked back with scorn on 'bigotry without religion, aestheticism without culture, and philosophy without common sense, dominant on the banks of the Spree'.[6]

For young Schleiermacher this was a wide world teeming with interest, though not without its moral dangers, past most of which he was guided by his carefully guarded lamp of faith. He soon became acquainted with distinguished families among the Jewish *intelligentsia* such as the Mendelssohns; he saw much of Dorothea Veit and Henrietta Herz—platonic friendships for which he was criticized by the staid leaders of the Reformed Church. He swore eternal friendship with Friedrich Schlegel, with whom he set up a joint bachelor establishment. He never wholly shared the outlook of his Romantic comrades, however. He felt that this was merely a phase in his mental and spiritual development. He decided to use his Berlin experiences of life and thought as the groundwork of appeal to 'the cultured despisers of religion'. He therefore published five 'Speeches' (*Reden*) in 1799. 'Let no one turn from religion for the sake of his spiritual independence.' The essence of Christianity was not dogma, but rather intuition and feeling. Philosophy, art, and culture were no substitutes for the soul—the 'cultured despisers' were as 'externalist' as creed-bound dogmatists and crass deists.

The *Reden* made a profound impression in Germany. Schleiermacher's British interpreter, Dr. Oman, questioned whether, after Kant's *Critique* and Goethe's *Wilhelm Meister*, any book of the period has had such lasting effects; 'there is certainly no question that it foreshadows the problems chiefly discussed among us today'.[7] Neander attributed to the *Reden* his conversion from Judaism to Christianity. Goethe, Schelling, and Fichte, dwelt on the author's significance for modern civilization; Steffens relayed his message to Scandinavia in his epoch-making lectures in Copenhagen. Klaus Harms, later leader of orthodox Lutheranism,[8] borrowed a copy of the *Reden*, immured himself, and reverted to his Bible and Luther-lore, confessing that Schleiermacher had stirred emotions that he could never satisfy. Friedrich Schlegel's comment was cryptic:

---

[6] cf. Brandes, *Main Currents in Nineteenth-century Literature*, Vol. II.
[7] *On Religion*, Oman's Introduction (London, 1894).   [8] See p. 195, *infra*.

The curtain is raised; the music must cease.
The Temple is gone; and far in the distance
Appears the terrible face of the—Sphinx.

Schiller, Schelling, and Steffens greeted the dawn of the nineteenth century with speeches and champagne. Schleiermacher honoured the occasion in a more lasting fashion by setting down his personal convictions in 'Soliloquies', which were 'virtually dictated to the printer'. These *Monologen*[9] are a unique contribution to the literature of self-revelation. As 'a lyric extract from the diary of his abiding self', this deeply personal confession is a complete contrast to Anglo-Saxon religious autobiography, enriched with copious Scriptural language. 'In thine own person, body forth humanity uniquely.' The free man is uncontrolled by any authority save his own soul, which should grow, blossom, and ripen like a plant. But free personality can only find full expression in fellowship with society; it does not thrive in isolation. These aspirations of Schleiermacher are unshadowed by any sense of sin or moral failure. The *Soliloquies* are inadequate when gauged by the standard of dogma, but they fortified the author's faith in dark days.

Dr. G. P. Gooch, in his *Germany and the French Revolution* (1920), has explained the bitter disappointment that followed its failure among the enthusiasts across the Rhine who looked for a new heaven and a new earth (not to speak of a new religion and a new mythology). Disillusioned Romanticists in Germany turned from unbelief to superstition. Reacting against rationalist intellectualism, which had proved so barren, they found little in Protestantism to appeal to their ardent imagination; they were repelled by the professorial attitude—'in the next lecture we shall proceed to construct God'.

Count Stolberg the poet set a fashionable example by becoming a Romanist in 1800. 'Mythology and Poetry, symbolic Legend and Art' were proclaimed 'one and indivisible' by Friedrich Schlegel. The 'Nazarenes', a brotherhood of ex-Protestant artists, settled at Rome in 1811 and astonished Catholics by their vagaries. This attitude was expressed by Overbeck's substitution of an altar for a table in picturing the Last Supper, where Christ stands apart and consecrates a wafer, instead of breaking bread with the Apostles. Recorded fact

[9] E. T. by Friess, well annotated, with good bibliography (Chicago, 1926).

meant nothing to such lovers of fiction. The mysticism of Schelling blended with the medievalism of Tieck and Novalis in pointing others to the *Una Sancta*—not the tolerant, lax Catholicism of the eighteenth century, but a new aggressive type, gilded indeed with medieval glamour, but girt also with Jesuit cunning. French conquests having robbed revolutionary ideology of its attraction for most foreigners, ecclesiastics took counsel with politicians in defence of Throne and Altar. 'Traditional Nationalism' on a neo-Catholic basis was set against the 'Jacobin Nationalism' of the French Revolution. Friedrich Schlegel, a pastor's son, the most notable convert to Rome, became a fanatical pillar of priest-ridden Austria. The historic Church was further linked to popular patriotism as a means of promoting morale and discrediting representative institutions. Schlegel even preached the racial superiority of the Germans and the unique purity of the German soul.[10]

Schleiermacher had not been long settled in a theological Chair at Halle before Napoleon attacked Prussia. He shared the hardships of the French invasion with his fellow-countrymen, refused a tempting call from a church in Bremen, and took his share in the task of national regeneration. He modestly submitted that he could do nothing for his country but preach. He preached to some purpose. In his pulpit addresses 'the Church militant' was no faded metaphor. His telling battery of words was discharged with tremendous effect. Trinity Church, Berlin, was crowded with people of all classes. Schleiermacher preached like a Pietist, *zelo ardentissimo*, but his full-orbed message attracted the public as the older Pietist preaching would never have done. Who could forget his Consecration Service, when the church was packed with soldiers leaving for the front in 1813? The Prussian people, encouraged by the retreat from Moscow, were rising against Napoleon. It was Schleiermacher's shining hour. His frail figure was far from impressive in the pulpit; like the Apostle Paul he had no 'presence'; yet his countenance beamed with radiant conviction as he reminded his hearers that the real issue was—not 'God is on our side', but 'Are we on the side of God?'[11] The Prussian people used to fight for dynastic interests: now they

---

[10] cf. C. J. H. Hayes, *Historical Evolution of Modern Nationalism* (New York, 1931), pp. 102-8.

[11] In 1714 Gottfried Arnold, the defender of the heretics, was celebrating Communion when recruiting sergeants burst in and seized all young men present. The shock of this intrusion caused Arnold's death three days later.

were fighting for national existence.[12] Schleiermacher voiced the religious aspirations of the Germans in their bitter need. In printed form his sermons[13] reached thousands of eager hearers all over the Fatherland; Baron Stein carried a copy, when he had to flee before the French in 1808, alone on a sleigh.

Schleiermacher was a new portent in the sky of German destiny—the Patriotic Preacher. He was a burning and a shining light, and there had been none like him since Luther delivered his 'Addresses to the Christian Nobility of the German Nation'. During the intervening centuries the Christian Patriot ideal had almost faded out of consciousness except in Prussia. When Madame de Stael wrote *De l'Allemagne* in 1810 in honour of the nation which Napoleon had humiliated, she painted too flattering a picture. Not content with eulogizing German romanticism, individuality, and 'poetry of the soul', she discovered that the Germans were actually deficient in 'national prejudice and egotistical patriotism'! To be sure, Goethe accepted Napoleon's tribute and Hegel described the Corsican as 'the world-soul riding'; but Prussia had consistently cultivated the military virtues. If these had grown rusty since the death of Frederick the Great, a band of experts were working hard at Berlin to refurbish them. Fichte roused 'the German nation' to self-consciousness by his famous *Addresses*; Scharnhorst reformed her army; von Humboldt modernized her educational system; von Stein abolished feudal privileges, and Arndt stirred her heart in song. Organizing a 'nation in arms' involved a return to Prussian disciplinarianism, also a touch of 'uplift' propaganda from the 'German Youth Movement', which was opposed to foreign influence and talked of the resuscitation of ancient Teutonic ways and customs.[14] Schleiermacher represented a luminous Christian strain in this movement of national regeneration[15] (he saw its progressive possibilities, unlike his friend, Friedrich Schlegel, who looked for a revived

[12] For a vivid contrast between social life before and during the War of Liberation, see Sarah Austin's *Germany, 1760-1814* (London, 1854), compiled from memoirs of the period.

[13] See *Selected Sermons of Schleiermacher*, Introduction by Robertson Nicoll (London, 1890).

[14] In 1810 a young Dane was reading Kotzebue's *History of Prussia*, which referred to the 'dry and withered cross', doomed to overthrow 'the nobler pagan worship of the Germans'. Gruntvig shuddered, hurled the book away, and dedicated himself to Christian service. As 'Prophet of the North' he felt called (like Schleiermacher in Germany) to regenerate the Danish people as well as their Church.

[15] W. Baur, *Religious Life in Germany during the War of Independence* (London, 1872).

Reich under the retrograde and Catholic sway of Austria).

Frederick William the Third sought the advice of Reformers when the very existence of his kingdom was at stake; once he was secure, after the fall of Napoleon, he dispensed with their services. Baron Stein and other forward-looking patriots soon found themselves in opposition to the royal reactionary.

Schleiermacher was among those who regarded the Peace of 1815 as a point of departure rather than as a full stop. He had no intention of consolidating discredited authoritarianism, to please the King of Prussia and Metternich. As a Christian reformer he held on to his lofty, comprehensive ideals. He did not entirely discard the spacious universalism of the *Aufklärung*. He was a debtor, also, to the Romanticists' discovery of individuality; but, he maintained, men found their 'larger selves' in the family, the local community, the province, and the Fatherland. Monarchy was the best form of government because the One integrates the divergencies of the Many. 'Man is social through and through', but the genuine *Volkstaat* is 'an organic, planetary work of art', built up of free personalities.[16] Ancient customs are not to be lightly abandoned (as by superficial rationalism); they are to be gradually adapted to a changing social order.

Language is an essential bearer of national character; only the mother-tongue can transmit essential social traits. Hence the need of a national system of education that should train men for the duties of a common citizenship, not merely for the requirements of their particular 'station' (*Stand*) in the social hierarchy. Education can only transcend class distinctions, however, in so far as it is genuinely Christian. Every child is born with a capacity for religion. Christian education consists, not in implanting dogma, but in assisting the healthy growth of the soul by removing obstacles and providing every opportunity for expansion. Like Francke, the Pietist educator, Schleiermacher emphasized the re-moulding of the will by means of the new birth and Christian nurture. Setting aside the catechetical method so rooted in Lutheran tradition, he preferred 'to form the heart by the understanding and the understanding by the heart'. Not indoctrination, but the creation of a free Christian personality was his ideal.[17] He started with the

[16] Koppel S. Pinson, *Pietism as a factor in the Rise of German Nationalism* (New York, 1934).

[17] In one notable instance Schleiermacher failed; he prepared Bismarck for Confirmation!

tradition of enlightened Pietism; he matured it with psychological insight and enriched it with romantic colour. He was not merely the pioneer of Sunday-schools but of the 'Religious Education Movement' which has made such progress of recent years in the United States and Canada.[18] He would have agreed with Bushnell that 'the Gospel is a gift to the Imagination'.

Schleiermacher was in some respects a true son of the Reformed Church. The predominant Lutheranism of the Fatherland acted like a dead weight of officialism, subservience, and convention. He felt sorely frustrated by the Church's lack of freedom, as we shall find when we examine his views on Church and State.[19] One of his aims was to make real the *original* Lutheran ideal of the priesthood of all believers. Every man was a 'priest' so far as he had specialized in leadership: every man was a 'layman' so far as he followed the direction of others who had mastered matters with which he was personally unfamiliar.

We think of Schleiermacher and Hegel as ill-yoked colleagues in the new University of Berlin during the post-Napoleonic era. One stressed the soul, the other the mind. Hegel's influence was the more extensive, reaching from philosophy to theology and politics (with baleful consequences). Schleiermacher's power was supreme in his own sphere as an emancipating and creative spiritual influence.

It is a hopeless task to summarize in a few paragraphs Schleiermacher's *Christliche Glaube*. It may be profitable, however, to mould in relief the salient points that stand out in relation to the scale of the German Protestant panorama. This *magnum opus* appeared in 1821, the 1830 edition being considerably altered. We expect much from the title: *The Christian Faith set forth according to the Principles of the Evangelical Church*. The title is a misnomer. One might suppose that a theologian like Schleiermacher, nourished in the tradition of the Reformed Church, would have built his system on symmetrical, architectural lines. Instead of Calvin's sharp outlines, we find blurred edges. 'The shadow of psychologism' rests on his theology. Clouds and mist hide the classic mountain-peaks of the Trinity, Sin, and Grace. He is over-fond of the smooth sequences of natural law, and allergic to the idea of

[18] A. R. Osborne, *Schleiermacher and Religious Education* (Oxford, 1934).
[19] See p. 199f., *infra*.

Divine irruption. The *Christliche Glaube* is much harder reading than Calvin's *Institutes*. One reason is the fact that in maturity Schleiermacher worked into a synthesis the great thoughts of outstanding men in theology, philosophy, and psychology. Plato, Spinoza, Leibniz, Lessing, and Kant, etc., passed through the alembic of his creative personality. In spite of a critical and scientific bent, he could say with deep conviction: 'My religion is so through and through heart-religion, I have no room for any other.' Religion was feeling, belief was dependence on God, doctrine was the interpretation of belief, and Christ was central for theology.[20]

This accent on religious experience relieved pressure by shifting the emphasis from the authority of the Bible and Confessions to an immediate sense of the Infinite and Eternal. The miraculous need no longer be a stumbling block to belief. The apologetic advantages of this new strategy were obvious in the early nineteenth century, but it indirectly opened the floodgates of pantheism. The danger may be illustrated from a passage of Goethe's *Faust* (Part I, xvi, 1808). Margaret recognizes Faust's language, but finds the emphasis new. He extols 'Heart', 'Love', 'God'; and he concludes: 'Feeling is all in all.' She replies:

> 'Tis plausible—yet must it be unsafe;
> Thou art no Christian.

With the subsequent development of German thought in mind, Mr. Gwilym O. Griffith asks pertinently:

If religion and piety are fundamentally a state of feeling, and if this feeling is itself the raw material of dogma, how shall the Church which indoctrinates its people in this belief safeguard them against the errors of 'strong delusions' which may arise at any time of widespread emotional eruption and mass hysteria? Under the powerful influence of some dominant personality, or of national propaganda, millions of religious-minded people may be swept into frenzied enthusiasm and feel—really feel—themselves religiously exalted. . . . What is to be the answer of the Church which has taught them insistently that religion *is* feeling, that revelation *is* intuition and that experience *is* the basis of doctrine?[21]

[20] Some of Schleiermacher's minor works were translated before 1850. His charming book on various reasons for celebrating Christmas was translated by Professor Hastie in 1890 (the *Weihnachtsfeier*). The *Christliche Glaube* had to wait till 1928. This E.T. was by H. R. Mackintosh, J. S. Stewart, and other Dr. Oman, reviewing it at length in the *British Weekly* (28th February 1929), explained the difficulties of Schleiermacher's style and terminology. Dr. Cross did a useful service in offering 'a condensed presentation' in his *Theology of Schleiermacher* (Chicago, 1911).

[21] *Interpreters of Man from Hegel to Barth* (London, 1943), p. 24.

No theologian since the Reformation has had more wide-spread influence than Schleiermacher. Even experts who deprecate his subjectivity admit that he wrote the most cardinal, thought-provoking theological classic since Calvin's *Institutes*. Theology is dated 'before' and 'after' Schleiermacher.[22] 'Not so discredited as some experts think,' says Dr. J. S. Whale; 'The only great theologian of the nineteenth century' is the considered judgement of Professor Brunner. Pusey, who attended his lectures at Berlin, spoke of him as 'that great man, who, whatever the errors of his system, has done more than any other . . . for the restoration of religious belief in Germany.'[23]

On the Continent Schleiermacher's influence over the educated laity has probably eclipsed that of any other religious thinker. Dr. Laurie Magnus, in his *Dictionary of European Literature*, praised him as 'incomparably the most literary theologian of modern times'. His attitude was questing, critical, 'Socratic'. Like Aquinas, he could truly confess: '*Theologus sum, humani nihil a me alienum puto.*'

The late Professor John Dickie, in his *Organism of Christian Truth* (1931) criticized a 'strain of sentimentality in Schleiermacher—to my mind rather womanish'. On the other hand, Robert Munro, in *Schleiermacher Personal and Speculative* (Paisley 1903), considered that 'the eternal womanly' in his hero was 'one of his most fascinating traits . . . like green turf covering hard granitic rock'. Readers who approach his theology through his life and letters will understand him better and appreciate his singularly engaging personality. He was remarkably modest in fame, patient in exhausting controversy. He fulfilled a resolution of his youth: 'I will never grow old in my soul.' Free from the arid intellectualism of some German professors, he believed that Christianity was a religion to be lived, not merely a set of doctrines to be discussed. So great was his respect for the views of others that his fellow countrymen are said to owe to him the word *Eigentümlichkeit* (individuality).

[22] F. Kattenbusch, *Die d. ev. Theologie seit Schleiermacher* (Giessen, 1926, 1934).

[23] Schleiermacher became a bogy to complacent, insular Englishmen. Carlyle's friend, Connop Thirlwall, met him in London, took him to the Zoo, and translated his minor treatise, *St. Luke* (1835). There was an outburst of expostulation. Thirlwall was marked as 'unsound'. Melbourne offered him the See of St. David's with some hesitation. ('What the devil made you translate Schleiermacher?') The seventy-fourth Oxford 'Tract' had an indignant post-script on the German heresiarch. Suspicion of German 'neology' continued to be a British characteristic for half a century afterwards.

When he celebrated the Lord's Supper with his family at his death-bed, he cried: 'Here light a sacrificial flame!' His life was a sacrificial flame, not 'a light that failed'.

Schleiermacher's critics accused him of shrouding Christian doctrine with the veil of vague idealism (his name meant 'veil-maker'). A fair-minded international scholar of the next generation, Dr. Philip Schaff, remarked:

It seems incredible that a man who removed from the New Testament the pedestal of the Old, who numbered the resurrection and ascension of Christ, among the things comparatively indifferent to saving faith . . . should have been a blessing to the Church and lead the rising generation to the fountain of life. And yet such is undoubtedly the fact and his lasting merit. . . . But Schleiermacher can only be understood and properly appreciated in close connexion with the two ages between which he stood, as the last in the generation of sceptics and the first in the generation of believers.[24]

The great 'renovator of German Theology' did not succeed in forming a school that stabilized Divinity on the 'left centre'. One reason for this was the counter-attraction of Hegel, Schleiermacher's colleague in the University of Berlin. In the Teutonic world of intellect Philosophy has often challenged Theology in her own realm.

We can understand Hegel better if we allow British admirers to introduce him.[25] G. W. F. Hegel (1770-1831) was a native of Würtemberg, where Pietism flourished so conspicuously. While still a theological student at Tübingen, he and Schlegel showed such enthusiasm for the French Revolution that they planted a 'Tree of Liberty' early one morning in the market place. When Hegel graduated in 1793 his certificate attested that he was well up in theology, but was 'without ability in philosophy'. In spite of this, he determined to devote his life to metaphysics. He settled at Jena on a legacy of under £300, satisfied with simple food, abundant books, and '*ein gutes Bier*'. A tireless student, he laid the foundations of immense erudition, stimulated by such Jena celebrities as Fichte and Schelling, Schiller, the Schlegels, and Tieck. Napoleon's soldiery broke into this academic paradise in 1806, and Hegel was forced to flee. Bitter experience made him reverse the Gospel precept: 'Seek ye first food and clothing and the kingdom of heaven

[24] *Germany: its Universities, Theology, and Religion* (Edinburgh, 1857). It is pleasant to mention that Karl Barth, exploring ruins in the University of Bonn after the Second World War, and finding a bust of Schleiermacher, replaced it in a niche of honour.

[25] For biographical data, J. H. Muirhead, 'Hegel', in *Ency. Brit.* (11th ed.); Edward Caird's *Hegel* in Blackwood Philosophical Classics.

shall be added to you.' After holding administrative and academic posts in Southern Germany, he was promoted to Berlin in 1818. In the Reconstruction era he ruled the philosophic realm, like Beethoven in music and Goethe in literature. An absent-minded genius, he achieved fame abroad as the typical German professor. A Frenchman once asked him to put his philosophy into one sentence—unlike the monk, who, asked to define Christianity on one foot, replied, 'Thou shalt love thy neighbour as thyself', Hegel replied in ten volumes. When these were all published, he complained: 'Only one man understands me, and even he does not.' Whether the story is apocryphal or not, its meaning is true. His writings are darkened by abstraction, condensation, and qualification, and largely consist of lecture notes (and his students' notes!). He described his work as 'an attempt to teach philosophy to speak German'.

The obscurity of Hegel was illumined by one master-thought that made an irresistible appeal, and not only in Germany. This was his neat mental process of Thesis, Antithesis, and Synthesis. It was guaranteed to operate in any sphere of life, e.g. the friction between conservatism and radicalism is liberalism; Romanism, in conflict with unbelief, breeds Protestantism. The theory satisfied believers in Aristotle's 'golden mean'— 'the knowledge of opposites is one'. It appealed to those who had become conscious of the significance of History and Progress; only dead things cease to be moved by the alternation and friction of opposing tendencies. 'The real is rational and the rational is real.' Here was a lever capable of opening all closed doors, a mental mechanism that lent itself to the rationalization of the most diverse schemes, ranging from the neo-Prussian theory of State Absolutism[26] to the economic materialism of Marx. Hegel himself was more interested in *processes* than in origins or ends.

Thus he would explain the Trinity as God the Revealer, Christ the Recipient, and the Spirit as the Revelation. From the Christian point of view, the most questionable feature of Hegel's is the relation of the finite mind to the Infinite. 'God

[26] Dr. Ehrenberg, confined in a concentration camp in 1938, was asked by an unhappy expert in philosophy: 'Do you attribute the fact that we have to suffer here to Hegel?' 'In such a place I wasn't in the mood to go into this question; but after all, wasn't he right? Were we not there as a result of Hegel's philosophical totalitarianism? . . . "Whatever is rational is real and whatever is real is rational" ' (*Autobiography of a German Pastor* (S.C.M., 1943), p. 101f.).

is God only in so far as He knows Himself; His self-knowledge
is His self-consciousness in man, is the knowledge man has *of*
God, which advances to man's self-knowledge *in* God.' This
ingenious theory would ascribe reality to the Absolute only in
the mind of men who believe in Him. Again, the different
religions of the world appear as stages in the unfolding process,
religion being 'the Divine Spirit's knowledge of itself through
the mediation of finite spirit'. In the light of this philosophy of
religion, heathenism appears in fresh, alluring vestments, as
each faith is directed to its appropriate niche in the hospitable
pantheon of world-religion. Here was a gleam to inspire
future investigators like Max Müller, scientific pioneers of
'Comparative Religion'.

Hegel undertook to reconcile faith and truth, to interpret
such doctrines as the Divinity of Christ and the Atonement so
that they might be tenable. This accommodation was bought
at a price, settled by Philosophy as the supreme court of appeal.
The price consisted in surrendering the conviction of the historic
Church that Christ is unique. Professor H. R. Mackintosh has
stated the Hegelian implication:

His death, resurrection, and exaltation . . . are parabolic statements of
the fact that finite man . . . is inevitably the prey of negation and decay;
yet view him in the light of his unity with the Infinite, and straightway he
rises and mounts to a lofty and positive participation in the pantheistic
world-process. Thus the story of man is . . . the self-evolution of Absolute
Reason spelling itself out in the medium of space and time. In this sense,
but no other, the Word took flesh and dwelt among us.[27]

Several theologians used Hegel's key of knowledge[28] to the
satisfaction of themselves and their followers. Four years after
his death appeared epoch-making books by Baur and Strauss
(1835).

A great impression was made by Ferdinand Baur's *Pastoral
Epistles*. Baur was appointed to a Chair at Tübingen in 1826
and died there in 1860, so that he had an ample opportunity
of founding 'the notorious Tübingen school', which caused
such consternation among the orthodox.[29] Lord Acton has
characterized him as an historian skilled 'in tracing the march
of ideas through the ages, over the heads of men—a thing new

[27] *Types of Modern Theology* (London, 1937), pp. 107f.
[28] Elizabeth S. Haldane, *Wisdom and Religion of German Philosophy, being Selections
from Hegel* (London, 1897).
[29] R. W. Mackay, *The Tübingen School and its Antecedents* (London, 1863). In
agreement with its findings. Cf. Mark Pattison's 'Present State of Theology in
Germany', 1857, reprinted in his *Essays* (Oxford, 1889).

to literature'. Baur used to repeat: 'Without philosophy, history is dead and dumb.' Unfortunately he carried his favourite saying so far as to become an architect of ideas, to whom facts were secondary. He found the key to the New Testament in Paul's conflict with judaizing Christians. He set Paul's 'universalism' against Peter's 'particularism', Paul's 'antinomianism' against Peter's 'legalism'. In approved Hegelian style he found a synthesis for the Petrine-Pauline antithesis—viz: the Catholic Church. Professor H. J. Cadbury has outlined Baur's method:

He assigned the several New Testament writings to one or other of these 'tendencies', laying stress on the polemic or conciliative purport of the authors, and settling questions of date and authorship to suit this formula. His pioneer application of the principle of development, his realization of the background of New Testament life as one of social movements, historic influences, and religious growth, is a permanent contribution, though his solution was too simple and too artificial.

On the negative side, Baur failed through not letting the individuality of the Apostles shine through the records; he sharpened divergencies till Peter and Paul almost appeared as though they were founders of rival German parties (*Richtungen*), complete with followers and acrimonious manifestoes. On the positive side, it may be claimed that the Tübingen School vindicated the unity of the New Testament by merging divergencies in all-embracing synthesis. These theories were in course of time corrected rather than disproved. 'They gave an incalculable impetus to research.'

David Friedrich Strauss (1808-74), the '*enfant terrible*' of the Higher Criticism, was a pupil of Baur. He was quite untouched, like his master, by the warm Evangelical ethos of his native Würtemberg. After some pastoral and teaching experience, he went north to sit at the feet of Hegel. Hegel, however, died just before he arrived. 'It was to hear *him* I came to Berlin,' he tactlessly explained to Schleiermacher. The eager student failed to catch the devout spirit of the great theologian, but Schleiermacher's lectures set him on the track of critical study of the life of Jesus. Strauss returned to Tübingen to write his *Leben Jesu*, which was not long in appearing (1835). His conclusions were sweeping. Myth formed the entrance and exit to the Gospel story; between them lay the crooked alleys of naturalistic explanation. His methods were up-to-date, like those of secular historians. What of Troy?

Had not F. A. Wolf of Halle proved that the *Iliad* was simply a patchwork woven by editors out of ballads derived from primitive folk-lore? Had not Niebuhr exposed the early history of the Roman State as a mere tissue of legends? The sacred must submit to the same critical text as the secular. There was no need to resort to the vulgar rationalist view that the Gospel was a fraud. Nineteenth-century speculation worked on the thesis of 'legend operating on a minimum of fact'. The expectation of a Messiah, maturing in the mind of an imaginative, oriental people, gradually clothed the earthly figure of Jesus with supernatural attributes. Thus the Gospel was reduced to an edifying myth. One thinks of Browning's German Professor in his close class-room (substituting 'Tübingen' for 'Göttingen'):

> So, he proposed inquiring first
> Into the various sources whence
>   This Myth of Christ is derivable;
> Demanding from the evidence
>   (Since plainly no such life was liveable)
> How these phenomena should class?
> Whether 'twere best opine Christ was,
> Or never was at all, or whether
> He was and was not, both together—
> It matters little for the name,
> So the idea be left the same. . . .
> When we looked for the inference and monition
> That our faith, reduced to such condition,
> Be swept forthwith to its natural dust-hole—
> He bids us, when we least expect it. . . .
> 'Go home and venerate the myth
> I thus have experimented with—
> This man, continue to adore him
> Rather than all who went before him,
> And all who ever followed after!'[30]

Strauss, however, did not even value the idea of the Incarnation. 'The idea loves not to pour all its fullness into one example'; only the race could answer to the ideal. 'Jesus symbolized the progress of mankind'; he deserved a niche in the humanist temple; 'but we have no real assurance that someone else may not appear equal to Him, or superior'. There was something so impersonal in Strauss that even his eulogistic biographer, Eduard Zeller, found it hard to humanize him.[31] The name 'Strauss' may mean 'an ostrich', or 'a bouquet', or 'a feud'. David Friedrich Strauss never buried his head in the

---

[30] *Christmas Eve* (1850), XV-XVIII.   [31] *Life*, E.T. (London, 1874).

I

sand, received few bouquets, and spent his life in controversy.
Few theological books have received such publicity as his *Leben
Jesu*. It was hailed with almost universal horror by professed
Christians—here was a Lutheran divine who actually assailed
the founder of the faith![32] Hengstenberg, pillar of biblical
orthodoxy, indeed declared that Strauss had done the Church a
service in frankly discarding fragments of conventional attire,
to which other rationalists timidly clung. The issue had been
brought to a head—'If the Lord be God, serve him, but if Baal
be God . . .'. Other opponents of Strauss called for government
action against the blasphemer. The gentler Neander pleaded
that his *Life of Jesus* be refuted by reason, rather than publicized
by persecution. Carlyle's friend, John Sterling, considered
Strauss 'exceedingly clever and clear-headed', with far more
insight than he had expected. 'It seems admitted that the
orthodox theologians have failed to give any sufficient answer.'

In Germany a country pastor from Holstein devised a novel
method of defeating Strauss—literally, he wrote a novel with
that object. If 'Higher Critics' could mistake a forgery for an
authentic document, might they not be capable of the converse?
So Wilhelm Meinhold wrote *The Amber Witch* in the pedantic,
quaint, and homely style of a seventeenth-century rural parson,
and passed off this anonymous novel as a genuine chronicle
of the period. How far was he successful? Lady Gordon Duff
commented: 'Meinhold went forth to refute Strauss, and found
on his way a new kingdom in the realm of Romance. It is a
repetition of the history of Saul.'[33]

Strauss made many enemies, but he was not without
friends. The radical government of Zurich thought that it
would be a shrewd stroke if they appointed a free thinker to a
Chair of Theology (1839). They miscalculated the temper of
their fellow-citizens. An insurrection led to the fall of the
cantonal administration, and Strauss was pensioned off before
he had started lecturing. After twenty years in literary work,
with excursions into politics, he returned to theology with a
new *Life of Jesus for the German People*.[34] It is surprising that this
'come-back' attracted any attention; to popularize the lifeless

---

[32] Renan, whose negative criticism was so much more seductive than Strauss's
owing to its literary charm, sometimes wished that he had been born a German
Protestant, who could be a philosopher without ceasing to be a Christian—though
'only just a Christian' (*Souvenirs*, Appendix).

[33] Introduction to *The Amber Witch*, E.T. (London, 1895).

[34] 1864; 13th ed., 1904.

shadow of his 'Jesus' would indeed be a miracle. 'Are we still Christians?' he asked in his *Old and New Belief* (1872). 'No, but we still have a religion,' he replied. Two years later he was dead, with nothing to cling to at the last but the materialism of contemporary science.

'It was the provocative character of the *Leben Jesu* which made 1835 so memorable in the history of Modernism,' says Professor H. L. Stewart.

Hardly anyone now reads it, except the professional theologian. . . . It has long since been superseded by books which contain all that is worth study in its argument, and omit what further analysis has rendered trivial. But in its time it forced the pace in theological thinking. It was the most sensational product of that German thought which had begun to drift to England a little over a hundred years ago, and in England even to Oxford —which some jester has well described as the place to which German philosophers go when they die.[35]

When we consider Strauss's life and teaching in the perspective of later Liberal Protestantism, we see him as a sceptic rather than as a pioneer modernist. George Eliot translated (1846) his *Leben Jesu* (4th edition, 1840, with concessions to Neander and other critics withdrawn). She also was a sceptic, but unlike Strauss, had reacted against a fervent, Pietist upbringing. 'Can we venture to call ourselves Christians?' her master asked in 1860, 'I know not, but . . . we shall remain Protestants; in fact we shall then only be true Protestants.' The name of Strauss has become a byword, but there is a danger of underrating his ability today, just as he was overrated by his followers a century ago. 'He was beyond all question a great writer,' Dr. H. R. Mackintosh reminds us, and 'as we contemplate his brave, sad, clear-eyed agnosticism, we may well say of him, *Utinam noster esses.*'

Nevertheless, the views of Strauss provided useful ammunition for Romanists who wanted to prove from the *ipsissima verba* of Protestant thinkers that Protestantism was merely a mild phase of incipient unbelief. Friedrich Nietzsche (1844-1900) used to say: 'The Lutheran pastor is the grandfather of German Philosophy, its *peccatum originale* is Protestantism.' Nietzsche's father was actually a pastor. He was of clerical descent on both sides of the family. His mother was a Puritan lady, of the same sort that had fostered Kant, and he himself remained a preacher to the end. His father, who had tutored several of the Hohenzollerns, rejoiced when he was born on the birthday of Frederick William the Fourth, and named him after that Romantic and Pietist monarch. The son was thus able to declare: 'My birthday throughout my childhood was a day of public rejoicing.' Unfortunately there was nothing in Nietzsche's teaching to rejoice the heart of a Christian, save the genuine conviction with which he preached his beliefs. He hailed Wagner as 'a Siegfried who has never learnt the meaning of fear. . . . Bayreuth signifies for us the morning sacrament on the day of battle': but he refused to speak to the opera king when in *Parsifal* he recognized the moral and aesthetic values of Christianity. Indeed, he boasted about finishing *Thus Spake Zarathustra* in that 'hallowed hour when Richard Wagner gave up the ghost'.

Passing over much that is of interest in Nietzsche's life, we should note that his system may be summed up in three basic concepts—the death of God, 'nihilism', and 'the will to power'. He was a radical atheist who questioned the very value of our traditional values, the morality of our morals. Yet in the writhing of his tortured soul, the longing for the death of the Christian god and the rebirth of pagan Dionysius, there was a religious urge quite lacking in the bloodlessness of Strauss. Dr. Karl Löwith comes to the paradoxical conclusion that 'Nietzsche's philosophy is indeed a Protestant event'.[36]

There is a curious mental twist in many German anti-Christian theorists, whose negations have seldom brought them peace of mind. Nietzsche became so miserable that he lost his reason in 1888. His earnest follower, Arthur Drews, who was an ardent monist, deviated from historic sense in denying the very existence of the founder of Christianity. His *Christ Myth* went into three German editions before it appeared in English (1910). An analysis of his theory will be found in Dr. Stanley Hall's *Jesus, the Christ in the Light of Psychology*.[37]

It is curious to compare the attitudes of Anglo-Saxons and of Germans who reject the Divinity of Christ. The former usually pay respect to the ethical teaching of Jesus, often patronizing Him as a prophet of progress: the latter find fault even with His character. A minister of the Church of Scotland writes: 'When I was at Bonn in 1905 I picked up a printed thesis by a German Ph.D., which argued that Jesus was a mental

---

[36] Article on Nietzsche, *Church History* (U.S.A., September, 1944).
[37] Vol. I., pp. 205-20 (London, 1921).

defective subject to hallucinations. It ended with the tragic words: "Danke dass du bist frei von Jesus." Germany has become "free from Jesus" and we see the devastating results today. There was good reason for Albert Schweitzer choosing as the subject of his thesis for the degree of M.D.: THE SANITY OF CHRIST.'

Going back to the middle of the nineteenth century, we catch a glimpse of Ludwig Feuerbach, the classical instance of the sceptic in theology, corresponding to Hume in philosophy. 'Atheist' as he was reputed to be, Feuerbach conveniently retained the theistic values of goodness, love, and justice.[38] It was his aim to change his readers 'from friends of God to friends of man, from believers to thinkers, from devotees to workers, from candidates for the next world to students of this one, from Christians whose creed makes them half animal, half angel, to men who are complete men'. The humanism of this lonely seeker after truth was destined to give way to a bleak materialism.

Karl Marx and Ferdinand Lassalle, like Feuerbach, had been swept into the current of radical Hegelianism. When they emerged and proceeded to formulate their own ideas, those founders of modern Socialism, far from proclaiming the Rights of Man, reduced him to an economic unit, functioning according to a soulless, deterministic mechanism. Strange that men of Jewish extraction, whose heredity was rooted in a highly personalized Jehovah, should have denied the value of personality! Surely a movement for human emancipation should have been coloured by a certain idealism and sympathy with the life of the spirit broadly conceived, despite inevitable anticlericalism. Unfortunately, scientific socialism in Germany never escaped from the particular philosophy of history where it originated. Marx and Lassalle, in offering a substitute for religion, drained it of emotion.

If Hegelianism was employed as a kind of conjuror's handkerchief in the economic sphere, it had a damaging effect on morals; to the average man it was reassuring to be informed that Sin was an inevitable phase in the evolution of good out of evil, raw material on the way to being 'processed'.

Hegelianism of the extreme left branched into two —atheism and pantheism. The latter was often more mischievous in its effects on individuals, through the blurring of moral distinctions in a mist of confused feeling. There is, to be

[38] *The Essence of Religion* (1841; E.T. by George Eliot, 1853).

sure, 'The Higher Pantheism', as Tennyson reminded his generation in a familiar poem; one recalls Schelling's haunting statement that 'it is the same spirit which sleeps in the stone, dreams in the plant, awakens in the animal, and becomes self-conscious in Man'. But there is also a 'lower pantheism', which had a wide vogue among young men in Germany. It was dramatically exposed by W. B. Robertson, a Scottish student at Halle in 1841. Robertson describes his experience, crossing the Alps through a narrow defile. It was a sublime scene, capable of arousing the deeper instincts of any normal man. 'Vanslow, did you ever pray?' he asked his companion. 'Pray!' said he, 'What's that? What's God? Yon cloud is God; that ground' (kicking it) 'is God, and I am made of that, and so I am God, and when I pray I summon up myself.' A thunder-storm broke out, as though to vindicate the divine 'I AM', but the scorner laughed. Shortly afterwards an Alpine wagon, heavily laden, suddenly broke loose, not far off, and crashed. 'Vanslow, had you been killed just now, where would your soul have gone?' 'Gone to the Absolute,' he replied, 'lapsed into the all, melted like a snowflake in the ocean, gone to feed the flowers, I suppose, the worms perhaps.' When the thunder-cloud had passed, Robertson turned with relief from 'that dark-souled blasphemer' to hooded monks and Alpine woodmen, who greet wayfarers with 'Praise be to the Lord Jesus!', expecting the answer 'For ever, Amen!'[39]

The rank growth of pantheism has been graphically des-cribed in a novel that is said to have made as big a sensation as *Uncle Tom's Cabin*. This tract for the times, *Eritis sicut Deus* (1853) exposed nature-mysticism. Not only did it fail to produce 'the God-intoxicated man' after the tradition of Spinoza; it was tinged with a yellow streak of selfish materialism and degenerate morals. One of the interesting features of the novel consists in a conducted tour to the University of Tübingen, where we are introduced to living characters like Baur and Strauss, well-meaning but blind leaders of German youth. Pantheism must meet the needs of many a Teuton, for it was in the ascendant again in the early twentieth century.[40] Nature-mysticism was destined to bring forth Dead Sea fruit later in the Nazi mythology.

[39] *German Student Life* (Glasgow, 1891).

[40] cf. Weinel, 'Religious Life and Thought in Germany Today' (*Hibbert Journal*, July 1909).

Hegel's 'Absolute' was 'relative' in the sense that it appealed to men of utterly different views. Conservatives as well as radicals marched under the banner of Hegel. Take for instance, the case of Philip Marheineke, Schleiermacher's colleague at Trinity Church, Berlin. He was a firm believer in historic Christianity, but claimed that it could only be understood by the application of the 'dialectic' method. The process of 'accommodation' was carried so far that, in spite of profound scholarship and loyalty to the foundations of the Faith, Marheineke produced a system more Hegelian than Christian.

Even more fantastic was the theology of Karl Daub, Professor at Heidelberg from 1795 till his death in 1836. Daub was influenced successively by Kant, Schelling, and Hegel (indeed he passed through so many different phases that he was dubbed 'the Talleyrand of German Thought'). Daub ignored historical criticism; it 'cramped his style'. He would gladly have subscribed to Fichte's credo that 'the metaphysical only, and not the historical, can give us blessedness'. He found what he wanted to find. 'Still climbing after knowledge infinite' (in Marlowe's famous phrase), he eventually reached some extraordinary conclusions. For example, he discovered that Judas Iscariot was the embodiment of Satan, corresponding to Jesus, the incarnation of God. He wrote an amazing book on the theology of his contemporaries, which Strauss called 'a veritable inferno'. Guided by Hegel, as Dante was led by Virgil, Daub sees 'naturalists' and super-naturalists suffer side by side.

It might be supposed that exact science would have dealt Hegelian speculation a mortal blow. In Germany such *a priori* interpretations were discredited half a century after the sage's death. Isaac Dorner's massive *Glaubenslehre* (1879) embodied as much Hegelianism as was consistent with historic Christianity. Dorner started his academic career at Tübingen in Strauss's time and had seen for himself at close quarters the havoc wrought by theory when it plays with facts. His work was marked by objectivity and fine appreciation of the moving ideas of history, with tolerance for diverging views. Dorner's ability as one of the 'mediating school' was aided by his lucid style. He had visited England in student days and thus acquired a better understanding of the Anglo-Saxon mentality than most German divines. Consequently his *System of Christian Doctrine* and *History of Protestant Theology* (E.T. 1871) were widely read.

It is surprising, however, to note the popularity of Hegelianism in Great Britain long after the movement had spent its impetus in Germany. In 1865 Hutchison Stirling, a Scottish doctor who had turned from physic to metaphysics, unfolded to the uninitiated his elusive *Secret of Hegel*. In the preface to the new edition (1893) he explains that he was first drawn to the study of Hegel by seeing his name in a review and afterwards by hearing it mentioned with awe and reverence by two German students! Another great Scotsman, Dr. John Caird, preached this message in clear and melodious language. His brother, Edward, saw Christianity, not as something exceptional in the history of mankind, but as the culmination of a lengthy process of cosmic development. George Matheson boldly applied Hegelianism as the key to the interpretation of the first sixteen centuries of Church History; his ambitious *Growth of the Spirit of Christianity* (1877) was a *tour de force*. Philip Schaff, called from Germany to a Reformed Chair at Mercersburg, Pennsylvania, familiarized the more scholarly American divines with Hegelian method; some of them were shocked at his 'Puseyite' theory that Romanism and Protestantism were but phases in the divinely ordered evolution. At Oxford T. H. Green used Hegelianism against scientific materialism and as a basis of constructive citizenship. 'Idealism' built Liberalism on a Hegelian foundation, whereas in Prussia it was usual to regard the State as 'the culmination of the historic process'. The Anglo-Saxon was apt to treat Hegelianism in its practical, sociological aspects; the German tried to soar into the presence of God (or the Absolute) *via* unsubstantial speculation, at the cost of disintegrating tested Christian convictions.

CHAPTER SIX

FROM HEGEL TO HARNACK

IF Hegel stimulated thought, Tholuck stirred both mind and soul. Friedrich August Tholuck (1799-1877) made Evangelical religion a living power in his native land, emancipated from narrowness and provincialism. Indeed, Professor Stalker went so far as to claim: 'What Wesley did for the Church of England, and Chalmers for the Church of Scotland, and Vinet for the Church of Switzerland, Tholuck may be said to have done for the Church of Germany.'

The danger to which Pietism was exposed in the early nineteenth century was twofold. It was apt either to contract into rigidity, or burst into morbid mass hysteria. The first tendency was expressed by Hengstenberg, whose influence we shall consider later. The second was an efflorescence of wild emotionalism, stimulated by the unsettlement of war, repression, and penury. Würtemberg in particular, was a hothouse of weird sects. Some, like the Rappists, professed community of goods; they rejected marriage, became vegetarians and adopted strange garments. Others, like the Muckers in Königsberg, were Manichaean in attitude; so questionable were the practices of Ebel that in 1835 a criminal prosecution ended his religious activities. Madame de Krüdener, a Baltic baroness, was converted from fashion to fervour. A well-meaning but excitable enthusiast, she had an unfortunate habit of getting into tow with shady adventurers who peopled the 'underworld' of Pietism and exploited the foibles of the feeble-minded. Mme. de Krüdener found many simple souls who responded to her Millennarian prophecies. She blended politics with her Pietism so effectively that for a time (c. 1815) she influenced the Tsar Alexander the First in his scheme of a Holy Alliance, to band Christian nations against the forces of revolution and infidelity. She afterwards plagued the governments of Germany and Switzerland with her peripatetic evangelism and her indiscriminate charity. Such crude crusades brought reproach upon efforts to advance the Gospel by appealing directly to men's hearts. Revivalism of *any* kind became anathema to sensible men on the Continent, just as 'Methodism' was like a red rag to Englishmen like Sidney, 'the Smith of Smiths'.

Tholuck's aim was to redeem the Gospel from the fanaticism that had discredited it, and to bring it into friendly contact with the best in contemporary civilization. His method was personal evangelism ('I have but one passion and that is Christ'). When deep consecration is linked with intellectual distinction and real interest in the lives of others, a man's magnetism is bound to tell.[1] Hundreds of ministers all over Germany owed their very soul to Tholuck. His influence spread abroad. In the 'thirties' and 'forties' his fame drew to Halle Scotsmen of the calibre of Lindsay Alexander, W. B. Robertson, and John Ker. From America came Charles Hodge and Calvin E. Stowe, the husband of the famous Harriet Beecher. In London John Sterling, a thoughtful young curate, devoted himself to translating some of his works. Carlyle, in his *Life of Sterling* (1851) remarked: 'I remember he talked often about Tholuck, Schleiermacher and others of that stamp; and looked disappointed, though full of good nature, at my obstinate indifference to them and their affairs.' Pusey made friends with Tholuck, who was able to help him with material for his weighty *Theology of Germany*.[2] The young Tractarian, re-acclimatized at Oxford, lost touch with his German friends, but never forgot the man who regenerated the soul of his people.

When Tholuck was appointed to a theological Chair at Halle in his twenty-seventh year (1827) the whole Faculty turned against him. It was as narrow-minded in its rationalism as it had been whole-hearted in its Pietism a century earlier. Tholuck's colleagues urged that his nomination be cancelled, but the government refused their petition. It appeared that his life would not last long; a brief tenure of office was indicated —which relieved his opponents. Yet he was spared to teach at Halle for fifty years. He attended to his labours joyfully as well as resolutely, like Mercury the celestial messenger who had wings to his feet. The old rationalism was vanquished and Halle was recaptured for Pietism through his agency. But it was not the Pietism that reigned there a century earlier. It was an expanded Pietism that found room for Biblical Criticism, discussing new theories with candour, proclaiming the need for world missions and welcoming the co-operation of foreign Evangelicals.

Tholuck was fresh, stimulating and suggestive, free from the

[1] See article by Stalker on Tholuck (*Expositor*, August 1912); cf. Witte, *Das Leben Tholucks* (1884).   [2] cf. p. 3, *supra*.

professorial pedantry of *Gründlichkeit*. For prose he offered poetry. He had a genius for striking illustrations and scintillating quotations; but he won the youth of Halle by more than rhetorical gallantry. He broke new ground in making his relations with the students intimate. He visited them in their lodgings, took them out for walks, and invited them to his home. His humour and geniality were as conspicuous as his determination to win them for Christ. To poor students and foreigners he gave special attention: nor did he relax these efforts when his classes became uncomfortably crowded.

Many of Tholuck's hearers had little first-hand knowledge of Evangelical religion; orthodox Christianity they dismissed with a smile. His aim was to lead young men from the tropical jungle of pantheism and the arid desert of rationalism to the green pastures and fresh fountains of the Gospel. A good impression of his method and personality may be gleaned from *Guido and Julius* (1825). This was a series of letters on the aberrations of two young divines, showing how they were eventually won to the Christian Faith. It is autobiographical. 'Julius' represented Julius Muller, afterwards Tholuck's colleague; 'Guido' was Tholuck himself; 'Father Abraham' was the Baron von Kottwitz, a Moravian, largely instrumental in his conversion. The sub-title, 'The True Consecration of the Sceptic', was an answer to a semi-rationalist tract by De Wette, published three years earlier, and entitled *The Consecration of the Sceptic*. *Guido and Julius* was the work of an historian who had a thorough knowledge of the *Aufklärung* and its antecedents. It was translated into English by Ryland. The following passage illustrates Tholuck's ironical style:

In the circuit of their Seminary there was no Emmaus; no spring flowers flourished there, nor groves of Academus. The new temple of Reason was built on the mouldering ruins of the old porch of the Stoics and the deserted walks of the garden of Epicurus. The Director of the Gymnasium, an aged man, revered the pineal gland as the seat of the spirit, and had often indulged the speculation whether the Creator might not have furnished man at creation with a third hand or a third foot instead of a heart. It was his office to teach religion. Most assiduously he dragged a skeleton, his own workmanship, day after day, into his lecture-room, and shook the thing of bones till a shudder ran through the school. Nor were the other masters of a better kind—philologists, who in all their vocabularies had not one word of life-giving power. What the preachers had of religion was picked up at foreign volcanoes. No wonder that the flame in the souls of these youths shone more faintly, as it vainly turned to the right and left, eager for fuel, but finding none.

The 'bold, mocking spirit of the age' was incarnate in Heinrich Heine, the German Aristophanes. In his censor-mutilated articles on 'Religion and Philosophy in Germany' (1834) he compares the mystical, Platonic temperament, and the practical Aristotelian attitude, through the centuries. He finds this conflict reproduced in Germany, but with a damaging qualification—'the Protestant pietists are mystics without imagination, and the Protestant orthodox are dogmatists without intelligence'. Professor Walter, in his critical study of Heine, has pointed out that 'he never ceased to deplore his loss of self-respect' in abjuring the Judaism of his forefathers and receiving Christian baptism at the hands of a Lutheran pastor, for whose Church he had but slight regard. Prussian Jews were in a disadvantageous position after 1815. Those who had been given full rights of citizenship in the Rhineland under the Napoleonic régime found themselves threatened with a return to ghetto conditions.[3] Those who had been combatants in the War of Liberation, far from being given the credit of rallying to defend the Fatherland, were denied a certificate entitling them to civil employment, which was issued to their Christian fellow-soldiers. Anti-semitism found expression in social discrimination as well as in legal enactment. Ridiculing Jews became as popular in the Press as on the stage.

In Goethe's youth, the Hebrew cause benefited during the era of the Enlightenment; yet large caricatures could still be seen in public places, representing the martyrdom of a Christian child. 'This still bore witness against them,' he explained, 'though wrought not through private ill-will, but by public order.' With the passing of the tolerant, universalist spirit of the eighteenth century, the demon of prejudice returned to Germany. Hatred of 'the Jewish intellectual' and 'the Jewish money-maker' was stimulated by commercial jealousy, particularly among the lower middle class.[4] This attitude contributed, along with hatred of 'the harlot Reason', to a kind of

---

[3] The desire for assimilation to German culture ('Christian') owed much to the cosmopolitan *Aufklärung*. Abraham, son of Moses Mendelssohn (1729-86) declared that, while not knowing whether God exists and while not personally leaving his ancestral Judaism, he intended to have his children brought up as Christians. This, after all, was 'the creed of most civilized peoples' which contains 'nothing that can lead youth astray from what is good'.

[4] These conditions are reflected in Raabe's *Der Hungerpastor* (1864; E.T., 1885). This once-famous novel, somewhat old-fashioned when published, points back to the early nineteenth century. The theme is jealousy. The son of a Jewish second-hand dealer becomes a Privy Councillor, while the son of an Evangelical schoolmaster only attains the status of a village pastor.

rancid, half-secularized Pietism. Börne used to say: 'He who cannot be an aristocrat so that he may look down on the burgher, wishes, at least, to be a Christian, so that he can have the Jews to look down upon.'

Among the educated Jews of Germany there was a keen realization that persecution in the past had cut them off from the best in civilization. Isolation from good society and disqualification from many honourable professions and callings had injured their temper as well as their prospects, producing what we would now call 'an inferiority complex'. A Jewish Reform Movement was therefore started in the early nineteenth century to keep educated Israelites in touch with modern ideas. Frederick William the Third might have welcomed a voluntary renunciation of 'peculiarities' by a certain section of his subjects; the removal of grievances would have promoted the unification of the kingdom and brought him new friends. Instead of taking this line, the Prussian king went out of his way to attack the Jewish Reform Movement. He would allow no German hymns, prayers, or sermons in the synagogue. Indeed, he issued a cabinet order insisting on the traditional ritual, 'without the slightest innovation in language, ceremonies, etc.' Complete segregation—with disastrous economic and cultural consequences—or complete assimilation to the State pattern, was the choice he offered. As the law of Prussia required everyone to belong to a definite religion, educated Jews had either to worship in a language they could not understand (and find themselves excluded from honourable public employment) or become Christians. The number of conversions, particularly at Berlin, became alarming.[5] Judaism in that city came within calculable distance of total extinction, and the realization of the dream of Frederick William and the Society for the Conversion of the Jews[6] appeared assured.[7]

In utter contrast to the conversion of Heine stands that of David Mendel, a young Jew who was captivated by Schleiermacher's *Reden* in his seventeenth year and was baptized in

[5] Karl Marx's father, a Jewish lawyer, was baptized with his family in 1824. Lassalle was also of Jewish extraction. Is it surprising that from families conforming to the official Church through social pressure there should spring militant Socialists who hated State Christianity?

[6] In 1801 a Berlin student, a Hebrew Christian named Frey, met pioneers of Jewish Missions in London. One of these, Lewis Way, met Tholuck, who was instrumental in starting a Berlin Society for the Conversion of the Jews (1822); this Society was supported by annual collections from all the congregations of the Prussian United Church.

[7] H. Walter, *Heinrich Heine* (London, 1930), p. 32.

1809, taking the name 'Neander' as a symbol of having become a 'new man' in Christ. Without warmth, Neander was convinced, there could be no theology: 'It can only thrive in the calmness of a soul consecrated to God.' This explains his favourite motto: *'Pectus est quod theologum facit.'* Neander was more permanently attached to the pietist tradition than to Schleiermacher's *via media*, but found himself in close sympathy with Tholuck's 'Theology of the New Life'. The end of the Napoleonic Wars saw Neander a Professor in Berlin. Under his inspiring influence, Church History came to life. After the Reformation it had passed through various phases. It started by being polemical with the *Magdeburg Centuries*. It became semi-pietistic and suddenly tolerant with Gottfried Arnold (apologist for heretics). Under the urbane Mosheim it assumed eighteenth-century garb—conventional, matter-of-fact, almost secular. Neander was quite interested in Church History as a process of institution-building: indeed, Möhler the famous Catholic exponent of the 'Theory of Development', was one of his hearers and praised him as the first German Protestant to understand the Fathers. Neander's chief service, however, was to paint with glowing colours the unfolding pageant of Christianity through the centuries; he was at his best when he portrayed great personalities like Julian the Apostate and St. Bernard. In this labour of love the Pietist and the Romanticist blended. To Neander, Church History was essentially a procession of witness, though he was more successful in portraying types that were congenial to his own temperament—the saint and the scholar rather than the man of action. His *General Church History* has long been superseded, but it was valuable as a pioneer work in claiming place for personality, thus relating the piety of the past to that of the present. History was a drama of flesh and blood, as well as an impersonal record of cause and effect. The voice of Neander was persuasive in pleading that History was an Art as well as a Science.

The 'Theology of the New Life' was attractively interpreted by Tholuck and Neander, but did not succeed in stabilizing a 'Liberal Evangelical' front. Rival parties sprang up, notably a scholarly group less indifferent than they to the 'pilgrims' dress' of particular 'confessions'. Tweston and Nitzsch were 'right centre' in their emphasis.[8] They both owed much to Schleiermacher, but went beyond his standpoint to a more

[8] cf. p. 202, *infra*.

orthodox, 'positive' position. In Twesten the scholastic Lutheranism of the seventeenth century was revived, but enlarged and liberalized by the scientific interest of Schleiermacher and the tolerant eclectic tendency of the Prussian United Church.

The indicator, however, swung from 'right centre' to 'right' with signs of veering even to the 'extreme right'. Theology, which had soared with Schleiermacher, losing sight of the creeds and (at times) even of the Bible, was inclined to exchange wings of speculation for the bonds of literalism. Was the authority of the Bible so discredited as Strauss and Baur had apparently demonstrated? A considerable public looked for guidance and turned back to the Word of God. Their oracle appeared providentially in the person of a Bible Commentator, ready to confute the rationalists.

Ernst Wilhelm Hengstenberg (1808-69) was not content with proving that the Bible was a trustworthy rule of faith and life. He re-forged the fetters of Verbal Inspiration, with particular attention to the links of Old Testament prophecy. Every opinion that did not tally with his views was 'deadly rationalism'. He made capital out of the disagreements of 'the Critics'. His fervour was reminiscent of the old German Pietists, but, unlike them, he was attached to a hard-and-fast theory of Biblical authority, which laid far greater emphasis on orthodox belief. This procured for his Old Testament Commentaries, translated and published during the 'fifties', an immense circulation in Great Britain and America (*Biblical Cabinet*).[9] Not all German theology was 'unsound'; Hengstenberg's father was a minister of the Reformed Church, but he himself was a staunch Lutheran. Professor Schaff believed that if he had been born in Scotland or New England, he would probably have lived and died a rigorous Calvinist. He considered him 'in some respects the most Puritan and Americanizing, and in other respects the most un-Puritan and un-American divine of Germany'.

An English historian, Archdeacon Cheetham, has described Hengstenberg as 'a man of real learning and ability who fought for the Evangelical party with unfailing courage and

---

[9] This series opened the door for more liberal theology. T. and T. Clark, having exhausted the conservative writers in the Foreign Theological Library, passed on to men like Dorner and Ewald. That led to the export of 'advanced' theology (e.g. Ritschl and Harnack) to Britain and America; their views were not generally accepted at face value, but did much to fertilize thought.

energy'. Unfortunately, his Evangelical dogmatism led him back to Lutheran Confessionalism of a reactionary type. We shall see him later as an uncompromising 'Church and State' partisan.[10] His influence caused the theological dial to register a pronounced swing in the opposite direction.

The Higher Criticism was not always linked with scholars of a cold, analytical type, the slaves of their own theories. Some of them were real personalities and men of ardent Christian faith. W. M. L. De Wette (1780-1849) was among these. De Wette, Schleiermacher's colleague in the University of Berlin, was converted from rationalism under Moravian influence. This 'Nathanical soul' (as Neander called him) was dismissed from his Chair in 1819 by the Government. He retired to Weimar, where he wrote *Theodore or the Conversion of the Sceptic* (1822). Soon afterwards he was called to the Chair of Theology at Basel, like another distinguished victim of political intolerance, Karl Barth. There he became popular among the citizens as well as in the University. His dramatic, musical, and artistic interests prevented him from becoming a Higher Critic with a one-track mind. Realizing in his own experience what the religion of today owes to the past, he brought to the study of the Old Testament a genuinely religious spirit as well as candour and exegetical skill. To Wellhausen he was 'the epoch-making opener of the historical criticism of the Pentateuch'.

The greatest Old Testament scholar whom Germany had so far produced was Heinrich Ewald (1803-75). His *Life* has been written by Professor Witton Davies (1903) and gives us a graphic account of his career. Like De Wette, Ewald suffered by trespassing on the forbidden ground of politics, but his troubles were partly of his own seeking, for he was temperamental, arbitrary, and intolerant. These defects, however, did not enter into the fabric of his scholarship. His Hebrew Grammar inaugurated a new era of scientific study in Semitics. His *History of the People of Israel* (1843-59) was the first attempt to gather up the various strands of Israel's past, and to present the result with imagination, accuracy, and breadth. Utilizing the findings of fellow-workers like Reuss, as well as his own research, he revealed in the books of the Old Testament a line of historic development, hitherto unrealized. Without being unduly biased by Hegelian presuppositions, he grasped and

[10] cf. p. 201, *infra*.

expounded an illuminating principle: Lessing's idea of 'the Divine Education of the human race' was shown to be supremely true through the medium of Israel. Under Ewald's sensitive touch, the early Hebrew records appeared as the incomplete expression of truths made explicit later; the historical books were seen to be the work of many minds in many centuries. The Prophets ceased to be unintelligible predictors of the shape of things to come; they became men of insight as well as foresight; and they fell into line as a procession of preachers, social reformers, and wise counsellors, with their faces toward the New Testament.[11] The Sages recovered their humanity. The poets came into their own again, freed from thraldom to the hard prose of both orthodoxy and rationalism. On the foundation of this 'noble work' of Ewald's, Dean Stanley built his stimulating *Lectures on the Jewish Church*, which made the Old Testament live for thousands of thoughtful English readers.

If Ewald unveiled the sublimity of Hebrew literary genius, his successor, Julius Wellhausen (1844–1918) accomplished valuable work on the technical side, analysing the Pentateuch into the four strands that still have to be grasped by students who make their first critical approach to the Old Testament ('J, E, D, and P'). Kuenen, the great Dutch scholar, accepted the '*Graf-Wellhausen* Theory' in its final form and did much to commend it abroad. He described Wellhausen's *History of Israel* as 'the crowning fight' in the long campaign for the scientific study of the Bible.

One of the leading orientalists of the nineteenth century, Professor Franz Delitzsch of Leipzig, owed much of his education to a Jew and had the satisfaction of seeing his benefactor baptized. Delitzsch became known as 'the Christian Talmudist'. He translated the New Testament into Hebrew and communicated his enthusiasm by reviving the *Instituta Judaica* (founded in 1728 by Callenberg the Halle Pietist). These were university societies, inspired by the twofold aim of training missionaries to convert the Jews and of studying Jewish life and thought, past and present. Delitzsch was a stiff Churchman, like most Saxons; two years before his death in 1890 he announced: 'By the banner of our Lutheran Confession let us stand; folding ourselves in it, let us die!' His attitude to new

---

[11] At the close of the century Cornill's *Prophets of Israel* had an immense influence abroad as well as in Germany.

K

ideas, however, became more liberal in later life; Cheyne even claims him as one of the pioneers of Biblical Criticism. His son, Friedrich Delitzsch, broke new ground in Old Testament Archaeology. When *Bibel und Babel* was published in 1902, thousands of copies were sold at home and abroad. Laymen as well as clergy were intrigued by the question: 'Did the Hebrews borrow the Flood-story from Babylon?' If his claims for the Babylonian contribution to the Hebrew religion were somewhat sweeping, his research was beneficial in stimulating a more careful study of Israel's neighbours and their influence.

New Testament study was ultimately advanced rather than arrested by the one-sided theories of F. C. Baur and the Tübingen School. Philosophical and theological bias was corrected by a fresh study of the documents, and by more exact methods. By the close of the nineteenth century German critics had thoroughly sifted such fundamental issues as the life of Jesus, the Synoptic Problem, and the significance of the Johannine writings. No agreement was reached on the dates and authorship of some New Testament Books, but the groundwork had been thoroughly worked over and it was possible to speak of 'the assured results of Modern Criticism'. One reassuring feature was this: despite tendencious extremists, the more conservative views were sometimes vindicated. Thus Harnack proved the Lucan authorship of *Luke* and *Acts*, remarking: 'On this, as on many other points regarding Early Christian Literature, tradition is right.'

In one important respect tradition was wrong. A scholar as progressive as Edward Hatch repeated the traditional maxim that 'Biblical Greek is a language that stands by itself'. Rothe could speak of it as 'a language of the Holy Ghost'. Even Viteau in 1893 thought of New Testament Greek as 'a variety of Hebraizing Greek'. Two years later a young German candidate for the Ministry, looking through the reproductions of some German papyri (published in parts by Berlin scholars), was struck by the resemblance between the Greek of the New Testament and the ordinary colloquial Greek of these everyday letters, discovered in Egypt. Adolf Deissmann pursued research in that tireless, objective manner so characteristic of German scholarship in his generation. He demonstrated his theory that New Testament Greek was none else than the common Greek (the κοινή) spoken throughout the Roman Empire in home and market, a non-literary dialect that made the New Testament virtually a 'people's book'. Deissman's *Bible Studies* (1895) and *Light from the Ancient East* were soon translated into English and other languages. In many respects his work revolutionized New Testament study, stimulating the demand for modern colloquial translations, especially in Great Britain and America.

The work of Albert Schweitzer and Johannes Weiss was important in emphasizing in a new way the eschatological element in Christ's Messianic consciousness. Schweitzer's *Von Reimarus to Wrede* (1906) not merely recorded brilliantly the procession of successive 'Lives of Jesus' from the *Aufklärung* to his own time; his *Quest of the Historic Jesus* (to quote the English title) made it clear that the mind of the Master differed profoundly from that of nineteenth-century Liberal Protestantism. His view of Jesus as a tense Messiah issuing an *Interim-Ethik* to his disciples for the brief interval before the End of the World-Order, was disturbing; it was out of focus, but it 'dated' the over-smooth contours of the accepted 'progressive' portrait of an idealized ethical teacher and social reformer.[12]

Some years before Schweitzer became famous, Weiss edited a New Testament Commentary that broke new ground by taking into account the whole circle of ideas and thought-forms that lay behind the Gospels in their final arrangement. Attention was focused on paragraphs and sections rather than on single words and sentences. Here in embryo was the substance of what was afterwards known as 'Form Criticism'. *Formgeschichte* owed much to Martin Dibelius and Rudolf Bultmann, and emerged into publicity after the first World War.[13] The important question was: 'What interests and activities of the early Christians moulded the material that eventually assumed literary form in the New Testament?' In the sifting and moulding of material the community counted for more than the individual writer. In the analysis of 'forms' the substance took shape in relation to particular requirements—the need for instruction, for passages to be read at services, etc. 'Blocks' were assembled in response to separate situations (*Sitz im Leben*). Despite the value of Form Criticism as a corrective, it has been over-driven, like many another theory born in Germany.

---

[12] It is tempting to say much about Schweitzer, but he was only a German accidentally, due to the fact that Alsace was incorporated in the Reich (1871-1918).

[13] E. Fascher, *Die formgeschichtliche Methode* (Giessen, 1924).

'In the general opinion of competent scholars', says Professor
G. H. C. Macgregor of Glasgow, 'this School has gone to
unjustifiable lengths in formulating judgements as to the
historical value of material from an analysis of literary types.'

Whatever our opinion of the varied movements in German
Biblical study in the past half-century, we cannot deny that
many of them are vital. What a change in the last hundred
years, when arid and negative theories were so prevalent!
Readers of Browning's *Christmas Eve* (1850) will remember
the poet's strange experience. Caught up in a flying vesture he
is flown, first, to an obscure bibliolatrist 'Bethel' in England,
thence to High Mass in Rome. A further flight sets him down
in a theological classroom at Göttingen. Fresh from living
worship, Evangelical and Catholic, he finds the ethos too
rarified to breathe; Papist and Dissenter had tainted the
atmosphere but the critic leaves no atmosphere at all to breathe,
though he be a right true man. 'Can't we respect your loveless
learning?' Browning was one of the few British Christians of
his time to honour the patient truth-seeking attitude of the
German theologians; but surely he had no need to depict the
extreme type of critic who reduced Christianity to a myth.
Earlier in the century Coleridge had introduced whiffs of
German thought. The 'sage of Highgate' exasperated most
Englishmen by his cloudy Teutonic mysticism, though he
could strike out incisive aphorisms, such as: 'He who begins
by loving Christianity better than truth, will proceed by loving
his own sect or church better than Christianity, and will end
by loving himself better than all.'

At the beginning of the nineteenth century Biblical Criticism in Britain was virtually non-existent, apart from a few
isolated and unrecognized scholars. Dons and Bishops were
more interested in the text of Greek plays than in the text of the
New Testament. Pusey sat under the most eminent German
Professors and was enlightened; but after his return to Oxford,
his eyes soon became readjusted to theological twilight and he
renounced the new learning (his German friends were astonished—they had considered him *ganz evangelisch*).[14] Against
the deluge of Strauss's *Leben Jesu*, the leaders of the Oxford
Movement provided no embankment but a chain of texts
from the Fathers and Schoolmen, identifying the new views
with ancient heresies. The brilliant Newman pathetically con-

---

[14] See Liddon's *Life of Pusey* (1893-9).

tributed *The Lives of the Saints* as Christian apologetic (one recalls Dean Stanley's remark: 'How different the fortunes of the Church of England might have been if Newman had been able to read German'). Bishop Knox, in his *Tractarian Movement* (1933) points out that Oxford had not even sympathy to offer to the orthodox Germans, whom W. G. Ward in his rashness had pronounced to be worse than atheists.

Even by the middle of the nineteenth century an Oxford education was no prophylactic against a morbid fear of 'German Neology'. The Curate in Kingsley's *Yeast* (1849) was warned against the Germans, for they were all pantheists at heart. Robertson of Brighton was among the few representatives of English Protestantism who called for discrimination and fair-play toward German theology.[15] A liberal writer in *Essays and Reviews* (1860) satirically defined religious doubt as 'a disease contracted by means of German inoculation'. When Colenso used his missionary experience as an empirical approach to Old Testament Criticism, educated Englishmen denounced him as 'the wicked bishop'.

In 1869 T. K. Cheyne, a Fellow of Balliol, began to study the work of the German Critics, although 'willing to concede to tradition anything that could without any plausibility be conceded'. For many years Cheyne stood alone in Oxford. In 1880 it was still heresy to hold that part of Isaiah was written by an unknown prophet of the Exile; by 1890 it was fairly safe to hold this opinion; and by 1900 it was generally accepted.

In the United States and in Scotland, the mere study of German theology was enough to gain the reputation of being *unsound*. In the early nineteenth century Professor Moses Stuart of Andover Theological Seminary taught himself German; he was influenced by Tholuck's ardent Evangelicalism, nevertheless, his 'unusual studies aroused much suspicion among his colleagues'. As late as 1893 Professor Briggs of Union Seminary, New York, was condemned by the Presbyterian General Assembly for teaching the results of the Higher Criticism, although he was unquestionably loyal to the Creeds. Eleven years earlier Robertson Smith had been removed from his Chair by the Scottish Free Church Assembly. 'There can be no doubt', said Dr. J. R. Fleming, the Church historian of modern Scotland, 'that Wellhausen was the chief teacher of Robertson Smith.' But for pioneers who were willing to study

[15] Stopford Brooke, *Life of F. W. Robertson*, Chapter 6.

German theology, teach it and take the consequences, British and American divinity would have remained even longer in provincial ignorance. Among lonely thinkers who wrestled with doubts raised by the more radical German theologians and philosophers, was a young country minister with defective eye-sight, afterwards famous as the author of 'O love that wilt not let me go'. George Matheson's *Aids to the Study of German Theology* (1874) was a fair and sympathetic guide to a *terra incognita*. Would that his understanding spirit had been more widespread!

Gratitude to Germany for the Higher Criticism must not, however, blind us to the fact that in spite of honest and arduous scholarship, the donor did not enjoy peace in his own household. It is true that the impact of Darwinism did not cause quite the same shock as in England (1859). Yet many conservative Lutherans were with Professor Luthardt of Leipzig in holding that the theory of Evolution contradicted Scripture: 'The idea of creation belongs to religion and not to science; the whole superstructure of personal religion is built upon the doctrine of creation.' Theological radicalism and right wing orthodoxy were bitterly opposed, though a considerable body of opinion had found a synthesis in the *via media*.

Tension was relaxed toward the close of the century by the Schrempf, Lisco, and Steudal cases, which were much in the public eye. Christophe Schrempf was a young Württemberg pastor, ordained (1884) although he could promise to preach only the Synoptic Gospels. In 1891 he was forced to resign his parish because he could not see his way to recite the Apostles' Creed at Baptism. An appeal was made to Harnack, who published his opinion, acknowledging the antiquity and value of the Creeds, but deprecating its enforcement.

Less popular sympathy was extended to the aged Pastor von Sydow, who tore up the Creed before his colleagues in the liberal *Protestantenverein*,[16] but continued to recite it in church ('I do not profess these articles, I read them,' he explained). In spite of this casuistry von Sydow was deposed. The Supreme Church Council of Prussia, however, reversed the verdict; he was merely reprimanded for saying in public what he should

---

[16] An extreme 'modernist' association, founded by Rothe, Schenkel, and Ewald (1863). It declared Creed-subscription contrary to the spirit of Protestantism. 'The higher reason only has unconditional authority, and the Bible must justify itself before its tribunal.' The *Protestantenverein* numbered twenty-five thousand members in 1910, grouped in twenty branches.

have kept private. Dr. Falk, Bismarck's instrument in the *Kulturkampf*[17] was largely responsible for this move (1877). The King-Emperor William the First rightly pronounced this judgement unworthy of an ecclesiastical court.

William the Second considered that in actively interfering in theological disputes he was treading in the noble paths of his Hohenzollern forefathers. The young Kaiser, in his speech to the German princes at the inauguration of the bronze doors at Wittenberg to commemorate Luther's 'Theses', declared himself the chosen champion of orthodoxy (31st October 1892). The sovereign having spoken, the Supreme Church Council no longer hesitated to act in the case of Professor Harnack, who had written an article in the *Christliche Welt* (18th August 1892) stating that the Virgin Birth need not be accepted as a fact but merely as an historic recognition of the Incarnation expressed in symbol. The Council deplored Harnack's views in a special circular (25th November 1892). It was hardly able to submit these views to academic Germany in time-honoured style, for the orthodox were a minority in the Divinity Faculties of thirteen universities; they could only count on a majority at Rostock, Greifswald, Erlangen, and Leipzig.

The attack on Harnack widened into a campaign against liberal theologians in general. Achelis and Herrmann were officially reproved for their published opinions on the Creed. The State appointed two orthodox professors at Marburg and Bonn (*Strafprofessoren* they were nicknamed). It was proposed to establish seminaries to shelter theological students from the heterodoxy of their professors. Another weapon was the compulsory use of the Creed at Ordinations and in public worship. In 1892 the Creed was excluded from the new edition of the Prussian Liturgy, but the professorial controversy led to its eventual inclusion two years later. Liberals had good cause to complain that its enforced use would merely promote clerical insincerity.

The *Apostolikumstreit* caused much bitterness. William the Second's intervention was resented and an ecclesiastical *coup d'état* was feared. Was the Church to be degraded into a *Zwangemeinschaft*, a community based upon force? This misuse of State authority merely provoked Modernists to radical utterances. At the Congress of the *Protestantenverein* in 1905 Pastor Fischer claimed the right to proclaim from the pulpit

[17] See p. 234, *infra*.

'the revelations of Science'. Some of his brethren went farther; one is said to have baptized 'In the Name of the Good, Progress and Science'.[18] Congregations were bewildered by preachers who asserted that it was a mere 'image or symbol' to speak of Jesus as Son of God; it merely means 'Elect of God'. (So Pastor Römer, preaching at Remscheid in 1906.) If some pulpiteers went scientific, others went literary, and not even the Christian Year kept them to Christian fundamentals; Pastor Burggraf of Brema turned his sermons into a course on literature, using Good Friday to interpret Schiller's tragedy, *Maria Stuart*. This kind of secularization reminds us of the *Aufklärung*. When Pope Pius the Tenth struck a mortal blow at Modernists in 1906, German Protestants were able to boast that no external authority could touch *them*. Martin Rade, editor of the *Christliche Welt*, acclaimed Protestant Modernism as 'the natural daughter of orthodoxy'. Pastor Cromer of Hanover retorted: 'You are the enemies of our Christian faith. If indeed it be corrupt, go and found a new religious community!'

A more positive, hopeful cycle of liberal advance began with Albrecht Ritschl (1822-89), whom Harnack hailed as 'the latest of the Church Fathers'. Reacting from metaphysics, which had soared into hazy speculation, Ritschl was a tonic to minds devitalized by the extremes of acrid dogmatism and arid modernism. As the late Dr. A. B. D. Alexander claimed: 'Ritschl's merit lies in investing theology with human interest. His teaching overflows with ethical enthusiasm. . . . He asks not, what is God in His celestial being, but what does God mean for us? Not what is Christ in His source and nature, but what difference for our life do His person and teaching make?'[19] It was something new to find a German theologian of the first rank who had no use for abstractions but preferred to think of religion in personal terms in relation to concrete situations.

When post-graduates returned to Britain and America after sitting at the feet of Ritschl in Göttingen, they resembled their predecessors in talking a language which (in Carlyle's words) 'excited no idea in the head, but much horror in the

---

[18] The optimism of some Liberal Protestants reminds one of the *Aufklärung*. The following passage, written by Condorcet during the French Revolution, might have been penned in Germany a century later: 'Human perfectibility is in reality infinite. . . . Doubtless this progress can proceed at a pace more or less rapid, but it will never go backward' (*Progress of the Human Spirit*).

[19] *Shaping Forces of Modern Religious Thought* (Glasgow, 1920), p. 299.

heart'. They were always contrasting 'judgements of fact' and 'judgements of worth',[20] denouncing 'mysticism', and announcing that 'Jesus Christ has the value of God'. It would be a risky business to attempt to elucidate Ritschl within the limits of a few paragraphs. From the historical point of view attempted in this book, we may claim that Ritschl corrected some plausible nineteenth-century tendencies. He saw the weakness of speculative rationalism that built its theories on cloudy Hegelianism. He saw the weakness of Natural Theology —'proofs' for the existence of God taken from outside Christianity that could never take the believer *within*. 'Every claim to teach us something concerning God in Himself, apart from some real revelation on His part, felt and perceived on ours, in vain.' Ritschl denounced the undue reliance on feeling, which flowed from Schleiermacher and resulted in a deluge of sentimental romanticism, pietism, and mysticism. The 'Christian consciousness' led nowhere. Clear and objective, 'towering o'er the wrecks of time', stood the Revelation of God in Christ. An age hungry for facts was taught by Ritschl that religion, like the arts and sciences, has its roots in bygone events and is nourished by their sap. The New Testament is the Revelation of God in Christ, whose personality is central for all theology; what we know of God, we know through His Son, the Founder of Christianity. 'Ritschl not only emphasized the religious experience of the historic Jesus, but refused to go beyond it.' This attitude appealed to a number of liberal Evangelicals in Great Britain.

Ritschl's grasp of the concrete made him too much of a pragmatist. He had the limitations and virtues of the masculine type of thinker, whose one aim is to make religion practical. He was a great contrast to Schleiermacher, whose temperament was essentially feminine in *feeling*. Ritschl claimed to return to the New Testament, read in the light of Luther; but he minimized the evil of sin ('judged by God as ignorance'). His *Christian Doctrine of Justification and Reconciliation* (1874) indicated an experience of man rather than an act of God; he stood, as it were, rather than knelt. He obeyed, but was not 'lost in wonder, love, and praise'. According to his sober ethical attitude, 'the Kingdom of God' was almost equivalent to 'the moral unification of the human race, through action

[20] e.g. A judgement of Fact: 'Jesus died on Calvary.' And of Worth: 'We have redemption through His blood.'

prompted by universal love to our neighbours'. This Kingdom, 'stripped of the eschatological transcendence that belongs to it in the Gospels, is now hardly more than (as with Kant) a realm of moral ends, a purely present and mundane commonwealth. From this total lapse Ritschl barely saves himself by periodic recurrence to the famous figure in which he pictures Christianity as like an ellipse with its two *foci*—the moral focus being the Kingdom of God, the religious focus, on the other hand, redemption through Christ.'

Professor Mackintosh, in a felicitous phrase, compared Ritschl to Tennyson, as a figure in 'the middle distance', behind a passing cloud today, 'too far for gratitude, too near for reverence'. Yet Ritschl created a greater stir in the Protestant world at large than Schleiermacher did in his lifetime. As regards Britain and America, much of this was naturally due to the fact that German was far more widely read in the last quarter of the nineteenth century; he had, moreover, an able interpreter in Dr. Garvie.[21] Not many German theologians took their stand on the Ritschlian Theology as a whole—there were too many gaps, for the author only dealt thoroughly with issues that interested him. Yet his work was significant. It opened up new lines of thought to followers and critics, which inaugurated a fresh phase of 'scientific theology'.

Two grave faults in the *Kulturprotestantismus* of the next generation may be traced to Ritschl. The first of these was the tendency to think of God as 'accrediting himself to our moral canons . . . rather than as breaking *creatively* into our life and making all things new—even our conscience and its standards'. Secondly, there was the danger of using religion as a mere instrument of social progress; a utilitarian attitude was apt to produce a 'this-worldly' religion, like the *Aufklärung*. Alas! the earth-works which Ritschl threw up to defend the Christian Faith did not prove formidable in the next generation. He had isolated Natural Science, shutting it off from theology, which was protected in a watertight compartment. He had insulated Christianity from other world religions (except the faith of the Old Testament). This apologetic naturally drew attention to artificially excluded areas, and into the vacuum swirled a welter of theories that treated Christianity as 'a syncretistic religion'. In the 'eighties and 'nineties students of Comparative Religion

[21] *The Ritschlian Theology* (Edinburgh, 1899).

had ceased to venerate Christianity as a 'holy isle' in the sea of history: they were inclined to explore it as though it were a jungle of ideas—Jewish, Hellenistic, Oriental. The 'Mystery Cults' moulded the development of the sacraments. The new science of religions was ready to take over theology! There was a new interest in the Psychology of Religion, a readiness to explain normal Christian experience by phenomena that expressed what was rudimentary, weird, or morbid; much was made of the religion of primitive races; prayer and other devotional practices were treated as though they denoted the same kind of religion in the Bible and out of it.[22]

How far is Christianity the final religion? Ernst Troeltsch (1865-1923) devoted his keen intellect to answering this leading question. Troeltsch taught theology at Heidelberg, and afterwards philosophy at Berlin. It would have been appropriate had he also taught history, for he aimed at embracing the world's civilization and religion in a comprehensive philosophy of History. He was thorough in his methods, well acquainted with 'the modern mind' in its complexity. He had scant sympathy with superficial attempts to 'reconcile' science and religion. Yet he had the defects as well as the virtues of the historian. 'Relativity' was his mental watermark. Christianity, seen through his spectacles, tended to lose its firm outline, dissolving into the Philosophy of Religion. Troeltsch almost gave the impression that the Church's energy was exhausted and her doctrines were museum-pieces. His conception of 'reduced Christianity' simply fails to account for the triumphs of the Faith on the Mission field. His conception of Protestantism was determined by the 'progressive' *Aufklärung* rather than by the Scriptural Reformation. Consequently, his spiritual experience is too shallow for a theologian of the first rank. He is too rationalistic, too subjective, and too confident in the ability of Man to work out his own salvation. Troeltsch's name was long unfamiliar to the British public (it does not appear in the index of the 11th Edition of the *Encyclopaedia Britannica*); but he was fortunate in his Scottish interpreter, Dr. R. S. Sleigh.[23] Troeltsch will probably be remembered for his

---

[22] Note the series *Religionsgeschichtliche Volksbücher*, by which scholars tried to convey their findings to the laity (Bousset's *Jesus* and Wrede's *Paul* were widely read in E.T.). Gunkel's book on the Holy Spirit (1888) was a characteristic product of the era.

[23] *The Sufficiency of Christianity*, praised by Vollrath as 'a penetrating and comprehensive study . . . such as Germany does not possess'.

monumental *Social Teaching of the Christian Churches* (1911, E.T., 1931). Even so his style is likely to limit his public, for his heavy tomes ignores Goethe's warning that 'the artist is known by selection'.

If Troeltsch emphasized the similarity of Christianity with other faiths, as fulfilment and completion, other followers of Ritschl magnified the uniqueness of the Gospel. Among the latter were Kaftan and Hermann. Julius Kaftan translated A. J. Balfour's *Foundations of Belief*. As an interpreter of Ritschl, he filled in gaps. What about a personal Devil, for instance? Kaftan elucidated: 'Faith can say nothing about it . . . this whole province must be left to the immediate world-view of the pious.' The ascription of temptation to Satanic agency weakened the sense of individual responsibility. Yet Kaftan softened the edges of Ritschl's ethics with mysticism. Wilhelm Hermann went farther in the direction of orthodoxy. 'I regard myself as infinitely nearer to Nicaea than either Schleiermacher or Ritschl. *They* put Christ alongside of God, and argued from one to the other; in Christ I find God personally present.' It was the radiant personal Christianity of Professor Herrmann that attracted British and American students to Marburg— the same spirit of discipleship drew them to Tholuck at Halle generations earlier.

The greatest Ritschlian was Harnack. And it is fitting that the foremost exponent of Liberal Protestantism should be presented before the thread of theological continuity is broken by the First World War.

Adolf Harnack (1851-1930) was born and educated at Dorpat, in the Baltic provinces of Russia. Like Ritschl, whose father was General Superintendent of Pomerania, Harnack was brought up in an ultra-orthodox environment singularly unpromising for the fostering of a progressive outlook. Theodosius Harnack, professor of Lutheran theology at Dorpat, was particularly interested in practical religion and gave his son a bent that had important results. Adolf began lecturing as a *privat-docent* at Leipzig in his twenty-third year, and was rapidly promoted to Chairs at Giessen and Marburg. His appointment to Berlin in 1889 was strongly opposed by conservatives. As we have seen, he was drawn into controversy over the use of the Apostles' Creed. He contended that in one sense it contained 'too much', in another 'too little'; he would have preferred a briefer statement for ordination candidates, to which 'assent could be rigorously exacted from all'.[24] So encyclopedic was his learning and so sound his judgement that his opinions were heard with respect, and his *Apostolische Glaubensbekenntnis* (1892) reached its twenty-seventh edition by 1896.

Harnack's *magnum opus*, the *History of Dogma*,[25] demonstrated on a massive scale his thesis that non-essential elements had penetrated and possessed official Christianity from the fourth century onward. Eastern Orthodoxy represented the incursion of Greek thought; Western Catholicism the inroads of Roman[26] organization. Protestants were not merely free to criticize dogma, but bound to do so, with the object of stripping accretions from the kernel of genuine Christianity. Harnack's aim was to re-state the Christian Faith in broad outlines, avoiding as far as possible theological jargon. He appealed to educated audiences in his famous Berlin lectures, which reached a wider public in printed form. *Das Wesen des Christentums* (1900) reached a fifth edition in 1901; under the title of *What is Christianity?* it was hailed in England as an epoch-making book.

Harnack felt that German Protestantism was thwarted by two tendencies that prevented it from producing the fruit of the Spirit.[27] The first danger was 'catholicizing'. By this he meant, not papal propaganda, but the pre-Reformation virus working within Protestantism so as to exalt ordinance, doctrine, and ceremony. What of the Gospel when living faith was 'transformed into a creed . . . devotion to Christ into Christology . . . prophecy into technical exegesis . . . the ministers of the Spirit into clerics?' The masses, however, showed little understanding of Evangelical Christianity. If they wanted religion at all, they wanted it cut-and-dry, 'something to lean upon' ('and a good deal else too', Harnack adds).

The second danger was State patronage, from which German Protestantism had suffered so much in the past. The Church was treated as a 'public utility', to the advantage of formal orthodoxy and the flourishing of authoritarian methods at variance with the free spirit of the Gospel. The masses, absorbed in practical paganism, would remain deaf to

---

[24] But what minimum? Harnack's own Christology was sadly lacking in Evangelical essentials: 'Jesus was only Son of God in the sense that he had a knowledge of God like that of no one before Him.'

[25] E.T., ed. A.B. Bruce (London, 1894-9), 7 vols.

[26] Edwin Hatch's Hibbert Lectures, *On the Influence of Greek Ideas and Usages on the Christian Church* (1888), moulded Harnack's views. Harnack translated Hatch's Bampton Lectures (1881) on Early Church organization.

[27] *Thought on the Present Position of Protestantism* (London, 1899).

the voice of the Gospel; they would be captivated by the siren of Socialism, until the Church itself was freed from the incubus of servile erastianism. Neither Catholicism nor Protestantism were truly representative of what Christianity should stand for: 'The nations are still waiting for a third kind of Church as the foundation of their higher life.' Doubtless, Harnack was think- ing of a democratic, non-hierarchical fellowship somewhat after the pattern of Mazzini's *Church of Humanity*; but unforunately there were political propagandists ready to adapt his ideas of 'simplifying the Christian Faith and adapting it to modern conditions'. One of them was a disciple of Ritschl.[28]

Harnack's *Kulturprotestantismus*, however, seemed sound and practicable to many thoughtful laymen alienated by the evasions of the more conservative theologians. A generation of eager teachers, trained in his *Seminar*, carried his method and spirit far beyond Germany. Here was reverence for knowledge —in detecting inconsistencies, linking phenomena, correcting judgements. Here was humanity—the sense of brotherhood, the ideal of social justice, the urge to build not just systems of theology but bridges to unite sundered classes, nations, and races in the Kingdom of God. Here was Good News—freedom from fear and every kind of coercion, trust in the Divine Fatherhood, progress under Jesus as Lord and Leader, whose abiding influence renewed men's lives in every age, as of old in Galilee. 'The Christian religion is something simple and sublime; it means one thing and one thing only: Eternal life in the midst of time, by the strength and under the eye of God.'

Harnack was no sinister arch-rationalist. When the critics have said their worst, there still remains much in his thought and spirit that is fresh, vital, ardent. Yet his contemporary, George Tyrell, exposed his weak spot when he declared: 'The Christ that Harnack sees, looking back through nineteen centuries of Catholic darkness, is only the reflection of a Liberal Protestant face, seen at the bottom of a deep well.' This 'Liberal Protestant' fatally underrated the latent evil in the heart of man. His hopes were blasted by the First World War, his dreams of progress were shattered, and his work 'dated'. Three years before his death in 1930 a German student was asked by an Englishman: 'What is the present position of Harnack?' Dean Inge has recorded the reply: 'We have

[28] See p. 163, *infra*.

conducted him to Olympus, from which he looks down upon a world which knows him no more.'

Professor Frank of Erlangen, writing at the close of the nineteenth century, summed up the contrast between its early promise and its later fulfilment: 'The spring is without doubt over and gone. The sun which we saw rising is dropping in the West. The fields once richly irrigated, in which a noble seed sprouted forth, have gradually become more parched and withered. There have been fruits, noble and fair, but not what we looked for from the promise of the bloom.' Compare with this melancholy *fin-de-siècle* soliloquy the brisk estimate of Mark Pattison, offered in 1857: 'German theology is no insulated phenomenon. Though generated in Germany, it belongs to Christendom. . . . It is only because there is fuller intellectual life in Germany than elsewhere—only because European speculation is transacted by Germans, as our financial affairs are by Jews—that German characteristics are impressed upon the substance of the Christian science. The capital of learning is in the hands of Germans, and theirs has been the enterprise which has directed it into theological channels.'

German divines have applied themselves with astonishing patience and thoroughness to the task of relating doctrine to current philosophies—or of rescuing theology from speculative metaphysics; they have wrought in modern times with the same thoroughness as their seventeenth-century predecessors, who laboured to impart to Lutheran orthodoxy its coping of finality. In over a score of fully staffed Faculties, a kind of continuous debate was carried on, 'each watching all the rest, and all throwing their knowledge into a common stock'. The emphasis on exact knowledge has led to over-minute analysis and hairsplitting definitions. When the theologians have soared in speculation or in mystic flights, they have inevitably lost touch with reality; in Barth's phrase, they have substituted 'the word of man' for the Word of God. Sometimes they have been deficient in sound judgement, disciplined imagination, and a sense of humour. Too often have the needs of Youth been recognized in terms that only inquiring students would understand.

On the other hand one realizes the difficulties that have beset attempts to relate theology and life the divided state of German Protestantism, the conservative officialism of the

Landeskirchen, the alienation of the masses in many areas from Christianity, the low ebb of Church consciousness. We have seen that there are vital elements, proving that German Protestantism is not as moribund as its critics have asserted. We acknowledge the debt of British and American theology to Germany. Yet we wish that the result had been more fruitful to German Evangelicalism itself. We recall the story of the priest who was showing the humanist Casaubon, the hall of the Sorbonne. 'Here the theologians have debated for three hundred years,' exclaimed the guide in triumph. 'Indeed,' replied the great scholar, 'and pray, what have they decided?'

CHAPTER SEVEN

FROM HARNACK TO BARTH

LIBERAL Protestantism in Germany was a major casualty in the War of 1914-18. Distinguished theologians survived Harnack, Weinel, Gunkel, Seeberg, Hermann, Schlatter—but they belonged to an extinct era. 'Scientific theology' had flourished in the past, but its defects were exposed by the shattering experience of national ruin. What men wanted was a religion that would reconstruct broken ideals, a dynamic faith that proclaimed the Christian way of life invincible, though all human institutions reeled from the shock of revolution. The imagination of the German people might have been captured by the presentation of Christianity as a glad Gospel of healing and reconciliation, 'optimism rooted in pessimism'. Admittedly Harnack and others had been keenly interested for years past in economic and industrial problems. Nevertheless, German Protestantism as a whole lacked creative leadership; as Dr. Piper has noted, it was 'without connexion with active Church life and in social isolation'.[1]

How had the First World War affected the mind of Germany?[2] The tendency before 1914 was for men to believe that they knew a thing if they knew its laws. However practical the Germans might be in running their country in peace and war, religion was one of the few spheres where theory was preferred to practice. The bureaucratic 'particularism' of the former *Landeskirchen* made the Church provincial rather than national, deprived its members of real responsibility and tended to maintain the old tradition of the universities as the focal centres of religious thought.[3] Theology was still unduly academic, illustrated by the playful paradox that if a German were confronted with two notices—'To the Kingdom of Heaven' and 'To Lectures on the Kingdom of Heaven'—he would infallibly prefer the latter!

'The Mind of Post-war Germany' (to use the title of an essay by Professor C. H. Herford) was to a large extent realist. The soldiers who returned home had discovered that knowledge

---

[1] *Recent Developments in German Protestantism* (London, 1934).
[2] cf. G. P. Gooch, *Germany*, in the Modern World Series (London, 1925).
[3] H. Weinel, 'Religious Life in Germany' (*Hibbert Journal*, January, 1924).

comes, not merely by means of discussion, but by experiencing the issue in a concrete situation, e.g. danger, fear, pain. The school of suffering had taught them that problems of life can be solved by comradeship, collectively rather than individually; that pure intellect is not the only way—a belief must lay hold on a man's *whole* personality in relation to the circumstances in which he finds himself. 'Existential' thinking became the new watchword.[4] The scientist or mathematician registers facts in a cold, disinterested way. He who deals with such living questions as religion, however, must make a *personal* decision; he cannot remain a mere investigator, or a balcony onlooker—he must *act*. Between 1914 and 1918 the German vocabulary had been enriched by a new *Haltung* (attitude), a new *Lebensgefühl* (sense of life) and a new *Wirklichkeit* (actuality). Isolation differentiated German thinking acutely from that of other lands. Defeat convinced them 'that they had not lost the War because they had been too German, but because they had not been German enough' (Professor Piper). Shattered dreams of world domination did not silence the apocalyptic note, but made it all the more strident. The German people were gripped by a neurotic fear of such sinister foes as Capitalism, Bolshevism, and World Jewry. A minority believed that the Weimar Constitution might facilitate the onward march of science, education, and democracy; but the irrational (*Das ganz Andere*) had a new lure for disillusioned minds who had once tired of Reason. Count Keyserling suddenly discovered that he was a prophet to seekers who saw in his *Travel Diary* light from the ancient East. Rudolf Steiner's school of 'Anthroposophy' (opened at Dornach in 1913) made a wide appeal after the War. Oswald Spentler's monumental *Decline of the West* was apocalyptic in its linking of World Power and Fate; the downfall of Germany was but the prelude to the collapse of Western civilization. 'We shall not make another Goethe, but we may yet make a Caesar'—prophetic words!

The defeat of Germany in 1918 had dramatized the limits of man's possibilities. Socialism had failed to usher in the good times once predicted. Godless Communism threatened the foundations of society. Naturalistic morals pointed to the disintegration of family life. 'Intuition', 'feeling', and 'action' were the vague watchwords of the day. The comradeship of

[4] For various interpretations—philosophical, theological, and sociological—see Paul Foulquié, *Existentialism* (E.T., London, 1947)

the trenches and the financial plight of the upper and middle classes had broken down class divisions, once so rigid. More than ever the Germans had been fused into one *Volk*, and in certain nationalist circles there was already some talk of 'blood, race, and soil'.

Suffering had educated the theologians as well as men in other walks of life. The bankruptcy of 'Culture-Protestantism' made them more humble, ready to listen to the Word of God before formulating it in theory and speculation.[5] The glittering temple of Theology was exposed as a prison-house, whose roof shut off the heavens, and whose pillars were of substitute-material (even the old orthodoxy was doctrine petrified). As Dr. Keller put it, the Christian soul of Germany, like Noah's dove, sought refuge in all manner of places; finding no solid foothold, she eventually flew back to the ark (God's Word). The Bible was rediscovered, not simply as the greatest devotional classic, not as a miscellaneous collection of documents, to be dissected and analysed by the critic, nor yet as the Fundamentalist's storehouse of texts to be applied in a rigid, mechanical fashion. The Bible was rediscovered as the Voice of God speaking to those who seek His revelation and are ready to hear it. *Ad fontes!*

This re-digging of ancestral wells stopped by the Philistines also involved a return to the Confessions of the Reformation era. These formularies were now regarded as neglected treasure of practical value—no longer as faded banners of obsolete warfare. When the four-hundredth anniversary of the *Augsburg Confession* was celebrated in 1930, certain Lutherans hailed it, not as a standard of militant Evangelicalism but as an inclusive, ecumenical document ('*pia et catholica confessio*' in Melanchthon's phrase). The *Augustana* was certainly a standard that exposed, as secularist in trend, the evolution of German theology since Schleiermacher; historic Christianity had been neutralized by 'autonomous reason, religious consciousness, and cultural ethos'. Over against a welter of philosophy, psychology, and sociology, there stood fast the sovereign grace of God as represented by Luther's *sola gratia* and Calvin's *soli deo gloria*. Both Reformers had faith in God—not faith in speculation, religious experience, mystical meditation, or philanthropic activity. Since the quater-centenary of the Reformation in

---

[5] cf. Adolf Keller and G. Stewart, *Protestant Europe, its Outlook and Crisis* (London, 1927); Keller, *Religion and the European Mind* (London, 1934).

1917, the personality and teaching of Luther have been much discussed in the light of recent research. On the one hand, he was eulogized as a master-theologian and prophet, whose message was definitely relevant to the modern situation;[6] on the other hand, he was criticized for his 'medieval residues' and his impulsive, obstinate temperament. Psychologically, Luther appealed to bi-polar elements in the average German—the urge to independence and the urge to subordination.

Revived interest in Luther mingled with a fresh craving for colour, pageantry, and symbolism in life and worship. The drabness of post-war existence stimulated this demand, and called into being the pre-Hitler Youth Movement. Out of this atmosphere of mysticism, archaism, and irrationalism sprang the vogue of *The Holy*, by Professor Rudolf Otto of Marburg. Germans, weary of the Liberal Protestantism's 'glory of the lighted mind', retreated to the 'dim religious light' in search for the '*Deus absconditus*' who dwelt in the uncanny depth of 'the Numinous'.[7]

Otto's popularity in Britain reminds us that German theologians took a fresh interest in religious thought across the Channel. There was Vollrath's notable survey of contemporary British theology.[8] In 1916 Hauck had published his Uppsala lectures.[9] After 1920 successive volumes on the Christian institutions of non-German countries appeared, under the able editorship of Dr. Siegmund-Schultze (*Ekklesia* series, publ. Gotha). German scholarship still counted for something abroad. In 1927 German divinity students numbered only two thousand, compared to four thousand in 1914; yet they constituted sixty per cent. of the ministerial candidates of Continental Protestantism.

Another well re-dug was the Church, stopped for centuries by Erastian Philistines. The abolition of the secular *Summepiskopat* in each German State revealed the urgent need of genuine churchmanship. '*Ecclesiam habemus*,' declared General Superintendent Dibelius. Older theologians like Reinhold Seeberg realized that 'without a community of believers Christianity is

---

[6] The more recent phase of Luther-study is indebted to Karl Holl's *Gesammelte Aufsätze . . . I, Luther* (6th ed., Tübingen, 1932).

[7] Post-graduate students at Marburg will recall the little old-world chapel where Otto held his mystical week-night service—a contrast to the more 'Catholic' service held by Heiler in another quaint sanctuary on the edge of that delectable university town.

[8] *Theol. der Gegenwart in Grossbrit.* (1928).

[9] *Deutchland u. England in ihrem kirchlichen Beziehungen.*

unthinkable as a world principle'. Friedrich Heiler, a convert from Rome (*rara avis*),[10] brought into Lutheranism unwonted zeal for the *Una Sancta*; his books on worship and symbolism were translated into many languages, and it was increasingly recognized that 'Catholic' and 'Evangelical' were not utterly incompatible. Altogether, the Catholic tradition of Church-manship (*Extra Ecclesiam nulla salus*) seemed more acceptable to German Evangelicals than it had proved for centuries.

The 'Theology of Crisis', associated with Karl Barth and his friends, grew out of this attempt to meet the Church's urgent need. It was no exclusive product of the study and the class-room, but was conditioned by an anxious concern for the Church's future. It was not enough for science to be 'scientific'; the theologian must be a Christian believer. Complacent isola-tion would never win men and women for the Evangelical Church—disowned, despised, disregarded. If theology was again to become 'Queen of Sciences', the Church must take the initiative by 'cleansing the Temple'. She must no longer permit the world to define her mission; she must decline to adapt her methods to 'the spirit of the age'. '*Finitum non capax infiniti.*' Relativism must give place to absolute claims. God is not 'the world soul', but 'the totally other'. Barth had no use for the generous Anglo-Saxon method that admitted science, reason, and human values as paths to the knowledge of God. He refused generous offers of 'All this and Heaven too'. His ruthless 'Either—or' cancelled the synthetic 'Both—and'. He would not hear of 'Revelation *and* Reason, God's Grace *and* Man's Activity'. Our present study of German Protestantism in its historic evolution makes it clear that rationalism, moralism, and other *isms* had penetrated religious thought so thoroughly as to deprive it of positive Christian vitality. German philo-sophy was an invaluable gift to civilization but its effects on German theology were questionable. Out of the ashes of Liberal Protestantism there sprang the phoenix of 'Dialectical Faith',[11] which the famous Jesuit, Erich Przywara, described as 'a genuine rebirth of Protestantism'.

It is surprising that a movement which caught fire so

[10] Among Protestant converts to Rome was an ex-History Professor at Halle, A. von Ruville (*Zurück zur heiligen Kirche*, Berlin, 1910).

[11] 'Dialectic'—a charm to recall the ghost of Hegel? On the purely human side, Barth admitted that truth is reached by the zigzag path of statement and counter-statement; but it lies behind the dogmatic 'Yea' and the critical 'Nay'. 'The synthesis is with God, who alone can speak the undialectic word, the Amen, beyond which there is no going' (McConnachie, *The Significance of Karl Barth*, pp. 79ff.).

ardently in Germany should have accepted the torch from a small country. Switzerland had remained neutral in the first World War, and was not therefore turned upside down, economically and intellectually; moreover Switzerland was Reformed, while Germany was predominantly Lutheran. Karl Barth and his associates, Brunner and Thurneysen, started life as Swiss pastors. All three were originally advocates of the 'Social Gospel'. The War of 1914-18 and the subsequent failure of Socialism disillusioned them. They discovered that they had been offering stones instead of bread to a people 'pathetically expectant, longing to be convinced of the reality of God in a world gone mad'.[12]

Karl Barth, son of a theological professor at Bern, was born at Basel in 1886. He sat at the feet of Harnack in Berlin and of Herrmann ('my unforgettable teacher') at Marburg. Having absorbed the best that Liberal Protestantism had to offer on the theological and devotional side, he opened his mind to the 'Social Gospel' that was being proclaimed by Pastor Kutter of Zurich—the ideal of 'Christianizing' the economic order. The 'Social Gospel' was built on the belief that Socialism was a kind of unconscious Christianity, that only needed to be inspired by the ethics of Jesus, the Supreme Reformer. In 1909 Barth became assistant to Dr. Adolf Keller,[13] pastor to a German-speaking congregation that worshipped in the gaunt *Auditoire* at Geneva, a church little changed since the day when John Knox held forth there to the English-speaking exiles. As the young Swiss dwelt on the theology of Schleiermacher and social idealism, did he give a thought to the Divine Sovereignty, which, according to Calvin, was the only source of power capable of generating a righteous community?

When Barth was appointed pastor of the quiet parish of Safenwil, Canton Aargau, he became less sure that Christian ethics and religious psychology were adequate. On the other hand, the older Protestant orthodoxy seemed irrelevant to the situation. The First World War precipitated the tension of mind and soul. In his study he meditated and wrestled in prayer. Like Carlyle, he saw 'death and eternity glaring in'. He reached the conviction that truth, beauty, and love were but human paths to the divine presence, blocked by the for-

---

[12] W. M. Horton, *Contemporary Continental Theology*, p. 97.

[13] For many years a household name for ecumenical circles; his periodic surveys of books on European Protestantism have sounded a warning blast to Anglo-Saxons for many years past of the impending crisis of the Continent.

bidding notice—NO THOROUGHFARE. There was no way from man to God, only a way from God to man, the way of Revelation and Grace. This ruled out any reciprocal relationship, or 'Federal Theology'. Barth found help in the writings of an almost forgotten theologian of the mid-Victorian period, Professor Franz Overbeck of Basel. Overbeck, a man born out of due season, denounced the theologians (both orthodox and liberal) for coming to terms with civilization, 'thereby denying the essentially eschatological character of the Christian religion'. It was in 1906 that Albert Schweitzer published (in German) his *Quest of the Historical Jesus*. That epoch-making book demolished the Liberal Protestant portrait of Jesus as religious genius and reformer: but it did not lead Schweitzer to formulate a 'Theology of Crisis' based on his apocalyptic-eschatological thesis.[14] The study of Kierkegaard in relation to twentieth-century needs was a cardinal event in Barth's development. The scales fell from his eyes; like the Danish 'Prophet of the Absolute' he glimpsed the Eternal in a 'moment', i.e. the point in which Time and Eternity touch. Indeed, he described his ancestral line as running back from Kierkegaard to Luther and Calvin, and so to Paul and Jeremiah: it certainly did not pass through that other eminent Dane, Martensen, to Erasmus and the Humanists; emphatically, it did not include Schleiermacher.

To Barth, Divine reality was related to humanity 'like another dimension, cutting across the earthly plane at right-angles'. What matters is—'not what we think of God, but what God thinks of us'. Had not Ecclesiastes made the position clear even in the Old Testament—'God is in heaven and thou upon earth, therefore let thy words be few'? This was strange doctrine to the rural parishioners of Safenwil, but the name of Barth soon became known in Switzerland. Wherever he preached, sparks flew. To his hearers he revealed such unfamiliar themes as 'The Strange New World Within the Bible' (to quote the title of one of his earlier addresses).[15]

Barth was not conscious of being the founder of a new and exclusive theology. He modestly described his contribution as 'a marginal note to other schools' (*Richtungen*). At most he was but a witness, 'a finger pointing to God'. His earnest desire was

[14] Paradoxically, it led him back to the liberal fold. See G. O. Griffiths, *Interpreters of Man* (London, 1943), p. 139.

[15] cf. *The Word of God and the Word of Man* (tr. Douglas Horton, London, 1928).

to save the Church from being secularized, albeit with good
intentions. The Church of 'the Good, the Pious, and the
Moral' must be converted into the 'Church of the Word of
God'. Subjective religious zeal, humanistic aspirations, experiments in ritual, social and charitable activities—had all been
mistaken efforts to help the world from below, rather than from
above. On the negative side, the War of 1914 and its aftermath
did much to destroy the imposing edifice of man's confidence
in himself; over the portal was inscribed 'in huge proportions
and in the utmost clearness a MENE, MENE, TEKEL'. The ground
was cleared for a positive theology, a Theology of Crisis. 'Crisis
may mean the turning-point of direction, or judgement. The
new Swiss divines saw the Church as well as the World under
the judgement of the Word of God.

Although Barth himself eschewed subjective individualism,
his personal experience, as well as his principles, brought him
disciples. He had studied the best that modern thought offered
and found it wanting—in sociology and psychology, as well as
in philosophy and theology. He was no mere escapist, taking
refuge from modern problems in the obscurantist byways of
tradition. Speaking to students at an international gathering
in 1934, he remarked: 'You may rest assured that I have a little
experience of my own. *I* too am a modern man also, and *I*
stand in the midst of this age too. . . . And I assure you that
exactly because I was called to live in a modern world, did I
reach the path of which you have heard me speak.'[16]

Barth was surprised at the publicity which came to him after
the First World War. He compared himself to a man who
mounts a dark church-tower at night, lays hold of the bell-rope
instead of the guiding-rope—and to his horror—hears the bell
peal forth.[17] It was in August 1918, within sound of the
German guns, that he published his *Römerbrief*, which 'fell like
a bomb on the playground of the theologians' (to quote Dr.
Karl Adam). This *tour de force* made him the storm-centre of
Continental Protestantism during the final phase of the War,
that apocalyptic year, 1918. It created consternation in the
camp of liberals and humanists. 'Like an Alpine torrent, it
brought down rocks and trunks that devastated fertile fields

[16] *God in Action* (1937), p. 133.
[17] Britain had already her own alarm bell (though few responded to its
summons). Marcus Barth said to Dr. McConnachie in his study: 'You did not
need my father in this country; you had Forsyth.' There is an admonitory *Un-
Barthian* ring in Donne's *locus classicus*, 'For whom the bell tolls'.

and pretty villages.' It was a blow for absolute faith in God as significant as Luther's *Romans*, published four centuries earlier. Within a few years fifteen thousand copies of Barth's *Romans* were sold, and this bold manifesto was soon translated into foreign languages.

In 1921 he was appointed to the Chair of Reformed Theology at Göttingen, and was promoted to Münster (1925) and to Bonn (1930). New phases of his changing thought were made known through the pages of the periodical *Zwischen den Zeiten*; its very title was significant—we live 'between the Ages'—the passing age and the coming age—hence the strain and tension of faith. In Germany, Holland, Denmark, and other Continental countries, even in Japan, there was widespread response to Barth. In many quarters, of course, there was criticism and dismay. His stiffer *Dogmatik* was less popular than his prophetic *Romans* (which he no longer wished to be taken as an authoritative source of his theology). His 'convoluted thought' puzzled divines used to 'closed systems'. His mind moved, it did not crystallize—a trial to pedestrians unaccustomed to 'theology on the wing'.[18]

In Great Britain, even in the United States, Barth was embarrassed by dubious camp-followers, though he was aided by judicious interpreters like McConnachie and Horton. The London *Times* described his doctrine as 'not easy to grasp, subtle, baffling'. The Welsh Eisteddfod in 1932 offered a prize for 'The Contribution of Karl Barth to Theology'. Dr. Hutton, Editor of the *British Weekly*, compared the great Swiss to Hildebrand—both were inspired with 'an exclusive fervour for the Church of Christ'.[19] These compliments evoked from Barth a modest doubt 'whether there was as much joy in heaven as on earth over the growth of the Barthian School'. He feared that the British were still tainted by the optimistic heresy of their ancestor, Pelagius. When German pastors fled to England from Nazi persecution, they were hospitably received by the British Churches, but sometimes complained that they were expected to accommodate their theology to insular conditions; they did not like the idea of this 'atmospheric assimilation'.

In Germany Barth's message met with varied response.

---

[18] Recalling the first edition of his *Dogmatic*, Barth afterwards excised everything that might be taken as a buttress of theology, if it was derived from the 'existential philosophy' so popular after the first World War (*Ch. Dogmatic*, E.T., p. ix).

[19] Adolf Keller, *Karl Barth and Christian Unity* (London, 1933).

Professor Karl Heim of Tübingen, interpreter of Reformation principles in modern terms, warmed by the glowing faith of Württemberg Pietism, approved up to a point. 'Barth swung the tiller of theology hard, so that the whole Church "came about".' Heim, however, as an exponent of 'Positive Christianity' wondered whether this 'theology of despair' was real, or only 'emotional thunder'. Further: 'Does Christian belief start with the authority of the Church—or, as Calvin taught, with an act of the Holy Spirit in the heart of the believer?'

Conservative Calvinists were not satisfied with Barth's attitude to historic Confessions, based on the plenary inspiration of the Bible. Still less did he please Lutherans by rejoicing that the Reformed fathers 'left no *Augsburg Confession*, no "symbolic books", which might come to possess an odour of sanctity. They left us only creeds' (more open to the fresh interpretation of Scripture and the living testimony of the Spirit). Conservative Lutherans saw in Barth an interloper, another Zwingli (a more formidable Zwingli) coming out of Switzerland to neutralize their ancestral Confessionalism. They saw in him an offshoot of the Calvinistic tradition in its bleaker phase; did he not try to revive a legalistic, ascetic attitude to life, alien to Luther's? Did he not widen the gulf between God and Man, in a bold and reckless way, unattempted even by classic Calvinism?[20] Barth disclaimed the charge of 'smuggling' Reformed articles across the frontier of Lutheranism. He came to the *Reich*, not as a critic of the indigenous form of Evangelicalism, but as a German-Swiss who shared in the heritage of Luther; Zwingli had indeed misunderstood Luther four centuries ago, but need that hinder a better understanding today? Barth is not a cold humanist like Zwingli; he has a warm, impulsive temperament like Luther. For a time he was amused rather than embarrassed by the opposition of the Lutheran stalwarts of Erlangen—Althaus, Sasse,[21] and Elert.[22] He described himself as 'scattering a pinch of spice on all the varied dishes of German Protestantism'.

[20] Professor G. T. Thomson of Edinburgh, translator of the *Church Dogmatic* (Barth's 2nd ed.), praised his treatment of the Trinity—'the greatest since the Reformation, by one whose faith has been put to the test and come out the stronger; I have read nothing like it except Martin Luther and John Calvin'.

[21] Hans Sasse, *Was heisst lütherisch?* (2nd ed., Munich, 1936) outlines Lutheran convictions of the exclusive wing. His Confessional anathema includes Lessing and Herder, Kant and Fichte, Goethe and Schiller, Schleiermacher and Hegel. 'That is all the old devil and old serpent, who made Adam and Eve enthusiasts' (pp. 56ff.).

[22] cf. W. Elert, *Morphologie des Lutherstum* (2 vols., Munich, 1931).

Barth's friends, Professors Bultmann of Marburg (a radical New Testament critic) and Gogarten of Breslau (his leading Lutheran supporter), were not long in questioning the transcendent isolation of God and man. Any attempt to build bridges between revelation and human experience has been resisted by Barth with the uncompromising reply—'Thou shalt have no other gods before me!' His 'lack of respect for everything human' alienated Emil Brunner, who was called to a Chair at Zurich. Brunner, who had studied at the Union Theological Seminary, New York, never lost this broader impress. To Barth, he seemed incorrigible, nor was his patronage of the 'Oxford Group' acceptable (though he warned them not to be 'theological gypsies'). Brunner saw that the theology of revelation needed *some* contact with science and sociology. His book, *Das Gebot und die Ordnungen*[23] gives the Theology of Crisis an ethical reference, hitherto lacking. 'Creation, though fallen, had not entirely lost the mark and image of the Creator.' There must therefore be a general revelation of God in nature, conscience, and history. Barth's failure to allow for this had the result of cutting off Christianity from the ordinary social and ethical life of the world. Fear of Anglo-Saxon 'activism' prevented him from advocating any Christian solution for industrial and social problems. His critics thought that he lived in too rarefied an atmosphere; the scholar's pride blinded him to the real world and its problems outside the study; the people needed the practical comfort of the Gospel, not the stones of hard theology. A Scottish student, thinking of that ultra 'activist' American hymn, 'Rise up, ye men of God, . . . Bring in the day of brotherhood', wrote the following parody of the Barthian attitude to social problems:

> Sit down, O men of God!
>   His Kingdom He will bring,
> Whenever it may please His will;
>   *You* cannot do a thing.

Barth claimed that his theology was effective because it was absolute, objective, and no human product like the pre-war 'scientific theology'. Yet Barthianism, before Hitler's appearance, did tend to be academic—and limited, at that, to one Faculty. Dr. H. C. Lefever, who studied at several German universities in 1932-3, said that Divinity students marvelled that he should attend lectures in philosophy as well as theology.

[23] E.T., *The Divine Imperative* (1937).

'What has *that* got to do with Christianity?' they asked. Indeed, he was the only theologue at Jena to attend the classes of one of the greatest living exponents of Kant. Dr. Lefever goes on to say: 'As the Church became more and more influenced by Barthian teaching, sermons became more and more dogmatic —rather poor imitations of proper theological lectures. When I pointed out that in England we stressed more the "practical application" of the text, the retort was immediate: "But that is *Bergpredigt* (the Sermon on the Mount), i.e. pure ethical teaching; "our task is to lead the people to faith".'[24]

British students who have met Barth find in him no trace of the neurotic recluse, but a genial, kindly personality with the hope and vigour of youth written in his features. In view of his humanity, his uncompromising attitude is all the more remarkable. When his theology ceased to be a novelty, he tended to lose ground among the clerical rank and file; Karl Heim attracted a larger following to his 'positive theology'. Then came the Nazi Revolution. Barth refused to tone down his opinions and was dismissed in 1935 from his Chair at Bonn. Called to Basel, he continued to be the inspiring figure in the background of the German Church struggle for a pure Gospel. Thus in a Swiss city a prophet of the Living God became sentinel, as Calvin had made Geneva his watch-tower in the century of the Reformation.

In Part Two the emergence of the German Confessional[25] Church will be sketched. Barth warned his friends who were struggling for spiritual independence that they must be on their guard against the intrusion of political issues. In his *Theologische Existenz heute* he blew a blast of admonition. 'God can be found nowhere save in His Word. This Word is Jesus Christ. Christ can be found only in the Bible of the Old and New Testaments. The heart of the Church must not be divided between her political and ecclesiastical interests and the cause of the Gospel. The Gospel alone is her care and great concern.'

Was Barth unduly suspicious of Natural Theology and mysticism? His apprehension was confirmed by the mushroom growth of heretical sects, as soon as National Socialism became fashionable.[26] *The Myth of the Twentieth Century* (1930) offered

---

[24] Article, 'The Trend of Modern Theology' (*Presbyterian Register*, December 1943).

[25] We shall use the translation 'Confessing Church'. In Germany the term 'Confessional' has acquired associations clustering round the elaborate doctrinal formulas of the sixteenth- and seventeenth-century Scholasticism.

[26] N. Micklem, *National Socialism and Christianity* (Oxford, 1939).

a syncretist religion to those who proposed to build a Third *Reich* on the basis of Nordic race and German blood. The author, Alfred Rosenberg, was a Balt, subsequently notorious as a Nazi war criminal. One half of his *magnum opus* (no English translation) was polemical, the other a *summa de omni scibili et de quibusdam aliis*. From Eckart, the medieval German mystic, Rosenberg borrowed the idea of God immanent in the soul, for which he substituted the Nation. Following ultra-modernist suggestions of 'a Larger Bible', he would incorporate Nordic Myths and Sagas.[27] The works of Marcion, Paul de Lagarde, Schopenhauer, Nietzsche, and Houston Chamberlain were to contribute to the canonical literature of the new dispensation. For apostles, saints, and martyrs he substituted 'heroes'— Odin, Siegfried, Wagner, Frederick the Great, and Hitler. He repudiated humanist values as well as historic Christianity, he welcomed the irrational and eulogized Myth as 'the product of the self-conscious collective mind'.

Rosenberg's journalistic welter of nonsense might be ignored, but for the fact that defunct Liberal Protestantism had prepared the way by urging that Christianity must be disengaged from its Greek and Roman envelopes and presented in modern terms. For instance, take the case of Bousset, a respectable Ritschlian who claimed to be led by the hand of Jesus in emancipating the Church from dogma. In *What is Religion?*[28] he amplified Harnack's suggestion that 'Christianity must incorporate more of the modern way of life'. The survival of Christianity was to depend on placing the teaching of Goethe and Bismarck side by side with that of Christ! Thus the advocate of the simple Galilean Gospel turned to syncretism. Culture-Protestantism, by humanistic emphasis minimized revelation and prepared the way for materialism, paganism, pantheism, and titanism, all garbed as angels of light.

Another heresiarch, Professor Hauer, an ex-missionary from the Palghat, came to the conclusion that a religion of Semitic origin was uncongenial to the German genius; he preferred a selection of elements common to Aryan religion in India, Persia, and Northern Europe. Hauer was a sincere crank. He resigned the leadership of the 'German Faith Movement'

[27] Ludendorff was the link between the Second and Third *Reich*, in seeking to resuscitate the German paganism idealized by Wagner.

[28] E.T. (London, 1907), p. 274.

as soon as he realized that it was merely being utilized as a subsidiary gadget of Nazi ideology.

More dangerous were the 'German Christians', who were adepts in 'taking the name of God in vain', to mislead the simple and ardent. Dr. Goebbels found that his Jesuit education had served him well as a propagandist. Familiar Christian terms were plastic and capable of exploiting religion as well as sociology to serve Nazi ends. This cult appealed to those who could not be bothered to think about anything that antedated the Revolution of 1933. Under the Führer, 'contemporary history is being used by Providence for a fresh continuous revelation'. When we come to the struggle of the Confessing Church, we shall see how the Nazis trusted the 'German Christians' to capture the machinery of the German Evangelical Church. They completely identified religion with the *Volksgeist*. The ablest 'German Christian' theorist, Emanuel Hirsch, announced that 'the meeting with God in national existence . . . is the only preparation for the meeting with God in the Gospel'.

Barth was convinced that events in Germany had justified his drastic action of shutting 'the little back door of Natural Theology'; humanism, materialism, and finally Nazi paganism found access, for previous entry had already been effected by the apparently innocuous ideas of Liberal Protestantism. The Water of Life must flow uncontaminated; it must not be concocted with synthetic substances to form a specious 'lemonade'.

On the other hand, the orthodox Lutherans entrenched in their traditional fastnesses of north and east Germany, were 'conditioned' by their past to respond to authority (*Obrigkeit*). The doctrine of personal obedience to a personal ruler was easily transferred from a secular *summus episcopus* to a *Führer*. Ferdinand Gogarten, Barth's erstwhile ally, was willing to go a considerable distance with the Nazi philosophy, basing his theory on despotic sixteenth-century practice. Had not Luther, in his classic Reformation Addresses, shown a marked antipathy to 'Welsches, Wends, Turks, Jews, and other inferior races'? What objection could there be, then, in discriminating against lesser breeds without the law? Dr. G. Kittel wrote a notorious tract advocating the exclusion of Christian Jews from Church offices.[29] Professor Burkitt placed two copies in

---

[29] Before the First World War the *Ency. Brit.* noted a phenomenal increase in the number of German Jews converted to Christianity (11th ed., Vol. XI, p. 822). 'The impulse is less from religious conviction than from a desire to associate on more equal terms with their neighbours.'

the library of Cambridge University as an instance of 'tendencious scholarship'. Kittel reasoned quite seriously: If the Jew claimed to be the Suffering Servant of Scripture, it was the Christian's bounden duty to make him fulfil his prophetic function. When the 'Aryan paragraph' expelling pastors and professors of Jewish descent from their pulpits and chairs, was submitted to the German universities, most of them censured it as an un-Evangelical discrimination between first and second-class Christians. The ultra-Lutheran University of Erlangen, Bavaria, affirmed that the State had the right to emphasize biological and social distinctions according to circumstances; and these *Ordnungen* the Church was bound to accept. This policy of appeasement was characteristic of Lutheranism in varying degrees. It was a profound disappointment to Barth. He of the Reformed faith, could reproach those Lutheran 'neutrals' in the historic words of Luther to Zwingli (but with much greater justification): 'Yours is a different spirit from ours!'

The creed of the Confessing Church, adopted at Barmen in January 1934,[30] was a clarion. Its intensity recalls a saying of the great South German preacher, Ludwig Hofacker, who, a century ago described the Gospel trumpet as 'more powerful and piercing when it does not follow the range of the scale, but keeps at one penetrating note'. The Barmen Declaration did not claim to cover the whole field of theology like its predecessors, the classic Reformation Confessions. It was a specific, downright answer to the 'German Christian' challenge. As to whether there was any place for Natural Theology, it did not go so far as Barth's emphatic 'No!' Barth himself was among the leading spirits in convoking the Synod. His uncompromising attitude was justified by the course of events. In February 1937, Reichminister Kerrl, addressing the assembled heads of the German Evangelical Churches, made it clear that the Nazis intended to build their religious propaganda on the convenient foundation of pre-1914 Liberalism. 'There is a saying of Pfleiderer's,' remarked Kerrl, 'which I consider important: "God reveals *Himself* in history, but *dogmas* he reveals in the work of men."' In an open letter Dr. Otto Dibelius replied: 'Perhaps you know that in countless Evangelical churches today the congregations repeat on their own initiative the Apostles' Creed when the *Pfarrer* reads it at the altar. This

---

[30] Appendix III, Adolf Keller, *Religion and the European Mind* (London, 1934); *The Significance of the Barmen Declaration for the Ecumenical Church* (S.P.C.K.).

has never been done before. Now congregations must feel they
must show the anti-Christian world that they are determined to
hold fast to the Confession of Faith affirmed by their forefathers.'

The Creed was no longer a yoke, as in Harnack's heyday,
but a blast of the trumpet against the world, the flesh, and the
devil.[31] Barthianism, in Dr. Keller's phrase, became 'The
Arsenal of Theology' for the Confessing Church. Barth forged
the doctrinal weapons for their Crusade, though some of his
supporters reproached him with being an 'activist' in 1938;
during the Munich crisis he challenged Czech and British
Christians not merely to wait for 'the eschatological coming of
the Kingdom of God', but to fight for it. When war finally
broke out in 1939, Professor Martin Dibelius of Heidelberg
published a brochure giving a critical analysis of British
Christianity from a German Lutheran point of view. He
tried to explain political tensions by the different structure
of the German and the British soul; it was not as unfriendly as
might have been expected under the circumstances. Dibelius
blames the semi-Pelagian tendency of Anglo-Saxon Protestantism—the very antithesis of the Lutheran doctrine of salvation
by faith alone (*sola gratia*). He is suspicious of the self-assurance
that is apt to identify the interests of the British Empire with
the Kingdom of God. Dr. Garvie and other British theologians
replied by criticizing German Lutheranism, its subservience
to the State, its escape from moral and social responsibility by
'eschatological' flight into eternity.[31]

The leaders of the Confessing Church certainly did not look
'beyond' to a remote eternity. Far from being escapists or
fatalists, their attitude was 'here and now'; they were prepared
to face not only God's judgement, but that of *Obrigkeit*. Was
the Church to be bound to the Nazi juggernaut *Wagen*? A
certain Lutheran section, 'Confessional' as well as 'Confessing',
swayed by patriotic motives and hereditary tradition, was
inclined to make concessions that practically spelt surrender of
principle. Even the more intransigent German Barthians were
driven by the pressure of war conditions to 'a theology of
silence', though not of compromise. Barth himself, while
affirming his belief that the Allies stood for a just cause (in his
letter to British Christians) did not feel that the world crisis

---

[31] Barth's more popular expositions are based on the Apostles' Creed, e.g.
Dogmatics in Outline (E.T., London, 1949).

should involve the suspension of theological convictions;[32] hence the continuation of controversy between 'Natural Theology' (rightly understood) and what the Bishop of Truro called 'the unnatural theology of Barthians'.[33]

The late Principal Selbie described the Theology of Crisis as 'a tonic for a neurotic age', remarking that something better was required for human nature's daily food. It has certainly put iron into the blood of the Confessing Church, as the only group capable of salvaging the remains of German Protestantism. Lack of logical, psychological, and sociological relevance has not prevented Barthianism from making a strong appeal to the will and the imagination. God is Sovereign Will—irresistible, dynamic, absolute, and above all, personal. Certain Zurich theologians asked Barth: 'Tell us, Professor, *is there* (*gibt es*) any certainty of faith?' Barth replied: 'No, *there is* (*es gibt*) no certainty of faith—*He* gives (*Er gibt*) certainty of faith.' Barth forged the shining blade of the Theology of Crisis. The response of the Confessing Church to his prophetic leadership was immediate. It might well have appropriated the words of David to Ahimelech the priest, when he demanded the sword of Goliath: 'There is none like that; give it to me!'

A reviewer in the *Times Literary Supplement* characterized Barthianism as 'an *interim* theology'. Barth himself did not claim that it was a classical system, like Calvinism, meant to last. He never claimed that it was final,[34] and was not at all worried when critics accused him of shifting his emphasis annually. The Theology of Crisis was wrought out on the anvil of the world's need at a particular crisis in world history. It was meant to be 'a pilgrim's theology', *Theologia Viatoris*. 'The so-called Barthian theology will one day go as it has come, and justice will be done to it.'[35]

It may be generations before German Divinity recovers its balance. Abnormal times produce abnormal theologies.[36] The high dogmatic note is strident, the nervous tone strained,

---

[32] After the war a group of British theologians paid tribute to Barth in *Reformation Old and New*, ed. F. W. Camfield (London, 1947).

[33] Dr. Ehrenberg, refugee pastor, in his *Autobiography* (p. 63), asked British Christians how they could honour Niemöller and repudiate Barth; Barthianism tied up with the Confessing Church, and this obliterated the almost accidental circumstance that Barth was reared in the Reformed and Niemöller in the Lutheran Church.

[34] *Karl Barth: Dogmatics in Outline*, tr. G. T. Thomson (London, 1949).

[35] *Zwischen den Zeiten* (1926), Vol. I, p. 36.

[36] See article by Dr. Wilbert F. Howard, 'Continental Theology after the War' (*London Quarterly and Holborn Review*, January 1946).

M

the perspective out of focus. We recall the words of Scott in *Marmion*:

> But oh my country's wintry state
> What second spring can renovate?

If and when relatively normal conditions return to Germany it may be expected that the people of the Fatherland, like the house of Jacob, 'shall possess their possessions'. In other words, they will revalue their spiritual heritage, without being carried by the gusts of doctrine from cloudy speculation to the lonely peak of neo-orthodoxy. There is a legitimate form of 'German Christianity' represented by the *Chorales* of Luther, the woodcuts of Dürer, and the Cantatas of Bach, just as the flavour of English Christianity is represented by the *Prayer Book*, the *Pilgrim's Progress*, and the hymns of Watts and Wesley. If German Evangelicalism has certain obvious failings, it has escaped some of the faults of the British Churches—the devastating taboos of Puritan ethics, the superiority-complex of Anglicanism, and undue emphasis on the use (or disuse) of certain liturgical practices. The United Kingdom shares with the Fatherland a privilege few other nations possess—a classic version of the Bible that is their greatest national Book. During the First World War, German soldiers treasured the Scriptures like their enemies (though they also treasured Goethe's *Faust* and Nietzsche's *Zarathustra*, as Professor Deissmann admitted). During the Second World War the Bible Society of Prussia, in spite of official opposition, sold more copies of the Bible than of *Mein Kampf*. If the German people are to rediscover the Word of God in their present tragic situation as their forefathers rediscovered it in Luther's day, they will find a sure light in darkness. Intellectuals will need to be more humble and study God's Word with expectant interest and humility. In the provinces of the Lower Rhine, in Württemberg, and elsewhere, the Bible is known and loved, as it was centuries ago. It is studied prayerfully by the faithful, personally and in groups. The fountains of God's Word, closed so long by secular interests, must be unsealed all over the Fatherland. German Pietism at its best, like Methodism, has rejoiced in a deeply personal, intimate bond between Christian believers. It is *Gemeinschaft*. There is no exact English equivalent for it in the New Testament. It means more than 'community' or 'fellowship'. Luther used it to translate κοινωνία (sharing) in the New Testament.

This spirit is found in informal meetings for prayer, but also to a considerable extent in the church services of the villages and smaller towns. Reverent worship blends with 'the priesthood of all believers'. The pastor stands before the altar, with its lighted candles and crucifix, but he wears no vestments, only a gown with bands or ruff. The altar is the Lord's Table, free to all who love the Lord Jesus; it is not a 'Lutheran altar' as certain Anglicans speak of 'our altar'. The man of God stands near his people, not at the back of a distant chancel. Pulpit, font, and altar are grouped, as far as possible, together, for they are all instruments of the Word. The people join heartily in the ancient responses; they need no surpliced choirs to lead their worship for them. Although German services are usually liturgical in framework, they maintain an element of spontaneity.[37] The people stand for prayer, like their forefathers, and sit for praise. The *Chorales* may be slow and old-fashioned, but what they lack in breadth they gain in depth; they are mystical and experimental, with deep roots in the national consciousness.

What Professor Schaff said of German devotional life nearly a century ago is still, in some districts, true, and we pray it may become more widespread. 'Lutheran piety is the charm of Mary who sat at Jesus' feet and heard His Word. . . . If it is deficient in *outward* activity and practical zeal, it makes up for it by a rich *inward* life. It excels in honesty, kindness, affection, and *Gemüthlichkeit*—for which other nations have not even a name.'

[37] H. H. Kramm, 'Church Services in German Lutheranism' (*Church Quarterly Review*, No. 268, 1942).

Part Two

CHURCH AND STATE

CHAPTER ONE

THE TERRITORIAL SYSTEM EXPLAINED

ET erunt reges nutricii et reginae nutrices tuae. . . . In the castle of Coburg there is a singular emblematic fresco of the seventeenth century. It depicts the wedding procession of Duke John Casimir, which is led by knights, falconers, and musicians. Then, drawn by the nuptial car, defile two sets of attendants—four councillors for civil affairs and three for ecclesiastical. So the Duke sets forth for Cythera, the isle of Venus. Here is a graphic symbol of the twin bureaucracy at the service of every German prince great and small. Pleasure, convenience, and power too often became the motives of administration, sacred as well as secular.

'Lutheran polity is Caesaro-Papalism,' said Flacius Illyricus, the champion of Lutheran orthodoxy in the sixteenth century. Over two centuries later Schleiermacher compared German Erastianism to the 'horrible head of Medusa . . . everything is petrified as soon as it appears'. In the twentieth century a French Catholic, Maritain, thought of German Protestant administration in terms of mechanism: '*L'appareil césaro-ecclésiastique du lutheranisme.*' What are the grounds for this indictment?

'I see in the future', said Melanchthon, 'a tyranny more intolerant than ever existed before.' This was the principle of *cujus regio, ejus religio*, which put the people of the Fatherland at the mercy of innumerable princes, who fixed the religion of their subjects as they thought fit. *Ubi unus dominus, ibi una religio*. This theory of princely rights was incorporated in the 'Religious Peace' of Augsburg (1555), and was the dominating factor in the centuries that followed.[1] The *jus reformandi* was often exercised in an arbitrary manner. If subjects disagreed with the religion of their rulers, they would have to remove to another principality. The rights of Calvinists were not officially recognized till the Treaty of Westphalia (1648). Dissenters

---

[1] General Church Histories, dealing mainly with Germany: J. H. Kurz, *Kirchengeschichte* (Vols. II, III; E.T., 1893): K. Müller, *Kirchengeschichte*, 2nd ed., 2 vols. (Tübingen, 1924). In G. Krüger's Handbuch der *Kirchengeschichte*; H. Stephan, *Neuzeit* (Tübingen, 1909, and subseq. eds.), Hermelink and Maurer, *Reformation und Gegenreformation* (1931).

from the official 'Confessions' had to wait till the eighteenth century, and in some cases till the nineteenth, for the removal of galling restrictions; conditions differed widely in this respect from State to State.

The principle of *cujus regio, ejus religio* inevitably broke down in the course of time. If a Protestant prince became a Roman Catholic he could not coerce his Protestant subjects directly, but there was nothing to prevent him from building an expensive Court Church. In spite of legal safeguards for the Church of the people, the ruler's religion was apt to become the fashionable faith (*religio regius, religion regionis*). Roman Catholic princes sometimes gained possession of traditionally Protestant States; in the eighteenth century this happened in Saxony, which was almost wholly Lutheran, in Württemberg, which was predominantly Lutheran, and in Hesse, which was mainly Reformed. From the early seventeenth century onward Reformed Electors ruled ultra-Lutheran Brandenburg. In 1857 Professor Schaff remarked that there was hardly a principality in all Germany where religion was not mixed, Catholics being subject to a Protestant, or Protestants to a Catholic sovereign.

When the Thirty Years War ended in 1648, Protestantism in Germany was a survival, limited to certain areas of what had once been a mighty movement sweeping through central Europe. As late as 1557 the Venetian Ambassador reported that seven-tenths of the German people were Lutheran, two-tenths were Reformed, and only one-tenth were Catholic. The Emperor Maximilian showed a certain amount of sympathy to the Reformation; there was no persecution in Austria, but the fact that the Emperor was a Papist was a potential threat to Protestantism. The *terrain* favoured the Counter-Reformation. The cardinal principle of *cujus regio, ejus religio* (1555) originally favoured princes who veered toward Lutheranism. Now it was turned against them except in overwhelmingly Protestant principalities like Saxony. The Emperor Rudolph the Second, who reigned from 1576-1612, was a fanatical supporter of the Counter-Reformation, which had gone on from strength to strength since the Council of Trent concluded its epoch-making sessions in 1564.

The Jesuits started operations in the Emperor's own domains, and then turned their attention to what is now Southern Germany. They persuaded insolvent princes that Rome was prepared to give them economic security and prestige in return for tolerating Catholics. Toleration, however, was merely camouflage for the planting of propaganda (as is the case with Communists today). As soon as a principality was ripe, the Jesuits struck, with the aid of converted princes. Executions and confiscation 'liquidated' areas once largely Protestant; banishment was considered a positive act of clemency; 'new Catholics' multiplied as in France under the dragonnades of Louis the Fourteenth. Rulers who were nominally Protestant were bribed to remain neutral during the Religious Wars, or even forced to fight for the Emperor. Thus Gerhard the Lutheran theologian lamented: 'It is sad that we must defend with our arms the religion of those whom we attack in our writings.'

Bavaria was the first-fruits of the Jesuit policy of reclamation; Protestantism was suppressed except in Reformation strongholds like Nürnberg. The ecclesiastical principalities of the Rhine were then purged of Protestant influence.[2] Gebhart, Archbishop of Cologne, tried to secularize his domains, but did not succeed, like prelates of an earlier generation. When he became a Calvinist, he was immediately repudiated by his Chapter, acting under Spanish control, and forced to resign. Southern ecclesiastical principalities like Würzburg and Bamberg followed suit in taking their orders from Rome. The clergy had to subscribe to the Decrees of the Council of Trent; schools and colleges were taken over by the Jesuits; and freedom of thought was extinguished. Baroque splendour reigned in Würzburg and Bamberg, but its cost must be estimated in terms of moral and spiritual degradation.[3]

Even in Catholic principalities where Protestants were tolerated there was no guarantee that their rights would be respected. Cupidity or fanaticism on the part of an arbitrary ruler might release the alert watch-dogs of persecution on a heretic-hunt. In 1728 the Prince-Archbishop of Salzburg

[2] At the Reformation there were seven Electors (*Kürfursten*), fifty Prelates, seventy Abbots and Abbesses, thirty-one secular Princes, 128 Counts, and eighty-one 'Free Cities'. As late as 1750 there were 350 principalities, enjoying considerable autonomy (cf. Bryce, *Holy Roman Empire*, 1880).

[3] Baroque was as much in evidence at Lutheran Courts, although most of the great Baroque architects were Catholics. Spengler was surely right in stressing the connexion of Baroque Art and Music. The undulation, the evanescence and the sparkle 'are nothing less than a victory of tones and melodies over lines and walls, of pure space over material' (*Decline of the West*, E.T., Vol. I, p. 285). Here is an intriguing instance of Schelling's definition of Architecture as 'frozen music' and of Music as 'architecture dissolved into sound'.

expelled twenty thousand Evangelicals at three days notice.[4] Goethe's poem *Hermann and Dorothea* is based on an episode in their heroic winter march. When General Oglethorpe founded Georgia as a colony for distressed folk in 1733, he welcomed as the most promising element a company of Salzburgers. Can we wonder at the conduct of the Prince-Archbishop when we consider that Louis the Fourteenth set a notorious example to Catholic Europe by the Revocation of the *Edict of Nantes*?

When Louis was compelled to leave the ruined Palatinate in 1697[5] he left the Jesuits in control and a Romanist on the throne. Protestants were forced to salute priestly processions on the streets, to allow their churches to be used for the Mass, and to surrender endowments; dragoons were quartered in the homes of recalcitrant citizens. The glory of Heidelberg was blighted. The Calvinists, being more independent than the Lutherans, underwent more intense persecution. Indeed, the Reformed Church would have been utterly crushed but for the appeal of Protestant Europe to the Emperor in 1703. Joseph the First intervened, just as his Catholic ancestor, Maximilian the Second, had interceded in the sixteenth century for 'crypto-Calvinists' in Saxony. The Palatinate appeal, however, only carried weight when backed by the threat of Prussia to close Romish churches and cloisters. The Elector Palatine, forced to make concessions, in revenge moved his capital from historic Heidelberg to prosaic Mannheim. Direct persecution gave way to a systematic campaign calculated to disrupt Protestantism. It was profitable to become a Romanist. 'If there be one Catholic in any community (and he a cowherd) he shall be the magistrate.' Differences between Lutherans and Reformed were deliberately exploited, to weaken the Protestant front. The Reformed Consistory was shamelessly corrupted by the Jesuits; educational and pastoral offices were auctioned. Everything was done to degrade the religion of the people, and nothing to improve the wretched social conditions caused by Louis the Fourteenth's devastations.[6]

The Electors of the Palatinate could not prevent their subjects from emigrating to America. The first swarm left in 1708; up to twenty thousand 'poor Palatines' being maintained

---

[4] E. B. Speirs, 'The Salzburgers' (*Engl. Hist. Review*, October 1890).
[5] See p. 26, *supra*.
[6] J. I. Good, *History of the Reformed Church in Germany*, 1620-90 (Reading, Pa., 1894).

in a great camp at Greenwich through the generosity of Queen Anne. Special collections were taken on their behalf in the churches of Great Britain, but most of these 'displaced persons' underwent considerable hardships on reaching Pennsylvania.[7] The *classis* of Amsterdam took a belated interest in their welfare. Michael Schlatter came over from Switzerland in 1746 and organized these struggling settlers, who afterwards became the German Reformed Church in the United States. Before American Independence was won, however, many a 'poor Palatine' was sent to America against his own will, sold by the Elector Palatine, to fight for George the Third.

At home, conditions became so bad that the Protestant States of Germany had to petition the enlightened Emperor Joseph the Second to intervene in the Palatinate. Despite persecution, penury, and misgovernment, over 190,000 Palatines remained faithful to the Reformation cause, of whom 50,000 were Lutherans. Jesuit propaganda did not succeed in increasing the Romanist population above 90,000. The long night of Jesuit oppression came to an end in 1802, when Napoleon remodelled the map of Germany. The Palatinate was united with Baden under a tolerant Lutheran as Grand Duke. The two Protestant Confessions, left to their own devices by the State, lived peacefully side by side. Even the joint use of village churches by Catholics and Protestants, originally imposed by arbitrary authority (the *Simultaneum*, 1698), grew into a recognized communal custom.

The tragedy of German Protestantism after the settlement of 1648 was the large number of self-contained, isolated Establishments at the mercy of their rulers. These resembled a series of inland pools, stagnant save for exceptional inundations. The Catholic Principalities were also pools, but the tide of a wider life flowed over them. There was nothing to remind the separate Evangelical *Landeskirchen* that they were part of a larger whole. The curse of Lutherland was *Kleinstaaterei*.

The 'Territorial' or 'Consistorial' System of Germany was a makeshift polity devised to take the place of a National Evangelical Church.[8] It admits considerable variety of detail under certain common features of organization. It was an improvisation, which rulers knocked together as best they could in a

---

[7] A. B. Faust, *The German Element in the United States*, Vol. I (1909).

[8] See *Encyclopaedia Religion in Geschichte und Gegenwart*. Also *New Schaff-Herzog Cyclopaedia of Religious Knowledge* (New York, 1908).

time of emergency, though its apologists prefer more elegant nomenclature. Luther's painful experience convinced him that the *jus episcopale* belonged, in the last resort, to the civil authorities, who 'took over' in principalities and free cities after the Diet of Spires (1526). Principal Lindsay has described the new system as an *ad hoc* structure suggested by the consistorial courts through which medieval bishops transacted diocesan business.[9] The term 'Superintendent' was taken over from the later Scholastics who had used it as a translation of *episcopus*. Prince John of Saxony, the first to improvise the new polity (1527) made it clear that his superintendents were not to be bishops in the Catholic sense. He assumed the title of *summus episcopus* and as 'High Magistrate' appointed a supreme ecclesiastical council, consisting of jurists, civil servants, and theologians. He nominated a 'General Superintendent' to preside over the Council and 'Superintendents' to administer the dioceses. The hierarchical principle was retained, but many administrative functions were transferred to the State. This provided a pattern for other principalities, leaving room for local modifications.[10]

If Luther regarded Church government as undefined by Scriptural authority, he certainly did not prefer the Territorial system as the *summum bonum*. In sanctioning State-appointed Consistories he was departing from his own ideal through force of circumstances. Böhmer rejects as quite unhistorical the view that State control of the Church corresponds most closely to Luther's ideals. 'On the contrary, we may assert that the territorial system stands . . . in direct contradiction to his principal conception of religion.' Luther was a 'Conciliarist', a believer in ecumenical councils—always provided that they were not coerced by papal authority. This principle of consultation and fellowship he intended to apply to the Church as locally organized. In May 1523 he defended the people of Leisnig in forming a congregation administered by a representative committee. His tractate bore the significant title: *That a Christian assembly or congregation has the right to judge all doctrines, to call, install, and dismiss teachers; proof and reason from the Scriptures*. Professor J. T. McNeill comments: 'This is a vigorous claim, on the basis of the priesthood of believers . . .

---

[9] T. M. Lindsay's *Reformation* (1906), Vol. I, Chapter 6.
[10] Richter collected 172 separate ecclesiastical constitutions (1846). Sehling published a complete collection, *Die Ev. Kirchenordnungen des 16 Jahrhunderts* (Leipzig, 1902).

to conciliarism in its elementary congregational form. All Christians are to be called priests, but they are to select those who shall exercise the ministry on their behalf. This is Luther's favourite idea of a representative priesthood in the specialized ministry as projected from the priesthood of the whole body.'[11]

The same year Luther expanded these ideas in his advice to the Estates of Bohemia.[12] The fact that he issued this immediately in German, indicates that in preparing it, 'he was thinking of Germany, and above all of Saxony'.[13] Those whose hearts God had touched should meet as a congregation and delegate the rites of preaching and administering sacraments to a pastor. When a sufficient number of communities have been provided with this organization, their pastors might select from among themselves superintendents, till the country finally returns to 'the legitimate and evangelical episcopate'.

Luther's theory of 'delegated power' was not implemented, and his projects to express the priesthood of all believers in ecclesiastical polity were indefinitely postponed. His faith in 'the common man' was decisively shattered by the fanatical excesses of the Peasant War and the Anabaptist Movement. Instead of viewing these rebellions as an inevitable, though regrettable, outburst against social injustice, he reacted violently against all attempts to organize the Church on democratic lines. Strong mistrust of the people overcame his generous instincts and warm human sympathies. In introducing his *German Mass* in 1526, he made the following reference to the proposed ecclesiastical constitution: 'I cannot and would not order or arrange such a community at present. I have not the requisite persons for it, nor do I see many who are urgent for it.

It is perfectly true that the minutely stratified, feudal organization of German society was not at all suited to a brand new democratic order in the Church. Experiments, however, might have been encouraged in the Free Cities and other towns where the presence of merchant and craftsman communities warranted a trial. Luther's disavowal of ecclesiastical uniformity surely allowed room for testing his own ideals within limited areas. Francis Lambert, in presenting a new draft constitution for the Church of Hesse in 1526,[14] recognized the great Reformer's principle that the Word of God, rather than

[11] *Unitive Protestantism* (New York, 1930), p. 122.
[12] *De instituendis ministris Ecclesiae* (October, 1523).
[13] Grisar's *Luther*, E.T., Vol. II, p. 112
[14] R. L. Winters, *Francis Lambert of Avignon* (Philadelphia, 1938).

Canon Law, ought to regulate ecclesiastical polity. Bishops (i.e. Pastors), elders, and deacons, were to be elected in each congregation and ordained according to apostolic practice; at least three clergy were to participate in the ordination of a minister. A synod, consisting of all the pastors and an elder from each congregation, was to exercise supreme authority. Luther feared that this constitution was too advanced for the age and wrote to the Landgrave of Hesse, admitting that he had not the courage to sanction it (7th January 1527).

The fact that Hesse afterwards adopted Presbyterianism (and was prepared to suffer for conscience sake) shows that Lambert's scheme was not altogether impracticable. It found ready acceptance at Emden, when Johannes a Lasco reorganized the Church on democratic lines (1544). The city of Bremen was also favourably disposed to the Reformed ideal of self-government. It was remarkable that Presbyterianism attained complete stature in the duchies of the Lower Rhine (Jülich, Cleve, Mark, and Berg). These provinces were united by a General Synod, whereas in most Reformed States the sovereign reserved for himself control of the upper Church courts. Non-liturgical worship flourished, also 'liberty of prophesying' in informal prayer-meetings.

Further south, the Nassau duchies (near Frankfurt) and the larger principality of Hesse-Cassel constituted another group. The Palatinate flanked the upper Rhine. Strasbourg came straight over to the Reformed Church, like Emden, not *via* Lutheranism. It did not, however, remain long in the path marked out by Bucer (whose influence on the English Reformation was so marked). It fell under a strict Lutheran régime in 1548, and Calvinists, who once possessed the Cathedral,[15] were obliged to worship outside the city walls till 1789. Western Germany was thus garlanded with a ring of Reformed Churches. Elsewhere, you might find a Calvinist *diaspora* like Anhalt (between Brandenburg and Saxony) or Liegnitz and Brieg in distant Silesia—islands in a sea of hostile Lutheranism.

In 1571 the Synod of Emden issued a manifesto that outlined the position of the Reformed Church against the hierarchical and Erastian tendencies of Lutheranism: 'No Church

---

[15] Strasbourg was betrayed to the French by the Roman Catholic Bishop and leading citizens in 1681. By the Treaty of Ryswick (1697) Louis the Fourteenth's conquest of Alsace was confirmed. Although Strasbourg Cathedral remained in Roman Catholic hands, Lutherans were allowed to hold certain churches with specified rights.

among the other Churches, no Minister among the Ministers, no Elder among the Elders, and no Deacon among the Deacons, shall obtain the primacy of sovereignty, but rather will guard against every appearance and occasion of such.'[16]   About three hundred and fifty years later Karl Barth reaffirmed this testimony in a notable speech at Emden. Had the religious life of Germany been more adequately leavened by the Reformed spirit, Lutheranism might have been safe-guarded against apathy, officialism, and passive obedience to secular authority.

There was nothing in Lutheran theology to prevent the growth of synodical government, granted tolerable conditions. Lord Acton was incorrect in asserting that Lutheranism could not exist unless buttressed by the civil power. Indeed, in North America, where Confessional Lutheranism triumphed and stood aside from Presbyterianism, an orderly yet democratic series of synods became the accepted polity;[17] no Superintendents were appointed, although the Methodists adopted this system of personal authority. Even the conservative Swedes made no attempt to import bishops, though they brought over their historic liturgy.

After Luther's death the German princes took a stronger line. Not content, like the Stuarts, with subservient bishops, they claimed the *jus episcopale* for themselves and branded those who wanted synodical government as 'Crypto-Calvinists', disloyal to a fundamentally German institution. One principality after another adopted the 'Territorial System'. What had been improvised out of sheer necessity came to be claimed as a prescriptive right.

Anglican writers have sometimes admitted that there were peculiarities in the situation of Germany which made it impossible to retain the Episcopate, however desirable—hence the apology of 'the judicious Hooker' for the constitution of Continental Protestant Churches. John Hales of Eton pointed out that 'the French Church being *sub cruce*, cannot well set up episcopal jurisdiction'. What about Germany where several Catholic bishops adhered to the Reformation? There were at least three, the number required by the Council of Nicaea for consecrating a bishop. These men were allowed to hold office till death. But they never took the lead, like Cranmer and his

[16] cf. J. I. Good, *Origin of the Reformed Church in Germany* (Reading, Pa., 1887).

[17] cf. R. Fortenbaugh, *Development of the Synodical Polity of the Lutheran Church in America* (Philadelphia, 1926).

episcopal associates, in regulating the progress of the Reformation and reaching a settlement to determine their place in the
Church's polity. The German Bishops were 'not called upon
to exercise their prerogative of ordination, nor do they appear
to have insisted on its necessity to a valid ministry. Melanchthon, and to a certain extent, Luther, had no objection to the
Episcopate as exercising a function of supervision over the
churches, if it could have been based upon human right, *jure
humano* and not *jure divino*'. Professor A. V. G. Allen (an
American Episcopalian) considered that Anglicanism perpetuated the 'secular Church' of the Middle Ages, as an inclusive institution closely related to the State. The Lutheran
Church he traced to the Augustinian Order, standing in the
Evangelical tradition of theology and piety. The Reformed
Church had its points of affinity with the Dominicans—in
its wide diffusion in every land, its emphasis on orthodoxy,
discipline, and organization.[18]

Passing from these suggestive speculations, we ask, what are
the facts as to Lutheranism and Episcopacy? The Swedish
Church retained 'Apostolic Succession' more by undesigned
circumstances than by conviction. The Church of Finland
possessed formal 'Succession' but lost it as late as 1884, owing
to an unusual situation arising through the death of all the
bishops. The German priest, Bugenhagen, ordained seven
Superintendents for Denmark and Norway (1527) who afterwards received the title of Bishop.

In Germany, little interest was shown in the historic aspect.
In 1542 Luther instituted Nicholas von Amsdorf, nominated
by the Elector of Saxony, to the See of Naumburg. He consecrated the new bishop himself, though he could easily have
obtained 'Apostolic Succession' through Roman Catholic
Prelates who had become Protestants.[19] Chillingworth in
1637 referred to Amsdorf, 'consecrated by Luther though he
himself was never a Bishop'; German Evangelical theory
indeed seemed to illustrate Tertullian's dictum: 'Today a priest
—tomorrow a layman.'[20] In 1544 Luther instituted George

---

[18] *Christian Institutions*, pp. 253, 275ff.

[19] The unpopularity of Bishops is indicated by the homiletic etymology of
Geiler, the great pre-Reformation preacher of Strasbourg. He used to say that
Bischoff originally meant *Bei den Schaffen* ('with the sheep'); it had come to mean
Beiss das Schaff ('bite the sheep'). When the title *Bischoff* was restored among
German Evangelicals in our own time, they experienced the 'biting species' in the
Nazi Primate, 'Rei-bi' Müller.

[20] *Religion of Protestants* (1866 ed.), pp. 401ff.

of Anhalt to the Bishopric of Merseburg, as he had installed
Amsdorf at Naumburg. No serious attempt was made in
Germany to link up the Lutheran Ministry with theories of
'Apostolic Succession'. This is somewhat surprising when
we consider Luther's attempt to demonstrate liturgical con-
tinuity by pruning the Mass and translating it into German.
The German princes, however, had no intention of allowing a
uniform, reformed episcopacy to take the place of the old
prelacy. Every prince wanted to be his own bishop—hence the
'Territorial System', the *Summepiskopat*.

N

CHAPTER TWO

ERASTIANISM AND LIBERTY IN PRUSSIA

PRUSSIA affords an instructive instance of the origin and working of the Territorial System, as modified between the sixteenth and twentieth centuries.[1]

Luther advised Albert of Hohenzollern, Grand Master of the Teutonic Order, to give up Romanism, transform the lands of his historic Order into a Duchy, proclaim himself Duke, and take a wife. He is said to have smiled, but afterwards adopted this practical advice to the letter. His first Church Ordinance (1525) admitted the right of the people to call their pastors and share in ecclesiastical administration. When actually in power, he lost no time in abridging the rights he had just proclaimed in theory. The neighbouring principality of Brandenburg identified Lutheranism with uncompromising 'Territorialism'. It was not behind Saxony in denying the rights of the ordinary layman. The *Corpus Doctrinale Brandenburgicum* (1572) gave a special place to a heated outburst of Luther's that Protestants who differed from him were not even Christians. 'Fill us, O Lord,' prayed Chancellor Distelmeyer, 'with hatred of Calvinism.'

The House of Brandenburg seemed committed to un-flinching resistance to un-Lutheran innovations: but this was not to be their destiny. By a failure of the ducal line of Prussia, Brandenburg and Prussia were united (1618). John Sigismund, the new prince, had certainly been trained in Lutheran orthodoxy; but he had travelled widely and had observed the beneficent effects of Calvinism in Heidelberg and the duchies of the Rhine. Convinced that Lutheranism was only a halting place between Rome and Geneva (the true Zion) he expressed his personal preference, first quietly, then more boldly. In spite of the protests of the clergy and his wife, he acted on the *jus reformandi religionem* and summoned Calvinistic divines from the Palatinate. He declared that he had no intention of coercion till he had given his people 'the opportunity of knowing Lutheranism purged of Papacy'. He therefore

[1] See K. D. Macmillan, *Protestantism in Germany* (Princeton, 1917), which has a good bibliography.

invited his Lutheran divines to meet the Calvinists. The Lutherans had almost to be dragged to the conference. They contended that the vernacular was undignified and demanded Latin; not unreasonably they argued that if Calvinists were imported from other lands foreign Lutherans should also be invited. There was dogged opposition from the nobility. As staunch Lutherans they refused to vote supplies in the medieval Diet, which still limited the Elector's power. The passive protest of the people and the active protest of the Electress Anna resulted in the project being abandoned. The Lutheran régime was now too deep-rooted to be torn up by the same potent instrument which planted it—the principle of *cujus regio, ejus religio*. Had John Sigismund enforced his demands *after* the Thirty Years War when the nobility had lost most of their power, it is quite likely he would have had his way, confronted only by passive opposition. As it was, he insisted on his own right to be a Calvinist (1614) and obtained full rights for other Calvinists; the cathedral of Berlin was henceforth Reformed, not Lutheran. The Elector's declaration (*Confessio Sigismundi*) that he would force no man's conscience in religion, publicly or privately, was much in advance of his times. As for the Electress Anna she died detesting Calvinism. Nevertheless, a Calvinist divine preached her funeral oration and utilized the occasion to prove that Calvinism was the true way of salvation.

Frederick William, the 'Great Elector' (1640-88), sought to make Lutherans and Calvinists agree to differ. To this end he forbade his subjects to study at Wittenberg, then the headquarters of ultra-Lutheran fanaticism. He imposed reasonable limits to the 'duty' which many preachers insisted on—'the duty of chastizing error, sinful Philippism, and wolfish Calvinism'. Thanks to his constructive skill and organizing zeal, Brandenburg, hitherto one of the poorest of German principalities, became strong and prosperous, an effective nucleus for the future Prussian State. It soon displaced Saxony in the moral leadership of Protestantism. Saxony, by taking the side of the Imperialists in the Thirty Years War, had lost prestige and had been more devastated than any other part of Germany. Saxony, forced to tolerate Calvinists at the Treaty of Westphalia (1648) owing to the un-wearying advocacy of 'the Great Elector', had to endure the mortification of being ruled by an Elector who threw off the Lutheranism of his fathers to secure the throne of Poland[2]—an unhappy venture which embroiled him in war with Charles the Twelfth of Sweden and caused international complications for most of the eighteenth century.

'The Great Elector' far outstripped the German rulers of his era in vision and energy.[3] Twice he refused the throne of Poland; unlike Henry of Navarre he did not consider any kingdom 'worth a Mass'. Scorning the subserviency of his contemporaries to Louis the Fourteenth, he married a Dutch princess. He allowed Roman Catholics more liberty than any Protestant sovereign of the seventeenth century. His welcome to the Huguenots, expelled at the Revocation of the *Edict of Nantes* (1685) was a wise as well as a magnanimous gesture. In spite of strong opposition among his own subjects to this French influx, he gave the incomers encouragement as well as toleration. He made Marshal Schomberg his Commander-in-Chief; he embraced Ancillon, pastor of Metz, and appointed him Court preacher. He gave Huguenots of rank a status similar to that which they had once held. He honoured professional men with positions of trust. He exempted business men from taxation and encouraged them to introduce the industries that had once made France rich. The Huguenot *diaspora*, originally sixty thousand in number, had now grown to about a million. Not only did it prove a veritable seed-bed of economic progress; its social influence acted as a leaven in heavy Prussian society. The French Reformed showed how the benevolent impulse might flow into hospitals, alms-houses, and orphanages. They showed their hosts a more excellent way in community life, by rising above the boorishness and pedantry hitherto dominant. A new elegance crept into literature and even preaching. The *Französische Dom* became one of the leading churches in Berlin. Only in one respect were the Huguenots disappointed in their benefactor. He claimed the right to nominate an upper Consistory and refused to allow free synods. 'Our crown is taken away,' the exiles lamented. Foreign infiltration did much to vitalize the German Reformed Church, which gradually absorbed the Huguenots as their language died out. In 1925 the surviving French congregations were

---

[2] Frederick Augustus the First (1697). He was obliged to confirm explicitly all the privileges of Lutheranism. Despite Court influence, Romanists were not allowed to acquire civil rights or landed property till 1806. Calvinists were not granted citizenship in Saxony till 1818.

[3] For middle-class life, see the racy autobiography of *Master Johann Dietz* (E.T., London, 1923). Dietz was surgeon in the army of 'the Great Elector' and Court barber.

organized in a synod, within the German Evangelical Federation. 'The Great Elector' is justly commemorated[4] in the international Reformation Monument at Geneva, where statuesque figures guard the wall that used to protect the city of Calvin. A panel in relief depicts him as the friend of the exiled Huguenots, whom he vows to aid even if he has to sell his household silver.

The Great Elector's son assumed the modest title of 'King of Prussia' in 1701 (Western Prussia being still Polish). Frederick the First crowned himself, the divine unction being bestowed by Lutheran and Reformed chaplains to whom he gave the honorary title of Bishop. His Calvinistic principles prompted him to remove 'Catholic remnants' from Lutheran churches—private confession, exorcism, crosses, vestments, etc. On the other hand, he gave no encouragement to the self-governing instincts of the Calvinists. He irritated both Confessions by dismissing doctrinal differences as matters of secondary importance. As a symbol of his ideals he built a number of 'union churches', on whose altar the Lutheran and Reformed Catechisms lay side by side. As the patron of Pietism, he founded the University of Halle as a 'school of the prophets'.

Ranging farther afield, the royal *Liturgiker* saw in the English Liturgy a rallying centre for the fellowship of all Protestants. 'Common Prayer' would prove a bond of Christian unity, which he confused with uniformity—did he not know that the restoration of the *Prayer Book* in 1662 had resulted in the resignation of two thousand English clergy? King Frederick thought it would be a good idea to send some of his Divinity students to Oxford or Cambridge. He decided to have the English *Prayer Book* translated, printed, and adapted for use in the Chapel Royal and Cathedral of Berlin (1704). Copies were sent to Queen Anne and the Archbishop of Canterbury, Dr. Tenison. This prelate made no acknowledgement of the gift, and no reference to the scheme for establishing Episcopacy in Prussia; he had evidently no great enthusiasm for exporting a service book that had been responsible for persecution at home.[5]

The King of Prussia, on receiving this rebuff, took no further steps, but in 1710 Grabe and Jablonski opened negotiations with Dr. Sharpe, Archbishop of York. J. E. Grabe,

---

4 See Carlyle's *Frederick the Great*, Vol. I, for his predecessors.

5 J. W. Legg, *English Church Life from the Restoration to the Tractarian Movement* (London, 1914), pp. 382, 404ff.

(1666-1711) was born at Königsberg and educated there at the University. Doubting the validity of Lutheran Orders, he applied to the Consistory of Sambia but received no satisfaction. Spener, the Pietist leader, advised him to go to Canterbury rather than Rome. He was accordingly ordained deacon in 1700, appointed chaplain of Christ Church, Oxford, given a D.D. and a pension of £100 per annum. Grabe found High Anglicanism profitable and loathed the Latitudinarians. Dr. Jablonski, Prussian Court chaplain, was quite a different kind of Churchman. A Moravian Bishop, he was willing to introduce Episcopacy and the English Liturgy into the Prussian Church. He believed he could supply the missing link of 'Apostolic Succession'—had he not consecrated the Bishops appointed by the King at his coronation (two Lutherans and two Reformed)?

Queen Anne and her advisers were interested, but the scheme for uniting the English and Prussian Churches fell through, owing to the death of King Frederick in 1713 and of Archbishop Sharpe in the following year. Jablonski's Moravian enthusiasm disarmed a good deal of suspicion. He worked hard at Berlin to include the Swiss Reformed Churches in a comprehensive union. The Courts of Berlin, Hanover,[6] and Gotha were interested, but the diffculties proved as insuperable as today. Leibniz, who had favoured the idea, turned against it when a Reformed pastor named Winkler brought it within the limits of practical politics by basing his proposal on the Lutheran maxim that a territorial monarch was the chief Bishop within his own dominion.[7]

Jablonski was a well-meaning idealist. He rather reminds us of the type of Broad Churchman satirized by Father Ronald Knox in his masterly parody of an irenic pamphlet, seventeenth-century style:

REUNION ALL ROUND, or Jael's Hammer laid aside and the milk of Human Kindness beaten up into Butter and serv'd in a Lordly Dish—Being a Plea for the Inclusion within the Church of England of all Mahometans, Jews, Buddhists, etc. (1914).

Frederick William the First, who ascended the throne in 1713, had no sympathy with the pomp and circumstance of Church and State. He had no desire to transform frugal

---

[6] The Union of Hanover with Britain under George the First would have facilitated the scheme, but advantage was not taken of it.

[7] cf. Leighton Pullan, *Religion since the Reformation*, pp. 87ff.; S. Cheetham, *History of the Christian Church since the Reformation*, pp. 153ff.

'superintendents' into lordly prelates. He had no interest in English institutions, still less in French fashions. He was proud to follow the simple ways of his forebears, drilling his subjects in religion as well as in military discipline. He demanded absolute submission to his principles of patriarchal loyalty, Spartan endurance, and Lutheran pietism. His new Garrison Church at Potsdam, with its four-square plan, tiers of galleries and ancestral vaults, was an appropriate symbol of 'the Church Militant'. His soldiers were issued devotional manuals as well as hymn-books, 'to direct correctly the prayers of the *Kriegsleute*'. This régime cemented the close relations of Church and Army which continued unbroken till the fall of the Hohenzollerns in 1918.

The King developed elementary education and assigned educational duties to the clergy. He doubled the revenue of Prussia and built up her backward economic fabric. He was a good steward as far as material was concerned, but relentlessly hostile to higher values unscheduled by Lutheran tradition. Winckelmann, apostle of truth and beauty, fled from this inhospitable Fatherland. Schiller confessed that it was 'better to be a eunuch in a Turkish harem than a subject of the King of Prussia'. The Court was a barrack, the Kingdom a combination of the farm-yard and the parade-ground; 'he viewed both with the eye of the non-commissioned officer and the stud-groom'.[8] When he lay dying, they read to him the immortal words: 'Naked I came into the world, and naked I shall leave it'—he interrupted the devotional exercise: 'No, no . . . I shall have my uniform!'

Frederick William the First dismissed theological controversies as 'parsons' disputes', and if any of the clergy had qualms of conscience he accepted their resignation with alacrity. Nevertheless, he followed his forefathers in eliminating with relentless vigour all medieval survivals in Church services; he had a hearty appetite for sermons, preferring homely Lutheran preaching to the polished discourses of his own Reformed divines, who modelled their style on the foreign patterns of Tillotson and Saurin. His reign was a transition era.[9]

The Crown Prince, brought up by his domineering father on a régime of piety, parsimony, and patriotism was loyal

[8] Marriott and Robertson, *The Evolution of Prussia* (Oxford, 1915).
[9] G. Pariset, *L'État et les Églises en Prusse sous Frédéric-Guillaume I* (Paris, 1896).

only to the last. Thirsting for a broader life, he broke with the
Christian tradition of his ancestors which had acted as a brake
on their worst propensities. When he ascended the throne as
Frederick the Second in 1740, the French *philosophes* came
into their kingdom. As the patron of Voltaire, he soon became
notorious. Even Tersteegen,[10] the mystic hymn-writer of the
Ruhr, felt moved to criticize his epicurean morals and loose
deism in his *Thoughts on the Philosopher of Sans Souci*. 'Can the
Quietists in the land do this?' the King asked. Yet he respected
Reformed princes and pastors who had the courage of their
convictions, unlike the more sycophantic Lutherans. Frederick
admired the attitude of Prince Charles of Hesse, who dined with
him daily: 'Now God be praised, I have lived to see one honest
man acknowledge Christ to the King's face.' He respected Dr.
Sack, the Court preacher, a man of human sympathies and
broad culture, who did not hesitate to criticize royal views
in his *Defence of Christianity* (1751).

The bad example of Frederick the Second did not unduly
alarm Europe from a military point of view. It *did* encourage
adventurers like Baron Pöllnitz, 'a regular Proteus', who
changed his religion six times; he served Prussia, the Pope, the
Emperor, the King of Spain; he was Canon of Cambrai,
gambler, spy, and news-monger.[11]

On the other hand, Frederick's scepticism made Prussia a
pioneer of toleration. Carlyle's hero offered complete freedom
to proscribed sects from bibliolatrist Mennonites to rationalistic
Socinians. After conquering Silesia, he insisted that Breslau
University (fanatically Romanist) should admit students
irrespective of creed. On the other hand, he forbade the
publication of a Bull issued by a progressive Pope against the
Jesuits because he valued their educational work. 'All religions
are equally good,' he maintained, 'if only the people who profess
them are honest; and if Turks and heathen came to Prussia and
were willing to populate the land, we would build mosques and
temples. . . . False religious zeal is a tyrant that depopulates
provinces; toleration is a kind mother that cherishes and
advances their property.'

The Prussian 'Land Law' of 1794 (*Allgemeines Landrecht*)
was the work of Frederick the Second, though published

[10] See p. 98f., *supra*.

[11] W. D. Robson-Scott, article on Pöllnitz, *German Life and Letters*, periodical,
No. 4 (1937).

after his death. It was a consolidation of the entire edifice of public and private law. The section dealing with Churches, their rights and obligations (Part II, xi) has been described as 'the most perfect expression of the collegio-territorial system then prevailing'. The ideal of the period was enlightened paternalism. The *Landrecht* was characteristically Frederickian in safeguarding the rights of conscience. No religious society was permitted to exclude its members 'for mere opinion deviating from the common confession of faith', provided that there was no occasion of scandal or interruption of worship. 'In all cases of dispute the decision rests with the State.' This conception expressed the ideals of the Enlightenment working through the existing channels of the Territorial System. It ran counter, however, to the very idea of a Church as a community united by a common creed. If Frederick the Second's 'Land Law' promoted toleration it also fostered casuistry. It invested many a preacher of Reason with the philosopher's *pallium* of State protection.

Prussian administration of the Enlightenment period treated the clergy as minor officials. They had instructions to enforce royal edicts, e.g. *re* extirpation of locusts, stopping post-boys on byroads, etc. In 1802 no less than forty-five such secular edicts were read from the pulpits of Brandenburg province. Spalding's two volumes *On the Usefulness of the Ministerial Office in the Country* had a wide circulation. The emphasis of the age was all on utility. Becker's popular handbook (*Noth-und-Hilfsbüchlein*) made it clear that 'man's chief end' was to be found in the career of his model husbandman:

> William Thinker is here entombed.
> While on earth his endeavour was
> To improve himself and everything.
> He now receives his reward before God's throne.

We have already noticed, in dealing with the religion of the Enlightenment, how its hard common sense drove imaginative people to mystical cults. Freemasonry[12] was patronized by Frederick the Second and eminent men in various walks of life. It was strange that rationalists who claimed to be emancipated from dogmas and rites should have revelled in the spurious symbolism of black chambers, grotesque vestments, fearful oaths, etc. The appetite for symbolism, when starved,

---

[12] The establishment of the Grand Lodge in London (1717) led to the first German Lodge at Hamburg (1733). Thereafter it spread rapidly.

is apt to turn to esoteric lore and mysterious orders (e.g. the
'Elks' and 'Kiwanis' of the United States). Those who fail to
find satisfaction in substitutes for religion sometimes turn back
to a hard orthodoxy. The strange fruit they have eaten in the
wilderness spoils their palate for the enjoyment of wholesome
fare. Such a person was Wöllner, who was to reverse much that
had been fashionable during the reign of Frederick the Great.

Frederick William the Second, who ascended the throne in
1786, was under the domination of Johann Wöllner, described
by Frederick the Second as a 'treacherous and intriguing
parson'. A poor tutor, he had married the daughter of a noble
patron, much to the scandal of the nobility. A plausible writer
as well as an ambitious schemer, Wöllner won a reputation
first as a Freemason and then as a Rosicrucian who dabbled
in alchemy and mystic arts. He had a flair for organization and
soon found himself *Oberhauptdirektor* of twenty-six 'circles' which
included in their membership officers, noblemen, and officials
of high rank. As a personal friend of the King while he was
Crown Prince, Wöllner enmeshed him in a web of mystery and
intrigue, condoning and furthering his immoral conduct.
Writing to a fellow-Rosicrucian, he declared that 'as an unworthy instrument in the hand of Ormesus' (the Prince's
Rosicrucian title) he might 'save millions of souls from per-
dition and bring back the whole country to the faith of Jesus
Christ'.

At the beginning of the new reign Wöllner was Premier in
all but name. Within two years he had attained his ambition
and in spite of strong opposition was entrusted with the portfolio
of Ecclesiastical Affairs (both Evangelical and Catholic). The
King was prepared to give him *carte blanche*, so long as he was
ready to shelter his private life from public inquiry.

No time was lost in declaring war on the 'enlighteners'
(*Aufklärer*)—'modernists' we would call them. The reign of
Voltaire was over in Prussia. By the famous *Edict* of 9th July
1788 pastors were ordered to preach according to the Confessional Standards; Biblical Criticism was banned; schools
were subjected to the control of orthodox clergy; strict censorship of books was imposed; rigorous tests were applied to all
academic and ecclesiastical appointments; Socinians, Deists, and
other rationalistic sects were forbidden to hold conventicles.

This order was issued by royal authority without any
attempt to consult the clergy. Even those who had no sympathy

with rationalism were struck by 'the crying contrast between the austerity of the *Edict* with its half pedantic and half unctuous tone and the immorality of the prince whose name it bore'. Here was a characteristic product of what H. von Schubert has called 'that deplorable growth, a Court theology'. Kant's *Religion within the Limits of Reason Alone* was banned by the government in Berlin and had to be published at Königsberg (with the consent of the Theological Faculty there). Kant, then at the height of his reputation, received a message of personal displeasure from the King, who exacted a pledge from him not to write or lecture on religion. He was only freed from this limitation at the death of Frederick William the Second in 1797, but enforced compliance had a most adverse effect on his spirits.

The immediate effects of Wöllner's *Edict* were disappointing from his own point of view. A Commission was appointed to enforce these regulations, to reward the subservient and penalize the independent. The students of Halle drove them from the town. 'They say we are all-powerful,' complained a member of the Commission, 'but we have not been able to depose a single preacher of the new doctrine—everything works against us.' As for the King, his zeal outstripped even that of his favourite. He blamed Wöllner's 'idleness and vanity' for the inevitable failure of the attempt to regulate religion from above; he even deprived him of his secular appointments in 1794, so that he might have 'more time to devote himself to the things of God'. Had this obscurantism started at the worst period of the French Revolution, Frederick William, like William Pitt, could have counted on public reaction against a rationalism that culminated in the execution of a King and the persecution of a Church. Wöllner's *Edict*, however, was issued a year before the Revolution broke out, when the spirit of reform was in the air generally. Reports were reaching Berlin concerning the disorders about to come to a head in Paris, with warnings about the pernicious effect of Voltaire's teaching in provoking discontent. In England the persuasive oratory of Burke roused public opinion to the danger of French ideas. In Germany harsh officialism was less successful. The smaller principalities followed the lead of Prussia in imposing 'compulsory religion' (as Bishop Thirlwall would have said). In the Duchy of Jülich-Berg absence from Church and Communion was punished with a fine, and if persistent, with imprisonment and even banishment. Frederick William the Second continued to publish 'recalls to religion' (backed by threats) to the end of his reign. A number of wolves donned sheep's clothing but few genuine conversions took place. Nor did the King's foreign policy reflect credit on the régime. Partnership with the plunderers of Poland led to Prussia's isolation and ultimately to her overthrow by Napoleon in 1806. Earnest Christians attributed this disaster to the fact that officers and men had fallen away from the army piety of Frederick William the First.

Frederick William the Third, who reigned during the troubled years that stretched from 1797 to 1840, 'had all the Hohenzollern tenacity of purpose without the Hohenzollern genius for using it'. Too distrustful to delegate his responsibility to his ministers, he was too infirm of will to strike out and follow a consistent course for himself.'[13] He did not coerce systematically like his predecessors; he intrigued spasmodically. His evil genius was Altenstein, Minister for Ecclesiastical Affairs. 'It is my chief joy,' purred this sycophant, 'to have revered in your majesty the determinate instrument of Providence, whose utterances became my convictions when my own intentions led me in another direction.' Not only did the King reject the wise counsel of men like Schleiermacher, but he had no patience with any view that visualized the Church as a spiritual organism. When he ascended the throne he was confronted with Frederick the Great's 'Land Law', which Förster had described as 'the first law book since the Reformation to recognize in a large way the ecclesiastical freedom of congregations and individuals'. By insisting on his rights as *Summus Episcopus* to supervise and inspect the Church, he robbed these concessions of real significance. His Decree of 1808, against which the head Consistory vainly protested, transferred ecclesiastical affairs to the Minister of the Interior; the Church practically ceased to be an independent organism.

This fusion of powers led to the next step, a fusion of denominations. By decreeing the Union of Lutherans and Reformed in 1817, Frederick William the Third deprived the new body of creative vitality. The Reformed minority felt that the King's Erastian attitude boded ill for the presbyteries and synods, which were guaranteed equal rights with Lutheran consistories. Many Lutherans were offended because the historic title of the Prussian Church was obliterated in favour of the

---

[13] 'Frederick William the Third', *Ency. Brit.*, 11th ed.

brand new label, 'United Evangelical'. They took courage from the bold example of Klaus Harms of Kiel, a former follower of Schleiermacher, who on the three-hundredth anniversary of the Reformation, issued a manifesto of his own in imitation of Luther's historic Theses: 'Pray do not perform the marriage ceremony over the bones of Luther; for they will be roused to life by the very act—and then, woe to you!' Church Union Harms denounced as a threat to the 'Gospel teaching' of Lutheranism. This was hardly logical, for it was among Lutherans that rationalism had swept the board; the Reformed never lost their heads over 'neology'. 'Reason' was arraigned by Harms as 'the pope of our time' who 'dismisses Christ from the altar and throws God's word from the pulpit'. He prescribed a return to Confessional orthodoxy. This 'bitter medicine for weak unbelief' was rejected by the humanists of Halle who sang: 'Strew roses on the way and forget Harms.' (*Harm* being the German word for grief.) Harms, however, knew how to adapt his message to popular needs (an almost forgotten art). He combined passionate evangelism with humour and quaint fancy, blending romanticism with old Confessional lore, and using racy anecdote with striking effect. When this sturdy Holsteiner returned to the pulpit of his native Kiel in 1816, the common people heard him gladly. The university circle scorned him as 'a darkener of the light of reason, a retailer of worn-out ideas—he and his Bible and Luther!' The authorities relegated his service to the afternoon,[14] but in spite of every hindrance he won fame as the foremost pulpit orator in Northern Germany. The Tsar wanted him to settle in St. Petersburg, the King of Denmark invited him to Copenhagen, the King of Prussia offered him the post of Court preacher, vacant by the death of Schleiermacher. He preferred to remain in Kiel, which became as closely associated with his name as Kidderminster with Richard Baxter's. The picturesque personality of Harms appealed to the rising generation, and his impassioned denunciation of rationalism won many of his hearers to the 'spirit of the Reformation'.[15]

[14] This expedient failed, just as it failed in Oxford to prevent Newman from getting a good congregation. Many people gave priority to food for thought over thought for food, and missed their dinners; others changed their dinner hour.
[15] In Southern Germany Harms's 'opposite number' was Ludwig Hofacker; wherever he preached 'heads bowed like a cornfield under the sweep of the wind'. This winsome young evangelist did not mix up the Gospel and ecclesiastical politics, like Harms; he had something of the direct evangelistic appeal of Murray McCheyne, his contemporary, and like him, he burnt out in his thirtieth year.

His appeal to the 'unbroken testimony' of Lutheran conviction added to the forces that fulminated against the very idea of Lutheran-Reformed Union in the German States.

Another firebrand who caused trouble was Professor Scheibel of Breslau, Silesia. He declared his intransigent opposition to the new Liturgy of the United Church of Prussia, sponsored by the King. His objection was different from Schleiermacher's. He declared that only the Lutheran doctrine of the Lord's Supper was orthodox: the Reformed version was 'an offspring of rationalism'. Scheibel refused to listen to royal admonitions. On being suspended he compared the King to Antiochus Epiphanes; whereupon he had to flee the country, and several pastors who supported him were arrested. Colonel von Arnim, of Blücher's hussars, when ordered to prevent the dissentients from assembling, declared that he was ready to sacrifice his life, but not the lives of defenceless worshippers. Persecution aroused sympathy at home and abroad. Several congregations asked permission to emigrate. Steffens, the friend of Schleiermacher, became a High Lutheran and an advocate of Pastor Scheibel. The Crown Prince offered to mediate and the controversy ceased to blaze. But it was not till he became King that a belated recognition was conceded to these 'Old Lutherans' (1845).

Frederick William the Third denied the right of any body that claimed to be Lutheran to separate from the United Church. Förster, the apologist of the Territorial System,[16] makes out that the King's personal intervention was something new and unique in Prussia. Treitschke the historian rightly perceived that his high-handed action was by no means unprecedented; it attracted attention just because it occurred in the open light of the nineteenth century, when liberal ideas were beginning to penetrate even the darkness of Prussian paternalism.

It was foolish of the King to rouse his docile subjects by ill-treating a divine whose opinions were only of interest to a small minority of Church people. He certainly overshot the mark when he turned a firebrand into a martyr. It was hardly worth it. In 1905 the 'Old Lutherans' dissentients numbered only 51,600 members and seventy-five pastors. On the other hand, the royal persecutor provoked whole congregations to emigrate

---

[16] E. Förster, *Die Entstehung der preuss. Landeskirche . . . Friedrich Wilhelms III* (Tübingen, 1905).

to the United States. Pastor Grabau of Erfurt, deposed as an incorrigible opponent of Church Union in Prussia, sailed from Hamburg with one thousand adherents in July 1839. His 'Buffalo Synod' remained apart from the earlier German Lutherans, of Pietist extraction, and now musters half a million communicants. Another wave of ultra-Lutheran exiles left Saxony in 1845. Within a century this body, 'The Missouri Synod', has attained a membership of 1,300,000 in spite of its rigid Confessionalism, anti-scientific prejudices and isolation from other Churches. Had the German State Churches of the early nineteenth century allowed reasonable latitude to dissentients, these groups of earnest Lutherans might quite well have calmed down and remained at home.[17]

We return to Frederick William the Third and the Prussian Union of 1817. Granting that it was engineered by an autocrat, there was not much wrong with the design; its relative failure was due to secular administration and the lack of spiritual leadership within the Church. That there was a strong case for Union, not many critics denied. The torrent of rationalism had submerged most of the differences between Lutherans and Reformed which seemed so insurmountable in the seventeenth century. The reviving Christian faith of the nineteenth century must flow through wider channels than those of antiquated Confessionalism if vast areas of Germany, long sterile with stale scepticism, were to be reclaimed for the fertilizing Gospel.[18]

These convictions were widespread and opposition only crystallized after the consummation of Union. It was said that 'the movement had fallen into the King's hands as the ripe fruit of his age'. It was an act of personal courtesy when he, whose ancestors were strictly Reformed, voluntarily partook of Communion in the Lutheran Church at Potsdam. In Berlin Cathedral the Reformed Communion table was so arranged that it could be converted into a Lutheran altar,[19] and vice

[17] A. R. Wenz, *The Lutheran Church in American History* (2nd ed., Philadelphia, 1933).

[18] cf. G. Ecke, *Die ev. Landeskirchen Deutschlands im 19. Jahrhundert* (Berlin, 1903); R. Seeberg, *Die Kirche Deutschlands im 19. Jahrhundert* (Leipzig, 1903).

[19] Dr. Charles Hodge, of Princeton, in 1827, described how Prussian pastors put the wafer into the mouth of each communicant, while an acolyte stood by with a blue cloth, to catch any precious fragment that might fall. 'Very few of the Lutheran clergy retain belief in Consubstantiation and yet the ceremonies which arose out of it are almost all preserved. I felt like a stranger here' (*Life*, by A. A. Hodge, p. 127).

versa. In 1817 there seemed a fair prospect that Luther's eucharistic breach with Zwingli would be repaired after nearly three centuries of isolation.[20]

Unfortunately Frederick William the Third ruined reconciliation by unbalanced zeal. On his visit to London in 1814, he was impressed—too easily impressed—by the Church of England as an institution, 'imposing, national, conservative, and pious'. Baron Bunsen explained that his sovereign matured the very idea of a Church Union and a new Liturgy in the Palace of St. James. This royal *Liturgiker* not merely concocted a service-book, but in 1822 imposed it on the newly United Church. He had already incurred ridicule by designing personally the silk gowns and pectoral crosses for his General Superintendents and Superintendents, now honoured with the venerable titles of Archbishop and Bishop. After attending to 'man-millinery' he proceeded to compile his new Liturgy, although only one-sixteenth of the clergy, when circularized, approved of the project. Every pastor received a copy of the service-book, with peremptory orders to use it; Superintendents received crucifixes and candlesticks (idolatrous *Nehushtan* to the King's ancestors).[21] Ordination candidates were informed that preferment depended on passive obedience.

The royal mail was swollen with protests. The new *Agende* was too like the Mass; there were too many responses, too much creed-recitation; and not enough time for singing and preaching. All this the King dismissed as *Geschwätz* (idle chatter). He refused to meet deputations and prohibited all discussion. Dr. Marheineke, of Trinity Church, Berlin, was among the protesters; but he afterwards wrote a personal note retracting: 'Your Majesty knows best.' His colleague, Schleiermacher, with a dozen Berlin clergy stood firm and pointed out that the proposed Liturgy was 'defective in literary style and theology, nor was it in harmony with evangelical freedom'. Premier Altenstein followed the example of Laud in Scotland by enforcing a brand-new Service-Book. Coaxing and coercion having failed, he asked royal permission to resort to law. Afraid that Schleiermacher and his friends might be acquitted, he

[20] Another *Kelchbewegung* was initiated by the Lutheran liturgiologists, Spitta and Smend, at the end of the nineteenth century. Reverting to a Zwinglian attitude, they recommended the 'individual cup' instead of the historic chalice.

[21] Schinkel, the great architect, was directed to design 'No more central pulpits'. He had good acoustic and functional reasons for this practice, despite his Romantic sympathies. He retaliated by flanking the altar with twin pulpits, to redress his offended sense of symmetry.

terminated proceedings after the case had dragged on for a year. The offenders were informed that they were guilty of 'insolence and criminal obstinacy', but could count on His Majesty's clemency. Schleiermacher showed no sycophantic gratitude, but questioned the right of royalty to interfere with Uzzah-like presumption in matters of worship. His independent attitude received much public support and shook the King's amateurish self-confidence. His constructive pamphlet, signed *Pacificus Sincerus*, led to a more acceptable edition of the Liturgy being issued in 1829, with an appendix containing alternative rites for those who considered it too 'High'.

The good intentions of Frederick William the Third were generally admitted. He restored to the United Church the Consistories which he had discontinued in 1808. He introduced Presbyteries and Synods into the backward eastern provinces, which had hitherto ignored the layman (unless he was a State official). These representative institutions were borrowed from the Rhineland, annexed to Prussia in 1815; they reflected the Reformed tradition and the liberalizing effects of the Napoleonic occupation. The King's ardour for reconstructing the ecclesiastical constitution soon flagged, partly because he feared that self-government in the Church might lead to a demand for political reform. In any case, the cunning delay-tactics of Altenstein and the *via inertiae* of the bureaucracy would have slowed down the zeal of any Nehemiah determined to rebuild Zion.

Schleiermacher did not see eye to eye with the German Youth Movement in identifying religious and political liberty. The students who processed up the winding path to the historic Wartburg in 1817 were too inclined to make Luther-celebration a democratic demonstration, aerated by beer and illuminated by fireworks. At the *Lutherfest* Youth was in a hurry and had to learn by experience that constitutions cannot be engineered; they ought to grow, as in England. Schleiermacher was one of the few public men to realize that one fruitful condition of political liberty—an active, independent Church—was sadly wanting. In his youthful *Speeches* (1799) he had denounced Erastianism as 'the terrible head of Medusa' which turns to stone everything that looks at it. Mature experience confirmed these gloomy convictions, and he was disappointed in the results of the Prussian Church Union, imposed as it was by the King. What was the antidote to petrifaction? He would willingly have

o

given up the advantages of 'Establishment' in return for the
freedom of the American Churches. Never did he retract his
anathema of 1799: 'Away with every union between Church
and State! That remains my Cato's utterance to the end.'

The spirit of compromise weakened the Prussian Union of
1817. The *Augsburg Confession*, the *Heidelberg Catechism*, and
their derivatives were to be accepted 'so far as they are in
agreement with one another'. This consensus method was
bound to raise dust in a land where theology was a major
intellectual interest. The Union was almost as external and
tenuous a bond as its secular equivalent, the Confederation that
in 1815 linked together the German principalities, now reduced
to thirty-nine in number.

Some of the smaller States followed the example of
Prussia in uniting the Lutheran and Reformed 'Confessions'.
Such were Nassau (1817), Baden (1821), Saxe-Weimar (1827),
and Württemberg (1827). These principalities had the
advantage of modern constitutions. Elected legislatures gave
the representative principle a fair chance in Church and State,
whereas Prussia was an autocracy, without a Diet, and only an
old-world feudal *Landtag* in each province. The liberal principalities were fortunate in not having the Union forced upon
them by an over-enthusiastic ruler. Further, liturgical differences were not too formidable in certain southern states where
Lutheran services approximated to Reformed simplicity.

No union took place in principalities where the Reformed
Church was numerically negligible, e.g. Bavaria, Saxony,
Mecklenburg, and Hanover. But even where no union was
effected, the stricter Lutheran element was galvanized into
activity, and Churchmen trembled for the ark of uncontaminated Confessionalism. The spearheads of resurgent
Lutheranism were active, determined men like Löhe of
Anspach, and Kahnis the historian of Leipzig.[22] In Bavaria the
ultras, with the support of most of the theological faculty of
Erlangen, attempted to reintroduce the high altar of Tridentine
Romanism, private confession and absolution; but these
efforts were strenuously opposed in Reformation strongholds,
like Nürnberg. Sixteenth-century liturgies were resuscitated,
as containing the essentials of the Mass; Gothic was extolled as
'the true Christian style'; indeed, it was '*altdeutsch*'—an affec-
tionate expression of medieval patriotism. English Tractarians

[22] *Internal History of German Protestantism* (Edinburgh, 1856).

heard echoes of voices in the Fatherland calling for a return to 'Catholicism'. They indulged in 'wishful thinking' about the probability of Lutherans asking the Archbishop of Canterbury for 'Holy Orders' in the near future. Little did they understand the spirit of Lutheranism!

Nevertheless, there were points of contact between High Anglican and High Lutheran. Both groups idealized the seventeenth century as a golden age of theology and ritual. Both were hysterically apprehensive of rationalism, liberalism, and dissent. The German equivalent of the 'stern, unbending Tories', rejuvenated by the Oxford Movement, were jurists like Stahl and aristocrats like the von Gerlachs. They stood for 'Church and King'.

Conservative Lutheranism, nevertheless, could not have thriven merely with the support of Prussian officials and Junkers. It depended on middle-class religiosity. Thousands of devout laymen were upset by the cacophony of rival theologies and deeply concerned at the negative view of experts who were supposed to teach the Christian faith. 'Back to the Bible!' was an effective rallying cry. Well-directed publicity was needed. Dr. Hengstenberg, the Commentator, whom we have already met,[23] was well qualified to offer a way of salvation to those who craved certitude, not speculation. A self-confident and adroit religious journalist, he was not afraid to hit hard at his opponents. From 1827 till 1869 he edited the Evangelical *Kirchenzeitung*, a paper which numbered Bismarck among its founders. Hengstenberg resembled some of the Tractarians in passing through liberal and evangelical phases before feeling at home in High latitudes. He advanced from a mechanical theory of the Bible to a mechanical theory of Church and Sacraments. He would have believed in the Divine Right of Bishops (had there been any); he believed whole-heartedly in the Divine Right of Kings. Reform in Church and State was anathema to him as to the Tractarians. Hengstenberg's influence in pious circles was considerable.

The 'right wing' of the Prussian United Church called themselves 'New Lutherans', as distinct from the 'Old Lutherans' who refused to enter the Union under any circumstances. These 'New Lutherans' were thorough-going Conservatives. Realizing that they could not dominate the United Church, they endeavoured to make it federation rather than fusion. By

[23] See p. 133, *supra.*

1852, they obtained a decision that 'confessional differences' be recognized in the *Oberkirchenrath*.[24] The Prussian universities protested against the threatened dissolution of the Union,[25] and Frederick William the Fourth declared he would faithfully defend the institution which his father had been instrumental in forming.

The Union survived largely owing to support from an influential central party, opposed to reaction in Church and State. The leading personality in this group was Professor Nitzsch of Bonn. Brought up as a loyal Lutheran, he valued the Reformed tradition of freedom and progress. His outlook was synthetic, though his critics objected that his creed was the *Nitzschene* rather than the Nicene. At all events he stood for the 'consensus ideal'. Tholuck, the theologian of 'the New Life' movement, who attracted so many British and American students, was also a strong supporter of the Union. So was Rothe of Heidelberg, a progressive thinker and a specialist on the relations of Church and State. To these we must add the name of Herzog, the pioneer of the modern *Encyclopedia of Religion*. The *Unions-Theologen* included some of the best brains of the Prussian Church and could count on a large measure of intelligent lay support: they had an excellent Press.

There was a smaller 'left wing' that supported the Union. This comprised what was left of the old rationalist school, along with those who held definitely radical views in politics. They accepted the Bible broadly as the rule of faith and conduct: they rejected all other doctrinal standards as *papiernes Papst-thum* ('paper popery'). Some of these radicals hoped for a favourable opportunity to apply the American solution of a complete separation of Church and State. Schleiermacher's son-in-law, Count Schwerin, was of this opinion. As Minister of Public Worship during the Revolution of 1848, he did not have much time to put his ideals into action.

Critics of the Union might complain that it was neither 'United' nor 'Evangelical'; it was a partnership rather than a Church; its shifting foundations provided a comfortable refuge

[24] This Supreme Church Council was constituted as follows: six members registered as Lutherans, two as Reformed; Stahl declared himself a 'pure Lutheran'; Nitzsch subscribed to both Confessions.

[25] Had this actually happened, the Reformed Church would probably have asserted itself with vigour, in alliance with 'left-wing' Lutherans, and the German-Swiss Churches.

for latitudinarians. Yet it weathered the storm of 1848 and the reaction that followed. Later in the century the High Lutheran element lost their opportunity of dominating the Union or demanding its dissolution. The mediating party by that time was strong enough to prevent extremists of either right or left from disturbing the centre of gravity. A large measure of self-government was conceded and liberal evangelical counsels prevailed.

Frederick William the Fourth, who reigned from 1840 till his death in 1861, is an interesting figure to the Church historian, because he was so impressionable, so subject to the *Zeitgeist*. D. F. Strauss, the author of the *Leben Jesu*, compared him satirically to Julian the Apostate.[26] Discerning critics thought that he would have been more successful as a Professor of Fine Art than a Monarch. Unlike his ancestors he had a dreamy, sensitive temperament; if grandiloquent oratory and theorizing could have saved Church and State, Frederick William the Fourth would have qualified as saviour of society. In boyhood he was much influenced by his tutor, J. P. F. Ancillon, great grandson of the Huguenot exile who set his mark on the Prussian Church. Unfortunately, this descendant of the Huguenots had none of the clarity, straightforwardness, and independence of his ancestors. Court preacher Ancillon revelled in sugary optimism, unctuous phraseology and opportunist philosophy; he was a henchman of Metternich, the Austrian Chancellor, who held the German States on his leash.

As the Crown Prince grew up, Romanticism fused patriarchal Prussianism, orthodox Pietism, neo-Catholicism, and pan-Protestantism into a weird amalgam. Frederick William claimed kinship with all who embraced his 'old German' patriotism: yet he was *weltbürgerlich* in welcoming a Christian internationalism. He would have agreed with Meinecke's maxim that 'it is un-German to be only German' (*Weltburgertum u. Nationalstaat*). Unlike many idealists whose eyes seldom leave the field of politics, he was an ardent 'Evangelical' (as the term was understood in England). He made religion fashionable. In aristocratic circles there was much talk of 'rebirth' and 'special calls'. Generals conducted Bible classes and prayer-meetings. Among the young men deeply influenced by the revival was Bismarck. Berliners were sceptical about the

[26] *Der Romantiker auf dem Thron der Caesaren* (1847).

alliance of Pietism and patriotism, but there was a sincere strain in the movement.[27]

The King's personal friend, Baron Christian Bunsen,[28] shared his enthusiasm for a regenerated Germany, a renascence of religious art and a fresh advance of European Protestantism under Prussian leadership. The Baron was an Anglophil, and had married the daughter of a Welsh squire. While they resided in Rome from 1817 onward their home became a salon for bringing British and American visitors into touch with the nobility and intelligentsia of the Holy City. The Chevalier, first as secretary to Niebuhr the historian and later as Ambassador himself, was in a strong position. For a quarter of a century he used his influence to promote the interests of enlightened Reformation piety. Protestant expatriates who were in danger of feeling the magnetism of the Roman Church found in the Prussian Legation a counter-attraction to the 'Nazarenes', and other perverts.[29] Bunsen organized a 'Capitoline Congregation', compiled a service-book, and appointed a succession of able young chaplains, some of whom afterwards attained fame, e.g. Richard Rothe.

Bunsen and the Crown Prince (Frederick William the Fourth after 1840) had many interests in common—enthusiasm for Liturgy,[30] hymnology,[31] and church architecture, also a desire to free the Prussian Church from the dead-weight of convention and officialism that neutralized initiative and voluntary effort. Neither Frederick William the Fourth nor his father sympathized with Bunsen's chivalrous attitude to the Roman Catholic population of the Rhineland who were being harassed by the Prussian State. As a lonely Protestant in Rome, he could sympathize with members of another communion under alien rule. He realized the injustice and folly of insisting on Roman Catholic soldiers being forced to put in a statutory number of parades at Lutheran churches.

The Chevalier was in his element when he accompanied

---

[27] cf. Treitschke, *Germany in the Nineteenth Century* (E.T., 1919), Vol. VI.

[28] cf. A. L. Drummond, 'Baron Bunsen, Pioneer of Pan-Protestantism' (*Evangelical Quarterly*, January 1941).

[29] See. p. 108f., *supra*.

[30] His *Prayers* (E.T., Cath. Winkworth) had a wide circulation. To Dr. Arnold he wrote in 1834: 'I claim liberty for extempore prayers, silent prayer, and free selection from fixed prayers.' This surprised Englishmen, accustomed to rigid liturgy or its complete disuse.

[31] He was a pioneer in burrowing into a corpus of eighty thousand German hymns and extracting the honey from three hundred collections in use (*Book of Hymns*, 1833, 2nd ed., 1844).

his royal master on a visit to Queen Victoria and Prince Albert in 1842. Frederick William the Fourth expressed his delight in the English *Prayer Book*, the English weather, and all other English institutions; he also rejoiced in the company of Dr. Arnold and Thomas Carlyle. He acted as godfather to the Prince of Wales—despite the official protest of Tractarian Oxford against a Lutheran heretic being thus privileged. He was inspired by the prospect of British and German Protestantism standing shoulder to shoulder—a counter-poise to Metternich and Catholic Austria.

Setting aside the lure of imperialist adventure[32] Frederick William looked East and considered the prospects of Christian Missions in conjunction with the promotion of Prussian interests. Bunsen was sent to London with powers to negotiate a proposed Anglo-Prussian Bishopric of Jerusalem. He had no difficulty in persuading Prince Albert of the advantages of this scheme, the appointment to be made alternately by the Prussian and English Governments. Lord Shaftesbury and other students of Prophecy saw a foreshadowing of the restoration of Israel. Historically minded English Churchmen hailed it as the revival of the primitive See of St. James. Newman and Keble were shocked at the very idea of fraternizing with a hybrid non-episcopal body; opportunist Churchmen thought it a first step toward the absorption of Lutheranism by Anglicanism ('the present King of Prussia is at heart an Episcopalian'). Eventually, most opponents of the scheme recognized it as tentative and innocuous. In 1841 Bishop Alexander was consecrated; he was a native of Prussia, a Jewish Christian, but Anglican by confession. With uplifted heart a great English philanthropist recorded in his *Diary*: 'The successor of St. James will embark in October. . . . The beginning is made, please God, for the restoration of Israel.' Lord Shaftesbury's dream was as vain as Baron Bunsen's, for the joint-bishopric was abandoned when it came to the turn of German Evangelicals to nominate a prelate. Thus Anglo-Prussian *rapprochement* came to nothing. Bishop Knox thought that solid results might have been achieved, if only the Church of England had shown a genuine desire for co-operation.[33]

[32] To Bunsen's disappointment, the King rejected a Mexican offer to sell him California (1842). Anglophil as he was, the Chevalier was amazed at English unbelief in Germany's future. 'They consider themselves as still in the ark, and look down from their Mount Ararat with Pharisaic self-satisfaction' (letter to Stockmar, 1848).
[33] *The Tractarian Movement*, Chapter 17.

Bunsen resigned his office as Ambassador at St. James in 1854. The King had rejected his advice to give a lead to Nationalism in the Revolution of 1848; and he afterwards associated himself completely with the triumph of reaction. But the Chevalier and his royal master were still knights-errant of Christian unity. Frederick William the Fourth considered himself the patron of pan-Protestantism. As his Hohenzollern ancestors had welcomed the exiled Huguenots, so he would gather under his wings the scattered brood of Evangelical Christendom. The World's Evangelical Alliance (1846) was largely his idea. The breadth of the brotherhood was restricted by ultra-orthodox articles of belief, but in the early days of the movement this certainly expressed the theological position of the constituent Churches. General conferences were held at Paris, London, and Geneva. The Berlin meeting (1857) was Frederick William's greatest triumph, with Bunsen as Master of Ceremony. Lutherans, Anglicans, Presbyterians, and men of nearly every Protestant sect attended. There were Hungarians and Swiss, Frenchmen, Americans, and Scotsmen, to name only a few of the nations represented. Appeals for Protestant Unity were applauded; fulminations against 'Puseyism and Popery' were carried with acclaim, as at the 'May meetings' in Exeter Hall. For the first time in history an Anglo-Saxon, Bishop Simpson (an American Methodist), preached in the Royal Garrison Church. Bunsen presented a series of distinguished foreigners to His Majesty. The final scene, on the green sward of the New Palace at Potsdam, was characteristic of the Evangelical, ecumenical spirit of the age. The ghosts of Frederick the Great and Voltaire must have gazed bewildered, and no doubt amused. After a number of short, stirring addresses, there was a resounding cry of *Lebe hoch!*—and then sudden silence. As the King entered the portal of the palace, the Germans formed a circle and greeted him with the strains of *Ein' feste Burg*. Frederick William the Fourth could not restrain his emotion. Nor could Sir Culling Eardly, who declared with fervour: 'There is no more North Sea!' Dr. John Cairns, the most eminent Scottish representative, made a profound impression at the Berlin meeting. Ever since his student days at Berlin a quarter of a century earlier, he had kept in sympathetic touch with German thought, communicating to the British public its vital and positively Christian aspects.[34]

[34] See A. R. Macewen, *Life and Letters of John Cairns* (4th ed., 1898).

Dr. Cairns was the interpreter of Krummacher, the inspiring leader of the 1857 meeting, as well as the translator of his famous sermons on Elijah.

F. W. Krummacher (1796-1868) was one of the few masters of the German pulpit who may be compared to great Anglo-Saxon preachers like Spurgeon, Beecher, or Parker. His eloquence and homely unction, as well as his appearance, reminded Scottish hearers of Dr. Guthrie. No Lutheran, he came from vigorous Presbyterian stock. When Krummacher went to his first parish at Ruhrort in 1825 he was welcomed with flags and the firing of guns. On being promoted to a charge near Barmen he was met by 'a procession of splendid carriages and stately horsemen'. This was the Reformed reception of a preacher as 'an ambassador for Christ'. Krummacher could say, like Paul: 'Wherever I go, thank God, He makes my life a constant pageant of triumph in Christ.' Krummacher fulfilled the promise of his youth. In Trinity Church, Berlin (empty since Schleiermacher's death), people of all classes stood in queues to gain admittance—a rare phenomenon in a city notorious for the reputation of being a spiritual cemetery. 'He that receiveth a prophet . . . shall receive a prophet's reward.' Those who heard Krummacher had their reward. They might not agree with his fulminations against ritualism, rationalism, and secularism; but they recognized in him a prince of the pulpit who possessed a secret rare in German preaching; he was a superb word-painter, who brought to life Bible characters with wonderful dramatic power. It was a striking tribute to his personality that Frederick William the Fourth called to the Court Church of Potsdam a preacher so independent, Evangelical, and outspoken.[35]

The promotion of Krummacher shows the King in a more attractive light than as an autocrat whose one ambition was to impose his own will on the Church. Professor H. Geffcken, writing with authentic royal papers before him, dismissed as 'a baseless rumour' the allegation that he intended to introduce 'Apostolic Succession' *via* England or Sweden.[36] He credited him with the sincere intention of renouncing State sovereignty

---

[35] His illuminating *Autobiography* (E.T., Edinburgh, 1869) unfortunately was broken off in 1848.

[36] *Church and State* (E.T. 1877) Vol. II, pp. 182-5. Geffcken's estimate of the King is rather too favourable, but Richter also made copious extracts from the royal essays in his standard work, *Friedrich-Wilhelm IV u. die Verfassung der ev. Kirche* (Berlin, 1861).

over the Church. Far from sharing Hegel's theory that the Church was merely the inner side of the State, he earnestly desired to restore the spiritual independence of the body of Christ. The Sovereign's right as *summus episcopus* he denounced as 'abnormal and irregular . . . the cause of German defence-lessness against Romanist pretension' and popular mistrust. 'It would be a glorious day for the Fatherland if the German Church of the Gospel were to stand on her own feet . . . and not at the feet of forty sovereigns.'

'*Nolo episcopari!*' With all his soul and strength Frederick William the Fourth renounced 'the hateful episcopacy of the territorial sovereign' (his Hohenzollern ancestors would turn in their graves at this apostasy). His one aim was 'to resign the Church supremacy into the proper hands'. The difficulty was, where could he find the proper hands? He resented the criticism of his father's advisers. He was afraid of his voluntarily surrendered powers falling into the hands of a brand new Presbyterian régime, in alliance with political democracy. Episcopacy was unacceptable to the King, for it had served as the 'basis of the Romish Church of the sixteenth century . . . certainly unevangelical and desperately unapostolic'.

A synthetic scheme was ultimately approved—of some interest in view of modern attempts to blend Presbyterian and Episcopal polity in South India and the United States. Deacons and elders were to be appointed in each congregation. The District Synod (*Kirchenkreis*) was no longer to be subject to a royal Superintendent; its moderator was to be a Bishop. Bishops were to receive their commission from the Church collectively and were to exercise their jurisdiction in a constitutional spirit in co-operation with the clergy of their diocese.

The new order was to be dramatically inaugurated by the King in the presence of the Archbishops of Canterbury and Uppsala. His Majesty was to deliver the crozier to the royal commissioner, who was to hand it over to the presiding Bishop; he would pass it on to elders, and deacons; the oldest deacon would present it to the oldest pastor, who would return it to the Bishop. The grand climax would be the installation of the crozier next the crucifix on the high altar—a symbol of the Church seeking the protection of the Cross.

This spectacular ceremony never took place. The medie-valism of the visionary on the throne was mistrusted by both progressives and conservatives. The former wanted reform, but not along 'hierarchical lines'; the idea of a Hohenzollern as the Church's liberator seemed too good to be true. The latter were satisfied with the existing constitution as 'national and necessary, essentially Lutheran'. The Consistorial party 'did not wish to patch up the old garment, but only to brush it; but the brushing of old garments profited the holes better than the cloth'. To entrust ecclesiastical power to the delegates of conflicting parties would be a remedy worse than the disease. So argued the conservatives, entrenched in the higher ecclesiastical bureaucracy. The King was not a man of action and his schemes, unwelcome to reformer and reactionary alike, proved abortive.

Baron Bunsen had encouraged Frederick William the Fourth in some of his visionary schemes, including the ideal of 'a Free Church in a Free State'. Bunsen had already determined to his own satisfaction the constitution of 'The Church of the Future'. The Revolution of 1848 seemed to present a heaven-sent opportunity of realizing these ideals. In France, Switzerland, and Germany a number of Protestants thought that the time had come for spiritual emancipation. A Revolution offered a speedier (and less sacrificial) method of achieving a Free Church than the Disruption of 1843 had just shown in Scotland.[37]

When the Revolution of 1848 broke out, the first German Parliament assembled in the great oval church of St. Paul, Frankfurt-on-Main. Veterans of the War of Liberation, fighters for political freedom like 'Father Jahn', were confident that their cause was now triumphant. A 'Declaration of Rights' was to clear the way for a new ecclesiastical constitution. It looked as if the old 'Territorialism' and 'orthodoxism' had gone, never to return. Karl von Hase, the Liberal historian,[38] presented to Parliament 'the Evangelical Protestant Church of the German *Reich*', ready even to the very house where the Imperial Synod was to meet. There was considerable support for a 'People's Church'. This implied—complete self-government, the abolition of lay patronage, and the security

[37] The King actually sent his Court Chaplain, Dr. Adolf Sadow, to report on the Disruption. Sadow's *Scottish Church Question* (1845) was welcomed by the Free Church of Scotland.

[38] Well known later as an able Protestant apologist. His *Handbook to the Controversy with Rome* (1862) was translated into English (Religious Tract Society, 1906, 2 vols.).

of rightful ecclesiastical property. The separation of Church and State was formally decreed as a means of releasing spiritual life from temporal domination; unfortunately, there were good grounds for concluding that a considerable number of deputies wanted to emancipate the German people from national profession of the Christian faith. The Frankfurt Parliament claimed to regenerate Germany, but declined to open its meetings with prayer, even though they were held in a church. An omen of failure!

In Ewald's graphic phrase: '1848 was Germany's shipwreck year.' The dreams of the Frankfurt doctrinaires melted into air when the Revolution was crushed by Austria. Frederick William the Fourth, offered the imperial throne by the Federal Assembly, had scornfully refused 'to pick up a crown out of the gutter'. Pride inspired this gesture, but the conduct of the Prussian King was subsequently ignoble and pusillanimous. 'Who knoweth whether thou art come to the kingdom for such a time as this?' The opportunity of leadership was rejected; 'enlargement and deliverance' would have to arise for the Germans 'from another place' and at a later time. The policy of Metternich triumphed. The German princes thankfully abolished the liberal constitutions forced upon them by the reformers. Ecclesiastical affairs also returned to the *status quo*. Theological liberalism, now discredited, was thrown back on such alliance as it could make with the remnants of political liberalism. There seemed no destiny for Prussia, save as Austria's deputy. The only constitution was a conservative grouping of nobles, peasants, and burghers round the throne, backed by an obedient army and a subservient Church. The Evangelical *Kreuz-Zeitung* accepted the humiliation of the Protestant power and the hegemony of ultramontanism as the only possible policy:

> Austria and Prussia hand in hand,
> Germany else must helpless stand.

The failure of Frederick William the Fourth to realize his theocratic ideals placed a lever in the hands of Dr. Stahl and General Gerlach; the Church was just an instrument to prevent reform of any kind. A political cleric, Provost Gelbsattel, organized the *Treubund* on semi-masonic lines, with a 'home appeal' and a 'girls' section'—skilful propaganda in the cause of reaction. Even religious education became a weapon in the hands of the governing class.[39] In this 'day of small things' the frustrated idealist on the throne indulged in a few pathetic outbursts of activity without achieving results worth mentioning. Heine's ironic lines sketch his futile course:

> I am not bad, I am not good,
> Not foolish and not clever;
> If yesterday I forward went,
> Today I backward travel!

Frederick William the Fourth became insane in 1858. He was succeeded by his brother, a man of action. William the First's annexation of the Schleswig-Holstein duchies in 1864 gave him 'a taste for conquest' (as Bismarck put it). Far from going helplessly 'hand in hand' with Austria, he returned in triumph to Berlin after a brief campaign culminating at Sadowa (1866). The virtual annexation of the northern principalities soon followed the Prussian victory. Would the Churches of Hanover, Hesse, and Nassau be absorbed into the Prussian United Church? The Union of 1817 had not been devised with such an enlarged Prussia in view. The immediate incorporation of other *Landeskirchen* in the Prussian United Church would have obvious disadvantages. Some kind of ecclesiastical equivalent to the 'North German Confederation' seemed preferable; the Prussian Minister of Ecclesiastical Affairs would in course of time be able to influence the affairs of the smaller churches, and so 'adjust confessional differences'.

While Prussia was pursuing the path of autocratic imperialism that culminated in the Reich of 1871, most of the princes found that it paid to carry out the orders of William the First. The South German States did not relish this idea (*'travailler pour le roi de Prusse'*, in the eighteenth-century phrase). They preferred Isaiah's prophecy that 'the liberal deviseth liberal things and by liberal things shall he stand'. Among the 'liberal things' devised in Baden was an ecclesiastical constitution that applied the ideas of political democracy to the Church. The Baden Protestant acquired full privileges of Church membership by the mere fact of residence in a parish, apart from baptism and confirmation. The Church Councils and the clergy were popularly elected—but not on the basis of spiritual qualifications having unquestioned priority. Education was

[39] Luther's *Little Catechism*, like the English *Church Catechism*, inculcated social subordination—obedience to 'governors, pastors, and masters . . . and all my betters'. The Prussian governing class were naturally good Lutherans as their 'opposite numbers' were good Anglicans. *Obrigkeit* was the watchword of Establishment.

secularized. Dogma was minimized. Professor Geffcken has pointed out that this Constitution of 1861 was popular with political Liberals and theological liberals (of the *Protestantenverein* type).[40] It did not make the Church particularly popular with the people, however, or strong in evangelism; one instance of its lack of vitality was the decrease of theological students at Heidelberg (now in Baden) from 110 in 1863 to nine in 1875.[41]

Baden, the ecclesiastical model for Liberals, was naturally not copied in essentials when the Prussian United Church was given a new constitution in 1876, incorporating the reforms of 1860 and 1873.[42] Confirmation as well as baptism, and the signing of a declaration of loyalty to the principles of the Church were necessary qualifications for laymen elected to serve on ecclesiastical councils. Nevertheless, the Baden system was adopted in so far as it was 'representational' rather than Presbyterian. The lay deputies were elected on a basis of population and by 'proportional representation': they were delegates, not elders, who had been solemnly ordained in their respective congregations. From the *Gemeinde* (parish) to the *Bezirk* (district) and the *Kreis* (literally 'circle'—province) there was an ascending scale of councils resembling sessions, presbyteries, and synods. But these elective bodies were not 'courts of the Church' in the Presbyterian sense, for Superintendents and General Superintendents were set over them with more than the power of a permanent Moderator.[43] A Supreme Ecclesiastical Council (*Oberkirchenrath*) was superimposed, with the Minister of Church Affairs in control. The edifice was crowned by a royal pinnacle, for the King retained his traditional headship as *summus episcopus*.

Here was the old Prussian model, with a few modern improvements ostentatiously added, to convey the impression that the architect was moving with the times. There was certainly an improvement in efficiency, exemplified by an overdue increase in clerical stipends and pensions. By 1911 the Prussian Union Church was regulated by twenty-four General Superintendents and 639 Superintendents; there were 9,390 parishes —about half the total number of Protestant charges in Germany. Certain civil provinces of Prussia that had been

---

[40] cf. p. 104*n.*, *infra*.　　　　　[41] *Church and State* (1877), Vol. II, pp. 391-4.

[42] Bismarck gleaned ideas from a report published at his request in German at Berlin and in English at Boston: *Church and State in the United States* (1873), by Dr. J. P. Thompson.

[43] This is illuminating in view of the recent attempt to restore 'Superintendents' in the Church of Scotland—a proposal defeated by a large majority of presbyteries.

absorbed by Prussia (e.g. Schleswig-Holstein, 1864; Hanover, 1866) retained their separate *Landeskirchen*. The Prussian Church, however, extending from Danzig to the Rhineland, was the most important Evangelical body with its twenty million members (a good show on paper). Over-centralization was avoided by devolution. Each of the nine ecclesiastical provinces had an executive council (*Konsistorium*); a lawyer was usually president and a pastor vice-president. An elected assembly (*Provinzialsynode*) also functioned, but the effective part of the machinery was bureaucratic, not conciliar. As each of the twenty-four General Superintendents had a diocese of nearly a million tax-paying Church members, their areas were subdivided into smaller districts, administered by Super-intendents who were known in some parts of North Germany as 'Provost' (*Propst*, as in Scandinavia) and in the South as 'Dean' (*Dekan*). These pivotal persons were charged with the supervision of clergy and congregations.

In Kressman Taylor's *Until that Day* (1945) we read of 'the Pontifex Maximus of the Lutheran Church, who was the Kaiser himself'. This title belongs to the Pope alone, but the Emperor William the Second considered himself a kind of Evangelical Pope, the real head of Continental Protestantism (a role to which Frederick William the Fourth aspired). We need not be surprised that the 'War Lord' considered himself as much more than 'the most eminent member of the Evangelical Church'. As *summus episcopus* he interfered in theological controversies, ecclesiastical affairs, and issues raised by the Christian Socialists. He could say Amen to the convictions voiced by Bismarck at the end of his career: 'We Germans fear God and nothing else in the world.' William the Second inherited from Frederick William the Fourth a pronounced bias to swelling rhetoric and self-dramatization. He even conducted services. *Punch* depicted the robed 'war lord' offering an invocation at an eagle-lectern: 'Let us prey!' This was on the occasion of the Kaiser's invasion of neutral Belgium in 1914.[44] One has to read between the lines in noting the cool, objective statement of the historian: 'He exercised his office as *summus episcopus* more freely than most of his predecessors.'[45]

[44] The German war-effort (1914) won frenzied support from clerical and academic quarters. This was objectively analysed by a Danish theological professor, an admirer of true German culture, J. P. Bang, *Hurrah and Hallelujah* (London 1915 and 1917).

[45] *Ency. Brit.*, 11th ed., Article on 'Establishment'.

CHAPTER THREE

THE 'SOCIAL GOSPEL' AND THE PEOPLE

WHEN revolutionary fury was at its height in September 1848 a movement of national regeneration was inaugurated in Wittenberg at Luther's grave. The leader was Dr. J. H. Wichern of Hamburg (1808-81). A pupil of Schleiermacher and Tholuck, he preached 'The Religion of the New Life'. Every tract of German thought and activity must be regenerated. The laity must be roused from their traditional apathy. The *Landeskirchen* must become the *Volkskirchen*, exchanging the folded hands of passive 'particularism' for the clasped hands of active fellowship. Voluntary effort might yet promote what centuries of State initiative had failed to achieve—the restoration of confidence between Church and people.

When Luther lost faith in the plain man, terrified by the prospect of social revolution, he yielded to the State far more than the medieval Church had conceded. 'The powers that be are ordained of God.' This authoritarian interpretation of Paul's principle (*Obrigkeit*) was systematized in orthodox Lutheran tradition as 'Ordinology'. A division of functions regulated the relations between Church and State. This dualism was developed to suit the interests of German princes, whose chief aim was the preservation of power sacred and secular. As regards trade and industry, however, medieval ideas of 'just price' and occupational status still prevailed. Luther's social theory was thoroughly conservative. He accepted the hierarchical pattern of society; he only kicked away the sacerdotal rungs in the ladder. His Pauline principle of *Beruf* (*vocatio*) hallowed work as a task set by God: 'Let every man abide in the same calling wherein he was called.' Luther's opposition to usury was quite medieval; a favourite text was Ecclesiasticus 11[20f]: 'There is he that waxeth rich by his wariness and pinching, and this is the portion of his reward . . . he shall leave (his goods) to others and die.' Modern Romantist historians like Jansen[1] have criticized with some justice the effect of the

---

[1] *History of the German People after . . . the Middle Ages* (E.T., 1910); cf. Gooch, *History and Historians in the Nineteenth Century*, pp. 562-5.

Reformation on Christian philanthropy, but they go far from facts when they make wholesale accusations against Protestantism of being responsible for the growth of Capitalism. The 'capitalist spirit' flourished in fifteenth-century Venice, in Catholic Flanders, and in Southern Germany (the Fuggers of Augsburg were supporters of the Counter-Reformation, as well as pioneers of modern capitalism). In our own days Max Weber had attributed the individualistic attitude to English Puritanism, not to Lutheranism.[2] Lutheranism took over, almost unchanged, the pre-Reformation idea of a 'Church-civilization' that regulated commerce and industry, as well as social life, in accordance with a traditional Christian conception of the law of God.

This traditional ethic was suited to the needs of a static society, but its days were numbered by the early nineteenth century. Economic change was heralded by the introduction of modern administration when Napoleon conquered the Rhineland; and the War of Independence precipitated reform even in Prussia, when Baron Stein improved the status of the peasantry.

Nevertheless, for many years after 1815 the economic structure of Germany was backward (Karl Marx in 1843 compared it to that of France in 1789). The entire urban population of the Fatherland in 1815 was less than that of Paris. There were no industries in the modern sense, only handicrafts; trade was hindered by archaic regulations, and the old burgher spirit of the 'free cities of the Empire' had decayed. Social life retained many medieval traits, such as minute class stratification and the maintenance of town walls.[3] During the quiet years between 1815 and 1848 academic and professional opinion became vocal in two-chamber legislatures, established in the more liberal States, in imitation of the French *Charte*. The rise of a prosperous commercial class is registered by Freitag's famous novel; *Soll und Haben* (1850) proclaims the superiority of the 'Christian' merchant over the impecunious

---

[2] *Protestant Ethic and the Spirit of Capitalism* (London, 1930).

[3] Sarah Austin, *Germany 1760-1814* (London, 1854). She mentioned the case of two travellers at Eisenach, surprised to hear outside the inn, a choir of black-cloaked scholars. Was it a festival? The waiter explained: 'It is an ancient traditional institution established by Dr. Luther (*eine alte her-kömmliche Anstalt, von Dr. Martinus eingerichtet*). We give two and a half Thalers a year, and for that the poor scholars must sing twice a week and for that they receive their learning (*und dafür bekommen sie ihre Studia*).' No English translation could do justice to this naïve, yet pedantic formula.

P

aristocrat.[4] The shape of things to come was foreshadowed by
the first railway in Germany which in 1835 linked medieval
Nürnberg with the manufacturing town of Fürth.[5] The signs
of the times indicated change.

In 1846 an anonymous book attracted considerable
attention, *German Protestantism, its Past History and its Present
Life-Questions*. This timely survey came from Professor Hundeshagen, a Hessian, who made Zurich his observation-post, to
escape the censor. Hundeshagen was convinced that the social
and spiritual life of the Fatherland had been stifled by political
repression, and nothing short of a Revolution could clear the
air. When this book reached its third edition (1850) the
Revolution had come and gone, leaving wreckage all over the
Continent. Reaction was triumphant in Germany. Political
refugees swarmed over to America, about a quarter of a million
a year. Idealism in universities gave way to crude materialism.
Education was throttled by reaction. The middle and upper
classes, frightened by the Revolution, rallied to Throne and
Altar. The Lutheran clergy resumed their role as supporters of
reaction and social subordination. Teachers, civil servants,
tradesmen, and employees discovered that 'it paid to be pious'.
It is not surprising that anti-clericalism, hitherto associated with
Roman Catholic countries, made itself felt between 1850 and
1871.[6] The working classes were apt to regard the clergy as
'the black police'.

During these fateful years Dr. Wichern provided the driving
power for a redemptive Social Gospel. By avoiding political
issues he was able to gather a team that included such different
types as Stahl, the orthodox Lutheran jurist, Nitzsch, the
'mediating' Lutheran divine, and Krummacher, the popular
Reformed preacher. It was agreed that the interest and
enthusiasm of the laity must be roused by the free discussions of
the practical social problems that confronted Germany. A
Church Congress (*Kirchentag*) was organized to carry the
message of social redemption throughout the Fatherland. The
Kirchentag met in different cities every year between 1848 and
1871. The secret of its success was largely due to the fact that

[4] E. Kohn-Bramstedt, *Aristocracy and the Middle Classes in Germany 1830-1900*
(London, 1937).

[5] J. H. Clapham, *The Economic Development of France and Germany, 1815-1914*;
A. J. P. Taylor, *The Course of German History . . . Since 1815*.

[6] See collected articles by the Rev. John Hunt, D.D., Special Correspondent of
The Times in Berlin, *Religious Thought in Germany* (London, 1870).

it was voluntary and not official. At the Lübeck meeting in 1856 the French and Dutch Reformed sent delegates, as well as the Irish Presbyterians and the Free Church of Scotland. Here we find the adumbration of a modern 'Life and Work' conference.

The main purpose of the *Kirchentag* was to focus attention on the spiritual regeneration of the German people. At every meeting Wichern gained more support and gave a fresh impulse to his scheme of 'The Inner Mission'. The purpose was much wider than the title suggests, if it be translated 'Home Missions'. It was a widespread organization, with innumerable activities, for applying Christianity to social and industrial life. It developed out of small beginnings. As a young man, Wichern started a school for vagrant lads in the village of Horn, three miles from Hamburg (1833). The neglected human material and the broken-down farmhouse that was to shelter and fashion it suggested the appropriate title of *Rauhes Haus* ('Rough House' or 'Austere House'). But it was not long before English visitors called it 'The House among the Flowers'. An orderly community life was organized on the farm, in the garden and in workshops for spinning, tailoring, and printing. The lads were grouped in 'families' of twelve, under theological students trained by Wichern. He was successful with youths of the most desperate character, for he realized far more than any reformer of his day the power for evil of a demoralizing environment. He made a special study of social problems in great cities, visiting Paris and London as well as Hamburg and Berlin. Through the publicity of the *Kirchentag*, infant schools and nurseries, reformatories, homes, and asylums were built. Sunday-schools, savings-banks, and Y.M.C.A's. were founded. Efforts were made to give ex-prisoners a fresh start, and to provide lodgings for vagrants.

Wichern's work was inspired by the ringing text: 'This is the victory that overcometh the world, even our faith.' He was one of the great Christian philanthropists of history, worthy of being classed with Vincent de Paul, August Francke, William Wilberforce, and Thomas Chalmers. Yet the *Encyclopaedia Britannica* does not even mention his name in the index of the fine 11th edition! To find an adequate account of his life we would have to turn to German biographies by Oldenburg (1884) and Wernle (1908).

Wichern's work was anticipated as regards women by

Pastor Fliedner, who founded his Order of Deaconesses in 1883, fourteen years before Miss Sellon started her Anglican Sisterhood. In the 1820's Fliedner had come into touch with Elizabeth Fry, who visited Germany on her prison-investigation tours. She roused in him an earnest desire to improve the condition of jails and to promote the welfare of convicts. Another Englishwoman, Catherine Winkworth, has told the story of his life (London 1867). One night a woman appeared at his parsonage at Kaiserswerth, near Düsseldorf; she was a discharged prisoner, but had nowhere to go. As he improvised a refuge for her on the roof of his summer-house, he determined to do his utmost for all unfortunates who needed a fresh start in life. First, out of his poverty, Fliedner formed a home for discharged prisoners. Then, as some of the female prisoners had children, he took up Oberlin's idea of an infant school, which Robert Owen had popularized in Great Britain; and as there were no teachers ready for this work, he added a normal school for training them.

The need for hospitals and nurses soon attracted Fliedner's attention. In 1836 he acquired the largest house in Kaiserswerth (despite his lack of funds) and opened it, with one deaconess and one patient. Some years later an English girl presented herself at the institution, explaining that she had come on the advice of Elizabeth Fry, and wanted to learn nursing. Dissatisfied with a life of leisure, she had slipped away from her mother and sisters, who were taking the waters at Carlsbad. Florence Nightingale found herself among rough, peasant women. 'The nursing was *nil*,' she wrote, 'the hygiene horrible.' She took the training, nevertheless, 'for there was none to be had in England'. She discovered something that excelled efficiency; 'Never have I met with a higher love, a purer devotion than there.' Her experience at Kaiserswerth 'formed the foundation of all her future action', says Lytton Strachey.

Pastor Fliedner's hospital outgrew its primitive beginnings. Like the mustard-seed, Kaiserswerth grew and flourished. At his death in 1864, Deaconess Institutions had increased a hundredfold. The movement spread like a network all over Germany. Even in 'Catholic Bavaria' Evangelical philanthropy radiated in all directions from its centre at Neuendettelsau, where Pastor Löhe, preacher and liturgiologist, had founded his school for training Deaconesses (1840). By the end of the nineteenth century the German Protestant Churches had nearly eight thousand workers in hospitals, homes for unfortunate women, almshouses, schools, and parishes.[7]

The relief of poverty was a subject that engaged the sympathetic attention of active Christians in Germany, who had heard of the work of Dr. Chalmers in Glasgow. In 1852 a town councillor of Elberfeld, named Daniel von der Heydt, was reading his Bible; impressed with Jethro's advice that Moses should delegate his authority to assistants, he applied this idea to the problem of poverty. Voluntary helpers were to be assigned the task of visiting a group of poor families and taking an interest in their welfare. Neighbourly supervision, inspired by Christian kindness, was a contrast to impersonal, official routine. This carefully graded method, co-operating with the public authorities, was adopted by many cities and was particularly successful in Elberfeld and Leipzig. Self-respect and good citizenship were thus promoted.

Pioneer work in treating nervous disorders was undertaken by Pastor von Bodelschwing at Bielefeld in Westphalia (1872). A modest institute, a 'Bethel' for epileptics, expanded into a series of settlements covering a whole valley. Vocational training was provided for people of all types—agriculture, gardening, domestic, clerical work, etc. Epileptics were grouped in 'families'—a novel experiment in Christian living. The object was to give a fresh start in life to folk who had lost (or never possessed) their proper place in the economic order. Von Bodelschwing was spared to see the fruition of his life-work, for he lived till 1910. His son's refusal to admit Nazi 'mercy-killers' sent to 'eliminate' the cripples, epileptics, and lunatics under his care, is an act inscribed in the annals of humanity.

The opening of new callings to women, under the Inner Mission as nurses, teachers, and church workers, led to the question: Could not something be done by men for men in the cause of Christ? One aspect of this work lay in the field of social service. In the middle of the nineteenth century Germany was much less industrialized than England. Innumerable journeymen still travelled up and down the land in search of work. It was a happy thought of Professor Perthes to initiate

[7] The institutions of the 'Inner Mission' were transplanted to the United States for the welfare of German immigrants, and in course of time were copied by the more individualistic Anglo-Saxon Churches—a contribution to the 'Social Gospel', erroneously attributed to American initiative alone.

the erection of rest-houses for these travelling artisans, where they could be assured of comfortable lodging and a Christian atmosphere (1854). Two years later the *Kirchentag* revived the Scriptural diaconate. Since the Reformation Reformed congregations had elected deacons, but the Lutherans had still, generally speaking, to learn the spiritual necessity of releasing the lay forces of Christianity. The gulf between pastor and people should be bridged by enrolling laymen, as a corps of active church workers and eager evangelists. In 1843 a 'Pastoral Aid Society' was founded by Otto von Gerlach, whose evangelistic zeal was oddly offset by his reactionary politics. This Society grappled with the problem of Church Extension, using English experience as a comparative background. In Germany conditions differed vastly from state to state. In the Lower Rhine and Württemberg the healthier tradition of Pietism prevailed; religion was personal and real. In Hesse and the Palatinate the Reformed tradition of lay activity persisted. Wherever Evangelicals had to reckon with Roman Catholic rivalry, they showed signs of life; but wherever Lutheranism was dominant, e.g. the east and north, the laity were passive and the Church's witness weak (a good illustration of Arnold Toynbee's law that vitality demands a certain amount of struggle against circumstances, provided they are not too adverse). Hanover was conventionally respectful to official religion, Brandenburg was '*Kirchlich*', and Mecklenburg was both orthodox and 'hierarchical'. The 'inside of the cup' was less promising. These states had a bad record for immorality. East Prussia and Saxony were under the control of a deeply rooted High Lutheranism, but the churches were poorly attended and congregational life was at a low ebb.

During the second half of the nineteenth century the growth of the industrial population outran all efforts to meet their spiritual need. Times had changed since the days of the celebrated Pastor Winckler of Hamburg. In 1688 Winckler asked if he was the true pastor of 30,000 souls. The University replied gravely that Jonah had 120,000 parishioners in Nineveh, and was able to give individual attention to each! Parishes of 30,000 were very exceptional in the sixteenth century; they tended to become normal in the mushroom towns of 'paleotechnic' industrialism. Berlin was the more notorious 'spiritual cemetery'. In 1858 only about 20,000 of her 400,000 inhabitants attended church at all. Henry Adams resided in

Berlin that year and described the city as 'dirty, uncivilized, primitive beyond what an American boy could have imagined' (that was significant when we consider that hogs roamed the ill-paved streets of New York and Chicago in those days). By 1880 Berlin had been transformed from one of the most insanitary towns in Europe into a well-ordered metropolis (800,000); yet the churches could hold only 25,000 worshippers. In 1906 an English economist described Berlin as 'a marvel of civic administration, the most modern and perfectly organized city there is'.[8] Yet this great capital with over two million inhabitants had only about a hundred places of worship, of which ten were Roman Catholic and nine were synagogues. One of the parishes (St. Paul's, Schöneberg) had seven clergy to minister to 140,000 people. As regards the externals of religion there had been some improvement since 1880. In that year twenty-six per cent of the children were unbaptized, fifty-eight per cent of the marriages were civil, and eighty per cent of the funerals were without religious rites. By 1893 only twelve per cent of the infants, thirty-six per cent of the married couples, and sixty-three per cent of the corpses escaped the attention of pastors.

Kierkegaard stated satirically that in Denmark the theory still prevailed in the middle of the nineteenth century that 'all are Christians'. His recent biographer, Dr. Lowrie, found that an 'indispensable' German book of etiquette devoted its longest chapter to the thesis: 'It is a requisite of good form to have one's children baptized.' It argued cogently that 'they were not likely to ask to be baptized when they had reached years of discretion, and that as unbaptized persons they would be exposed to social embarrassment . . . and civil disabilities'. In less degree, this also applies to Confirmation. The 'first Communion' of many young people was their last. Those who belonged to the working classes listened with interest to the advocates of a new and easy faith—Socialism. 'The first word of religion is a lie,' said Engels. 'The idea of God', said Marx, 'must be destroyed; it is the keystone of a perverted civilization.' 'Our revolution', said Bebel, 'differs from all its predecessors in this—it does not seek for new forms of religion, but denies religion altogether.'

After the establishment of the German Empire in 1871 Socialism became widespread among industrial workers. The

8 Dr. A. Shadwell, *Industrial Efficiency* (London, 1906).

Evangelical Church grew even more unpopular among the masses. Glib agitators linked up piety and property, exploited the prejudices of the proletariat, and boldly offered the materialism of Marx as a substitute for the Gospel of Christ. In 1905 12,000 Prussian Protestants renounced the Church, most of them being Social Democrats. One is surprised at the large number who remained in nominal communion, utilizing the Church's services for baptisms, marriages, and funerals, but otherwise showing little interest. In Saxony, a strongly Socialist kingdom, ninety-six per cent of the infants born in 1892 were baptized and over ninety-six per cent of the marriages were solemnized by pastors. Except in the smaller rural parishes of Germany regular visiting by the clergy is almost impracticable. City churches are not staffed with curates to anything like the same extent as equivalent English parishes. Country towns are often under-churched. To take an instance familiar to me at Marburg, Hessen: in this historic university town of 23,000 inhabitants, there are only three Protestant parish churches, compared to the dozen kirks normal in a Scottish burgh of the same size.

Due credit must be given to the zeal of William the Second and his Empress. They were so eager to erect new churches that it was said to be unsafe to leave a vacant space in Berlin, lest it be requisitioned! Erastianism, however, prevented a genuine appeal to the people 'to rise up and build'. In some *Landeskirchen* funds were raised by means of State lotteries. Such unethical expedients did not really help Church Extension.

Had Protestantism any remedy for the economic and social evils that were sapping the nation's life? Roman Catholic leaders did much to retain the allegiance of the working-class element by espousing the cause of social reform. The first German Protestant to follow in this path seems to have been Victor Huber. This learned and devout gentleman sought to promote the co-operative principle—in production and distribution, in building- and loan-societies. Huber had visited England and was impressed by the way in which the 'operatives' were improving their conditions by voluntary association, with the help of progressive clergy like F. D. Maurice and Charles Kingsley. Unfortunately, the social climate of Germany was blighted by class mistrust. Men of means and culture were suspected not only by the prosperous but by the 'lower orders' whom they were trying to help. The shadow of Erastianism fell bleakly on non-official initiative. Huber was an old-fashioned Liberal, opposed (unlike Roman Catholic reformers) to State interference in industry. An individualist, he was not much good at team-work. Frustrated, he withdrew from Berlin in 1851 to the seclusion of the Harz mountains. The results of his endeavours to advance the voluntary, co-operative principle were meagre and transient.

A quarter of a century later Rudolf Todt, a country pastor, invoked State intervention in the interest of the exploited. It was now obvious that '*Manchesterismus*' was a brand of Liberalism that benefited only business men. Socialism would continue to be anti-Christian so long as the Church continued to give its unqualified blessing to the existing order.[9] To be neutral was to 'pass by on the other side' like the Priest and Levite, when a Good Samaritan was urgently needed. Todt appealed to the New Testament: 'You are members of one another.' The Gospel was the key to the social problems. The Sermon on the Mount and the parables declared that wealth required Christian stewardship; further, the whole community (and the Church in particular) was responsible for social sin and maladjustment. These views were set forth in *Der radikale deutsche Sozialismus und die christliche Gesellschaft* (2nd ed., 1878). This important book was the result of a passing suggestion from the more famous Pastor Stöcker that Todt should examine the Socialist programme from the New Testament point of view.

The commercial crisis of 1873 led to the questioning of the moral foundations of Liberal individualism. Five years later Rudolf Todt joined Dr. Adolf Stöcker (1835-1909) the Prussian Court Preacher, in founding an association for 'Social Reform on Christian and Constitutional Principles'. It was hoped that the division between rich and poor might be lessened, with 'a greater economic security' resulting. For twenty-five years the eloquent and masterly Stöcker laboured to promote Social Christianity on a basis of Evangelical orthodoxy. He gained some supporters among the upper class and the intelligentsia, but these *Katheder-Socialisten* ('Socialists of the Chair') were not an easy team to drive. He had to face the undisguised contempt of the Social Democrats (whose principles he dismissed as 'impracticable, unchristian, unpatriotic') as well as the ridicule of 'the enlightened' who made sport of his orthodox theology

[9] Alexander Miller, *The Christian Significance of Karl Marx* (London, 1946).

—he called it 'positive' and they called it cant (hence the gibe, *Muckerei und Stöckerei*). The Pastor also had to reckon with the distrust of the Government, which was carrying through its own schemes for social reform on paternalist lines. The Emperor William the First expressed his own opinion candidly. If a clergyman of a State Church holds Stöcker's opinions, he will either lose his place by his freedom of speech, or will fail to gain the ear of the masses and address property-holders alone. His only escape from the dilemma is to abandon the Holy Ministry and found a Christian Socialist party to oust the Social Democrats. Professor Peabody's comment was incisive:

To abandon the Church for the sake of religion; to see in politics the field for a religious revival; to ally oneself with the Socialist party for the sake of supplanting them—this will seem to most observers like the charge at Balaklava, magnificent, but not war; and the withdrawal of these Christian preachers from their prophetic office does not, at present, appear likely to carry with it the assurance of a corresponding influence and leadership in the political world.'[10]

In spite of the social idealism of the young Emperor William the Second, Stöcker felt that his position as Court preacher was impossible and resigned in 1890. Since 1879 he had committed himself to politics.[11] He won a certain number of Conservatives to his ideal of 'Christian Socialism'. Bismarck recognized in him a serviceable instrument to divide the forces of Socialism: but there was always the danger of his heading a Protestant counterpart to the Catholic 'Centre Party'. Stöcker's candidates polled 40,000 votes at Berlin in the elections of 1881, and 53,000 in 1884. An unhappy feature of his activity was the Pastor's support of anti-Semitic propaganda, which synchronized with barbarous riots against Jews in Hungary and Russia. Treitschke, the historian, was the only prominent German to give any encouragement to this agitation: Mommsen and Virchow denounced anti-Semitism as a social virus. The better elements in the community were therefore alienated from Stöcker's 'Christian Socialist Party' (later the 'Social Monarchical Union'). The only class that continued to assist his campaign to any marked degree were the small tradesmen, whose welfare was threatened by big Jewish firms (they complained that most of the bankers, stockbrokers,

[10] *Jesus Christ and the Social Question* (London, 1907), p. 52. A book rich in references to the German literature of the subject.
[11] Stöcker's Memoirs, *Dreizehn Jahre Hofprediger u. Politiker* (Berlin, 1895).

editors, and Liberal politicians were Jews). Adolf Stöcker, like Adolf Hitler, drew much support from disgruntled sections of the lower middle class. Violent debates took place in the Prussian Diet on the question of excluding Jews from national schools, universities, and public positions. Rioting, boycotting, and duelling broke out. The Crown Prince Frederick declared that the agitation was 'a shame and a disgrace to Germany' (1880). Unfortunately Stöcker had set in action a movement that he could not control. His proposals to limit the power of the Jews and prevent them from dominating German life were outdone by the inflammatory appeals of demagogues like Böckel and Ahlwardt throughout the 'eighties. This racial anti-Semitism made considerable progress among the ignorant. 'It adapted itself better to popular passions and inherited prejudice than the academic conceptions of the Christian Socialists.'

Stöcker was discredited. The financial scandals connected with Förster's attempt to found a Christian Socialist colony in Paraguay, the conviction of Baron von Hammerstein for forgery and swindling (1895-6), covered the anti-Semitic party with the very obloquy with which they had pursued the Jews. The ex-Court preacher was expelled from the Conservative Party for refusing to modify the socialistic flavour of his journal *Das Volk*. On 28th February 1896 William the Second attacked him in the following telegram which was made public throughout the Empire:

Stöcker has finished as I predicted some years ago! Political pastors— an absurdity. He who is Christian is also social; 'Christian-Social' is non-sense which produces personal exaltation and intolerance. Pastors ought to attend to the souls of the faithful and cultivate charity, but let politics alone for it does not concern them.

History will probably exonerate Stöcker from the charges of personal ambition and hypocrisy, with which his enemies charged him. We cannot but admire his boldness, pertinacity, and readiness to leave a position of ease and honour for the arena of action: but his programme sounds suspiciously like a Nazi manifesto. He set himself against 'all unchristian and anti-German schemes of spurious Liberalism, oppressive Capital-ism, rapacious Hebrewism, and revolutionary Socialism'. These panaceas were popular slogans such as reactionary groups on the Continent have often used, masquerading under the name of 'Christian Socialist party'. In any case Stöcker stirred up worse evils than those he claimed to cure. In 1905-7 there was another revival of anti-Semitism, linked with aggressive Protestantism, Chauvinism, and Anglophobia. When the centenary of Stöcker's birth was commemorated in 1935, the process of 'liquidating' the Jews was in full swing.

The closing years of the nineteenth century were clouded with reaction. William the Second continued Bismarck's policy of forestalling the Socialists by benevolent social legislation; but this paternalism was combined with militarism and authoritarianism. In a speech addressed to the Prussian nobility at Königsberg (November 1894), the Kaiser summoned them to support him in his struggle for religion, morality, and order against the parties of Revolution (*Umsturz*); it was '*Umsturz*' to criticize the accepted view of monarchy, marriage, and national defence. Orations and appeals from the throne were as frequent and fervid as in the days of Frederick William the Fourth. The Conservatives strove to put repressive legislation on the statute book, to increase the powers of the police, to extend Press censorship to religion and even art (1895-1900). 'Big Business' had lost its liberal tinge and lined up with the army and aristocracy. Georges Goyau has given a brilliant account of the Church's part in these closing years of the century.[12]

In spite of all these setbacks, the 'Social Gospel' had still active supporters; the belief persisted that it could rejuvenate the Church.[13] The tenth Evangelical Social Congress recorded considerable progress in 1899; some of their ideals were already embodied in legislation. Consequently, the Church was less unpopular as an institution. The task of awakening active interest, however, had still to be faced. During the 'nineties there was a general recognition that theologians were too isolated from their fellow men. The 'questions of the day' that interested the pastor were not those that interested the common man. The fear of ecclesiastical discipline and failure to get preferment deterred the more timid and worldly section of the clergy; but there were others who were fired by the need of active 'Social Christianity'. Churchmen of various types sought the re-statement of the Christian faith, not merely in terms acceptable to modern thought, but in language that the

[12] *L'Allemagne religieuse: le Protestantism*, 'Crowned by the French Academy' (Paris, 1898).
[13] Sulze, *Die ev. Gemeinde* (Gotha, 1891).

people could understand, offering a solution to their personal and social problems.

It was a sign of the times when Herr Göhre, an ordination-candidate spent three months in a mill at Chemnitz. He reported bad working conditions, poverty so intense that many of the employees were tempted to add to their wages by dishonest means.[14] Göhre's aim was to bring to the educated classes the facts that had been revealed to him through his own experience. He pointed out that the language of the clergy was unintelligible to the workers. One great quality of religion, however, remained—respect and reverence for Jesus of Nazareth. 'He lacks the supernatural light in his eyes; the divinity assigned to him by theologians is a subject for smiles . . . but they all stand reverently and quietly before his great personality.' Public interest was stirred by this personal record, but Göhre did not find the landowners so sympathetic when he turned his investigations to rural labour conditions in conjunction with Professor Max Weber. The new ideals stood the test of group loyalty in 1895, when the Protestant clergy of the Saar area took the workers' part against Baron von Stumm, the big industrialist who treated his men with munificent paternalism, but denied their right to self-determination. 'We are living in the Von Stumm age' was a cliché of the time.

The pendulum of interest had swung sharply from a Christology which ignored the social question to one which discovered it at the heart of the Gospel. Professor Ritschl (1822–89) had awakened a new enthusiasm for the redemption of humanity; the 'Kingdom of God' was 'organized love', a practical programme. Friedrich Naumann, a Frankfurt pastor who was eloquent in the pulpit and effective on the platform, examined the situation realistically. 'Social Democracy turns against Christianity and the Church because it sees in them only a means of providing a religion founded for the existing economic order.' The Jesus of History was the key to the New Order, the hinge on which turned the door of access into the Kingdom of God. Jesus Christ was a man of the people.[15] He put human life before property and saw in wealth an obstacle to the attainment of true personality. What questions would men have to answer at the Last Judgement? Not, what dogmas did you accept? but—what did you do to relieve human need? In

---

[14] *Drei Monate Fabrikarbeiter u. Handwerksbursche* (Leipzig, 1891).
[15] *Jesus als Volksmann* (1894).

his suggestive essay on 'Christ in the Machine Age', Naumann indicated how the teaching and spirit of the Master could be applied in a mechanized, standardized civilization.[16] This 'Social Gospel' the author preached with passion, but less crudely than some of his imitators in England and America.[17] With persuasive power he proclaimed a magnified and not a reduced Christianity. 'Christ was neither philosopher nor statesman, nor yet economist. . . . He brings neither conclusions nor methods. He *lives*, and His life is the revelation of God.'

Naumann found that the Inner Mission, which had once been the object of his enthusiasm, was not radical enough to serve as a channel of Christian Socialism; the Protestant Church, with its 'particularism' and officialism was a broken reed.[18] Like Pastor Stöcker he took to politics. In 1895 he declared against the Conservatives. He did not become a Socialist; until his death in 1920 he edited the Radical paper *Die Hilfer*. Although a strong democrat, he linked up his social idealism with nationalistic convictions. To many fellow-Liberals such an attitude seemed inconsistent; this curious amalgam was afterwards to become familiar in the 'National Socialist' ideology. Naumann's personality has been described as 'noble and stimulating'.[19] It was a tragedy that the prophet who related the teaching of Jesus to modern urban civilization[20] should latterly have become an unbalanced preacher of conquest and hatred.[21] It was as if Dr. T. R. Glover, author of the epoch-making *Jesus of History* had transferred his allegiance to the British Union of Fascists. Germany was singularly unfortunate in the passing of Christian reform leadership to men like Stöcker and Naumann.

Spiritual unity was the watchword of 'the Social Gospel' according to the precepts of Harnack and the practice of the 'Inner Mission'. Their sunlit hopes disappeared in the war of

[16] *Was heisst Christlich-Sozial?* (1894).

[17] The German Social Gospel was not winged with song. It produced no stirring hymns, calling for the Kingdom of God such as Symond's 'These things shall be; a loftier race', or Merrill's 'Rise up, O men of God! Have done with lesser things!'

[18] cf. his *Sozialismus u. Religion in Deutschland* (Leipzig, 1921).

[19] Biography by Heuss (Berlin, 1937).

[20] The 'Back to Jesus' movement in Art was represented by Fritz von Uhde (1848-1911). He depicted the Master among plain folk of modern times, peasants, and workmen. His realism was a contrast to the conventional, orthodox sentimentality of Hofmann.

[21] See p. 266, *infra*.

1914. Pessimistic dualism returned in 1918 with defeat. Traditional Lutheran 'Ordinology' reappeared with a 'new look'. The 'Doctrine of the Orders' assigned to the State the sphere of the Law, and to the Church the sphere of the Gospel. Sinful man needed discipline: only within the Christian community sounded the note of Grace. God worked through the State as Creator and Preserver; Christ is in the midst of the Church as Redeemer. What are we to make of this irreconcilable dualism, with its old-fashioned conception of authority (*Obrigkeit*)?

In 1919 Germany was humiliated, defeated, threatened with Communism; she certainly needed an 'order of preservation' against external pressure and internal collapse. Pessimism secured a hearing for the traditional Lutheran view that Christian standards could only prevail within the circle of professing Christians: a social Gospel, designed to transform a community containing a large proportion of people utterly indifferent or hostile to the Christian faith, was an impossibility. The State could only compel self-centred man to fulfil outward obligations to his neighbour. Thinkers like Ferdinand Gogarten began by viewing the State as an emblem of the 'wrath of God'. In course of time, however, they regarded it not merely as an instrument to knock down civil disobedience, but as the 'supreme co-ordinator of life'. The negative attitude of Lutheran tradition gave way to a positive principle of admiration. Nineteenth-century enthusiasm for the 'Social Gospel' came back, but instead of depending on voluntary effort and the leavening of the community, it tended to lean heavily on State initiative and action. A movement that began with releasing the lay forces of Christianity culminated a century later in their enslavement.

D. R. Davies, in *On to Orthodoxy* (1939) has recalled the influence of Harnack's *Social Gospel*. 'We serious, socially minded young men looked upon it as revelation. It has taken me a quarter of a century to realize that it *was* a revelation, not of Christ's mind, however, but of Adolf Harnack's mind. I shall probably be accused of perverse paradox when I say that the logical end of Adolf Harnack and his Social Gospel is Adolf Hitler and his Nazism. But is it not a striking fact that Hitler should appear in the country where the adaptation of Christianity to a secularist philosophy had gone farthest of all?'

CHAPTER FOUR

CATHOLICS, PROTESTANTS, AND THE STATE

A<small>N</small> important factor in the social and religious life of Germany has been the presence of a considerable body of Roman Catholics varying in strength from one region to another, but embracing one third of the population. In 1555 and again in 1648 a definitive attempt was made to settle the 'confessional' map of the Reich. The north and east were overwhelmingly Protestant, while the west and south were largely Catholic, apart from scattered islands of Evangelical faith—certain Rhine duchies, 'Free cities', and principalities like Württemberg. The economic depression which resulted from the substitution of Atlantic trade for coastal commerce mainly limited to the North Sea and the Baltic, hit the Protestant cities with almost paralysing effect and completed the disastrous effects of the Thirty Years War; they lost their cosmopolitan atmosphere and prosperity, dwindling to provincialism and dominated by unprogressive burgher oligarchies. The Catholic cities of the south did not all flourish like Augsburg in the hey-day of the house of Fugger; but they, like the Rhineland towns, enjoyed a limited prosperity through inland trade in the seventeenth and eighteenth centuries. The business class was less exclusively Protestant than in the early Reformation period.

Economic conditions, however, modified the traditional alignment, after the Napoleonic Wars broke up the torpor of the Fatherland. Communications benefited Northern Germany, and manufacturing towns arose largely in areas under Protestant rule. The Catholic areas in the south remained peasant country; in the Ruhr, where Catholicism was strong, the employers were mostly Protestant.

The old static conditions yielded to dynamic change. Catholic patches of population appeared in regions Protestant by sentiment and tradition, and vice versa. These changes were significant. Berlin, which had scarcely any Romanists in 1800, contained 51,000 in 1870, 135,000 in 1885, and 150,000 in 1939. Munich and Cologne, almost without Protestants in 1800, had 48,000 and 34,000 respectively by 1900. It has been observed that Protestantism has been almost lifeless in those parts of Germany where the Reformation achieved its numerical maximum—Brunswick, Hamburg, Pomerania, and Mecklenburg. On the other hand, Protestantism has proved a vital factor in States where it had not hitherto held the field, e.g. Baden, where it can count on the allegiance of one-third of the population, and Württemberg, where the proportion is two thirds. In Ultramontane Bavaria there were as many as 2,014,000 Evangelicals by 1910 as compared to 4,865,000 Romanists. Prussia had a Catholic population of 12,341,000 in 1910, 23,420,000 persons being nominally Evangelical. The considerable Catholic minority live mainly in the Rhineland, transferred to Prussia in 1815. Here, Catholicism had undergone a change in spirit since the French Revolution.

The Catholic Church in eighteenth-century Germany had been 'Cisalpine' rather than 'Ultramontane' in outlook. The Jesuit drive of the Counter-Reformation had long lost its impetus. The ecclesiastical princes of the west and south resented Papal interference from beyond the Alps. These dignitaries (often lax in doctrine and easy in morals) insisted on being masters in their own house—and managed very well on their own, as Church and State were one in these old-world principalities; life went smoothly for the rulers in the Baroque *Residenzstadt*. Then came the challenge of 1789.[1] Within a few years the German princes were at war with France; Napoleonic conquests and the cupidity of the lay rulers of Germany liquidated ecclesiastical property on a big scale from 1801 onward.[2] The 'little corporal' and his agents succeeded where the 'advanced' Emperor Joseph the Second failed; they 'rationalized' Germany. The secularization of the Archbishoprics of Cologne, Treves, and Maintz meant that 3,161,766 people became subjects of civil rulers (mostly Protestants). The compensation offered was no real equivalent to the confiscation suffered. The higher clergy, deprived of their temporalities and independence, harassed by the State, had now to look for support to the Papacy. Parishes and monasteries lost their endowments in Bavaria and other Catholic

---

[1] G. P. Gooch, *Germany and the French Revolution* (London, 1920).

[2] 'A glorified estate office was set up in Paris under Talleyrand . . . the ecclesiastical States and free cities, with a few exceptions, were distributed in 1803. This was the great reduction from three hundred States to thirty so often wrongly ascribed to the Congress of Vienna' (*German History . . . since 1815*, by A. J. P. Taylor (London, 1945), p. 35).

principalities. Priests were now threatened with the yoke of State control, to which pastors had been subjected since the Reformation. It looked as if Catholicism in Germany was bound to become more dependent on Rome, and consequently less national. All this weakened 'Cisalpine' sentiment and strengthened militant 'Ultramontanism'. German Catholics were compelled henceforth to look for leadership south of the Alps. It will be realized that Napoleon was largely responsible for the upsurge of clericalism as well as for the leaven of liberalism in the Fatherland.

The old antagonism between Catholics and Protestants had broken down in many parts of Germany during the eighteenth century. For instance, in Brunswick 'the utmost good will' existed between the monastery of St. Ludger and the Lutheran University of Helmstädt. Gellert's *Hymns* (1757) were introduced in Catholic as well as Protestant churches, after the influence of the Emperor Joseph the Second authorized vernacular services. This era of good feeling continued into the early nineteenth century. Bible Societies were patronized by the Archbishop of Treves. Ceremonies of a superstitious nature, popular in Latin Catholicism, were discountenanced. In Bavaria Bishop Sailer (1751-1823), the well-known Catholic preacher, did not hesitate to read Protestant devotional books and to welcome Pietist activities; he was criticized for his friendship with Lavater and the Illuminists, but was protected by the House of Bavaria. In Breslau the Catholic Faculty of Theology attended disputations held by 'the Sister Church'. As late as 1828 the Catholic Theological Faculty of Tübingen awarded a prize, in open competition, to the notorious D. F. Strauss, of the Protestant 'extreme Left'.[3] Voices were actually raised in favour of a married priesthood, with civil service status similar to that of the Protestant clergy. Hontheim, the historian, even dreamt of a 'German Catholic Church', reconstituted by the easy device of ignoring several centuries of division and seeking its new basis in a 'constitutional Papacy'.[4]

These dreams were shattered by the Jesuits, who had gained

[3] J. A. Möhler, Catholic Professor at Tübingen, had been influenced by Schleiermacher. Many Evangelicals attended Möhler's lectures. In spite of the provocative attitude of Baur, which confirmed Ultramontane suspicions that Protestantism was a slippery slope leading to scepticism, he persisted in his fairminded attitude. His *Symbolik* (1832; E.T., 1843, 1906) was too advanced for many Romanists, who would admit no 'theory of development' which allowed for any change in Catholicism since the Early Church.

[4] Treitschke, *Germany . . . in the Nineteenth Century*, Vol. II, p. 338.

a footing in Prussia as far back as the time of Frederick the Great. The Order was dissolved in 1773 but reconstituted in 1814. In most parts of Europe it was the close ally of reactionary governments, but in the Rhineland its agents adapted themselves to the relatively democratic régime, introduced into Napoleon's 'Kingdom of Westphalia', and not entirely abrogated at the Restoration (1815). Catholicism became popular partly because of its zeal, partly because of its sympathy with the social aspirations of working folk. In 1835 Montalembert declared that Westphalia was 'the heart of Catholicism in Northern Germany, the Germanic Brittany'. The younger priests were gradually moulding the minds of the coming generation. They preached uncompromising Ultramontanism. The authority of the Holy Father was absolute: the German equivalent of 'Gallicanism' was disowned. Bible Societies were denounced as 'the work of the devil', and fraternization with Protestants was frowned on. This Jesuit control meant that the Roman Church was far stronger and more popular than in the old aristocratic days, when it was rich in endowments and temporal privileges.[5]

Now the Rhineland and Westphalia passed into the hands of Prussia in 1815, doubling its population. Frederick William the Third was not the man to conciliate provincials who clung to their local liberties and the Church of their fathers. He had not the tact to make graceful concessions when demands involved no more than liberty of worship; yet he allowed the Jesuits to overstep the mark when the authority of the State was really questioned. His mismanagement of the 'mixed marriages' question resulted in a resounding victory for his astute ecclesiastical opponents, though Bunsen did his best to solve the problem in 1838. Roman Catholic leaders were swift to read the signs of the times; and when the Industrial Revolution began to transform Westphalia, they pointed out that the Protestant employer was as ready to infringe the labourer's economic security[6] as the Prussian State to abridge his political rights. In 1847 Father Kolping founded 'Catholic Working Men's Associations', which numbered more than 70,000 members by 1871. Baron von Ketteler, Archbishop of Mainz from 1850 to 1877, was influenced by Lassalle's Socialist views

[5] G. Goyau, *L'Allemagne religieuse; le Catholicisme, 1800-48*, 2 vols. (Paris, 1909).
[6] Weber has noted that not only business magnates but the higher grades of skilled labour, are, as far as nominal membership affiliation goes, 'overwhelmingly Protestant' (*The Protestant Ethic*, E.T., 1930, Chapter 1).

during the 'sixties and urged the need for the State under-
taking unemployment insurance, and so on, in a spirit of Christian
idealism. Consequently the tide of Social Democracy was
stemmed in the Catholic areas of the Fatherland. When the
German Empire was established in 1871 no less than fifty
Catholic deputies were elected to the Reichstag on a basis of
manhood suffrage.

This 'Centre Party' had absorbed Kolping's 'Working
Men's Associations' and other Catholic groups. It consisted of
men of all classes, drawn together primarily by their zeal to
promote the interests of the Roman Church. It separated the
secularist Social Democrats from the traditionally Protestant
Conservative party, which drew its main strength from the
Prussian army and aristocracy. Chancellor Bismarck, however,
was not satisfied with the political moderation of the Centre.
For some years he considered it an erratic block which could
never be integrated into the structure of the new Empire like
the 'National Liberals'; it was definitely *reichsfeindlich*. Hence
the campaign known as the *Kulturkampf*.

In 1873 Bismarck gave Falk, a National Liberal Cabinet
Minister, authority to proceed with the 'May Laws'. These
aimed at imposing control on the activities of the Roman
Church. Priests must in future be German subjects and
German-educated; the State was to have the power to veto
Church appointments and to suspend ecclesiastics; severe
restrictions were to be placed on Church schools; and procedure
was to be speeded up for those who desired to sever their
connexion with Catholicism.

Goyau gives a graphic account of this campaign, popularized
under the title of *Kulturkampf*; it was to be presented as a struggle
of civilization against clerical obscurantism.[7] Within a year six
Prussian bishops were imprisoned and dismissed by the civil
authorities; the Archbishop of Trier suffered the same fate;
in 1,300 parishes the services were suspended, some of the
priests continuing their ministry secretly. Bismarck naturally
received support from Liberals and Socialists who were
avowed secularists, as well as from staunch Evangelicals.
Italian and French anti-clericals applauded, while Lord
John Russell acclaimed the Chancellor as 'a fellow soldier
of liberty'. Not all Catholics were anti-Bismarck. Some
of them were capitalists who mistrusted the Socialist element

[7] *Bismarck et l'Église* (Paris, 1911).

in the Centre party; others believed that their beloved Church was being manipulated by scheming Ultramontanist politicians. The subsequent policy of the *Zentrum* gives some colour to the objection that it was a party without any principle save denominational advantage, a party of expediency ready to bargain with any group prepared to pay the price in concessions to Catholicism. This opportunism was hardly conducive to the rise of genuine democracy in Germany.

On the other hand, Evangelicals of an independent type feared that this demonstration of State interference might have unpleasant repercussions in their own *Landeskirchen*. Hanoverian Lutherans bitterly resented the annexation of their country by Prussia; they felt that they were fellow-sufferers with the Catholics. Persecution usually closes the ranks of co-religionists who may differ from one another: it also evokes the sympathy of fair-minded outsiders who want to see justice done.

Bismarck exploited German Nationalism in opposition to a Catholicism which he claimed was Roman, not genuinely German; but in spite of rising opposition to Ultramontane Papal claims, only a small minority of German Catholics rejected the Vatican Decrees of 1870. Not even the alliance of Prussian Conservatives and Liberalism backed by distinguished professors and D.D.s could make the 'New Reformation' a success. By 1875 the 'Old Catholics' secession mustered only 47,737 communicants, one hundred congregations, and fifty-four priests. Fifteen million Catholics remained loyal to Rome in spite of every encouragement from the State to secede; many of them regarded the whole affair as a mere 'dispute in a study'. The new sect on a Catholic basis appealed to High Church Anglicans;[8] it had learning and culture, but few followers; Renan aptly compared it to 'a staff without an army'. The Old Catholic leader, Ignaz von Döllinger, had a European reputation. He was elected *Rector Magnificus* of the University of Munich; he received Doctorates from Oxford, Edinburgh, Marburg, and Vienna. He presided at Christian Reunion conferences that broke new ground in bringing together Anglicans and Greek Orthodox. But when the secession reached its crisis, Döllinger refused to be consecrated a Bishop; 'by conviction' he belonged to the Old Catholics, but never formally joined them, and his refusal lost Bavaria to the movement.

[8] cf. C. B. Moss, *The Old Catholic Movement, Its Origins and History* (London, 1949).

Had he initiated schism, it would undoubtedly have been achieved on a larger scale. Yet even admitting the likelihood of this expansion, the Old Catholics would have lost heavily through Bismarck's political patronage.

The 'Iron Chancellor' had sworn that he would 'never go to Canossa', but his plans miscarried. The *Kulturkampf* came to an inglorious end. Dr. A. W. Holland considered that failure to subjugate the Catholic Church gave the Papacy 'greater power than it had since the days of Wallenstein'. Bismarck the opportunist was now glad to conclude an alliance with the Church that he had just defied. The new 'Centre Party' might be persuaded to march in step with the military junto, in return for certain concessions; thus conservatism would present a united front against Social Democracy.

It was a symbol of Catholic victory when Cologne Cathedral, unfinished at the Reformation, was completed and consecrated (October 1880) in the presence of all the reigning German princes, headed by the Emperor William the Second, whose ancestors had stood firm against Popery. The growing strength of Romanism challenged the isolated *Landeskirchen*. The younger generation must therefore be reminded of the achievements and sacrifices of the Reformation. Let the sculptor touch the people's imagination in the historic cities of the Fatherland! In 1860 a colossal Reformation Monument was unveiled at Worms. Designed by Rietschel, it took nine years to execute. Luther dominates the scene, with his contemporaries on lower pedestals—Reuchlin the Hebraist, Melanchthon the Preceptor, Philip of Hesse, and Frederick the Wise. Between them are allegorical figures of Magdeburg (mourning), Spires (protesting), and Augsburg (confessing).

In 1883 the four-hundredth anniversary of the birth of Luther was celebrated with great *éclat* throughout Germany. The historic Schlosskirche at Wittenberg was restored (all too thoroughly!) and the first words of '*Ein feste Burg*' were cut in huge letters on the tower. The famous wooden doors to which Luther affixed his theses (burnt in 1760) had been replaced by bronze ones in 1858, bearing the original Latin text. But more than *Thesentur* were required, if Lutherland was to present a united front to Romanism, exhilarated by *Kulturkampf* victory. The proclamation of the German Empire in 1871 did not lead, as some hoped, to the establishment of one National Evangelical Church. The separate *Landeskirchen* continued to afford refuge to 'particularism', sacred and secular. Societies, however, were founded to bridge the isolated units and to impart some unity to the ineffective fragments that composed Protestant Germany. In 1887 the German Evangelical League was founded on the basis of accepting the Divinity of Christ. Its aim was to defend Evangelicalism against the Roman menace by emphasis on Christian essentials; the Word of God would prevail if the Church was inspired by a higher tone; the conversion of laymen to Rome, puzzled by the *isms* of theological speculation and wearied by party strife, would be effectively arrested.

As early as 1832 the Gustavus Adolphus Union had been inaugurated at the bicentenary of the battle of Lützen. The memory of the great Swedish monarch was to be perpetuated by an association for strengthening the Protestant witness in parts of Germany where it was weak. The objective was commemoration by active evangelism and 'Church Extension'. Starting in Saxony, Germany was gradually covered by a network of organizations. The want of a definite creed alienated the stricter Lutherans, but the Union's uncompromising hostility to Romanism aroused the admiration of practical Protestants who felt that Papal aggression called for more than fulmination. Between the Revolution of 1848 and 1914 over two thousand Protestant churches were built in areas where Protestantism was weak; five thousand struggling congregations were assisted to the extent of £2,000,000. There were nearly two thousand branches, with hundreds of local women's auxiliaries. The Gustavus Adolphus Union was a splendid memorial to 'The Lion of the North' who had saved the Reformation. Protestantism was a cause to be promoted, not just a product to be preserved.

Another instance of Church Extension undertaken by voluntary co-operation in spite of official apathy and 'particularism' was Foreign Missions. Eighteenth-century rationalism had killed the impulse that flowed from Halle Pietism, but in 1815 a fresh wave marked the turn of the tide. In the 'Basel Society' Lutherans and Reformed worked along with agents of the (Anglican) Church Missionary Society; industrial, educational, and medical work was combined with evangelism overseas. The 'Berlin Society' (1823) was identified with the Prussian United Church and found eager advocates in liberal evangelicals like Tholuck and Neander. The 'Dresden Society' received support from the High Lutheranism of Saxony and

north-east Germany. The 'society and party' basis of German
Evangelical Missions reminds one of the Anglican method—
canalization according to different brands of Churchmanship:[9]
the divided state of Germany made it impossible to organize
overseas evangelism as an integral part of the Church's work
(the Church of Scotland method). In view of these difficulties
and the fact that German missionaries did not have the
advantage of working under their own national flag till nearly
the end of the nineteenth century,[10] their Foreign Evangelism
deserves great praise.

Considering that German Evangelicals were successful in
surmounting so many difficulties (implying an organizing
ability not often credited to Continental Protestants) it may well
be asked: Was there no official attempt to bind together the
various *Landeskirchen* in their own interests?

The formation of the Germanic Confederation in 1815 did
not lead immediately to any ecclesiastical counterpart. Not
till the Revolution of 1848 was the question seriously faced. In
spite of the abortive character of the Church Constitution of
1848, an attempt was made soon after the restoration of the old
order to provide a joint organization for matters common to
the German Evangelical Churches. In 1852 the 'Eisenach
Conference' was instituted, meeting at Eisenach, that focal
centre of Reformation piety. The 'Inner Mission'[11] supplied
much of the enthusiasm, for this was the day of the *Bewegung*.
The Eisenach Conference differed from other similar movements in that all the *Landeskirchen* participated, although its
functions were only advisory. This was a step in advance of
previous societies. The shifting tendencies of the time were
reflected in debate, and the decisions of the Conference often
received the tacit consent of the States concerned. Discussions
and recommendations ranged over a wide area. Among the
questions of the day were—religious education in day-school
and Sunday-school, clerical efficiency and pastoral aid, the
'correct' attitude to sects, and the function of army chaplains.[12]
In 1861 the Conference registered the high-watermark of the
Gothic Revival; new churches should be cruciform and
conventionally 'chancelized', as Sir Gilbert Scott had

[9] Ranging from the High Church S.P.G. to the ultra-evangelical Bible Churchmen's Missionary Society.
[10] See Warneck's *History of Protestant Missions* (E.T., Edinburgh, 1901).
[11] See p. 217, *supra*.
[12] See E. F. Williams's *Christian Life in Germany* (Edinburgh, 1897).

demonstrated in his accepted design for the cathedral-like St. Nicholas', Hamburg (1844). 'Ecclesiology,' however, was no permanent settlement in Germany. The tide turned. In 1891 an influential congress of architects and churchmen approved of the 'Wiesbaden Programme' which restored the 'lost tradition' of the eighteenth century, making the pulpit central as well as the altar. A lasting achievement of their Eisenach Conference was the Revision of Luther's Bible. Work was started in 1870 and completed in 1892. Published at Halle, associated with Francke's famous Bible Institute, this new version of the Scriptures was approved by all the German States except retrograde Mecklenburg. Although a noteworthy achievement, it aroused less public interest than our Revised Version of 1881.[13]

In 1900 a Commission was appointed to see if the decisions of the Eisenach Conference could not be given more authority. Three years later a standing committee was elected to represent the constituent Churches more effectively. Most of the members felt that a committee was of little value when power rested in the hands of the secular heads of the jealous *Landeskirchen*. How could the petty restrictions of 'particularism' be overcome? It seemed to some observers that the only effective link would be a personal one. If the Kaiser headed the federation of German princes, might he not likewise crown the federation of State Churches? Nothing was done, however, and a quarter of a century later there was no Kaiser left to lead a procession of *Landeskirchen* into the stately temple of a *Reichskirche*. Aggressive Romanism welcomed a papal nuncio to Berlin, and in a few years the Unter den Linden witnessed a sight that would have seemed incredible before 1914—the Chancellor and dignitaries of the *Reich* marching in procession on Corpus Christi day. Stranger events were still to happen. The National Socialist attack on Christian faith and ethics was one destined to make Protestant and Catholic march side by side in a 'procession of witness' that was more than ceremonial. The outcome of the Second World War upset the historic balance of German religion by assigning the predominantly Protestant part of the *Reich* to the Russian conquerors.

[13] See *New Schaff-Herzog Cyclopaedia*, article 'Bible Versions'.

CHAPTER FIVE

THE EFFECTS OF THE TERRITORIAL SYSTEM

A DISTINGUISHED Anglican, Dr. Edwyn Bevan, writing of the State Church theory in 1929, expressed himself in terms that would have astounded his predecessors a century ago. 'Such a view', he concludes, 'is worse than a corruption of Christianity; it is a denial of the very essence of the Church. . . . It is an assimilation of Christianity to the State religions of paganism.'

What are we to say of the Territorial System in view of its evolution? Our survey has shown us the truth in Luther's pessimistic remark that whereas *before* the Reformation 'the devil had injected the Church into the State, *now* he was injecting the State into the Church'. Tholuck and other German scholars have used the term '*Caesareopapie*' to denote utter subjection of the Church to the State. Perhaps the only English equivalent is 'Erastianism'. 'Erastianism' has been used in Britain without much discrimination as a barbed invective culled from the rich vocabulary of ecclesiastical vituperation. In Scotland the supporters of the Disruption hurled it against the 'residuary Establishment' just as their Covenanting forefathers renounced it in their impassioned testimonies against a backsliding age. In England Anglo-Catholics have cast it in the teeth of their Low Church brethren who have sought to restrain ritual excesses by Act of Parliament. Dr. John Lightfoot was one of the few historic Puritans who had the courage to declare themselves Erastians.

It is worth noting that the term 'Erastianism' can be traced to Germany. Erastus was a Zwinglian divine who flourished at Heidelberg between 1560 and 1570. He contested the Calvinist claim to theocratic rights. The following were the circumstances. George Wither, an English Puritan, had written a thesis for a doctorate in theology, which had been sustained by the University; he affirmed the power of presbyteries to excommunicate. Erastus replied in a treatise which was translated into English in 1659 and revised by Dr. R. Lee in 1844. The gist of his argument is that professing Christians are to be punished by civil authority, and not by the clergy withholding sacraments. Erastus was even more out of sympathy with the sacramentarianism of the Lutherans than with the views of their Reformed opponents. He was opposed to the establishment of Genevan discipline at Heidelberg. His own background was German-speaking Switzerland where the government of the Cantons refused to allow the Reformed Church excessive privileges that would infringe the authority of the civil magistrates. Erastus has been fathered with diverse conflicting interpretations.[1] He would certainly have repudiated 'Erastianism', as coarsely conceived by German princes who maintained their Divine Right to absolute authority over the Church.

Turning to the standard Lutheran theologians, we find that they theorized considerably on the relations of Church and State. Gerhard in his classic *Loci theologici* (1610-20) carried the generally accepted principle to logical extremes: 'To the magistrate has been committed by God the custody of the divine law, to which belongs not only the second table of the Decalogue . . . but also the first table, regulating the public worship of God.'[2] Chemnitz, an ultra-Lutheran, like Gerhard, qualifies the theory of State control by disallowing the ruler's right to call and install a pastor 'without the will and consent of the clergy and the rest of the Church'.[3] Reininck reminds the prince that he is 'not the whole Church, but a member of it; not its lord, but its nurse'. This was an advanced opinion, however, and diverged from the norm of sixteenth- and seventeenth-century theory. The Prince was commonly regarded as *summus episcopus*. He was often ascribed Divine Right in his ecclesiastical as well as in his civil capacity. Thus Principal P. T. Forsyth considered that 'Luther only succeeded in restoring the Byzantine State Church, with its religious parasitism'.[4]

Even when German princes were convinced Pietists, they rarely modified their theories of personal authority. Spener's warm plea for spiritual freedom must, however, be recorded: 'The power of the ruler extends over earthly things and the external man . . . but conscience itself and the inner man

[1] See *Ency. Brit.* (11th ed.), 'Erastus'. He appears in the historical novel, *Clytia* (E.T., Low, 1883), by 'Geo. Taylor' (Professor Hausrath of Heidelberg).

[2] Even in Congregational New England this was axiomatic. 'The magistrate is *custos* of both the Tables of godliness.'

[3] *Loci Theologici* (1592).

[4] *Church and Sacraments*, p. 72.

remain free. . . . When the ruler attempts to use such power in this sphere, God is greatly offended and in such cases the subjects are not bound to obey him.'

The Pietist plea for conscience was also reflected by seventeenth-century writers on law, who would soften authority with a certain tincture of consideration for the individual; one thinks of the international influence of Grotius in this connexion. There was a steady shifting of emphasis from Divine Right to political utility with the advent of the eighteenth century. Thomasius (1655–1728), following the great jurist Puffendorf, urged: '*Religiones debent dirigi secundum utilitatem singularum rerum publicarum.*'

This enlightened theory was often debased in practice by princes who interpreted the common good in terms of their own interests. They found the 'relativity' of truth and individual rights a convenient means of breaking through inconvenient barriers of absolute principle. The clergy could be employed as the 'black police' of the *Polizei-Staat*. Even in the early nineteenth century Frederick William the Third imposed the following oath of loyalty on the Prussian clergy:

> With life and blood, with doctrine and example, I will defend the royal power . . . as established in our wholesome monarchical form of government. Likewise, I will make it known in good time, if I discover anything aiming at its alteration or abolitition . . . and I will admonish my parishioners to think and speak rightly at all times, of the secular authority which is ordained of God.

Various improved versions of the Territorial theory were propounded. The most sensible adaptation was devised by Dr. Mathäus Pfaff of Tübingen (1686-1760). Pfaff absorbed the best ideals of Pietism. His 'collegial system' sketched in *De Origine Juris Ecclesiastici* (1719), was an attempt to safeguard the spiritual rights of the Church without destroying the Establishment basis of the *Landeskirchen*: (i) Certain rights were reserved for the sovereign, dealing mainly with finance and property (*jus circum sacrum*); (ii) All other rights (doctrine, worship and ecclesiastical discipline) belonged to the community of Church members who might delegate their authority to representative synods (*jus in sacra*).

It was not till the nineteenth century that a few shoots of synodical consultation were grafted on to the tree of Territorialism. These modifications did not change the essence of the existing system, whereby the prince was *summus episcopus*.

The theory of 'dyarchy', reserving certain rights to the authority in command and extending others to bodies without power,
did not work more smoothly in Protestant Germany than it did
in British India. As late as 1893 William the Second of Prussia
claimed the right to revise the Liturgy in spite of the spirited
protest of the eminent liturgiologists, Spitta and Smend. This
was obviously a *jus in sacra*, a spiritual privilege, and not a *jus
circum sacra*, a matter affecting the Church's material organization. Sehling, writing in the twentieth century, made it perfectly clear that the crass Territorialism of the past was not
dead. Whatever theorists thought of the division of powers, the
Prince was the absolute ruler of the Church. He was more than
'its most illustrious member'. He could issue ordinances,
arrange visitations, enforce discipline and decide appeals.
What Maitland said of Henry the Eighth fits the German
summus episcopus completely: 'He not only *personified* the State,
he *parsonified* it.'

Is there anything to be said for the Territorial System judged
by its effects? It is an understatement to observe that rigid
Lutheran orthodoxy yoked to Erastianism had little influence
in ameliorating social injustice, 'rugged individualism' in
business, and lack of humanity in the treatment of Jews,
heretics, and criminals. Allowing for the exaggeration of an
Ultramontane, there is much in Jansen's charge that Territorialism, linked to the doctrine of justification by faith alone,
made Lutheranism sterile in social ethics and philanthropy;[5]
the medieval Church had a far better record for practical
Christianity. Despite the formally patriarchal ethics of the
'God-fearing prince' in German tradition, selfish individualism
ousted corporate religion and invaded economic and social life.
Only fear of 'the powers that be' imposed restraint. 'I recom-
mend to my children submission to authority,' said the zealous
Lutheran Bartholomew Sastrow, 'no matter whether Pilate or
Caiaphas governs.'[6]

Audi alteram partem. Augustine's plea for the right of reply
must not be overlooked. It may be claimed, in the first place,
that the Territorial system has advanced freedom of thought.
This has been partly due to rulers like Frederick the Great

---

[5] *History of the German People* (E.T., London, 1910), Vol. XVI.

[6] H. A. L. Fisher, *Social Germany in Luther's Time: Memoirs of B. Sastrow* (London,
1902).

who valued toleration; and it has owed much to the accident of
Germany being a mosaic of different states with their own 'par-
ticularist' traditions. The process of intellectual liberation has
been very slow. In the sixteenth and seventeenth centuries
the German universities were the preserve of Protestant
Scholasticism, complete with 'Professors of Controversy'.[7]
A rarefied theological atmosphere was quite consistent with
boorish manners. Tholuck, in his *Deutsche Universitäte*, has
cited astounding incidents. The Chancellor of the University
of Tübingen addressed thus a speaker at a public disputation:
'Thou hog! Thou hound! Or whatever thou art, thick-headed
mule!' On another official occasion, a Wittenberg scholar,
irritated by hearing the authority of Melanchthon quoted
against him, tore down his portrait and trampled it underfoot.
Shakespeare sent Hamlet to study at Wittenberg, little realizing
how intolerable his reflective individualist would have found
the Mecca of High Lutheranism (actually, Danish students
went there just as Welshmen at Oxford were drawn by tradition to Jesus College). Wittenberg, a shadow of its former self,
lingered on till the Napoleonic War when it disappeared along
with Helmstädt, once a beacon of liberal Lutheranism. In
1815 Wittenberg merged with Halle, which had been founded
as a nursery of Pietism (1694), but became a centre of Illumin-
ism before the middle of the eighteenth century. If Halle
emphasized what was utilitarian, Göttingen (founded in 1737
by our George the Second) was humanistic, for Mosheim, the
Church historian, saw that freedom from ecclesiastical control
was written into its charter. Marburg, the first Protestant
foundation (1527) remained faithful to the ideals of Philip the
Magnanimous but Giessen was established in opposition as a
strict Lutheran University (1607).

In the South, Tübingen (dating back to 1477) was influenced by Melanchthon's liberal tone. This tradition was
carried to rationalist extremes in the days of Baur and Strauss,
but in recent years the critical approach to theology has been
corrected by the warm spirit of Württemberg Pietism. Erlangen, in Bavaria (1742), became famous in the nineteenth
century as the stronghold of High Lutheranism. At Bonn
(1818) Protestants and Catholics worked amicably side by
side. Leipzig (1409) was ultra-orthodox in the sixteenth-

---

[7] Even in the twentieth century, American theological seminaries of the Calvinistic tradition still glory in 'Chairs of Didactic and Polemical Theology'.

century, went rationalist in the eighteenth century, and returned to orthodoxy in the nineteenth century. Berlin (1809) rapidly rose to academic distinction despite the discouraging circumstances of its inception. It was expressly independent of any particular creed or school of thought; but Schleiermacher, the first Dean of Divinity, by the sublimity of his genius and character, gave theology a pivotal place in the University that few could challenge. There were, of course, sceptics like Strauss, who had come to the conclusion that theology was 'a product of the imagination, not a science or branch of human knowledge'—and therefore did not deserve any place in the academic curriculum.

Eugen Rosenstock-Huessy has pointed out that the collapse of the Medieval Church and the erection of several hundred *Landeskirchen* by princely 'High Magistrates' gave the universities an authority and influence unknown elsewhere.[8] The Professor's Chair (*Katheder*) became heir to much that was derived from the Bishop's Chair (*cathedra*). The 'territorial' Churches were not 'established' in the Anglican sense, because they were all based on a foundation broader and larger than the principality in which they were set. For instance, the Elector of Saxony acknowledged the sovereign claim of the Wittenberg Faculty of Theology to adjudicate in matters of religion. The professors were officially civil servants of His Highness the Elector, but they were also the Christian representatives of the German nation within his principality; it was their privilege to interpret Christianity in terms of the *Augsburg Confession*. It was the duty of princes to rule in the secular sphere, even to administer church property and patronage; but in the higher sphere of Christian belief, they had no standing ('Princes are God's hangmen and jailors', said Luther).

Rosenstock-Huessy symbolizes his theory by illustrating a medal commemorating the Bicentenary of Wittenberg University (1702) and comparing it with one struck in honour of the Supremacy of Henry the Eighth in 1535. Both medals bear the sovereign's likeness. But the obverse side is different in each case. Wittenberg is depicted as being divinely illumined by the University: Henry the Eighth is proclaimed Head of the Church in the three sacred tongues—Hebrew, Greek, and Latin. The Lutherans thus represent a normal relation of Church and State by the co-partnership of 'sovereign prince and sovereign

[8] *Out of Revolution, Autobiography of Western Man* (London, 1938), Chapter 7.

seat of learning': the Anglicans represent an abnormal situation by allowing a king to concentrate in his own hands, by despotic decree both secular and sacred sovereignty.

One feels that Rosenstock-Huessy draws too sweeping a contrast, far too flattering to Lutherans. The crass Erastianism of Henry the Eighth was afterwards modified by the retention of Catholic Tradition and Church Order, not to speak of the constitutional effects of England's struggles for political freedom and individual rights. Whereas the German stress on the condominium of sovereign prince and sovereign university was largely limited to theology; in practice as well as in theory, the prince was '*summus episcopus*'—the Head of the Church, its supreme manager and 'most conspicuous member'.

Even in the nineteenth century there were deplorable instances of theological professors being dismissed for their political views. One thinks of De Wette of Berlin[9] summarily discharged for writing a consolation to the mother of Karl Sand, the unbalanced student of radical opinions who murdered Kotzebue, popular play-wright and enemy of political reform. Another Old Testament authority, Ewald[10] was expelled, with six other professors, from the University of Göttingen (1837). Their 'crime' consisted in making formal protest against King Ernest revoking the liberal Constitution of 1833, granted before Hanover's separation from Great Britain. Ewald became so reconciled to his successor on the throne, that he would not take the oath of allegiance to Prussia, when Hanover was incorporated. It must be admitted that in his later years Ewald's temper as a controversialist was violent. In 1874 he was sentenced to three weeks' imprisonment for comparing Bismarck to Frederick the Second—for his unprovoked attack on Austria.

Nevertheless, the German universities certainly acted as a brake on ecclesiastical tyranny. Professors were respected more than in other countries because their teaching was considered a public trust; they were charged significantly with *Wissen und Gewissen* ('science and conscience'). If the Faculty of Divinity was sometimes reactionary the Faculty of Law was often humane and progressive. Puffendorf (1632–94) was repelled by the narrow dogmatism of the Leipzig divines: he found that by legal studies he was able to advance the true interests of his fellow men. Pfaff of Tübingen, a legally-minded

[9] See p. 134, *supra*.   [10] See pp. 134, 210, *supra*.

theologian who sought to liberalize the constitution of the State Churches, issued an irenicon as early as 1720 in favour of more breadth in religion. 'If the Apostles should return among us,' he supposed, 'and should be called to professorial Chairs, they would evince a woeful ignorance about the things which are the themes of strife among our theologians.'

In the judicial sphere the true spirit of Christianity was advanced by jurists. The Faculty of Law was inclined to be progressive in outlook. Thus Professor Schlözer of Göttingen was known in the eighteenth century as 'the European Conscience'.

When professors entered political life, however, in the nineteenth century, they often proved ineffective. The university leadership of such men as Dahlmann, Gervinus, Uhland, and Sybel, did not prevent the 1848 Parliament from proving a fiasco. It included forty-nine professors, fifty-seven schoolmasters, sixty-six lawyers and sixteen priests. The Weimar Republic was also inaugurated by some of the best brains available, but academic ability counted for little. The régime of the 'National Socialist' State abolished the universities as seats of learning standing for the public recognition of truth and justice; it dismissed the distinction between equity and party principle; it called the police into the academic cloister, where tradition admitted only the authority of the Rector; it assigned absolute authority to an ex-corporal whose 'intuition' was 'inspired'. We may smile at Rosenstock-Huessy's classification of Hitler, but what he says is worth noting:

Hitler is a pre-Reformation type by race, instinct, and character. He is immune to the last four centuries of German history. He is neither a Protestant nor an academic person nor a civil servant nor an army officer. With true instinct, he has declined any honorary degree in a university . . . he is the unknown soldier of the rank and file, and for that reason he is able to begin all over again like an unreformed man.

Looking back on the German universities as they once were, we can see how their privileged position in the sixteenth and seventeenth centuries acted as a bridge between rigid orthodoxy and intellectual emancipation. Their influence was inter-national. Students from Scandinavia made their way to the Lutheran universities; Huguenots, Hollanders, and Swiss, flocked to the Reformed universities; exiles like Comenius the Czech Reformer were indebted to Germany for their higher education. Since the Enlightenment of the eighteenth century

R

Germany has rejoiced in an academic freedom that was not attained in other lands till well on in the nineteenth century.[11] Had the Presbyterian system prevailed throughout Germany and professors had been subjected to ecclesiastical discipline, it is doubtful whether such giants as Schleiermacher and Ritschl would have been tolerated in a theological faculty. However defective the 'Territorial System', it did not crush genius by insisting on conformity to the Westminster Confession. No wonder British and American students, finding little light in their own creed-bound colleges, flocked to sit at the feet of world-famed German professors. Foreigners were impressed by the fact that these scholars not only pursued research with *wissenschaftlich* thoroughness, but did not consider it necessary that they should see eye to eye with their colleagues. On the other hand, specialism in German universities has been carried too far; the expert has been an isolating factor, carrying to a logical conclusion Luther's emphasis on *Berufstreue* (fidelity to one's particular vocation). A notable instance of a specialist retaining the Humanist interest in all knowledge was Harnack's appointment as President of the federated Institutes of Research established at Berlin-Dahlem in 1900. 'For the last time', says Rosenstock-Huessy, 'a theologian had played a central role in the interplay of government, universities, public opinion, and progress in Germany'. Eleven years earlier Harnack, the arch-liberal, had been promoted to a Berlin Chair by the Minister of Public Instruction, in spite of the Empress's emphatic protest. Only occasionally has academic honour been influenced by the promise of preferment or threat of official penalization, e.g. the case of the pioneer rationalist, Semler, who defended the notorious Prussian *Edict* of 1788 ordering an immediate return to orthodoxy.

It cannot be denied that the Protestant rulers of Germany have fostered the ideal of a well-educated ministry, but for at least two centuries after the Reformation, the Christian ministry offered little encouragement to students without money or influence. There was much evidence to justify the proverb, 'Luther's shoes do not suit every small-town pastor'. Balthasar Schupp, that keen seventeenth-century observer, has described

---

[11] We must not forget that the small Courts often furthered the freedom of mind and soul, though not every *Hof* was a Weimar. Steffens, the friend of Schleiermacher, considered that anyone who prized freedom and culture would be happy in the surviving small states of Germany; this applied to all classes in their *'fürstlichen, bürgerlichen, amtlichen, hauslichen Leben'*.

the hard lot of the German theological students of his generation. After exhausting his financial resources at the university, he was faced with the problem of finding a parish. Unable to gild the palm of a prospective patron, 'he must doff his hat to some ink-boiler, secretary, or boot-black', who gains him an interview. 'Yes, dominie, Johannes,' replies the patron, 'you shall have the parish—but you must marry Margaret, my wife's maid!' A dissolute landowner might compel the parson to wed his cast-off mistress, to exercise 'the lesser excommunication' against his personal enemies, and to fix the hours of service to suit his own dissolute convenience. A patron's power was almost unlimited, and if he did not get his own way he might just lock the church door. Drews gives a depressing account of uncomfortable parsonages and the problem of eking out a miserable stipend by teaching and petty farming.[12] Well into the eighteenth century the country pastor had to struggle against local traditions. Pre-Reformation prejudice against a married clergy lingered in some districts and in others a young minister was expected to marry the widow of his predecessor!

It is not surprising, then, that the Lutheran ministry was dogged by social disadvantages even when its material condition had improved. 'Divinity is a *Brodstudium*,' said Dr. Smith, English lecturer at Erlangen University in 1914, 'theological students command a minimum of respect in the social scale.' The clergy of the Church of England have been described as 'cultured but not educated': conversely, the pastors of the German State Churches may be classified as 'educated but not cultured'. Whatever else may be said of this generalization, the German pastor *has to* study Philosophy and Literature at a university, along with men intended for other vocations, while the English clergyman (and Nonconformist minister) need only pass through a theological college where 'seminary professionalism' is the danger.

The German Territorial System did not produce a social cleavage of 'Church and Chapel'. Originally it appeared likely that the Reformed Church, as an offshoot from Lutheranism, would be forced into an inferior status of dissent. The patronage of princes prevented this; in Hesse, the Palatinate, Brandenburg, and many small principalities, the Reformed Church gained control. Free Cities like Bremen and Emden responded to the Presbyterian call, whereas rural folk, rooted

[12] *Der ev. Geistlicher in der d. Vergangenheit* (Jena, 1924).

in regional tradition, tended to be Lutheran or Catholic. The Reformed were at last recognized as an official 'Confession' by the Treaty of Westphalia (1648). Where they were in a minority, they usually won a tolerable status as a *religio licita*. This was not the case everywhere. In Lutheran Frankfurt they were not permitted to worship within the city bounds; but as Goethe remarked: 'When they drove out in fine equipages to their service in Bockenheim, it was a triumph over the citizens' party, who are entitled to go to church on foot in good weather and in bad.' Where the Reformed constituted the Established Church, their record for tolerance was much better than that of their Lutheran brethren, with whom they were usually ready to associate on neighbourly terms. The French Reformed Synod of Charenton (1631) admitted Lutherans to inter-Communion and inter-marriage.

The Reformed Church, even on the monarchical soil of Germany, has produced the fruit of freedom that may be gathered wherever true Presbyterianism is at work. One instance out of many may be cited. After the failure of the Revolution of 1848, Dr. Vilmar, a prominent Marburg divine, did his best to prove that the Church of Hesse was not really Reformed at all but 'Melanchthonian', i.e. semi-Lutheran. His object was practical, to make the Church subservient to the State. The University of Marburg had no difficulty in confirming Professor Heppe's view that the Church had been Reformed for two hundred and fifty years in spite of encroachments on its spiritual independence. Premier Hassenpflug threw all his influence on the side of Vilmar. So unpopular did the Premier become that he became popularly known as *Hessens Hass und Fluch* ('Hesse's hate and curse'). 'Even more than Metternich' he made himself 'the Mephistopheles of Reaction to the German People.'[13] Hassenpflug lived just long enough to see the restoration of the Constitution, which it had been his life's mission to destroy. But for the uncompromising position of the Reformed Church, Hesse and other principalities would have had an even harder ordeal to win and maintain civil and religious liberty.

The Union of 1817 in Prussia and other States had the effect of neutralizing the witness of the Reformed Church, which was now exposed to the danger of being absorbed in a predominantly Lutheran combination. In 1884 the *Reformierte Bund* was

[13] *Ency. Brit.*, 11th ed.

founded to safeguard the interests of the Presbyterian minority
in full freedom of pulpit, press, liturgy, and synods. Ten years
later the *Bund* reported a membership of 450,000 members
within the Prussian Union, besides 750,000 in States where they
retained separate confessional status (whether a minority in a
Lutheran principality like Hanover, or as the only Church in
an entirely Reformed principality like Lippe). The Reformed
League entered the new German Church Federation in 1922,
but retained its identity. In 1939 it numbered 2,930,000
members, in addition to the Reformed section in the Prussian
United Church. This membership is small compared to that of
the Lutherans, but contains a larger proportion of active,
interested members. The Reformed Church was well qualified
by its history to act as spearhead of the 'Confessing Church'
when Hitler laid his unhallowed hands on religion.

Till the advent of the Weimar Republic it was not easy to
change one's 'Confession'; in some principalities it involved
making a declaration before a magistrate. The way of the
dissenter was hard, if he wanted to join some other sect than the
official bodies—Catholic, Lutheran, 'United', or Reformed.
Since the Anabaptist revolt in the age of the Reformation,
there have been no separatist movements of any magnitude in
Germany. One of the few bold attempts to canalize political
and religious discontent was a movement potent in the 1840's,
led by Ulich of Magdeburg, a forceful preacher and skilful
organizer. These 'Friends of Light' (*Lichtfreunde*) aimed at
establishing democracy on a basis of Christian idealism.
They succeeded in starting a number of congregations among
radical elements, but these were largely swept away by the
failure of the Revolution in 1848.

There is nothing in German tradition comparable to the
militant Nonconformity of England, acting in alliance with a
Liberal party. Before the war of 1914 the National Council of
Evangelical Free Churches hoped to cement Anglo-German
relations by sending fraternal greetings to their German
brethren. They were blissfully ignorant of the situation.
Methodists and Baptists in the Fatherland were in no position
to influence public opinion. A liberal estimate reckoned that
the 'Free Churches of Germany' could only count on 150,000
supporters.[14] Even Hitler left them alone, except those of a
definitely pacifist tinge.

[14] T. F. A. Smith *The Soul of Germany* (London, 2nd ed., 1915), pp. 327ff.

Examining the bodies known as *Die Sekten*, we note that many of them are foreign in origin. The picturesque Mennonites, bound by their own sumptuary laws to Biblical simplicity of dress and custom, came up the Rhine Valley from Holland and northwards from Switzerland in the seventeenth century;[15] at the end of the nineteenth century they had only 18,000 members in Germany. The modern Baptist movement in the Fatherland was initiated by J. G. Oncken, a German-American, at Hamburg in 1834. The American Methodists sent Dr. Jacoby to Bremen in 1850, to shepherd German immigrants into their fold before crossing the Atlantic. Methodist and Baptist congregations were started in the larger cities, consisting almost wholly of the working class. The Irvingites ('Catholic Apostolic Church') on the other hand made some distinguished converts, including the Church historian Professor Thiersch of Marburg. Thomas Carlyle, a lawyer and schoolfellow of Edward Irving, was appointed 'Apostle to Germany' (identified with the tribe of 'Simeon'). When he presented his testimony at the Prussian Court, Frederick William the Fourth (alone among all European monarchs) welcomed visionary projects that harmonized with his own ideals of ceremony and symbolism.

Most of the sects, however, were small groups of humble folk who were needlessly harried by the authorities of the more reactionary Lutheran states, e.g. Mecklenburg. Officials like Stahl of the Prussian *Oberkirchenrath* were unduly suspicious of harmless sectaries who merely asked to be left alone. Baron Bunsen, a believer in a National Church, advocated complete toleration; Protestantism allied to persecution involved 'an inner contradiction'. If dissenters were apt to be narrow bibliolatrists they would grow broader in their outlook by being understood; persecution simply embittered them. Troeltsch undoubtedly won greater respect for *Die Sekten* when he explained to the educated public that they bore a close resemblance to the Early Christian churches—informal groups of simple believers meeting in drab halls in back streets.[16]

The failure of dissent to make its influence felt in German life

---

[15] cf. p. 62 n. *supra*.

[16] Professor W. R. Forrester, commenting on Troeltsch's *Social Teaching of the Christian Churches*: 'The Church, the Sect, and Mysticism represent the three *dimensions* of a truly Catholic Church. . . . It must not only put up with, but provide for people of a catastrophic, apocalyptic type. . . . If we do not build our synagogues inside our temples they will be built outside. . . . True Catholicity comes from cross-fertilization of the Church-type, the Sect-type, and the Mystic-type.'

through 'the Nonconformist conscience' was not entirely due to legal restrictions and disqualifications (which were harsh enough in England from 1662 till 1828). The German temperament, being reflective, has never been disposed to embody religious differences in outward form and separate organization, provided the mind was free. Freedom of thought more than compensated for lack of freedom to run the church oneself. Theology in Germany since the eighteenth century has enjoyed much wider scope than in England. Even in the *Landeskirchen* formal, read sermons have not been part of the Sunday routine as they have been so often in the English Church. Furthermore, not all the German Churches have suffered from the yoke of a uniform liturgy, considered as part of the constitution. High Lutherans have emphasized ritual, but there are many regions of Germany where the Liturgy is quite simple and contains a place for free prayer. The German Churches have lost comparatively few members through dislike of liturgy, while in England a rigid, inflexible form of service has alienated millions from the National Church.

The union of Church and State, axiomatic with Conservatives, has not been challenged by any large body of opinion apart from Social Democrats. Indeed, it has been supported by some progressive thinkers. Dr. Richard Rothe (1799-1867) was one of them. This 'very modern Christian', as Tholuck defined him, considered that 'Establishment' might be an instrument of progress as well as reaction. Stimulated theologically by Schleiermacher and politically by Hegel, he held that as civilization became more complex, men would crave spiritual as well as economic satisfaction in organic co-operation; collectivism would inevitably replace individualism. Rothe's views on the potential regeneration of the State by the Church resembled those of Dr. Arnold in England. Unfortunately, these ideals of 'integration' were afterwards destined to be perverted by Nazi propaganda; the fundamental error was due to thinking of the Church as a human institution rather than as the body of Christ.

A considerable number of Germans who feel that the State Church does not satisfy their religious needs have retained their formal connexion but followed Spener's precedent of forming an *ecclesiola in Ecclesia*. 'Fellowship groups' (*Gemeinschaften*) exist all over the Fatherland. Like the old-time Pietists they meet regularly for prayer, Bible study and mutual edification.

Intellectually, they hold tenaciously to the Verbal Inspiration of the Bible and all that this implies. They have isolated themselves from modern thought. They have either stood aside from public life or blindly supported 'the powers that be'. In some districts their attitude to the Church has resembled that of the sectarians rebuked by Isaiah: 'Stand by thyself, come not near me; for I am holier than thou' (65⁵). Elsewhere, the *Gemeinschaften* have awakened the Church to her spiritual tasks by good example and co-operation. Indeed, they have developed a quite American flair for 'activism' in organization and publicity. These *ecclesiolae*, at their best, have leavened the *Ecclesia* with wholesome results. This situation might have existed in England had the Methodists not been driven out of the Establishment.

Another good point of the German Territorial system (from a modern democratic point of view) is the fact that the dignitaries and clergy of the *Landeskirchen* did not constitute an ecclesiastical counterpart to the 'nobility and gentry'. Even in the deadest day of Lutheranism 'the fox-hunting parson' was unknown. Superintendents performed most of the functions of Anglican Bishops, but they did not live in palaces. There were no 'fat livings' in the countryside reserved for the younger sons of the squire.[17] We have noted the abuses of lay patronage in rural parishes; German landowners wanted pliable parsons at all costs and treated them just like superior peasants. During the eighteenth century pastors gradually ceased to be dependent on patrons—but they became State officials, poorly paid[18] and lacking the security of the 'parson's freehold' that means so much to the English Rector.[19] Still, it can be claimed that a modest social status did something to allay the bitterness of Socialists against the clergy of a State Church. Not even the highest dignitaries of the *Landeskirchen* commanded the princely revenue and social prestige of Anglican bishops.[20]

[17] The improved social status of the English clergy in the later eighteenth century was due to a rise in agricultural prices. In Germany the Church lost its land endowments generally, except in Württemberg.

[18] The minimum stipend in the Prussian United Church in 1908 was M.2,260 (then equivalent to £113 p.a.).

[19] Before 1918 the State appointed 56 per cent of the German Protestant clergy; 34 per cent of the benefices belonged to private patrons and municipalities; in the remaining 10 per cent of the parishes the people elected their pastor (but even this percentage compares favourably with the Church of England).

[20] For a subtle comparison of parish psychology in East Prussia and in England (late nineteenth century) see *The Pastor's Wife* (London, 1920), a novel by Countess von Arnim, an Englishwoman, author of *Elizabeth and her German Garden*.

In the third place, the Territorial System, rigid as it was in many respects, has not encouraged exclusive theories of the Christian Ministry. During the sixteenth and seventeenth centuries Lutheranism was sharply polemical. But this false 'orthodoxism' (as Pusey called it) was reduced by the impact of Pietism and the Enlightenment to the limits of a fairly charitable orthodoxy. Now and then a King of Prussia has envied England her stately hierarchy, but every attempt to borrow 'Apostolic Succession' from Canterbury has encountered such overwhelming opposition that it has had to be abandoned. Most Lutherans realize the havoc that theological and sacramental disputes have wrought in their past religious history. They are not prepared to import new controversies that would develop out of over-rigid theories of Ministry that cut right across Luther's principle of the priesthood of believers. It is unity of belief and the resulting spiritual experience that matters, not uniformity of ritual and ecclesiastical polity.

Admitting the dead hand of bureaucracy in the Territorial System, and the need for giving the laity an active share in church administration, we can hardly assert that the system itself is entirely responsible for lack of breadth and vision. We have already noted that the polity of German Lutheran Churches in the United States is practically Presbyterian, enjoying complete freedom from the State. But this representative government is consistent with the dominance of a Confessional Orthodoxy far more tyrannical than any that has existed in Germany for many years past. In spite of their freedom from the State, American Lutherans tend to be ecclesiastical isolationists: even Episcopalians are more co-operative. There is evidently a dogmatic element in Lutheranism that is exaggerated rather than lessened by self-government, and becomes more pronounced when transplanted far from the humanizing modifications of European culture.

Making generous allowance for the better side of Territorialism, it cannot be claimed as a form of Church government that makes for spiritual maturity. 'Kings shall be thy nursing fathers.'[21] Too literal an application of this Old Testament principle has produced a race of Church children who never grow up:

[21] That fundamental Puritan document *The Cambridge Platform* also affirmed that 'the Magistrates are nursing fathers and mothers to the Churches' (1648).

And always keep a hold of nurse
For fear of finding something worse.

As late as 1857 Professor Philip Schaff stated that in north Germany, where Lutheranism was strongest, 'the congregations are almost as passive, dependent, and incapable of self-government, as in the Roman Church; Luther's complaint of the want of material for elders and deacons must be repeated in this nineteenth century, after Protestantism has been in operation for more than three hundred years'.[22] If sectarianism has made the Church a walled garden, cut off from the field which Jesus said was the world, Territorialism has exceeded the order to cast the net into the deep—fish clean and unclean have been treated indiscriminately. The Lutheran Church was so secularized that even Baptism and Confirmation lost their holiness by being lowered to the status of civil obligations. Zealous princes have failed because they have imposed their reforms from above instead of encouraging them to come from the people. Frederick William the Fourth admitted that the traditional Hohenzollern policy had blighted Church-consciousness, but that did not make him alter his own ways. He was not enough of a realist to see that a 'Free Church' could only exist in a 'Free State'.

The Territorial System did not merely give the prince the title 'Head of the Church' in the English Protestant sense. He was more than 'Defender of the Faith'. He claimed the right of *summus episcopus*. Strange bishops, indeed, who never studied theology, were never ordained to the holy Ministry and never consecrated to episcopal office! Yet they claimed to regulate the religion of their subjects, to fill the highest spiritual offices, and to control the standards of doctrine and worship. The holder of the *Summepiskopat* might be a Romanist like the later kings of Saxony, a notorious adulterer like William the First of Württemberg, a professed sceptic like Frederick the Great. Inbreeding and absolute power (within the limits of a principality) produced many temperamental, eccentric despots. *Summi Episcopi* of these varied types were hardly qualified to guide the Church of Our Lord Jesus Christ. 'All power corrupts and absolute power corrupts absolutely.'

Centuries of servitude prepared the German Evangelical Churches for the fate of incorporation (*Gleichshaltung*) in the National Socialist State. Luther had to deal with 'Christian

[22] *Germany: Its Universities, Theology and Religion.*

princes'. He did not visualize a situation in which criminals would capture the State machinery and work it at high pressure for their own profit. Yet, even in Luther's time, many of the German princes were 'godly' only in documents or in the presence of courtiers. 'If they do these things in the green tree, what shall be done in the dry?' *Quis custodes custodiet?* Territorialism even in a modified form, paved the way for Totalitarianism. Churchmen who welcomed Totalitarianism as a welcome change from democratic disintegration, lived to regret their choice. 'My father chastised you with whips, but I will chastise you with scorpions.'

CHAPTER SIX

RECONSTRUCTION AND REVOLUTION, 1918–48

'THE disappearance of the princes in 1918 and the appearance of a State whose government was not legally bound to any form of Christianity "disestablished" the German Protestant Churches almost automatically.'[1] Dr. Kramm, an eminent divine who ministers to a German congregation in England, presents an admirable conspectus of ecclesiastical polity; but in the light of our present study of Church and State in historic relationship, we must respectfully differ from his interpretation of the Territorial System. He contends that the Lutheran Church, when loyal to its principles, has never given the State the right to govern the Churches, but reserves this privilege for 'the Christian prince' or 'Christian government'. He holds that the first case of a real 'State Church' in Lutheranism occurred when Reichsminister Kerrl established his dictatorship in 1935. It seems mere quibbling to limit the term 'State Church' to countries where the political régime is neutral or even antagonistic to orthodox Christianity. Even if we concede to Dr. Kramm the term 'Royal Church' to describe such denominations as the Prussian Evangelical Union, that does not exonerate the 'godly princes' from the charge of bending the Church to their own ends which was not uncommon between the Reformation and 1918. While Lutheranism has prospered in the free atmosphere of America, in Europe its pivot has been the State. It would be possible to paint an attractive picture of a 'royal Church' in Scandinavia,[2] which is also a 'people's Church',[3] the sovereign being *nutricius* rather than *summus episcopus*, but it is only in recent years that the ideal of the Church's spiritual independence has developed, parallel to the evolution of parliamentary government. In Germany, however, the tradition of government from above was too

[1] H. H. Kramm, 'Organization . . . of the German Protestant Churches (prior to 1918)', *Church Quarterly Review*, No. 275 (1944).

[2] Dr. Söderblom became Archbishop of Uppsala only because the King of Sweden had the right to choose between three candidates. He chose the best man, although he had the smallest number of votes.

[3] A somewhat different conception of Churchmanship is indicated by the titles: 'The Swedish Church', 'the Christians of Norway', 'the congregations of Denmark'.

strong to allow much scope in Church and State for the genuine growth of government from below.

Instead of prolonging the *post mortem* of Territorialism, let us pass on to the radical changes wrought by the Weimar Republic and embodied in the constitution of 1919. The separation of Church and State was welcomed by Socialists and democrats, as might be expected. 'Babylon is fallen!' This fate was accepted as inevitable by Evangelicals, but some of them found that the indifference of the public was a harder judgement than persecution. Roman Catholics who had confidently foretold the complete collapse of Protestantism, deprived of State support, were disappointed by the success of negotiations whereby *Landeskirchen* secured State support with a minimum of State control. The civil authorities continued to pay certain subsidies, the interest on Church property secularized during the Napoleonic Wars, parochial endowments, schools, and charitable foundations. Only Saxony refused to honour this obligation, but was condemned by the Supreme Court of the Reich. As the German States could not restore Church property, and self-support could not be improvised in an impoverished country, the old *modus vivendi* continued. Had the Evangelicals possessed initiative and enthusiasm, they might have built up a 'Sustentation Fund' on the analogy of the Scottish Free Church: the spirit of sacrificial voluntaryism cannot, however, be suddenly conjured into existence by a crisis—it must grow out of a conviction that 'it is more blessed to give than to receive'.

The United Evangelical Church of Prussia was the largest Protestant Church in the world with twenty million members. A modest weekly freewill offering, even allowing for a large number of defaulters, would have gone far to reconstruct Church finances on a healthy New Testament basis, but the majority of members were nominal—a vast constituency who wanted pastoral care only for baptism, marriages, and funerals.[4] All persons registered as Protestants had to pay a church tax, unless they declared before a magistrate that they renounced the Church. The Revolution of 1918 accounted for a marked increase in the number of persons contracting out of the Church, more noticeable in northern and central Germany than in the

4 *World Dominion* mentions a rural parish with over 20,000 Protestants, only 400 being regular attenders at Church; for a Berlin Church with 30,000 Evangelical parishioners the figure was 600 (World War II, *Survey*, No. 6, p. 16).

south and west; in a few years, however, the breakaway lost impetus.[5]

The Roman Catholic Church was in a strategic position to bargain with the State authorities, owing to her political party, the Centre, holding the balance between the Left and Right; Protestants on the other hand, were mainly associated with discredited Conservatives. As an international body, the Church of Rome was able to profit by the rate of exchange and 'buy up the opportunity'. The financial ruin of the propertied class offered bargains to those with ready money. Many monasteries and convents, secularized for centuries, were proudly reopened. Between 1919 and 1927 over seven hundred new religious houses were founded. In 1924 alone no fewer than eighty-eight Protestant institutions were closed for want of funds. The baser Romanists were jubilant.

Was German Protestantism moribund? The reports of its death were, as Mark Twain said of himself, 'much exaggerated'. English High Churchmen like Dr. Leighton Pullan might rejoice that it was 'in a state of complete disintegration', but they were unaware that the spirit of Wichern was still alive. The machinery of the Inner Mission was now more mobile owing to the closer relations between the *Landeskirchen*.[6] A strenuous effort was being made to give reality to the new official name of *Volkskirche*. Statistics certainly disproved assertions of mass conversions to Rome.[7] The pastoral Letter of the German Catholic Bishops in 1919 admitted an average loss of 75,000 a year.[8]

Within the Evangelical Churches there was a 'Catholic revival'. In 1917, the Jubilee year of the Reformation, Pastor Löwentraut of Lausitz published an irenicon, 'One holy Catholic (*allegemeine*) Church', in which he minimized the difference between classic Lutheran doctrine and Romanist dogma (the Protestant authorities at Berlin ordered it to be suppressed). In the same year Pastor Hansen of Schleswig

---

[5] Numbers leaving the Church: 12,000 (1910), 305,000 (1920), 246,000 (1921), 111,000 (1923).

[6] By 1920 there were about 47,000 Home Mission workers in Church institutions and Youth activities; the Y.M.C.A. had 185,000 members.

[7] Comparing the columns of conversion from Protestantism to Romanism and *vice versa*, the balance was on the Protestant side, viz. 3,491 (1910), 3,432 (1921).

[8] Professor Hermelink of Marburg was the ablest Protestant apologist. His *Katholicizmus u. Protestantismus* (3rd ed., Gotha, 1926) deals with Germany in particular.

emulated Klaus Harms, who in 1817, had drawn up a new version of Luther's ninety-five theses, setting forth conservative Lutheran views. Hansen's manifesto called for a return to the Catholic Church in sackcloth and ashes. In contrast to Löwentraut, however, he drew a clear distinction between 'Catholic' and 'Roman Catholic'. He launched a 'High Church Union', which issued a periodical *Die Hochkirche*, edited latterly by Heiler.[9] This *Hochkirchliche Vereinigung* demanded the restoration of Episcopacy on the basis of Apostolic Succession, the elevation of the Eucharist as the central act of worship, and the foundation of religious brotherhoods. In 1924 the Movement split. One wing remained Catholic in the orthodox Lutheran sense, and therefore isolationist; the second sought contact with other 'Catholics' (Anglican, Roman, and Greek). The latter group issued *Una Sancta*, which took the name of *Religiöse Besinnung* after being banned by Rome.[10]

The High Church Movement did not make much headway. The fundamental Lutheran doctrine of the Priesthood of Believers blocked the sacerdotal approach. Rome demanded unconditional surrender, and not many German Evangelicals were prepared to kneel before the Archbishop of Canterbury.

The fall of monarchy in the German States in 1918 raised the question: who was to take the place of the Prince as *summus episcopus*? Evangelicals with synodical sympathies believed that, at last, Luther's ideal of an autonomous lay-controlled Church might be realized in the Fatherland; a federal structure on Presbyterian lines was indicated. Men like Martin Rade, a veteran editor of the *Christliche Welt*,[11] felt that the time had come to embody democracy in the Church as well as the State. Lutheranism must shed its conservative vesture, cease to look back like Lot's wife, and march in step with the idealists of the Weimar Republic. On the other hand, those who inherited the dominant authoritarian tradition of Lutheranism considered that a united Evangelical Church could only be formed on an

[9] Professor at Marburg. A lay convert from Romanism. See *Der Katholicizmus: seine Idee u. seine Erscheinung* (Munich, 1923).

[10] Heiler's essay in *Northern Catholicism*, ed. Williams and Harris (London, 1933).

[11] The *Christliche Welt* was founded, like the *British Weekly*, in 1886. Rade was as great a personality as Robertson Nicoll, but his policy (like the American *Christian Century*) was oriented toward 'Modernism', and 'Progress'. Rade would have said Amen to Dr. Duncan-Jones's definition of the Church of Luther as 'the Church of laymen'. The *Christliche Welt* was not suppressed by the Nazis till 1941.

episcopal basis, with the emphasis on the 'office' rather than the 'order'. How could these rival plans be dove-tailed so as to provide a German Church constitution that was workable, and acceptable to the State?

A beginning was made in the task of reconstruction by linking the *Landeskirchen* (now reduced in number from thirty-eight to twenty-two)[12] into a German Church Federation. The new body could take concerted action in matters of common concern, and present a united front to the world. Evangelical Germany would be officially represented by delegates at ecumenical conferences for 'Faith and Order', 'Life and Work', etc. If the tendency of the Weimar Republic was to strengthen the central government at the expense of obsolete 'particularism' in the constituent States, might not a genuine National Church gradually mature in the egg of the Church Federation, and one historic day emerge impressively? The *Kirchenbund*, analogous to the American 'Federal Council of Churches' was inaugurated in the hallowed *Schlosskirche* of Wittenberg on 25th May 1922.

The new Federation was to function on familiar parliamentary lines. An assembly (*Kirchentag*) was to be elected, the vote being extended to all baptized Protestants. There were to be two clergy to every lay delegate (in contrast to equal representation, e.g. in the General Assembly of the Church of Scotland). The *Kirchenbundesrat* corresponded to an Upper House, and the *Kirchenauschuss* to a Cabinet or executive committee. Churchly dreams and democratic vistas fired the imagination of ardent coteries (as in 1848), but there was no general enthusiasm for 'the Church of the Future'. The *Landeskirchen* were largely staffed by consistorial officials, who looked backward and not forward. It was the same in the ecclesiastical sphere as in politics. The Weimar régime constructed up-to-date machinery, but it was worked by 'the old guard'. .

It was obvious that 'Disestablishment' left many unsolved problems. As President Masaryk has said: 'An *absolute* separation of Church and State exists only in theory.' In Germany there were many marginal matters to be settled. The Churches

---

[12] The boundaries of regional Churches and the civil provinces do not always correspond. Thus, principalities added to Prussia since 1866 retained their own Churches, e.g. Hanover. They were not absorbed by the 'Prussian Union' denomination of 1817. Conversely, regional Churches outside Prussia, even outwith the Reich, continued as integral parts of the Prussian United Church, e.g. Posen, Upper Silesia, Dantzig. There were clearly political advantages in this policy.

were anxious to safeguard religious instruction in the schools and to prevent 'unsound' professors being appointed to the eighteen Theological Faculties in the universities. The State was willing, as a rule, to grant the guarantees that were asked, provided the Churches would appoint no General Superintendents without due consultation; this was considered essential in the interests of the Republic: pivotal persons in the hierarchy must not be inimical to the régime. All over Germany, separate Concordats were negotiated with the State, similar to those concluded by the Catholic authorities. This involved a good deal of bargaining, for Church and State could not afford to ignore one another.

Might not cohesion, prestige, and a sense of continuity be promoted if 'General Superintendents' (in States where there was only one) assumed the ancient title of Bishop? 'Since the Counter-Reformation, and through the influence of Calvinism, there is a deep distrust in the minds of many German Protestants against the word "Bishop",' says Dr. H. H. Kramm. It is not so much the authority and prestige of the office as its Catholic associations that has stirred up suspicion. Since 1920 the suggestion of restoring the title has been favourably received, on the understanding that they should be installed and not consecrated.[13] 'Bishops' were adopted in Saxony, Mecklenburg, Hanover, Schleswig-Holstein, Württemberg, and Bavaria. The Reformed element may have prevented the title being used in the Prussian United Church, the largest *Landeskirche*. Many north German Churches were High Lutheran and had no difficulty about the new nomenclature. The Lutheran Churches of the south, however, made it clear that their new Bishops must be strictly constitutional. As outposts of Protestantism in lands largely Romanist, they were on the defensive; indeed, they maintained a more active and ardent Church life than the northern *Landeskirchen;* the competition of Catholics tended to stimulate the growth of a healthy Evangelicalism able to cope with opposition.

Into a room 'swept and garnished' by the Weimar Republic came a Nazi *Reichsbischof* 'with seven unclean spirits more wicked than himself'. When Hitler assumed power in 1933 he declared that he only sought to promote 'the genuine interrelation of Church and State'. His advisers explained that the

---

[13] American Methodist Bishops enjoy power, if not pomp.

Führerprinzip was already in action, as many of the old *Landes-kirchen* now had bishops. It only remained to add a *Reichsbischof*, to act as keystone of the ecclesiastical arch. Lutherans gener-ally, and the Reformed (with reservations) saw the value of a functionary who should be a personal bond of union between them, and represent German Evangelicalism in relation to the Reich as well as to foreign Churches—why should there be no German equivalent of the Archbishop of Canterbury, or at least of the Scottish Moderator? The *Reichsbischof*, they soon dis-covered, was invested with very real powers (although the Nazis disclaimed a State Church). The 'Spiritual Ministry' that assisted him was packed with his supporters: a 'National Synod' of sixty members was elected under such pressure as to yield a 'German Christian' majority.

The new Church Constitution was inaugurated on 21st September 1933 at Wittenberg, cradle of Lutheranism, a swastika background providing a significant symbolism.[14] The trumpet gave forth no uncertain note. The first *Reichs-bischof*, '*Rei-bi*' Müller, blew his first blast by announcing: 'The political Church struggle is over, the struggle for the soul of the German people now begins.'[15]

Ludwig Müller was Primate of Prussia as well as *Reichs-bischof* (on the significant analogy of Hitler being Prussian Premier as well as German Chancellor). He lost no time in making it clear that he intended to reward the subservient and punish any who questioned his authority. An army chaplain, fifty years of age, he had the instincts of a martinet rather than the devotion of a Christian and the loyalty of a Churchman. He resented the fact that several months before, he had been set aside by the representatives of the German Churches assembled to choose a *Reichsbischof*, although he was Hitler's nominee. Instead, they selected Pastor von Bodelschwing of Bielefeld, a non-party man who had been in charge of the social work initiated by his famous father.[16] Von Bodelschwing, with characteristic humility, said he would have preferred the title of *Reichsdiakon*, as more suggestive of Christian service. But he found the Prussian Church at the mercy of Herr Jäger

---

[14] The Catholics, once their Centre Party was smashed by Hitler, struck a bargain with the Reich (Concordat of 20th July 1933). This opportunism did not guarantee any immunity from persecution.

[15] cf. *It's your Souls we Want*, by Stewart W. Herman, Pastor of the American Church, Berlin (London, 1943).

[16] See p. 219, *supra*

(well named, for he hunted all who did not do his bidding). Jäger was a Commissar who carried out the orders of Dr. Rust, Minister of Education.[17] The situation was impossible for a man of von Bodelschwing's temperament and he soon resigned, giving place to Müller, who was devoid of *Nolo episcopari* scruples.

The Nazi *Reichsbischof* had been a whole-hearted admirer of Hitler, whom he first met in 1926. Like Paul, he could declare with apostolic fervour: 'This one thing I do.' He was not formally installed till 23rd September 1934—one could not call it 'consecration' owing to the absence of all the Bishops who had held office since his appointment (save one, the Bishop of Baden). The scene was appropriate to the occasion—that soulless Baroque edifice, the pretentious *Dom* of Berlin (vintage 1891). There were the usual swastika flags and Nazi salutes. The new *Reichsbischof* recited the creed, extolled Luther, and affirmed the Confession of Faith: but this lip-service to historic Christianity bore no relation to his policy of cajoling and coercing the clergy.[18] Ludwig Müller became known as Lügen-Müller ('lying Müller').

When the appointment of a Primate was first proposed, Dr Weber, the Reformed member of the 'Spiritual Ministry', declared that he could only follow the *Reichsbischof* so far as that dignitary followed Christ. He certainly wore a conspicuous pectoral cross ('abdominal ironmongery' to Edward the Seventh). Müller's policy was so high-handed as to provoke even the mildest of Churchmen. It is not intended in these pages to tell in any detail the complex story of the Churches' struggle.[19] Certain factors, however, stand out against the background of German Protestant History.

There was nothing essentially new in the make-up of 'German Christianity', featured by the Nazis. The very expression became a catchword of noisy patriotism during the Napoleonic struggle, and was afterwards taken up by the young

[17] Dr. Otto Dibelius, General Superintendent of Kurmark, first heard of his dismissal by reading it in the papers; not even the fact that he had been the special preacher at Hitler's inauguration in Potsdam secured him immunity.

[18] Kressmann Taylor gives a stirring account of divinity students during the crisis. In Berlin the '*Rei-bi*' had few supporters among a thousand theologues; some of the professors, e.g. Lietzmann, yielded to official pressure. Karl Hoffmann, son of a cathedral pastor, organized a students' 'Underground', till spirited away by his friends to America. *Until that Day* (London, 1945) seems to exaggerate the popular support accorded to the Confessing Church.

[19] A. S. Duncan-Jones, *The Struggle for Religious Freedom in Germany* (London, 1938).

*

reformers (*Burschenschaft*), who mixed their politics with mysticism and pantheism. 'German blood and soil' came to the fore again when the *Reich* was established in 1871. A theological professor, Dr. Paul de Lagarde of Göttingen, looked for a German Imperial Church that would surmount all confessional differences, and also find room for vital elements in Teutonic paganism. This '*deutsches Christentum*' was linked up with a programme of 'expansion which cannot be accomplished without war'. It was no East Prussian Junker but Pastor Naumann, a radical apostle of the 'Social Gospel',[20] who advocated the enslavement and transportation of conquered populations, following Assyrian precedent. Pastor Naumann's proposal was a useful present to Corporal Hitler, who exploited the idea literally. Naumann's *Mittel-Europa* was a best-seller in 1915; in 1940 it was still relevant.

In the early days of Nazi power a 'German Christian group' emerged sponsored by Princes Eitel Friedrich and August Wilhelm of Prussia, inspired by Goebbels and Kube. 'A couple of divorced princes and Nazi editors were not perhaps a promising seed-plot for revival,' reflected the Bishop of Chichester, 'but they had with them a Pastor, Dr. Wieneke, and he showed how the Cross and Swastika could be combined.' Hitler thoroughly approved of the idea: 'Let them be called "German Christians", because it is the soul of the people that must be born again.'

This *Glaubensbewegung Deutsche Christen* soon found a leader— Joachim Hossenfelder of Kiel, a combatant in 1917, ordained in 1929. Hossenfelder was an adept at stimulating interest among nominal, ill-informed Protestants. Strangely enough he was most successful in Luther's land,[21] Thuringia, now highly industrialized. The 'Thuringian Church' was an artificial 'merger' of small *Landeskirchen*, which offered a fair field for radical Nazi propaganda. There Hossenfelder held forth on the need for a 'People's Church' standing for 'positive Christianity'—i.e. uncompromising hostility to Jews and godless Marxists: 'God speaks in Blood and Folk a more powerful language than he does in the idea of humanity.' Hossenfelder

---

[20] See p. 227f., *supra*.

[21] Bremen, despite its Reformed and Pietistic traditions, also capitulated to the 'German Christians'. Only four of thirty-nine congregations remained 'intact'; among fifty pastors, five were loyal to the Gospel. The Bishop's morals were even worse than his theology. Not even his Nazi friends could save him from a criminal conviction following divorce.

was more successful as a propagandist than as 'Church admin-
istrator' under Archbishop Müller. In the autumn of 1933 he
was sent to London to give a plausible interpretation of Nazi
ecclesiastical policy. 'Hossenfelder and I are inseparable,'
declared Müller on his return to Berlin; but by Christmas
Hossenfelder had resigned all his Church offices.

Like many fanatical sects, the 'German Christians' showed
cracks in their united front. They were at one in sharing
Stapel's conviction that 'Christ and Caesar belong together'.[22]
The 'right wing' selected what they wanted from the New
Testament, giving it the necessary twist. The 'left' went all the
way with Müller's deputy, Engelke: 'God has manifested
himself, not in Jesus Christ, but in Adolf Hitler.' Indeed, a
Nazi plan was outlined for the liquidation of Christianity and
the establishment of an *ersatz* State cult, symbolized by a sword
and *Mein Kampf* on every altar. In 1936 a striking scene
occurred at a Westphalian Labour Camp. A girl of seventeen,
seeing a large portrait of Hitler on the altar of the assembly
hall, publicly smashed it—'Thou shalt have no other god before
Me!' She was not punished, but next Sunday the girls were
marched to their own Churches.

The more sophisticated Nazis, realizing that the half-baked
heresies of the 'German Christians' would merely shock
Church-going conservatives, saw the advantage of exploiting
the German ecclesiastical tradition of subservience to secular
authority. They encouraged Lutheran divines to develop their
doctrine of the State as 'the supreme co-ordinator of life'.[23]
Thus, Paul Althaus[24] advanced from Gogarten's[25] approval
of the State in general as a beneficent institution to a benedic-
tion on 'the concrete reality of the *Volkstaat*', as a unique corporate expression of National Socialism. H.D. Wendland went
farther still. The authoritarian character of the new German
super-State was 'self-evident for Christian doctrine'; it was
even 'an instrument of Divine Love'.[26]

In view of the fact that a certain type of Lutheran collabor-
ated with the Nazis and enjoyed the benefits of publicity, which
was steadily being withdrawn from the more independent

[22] *Der christliche Staatsmann* (Hamburg, 1932).

[23] N. Ehrenström, *Christian Faith and the Modern State* (E.T. 1937) Chapters 7 and
8; bibliography. cf. A. Keller, *Church and State on the European Continent* (London,
1936).

[24] *Kirche u. Staat nach lutherischer Lehre* (Leipzig, 1935).

[25] *Politische Ethik* (Jena, 1932).   [26] *Die Nation vor Gott*, pp. 187, 191.

Christian groups, it is not surprising that the laity took time to understand the real issue. However, by the autumn of 1933 Church opposition to the policy of 'integration' (*Gleichshaltung*) crystallized in the *Pfarrernotbund*. This 'Clerical Emergency League' numbered three hundred pastors, who made it clear that they opposed the State only so far as it usurped the rights of the Church. Under ministerial leadership a 'Synodical Movement' began in West Germany where the Reformed were strongest. A 'Free Synod', held at Barmen in January 1934, adopted a clear-cut Confession of Faith prepared by Barth. Free Evangelical Synods were then constituted in the Rhineland and Westphalia—oases of definite Christian convictions in the midst of an arid waste, the United Church of Prussia.

In the pages of Frey's *Cross and Swastika* and Nygren's *Church Controversy in Germany* (1934) we read the thrilling story of resistance to totalitarian demands. The ideal of a 'Confessing Church' (*Bekenntnis Kirche*), founded on the impregnable rock of God's Word, gained adherents among the laity, once they realized that the more inclusive ideal of a *Volkskirche* embracing people of varied views, was being manipulated to non-Christian ends.[27] A 'Confessing Synod', drawn from various sections of the German Churches, met at Barmen in May 1934. Its successor, convened at Dahlem in October, announced that it had taken over the leadership of the *Reichskirche*, and at the end of November appointed a 'Provisional Church Administration' in view of Müller's refusal to resign. The '*Rei-bi*' was concerned at the strength of the opposition, undaunted by wholesale arrests and fines. He was confounded when the Court of Appeal in Berlin rejected his application to prohibit the title 'Provisional Church Administration' (*Vorläufige Kirchenleitung*). The Court gave a ruling that it was merely a private association;[28] moreover, a number of legally recognized Churches had accepted the leadership of Bishop Marahrens of Hanover. Müller only gained his point by setting aside the Courts of Justice where there were points at issue between the *Reichsbischof* and his critics; such disputes were to be referred to a

[27] For the Church's struggle in a rural parish, see Maarten's *Village on the Hill* (4th ed., S.C.M.).
[28] Strictly true. Translating into Anglican terms the analogy would be: the claim of the Evangelical 'Church Association' to take over the National Church on the ground that it had lost its Christian character through 'Modernist' manipulation—in which case the larger body corresponding to the 'neutral' Lutherans would be the 'Central Churchmen'!

Special Bureau (*Beschlusstelle*) set up at the Ministry of Justice. The Confessing Church was thus deprived of legal assurance.

In addition to the German Christians and the Confessing opposition there was a neutral party, predominantly orthodox Lutheran;[29] it was in a strong position in those *Landeskirchen* which were not yet integrated into the official *Reichskirche*. One by one, these regional Churches were absorbed—Saxony, Oldenburg, Schleswig-Holstein. Bishop Marahrens of Hanover refused to admit the right of the Church Senate to vote for Union, as it was dominated by German Christians. The Act of Union was signed, for all that—'in the Bishop's unavoidable absence'! As 750 out of 1,000 clergy stood by Dr. Marahrens, the Church of Hanover remained 'intact', though afterwards weakened by the Bishop's readiness to yield to Nazi pressure. Bavaria and Württemberg retained 'intact' status, but did not secure immunity from Nazi encroachments.[30] Bishop Meiser of Bavaria roused his people by a trenchant sermon that had something of Luther's spirit: 'We can do nothing against the truth, but only for the truth.' Thousands of his followers marched through the streets, singing hymns; when he was removed from office by Dr. Jäger and the secret police, the faithful actually demonstrated in front of the notorious 'Brown House' at Munich, spitting in unison and shouting '*Pfui*'! No less than twenty thousand loyal Evangelicals assembled in Nürnberg, that old Reformation stronghold in Catholic Bavaria, to welcome their bishop; released from 'house-arrest', he had come to celebrate the four-hundredth anniversary of Luther's translation of the Bible. Bishop Wurm of Württemberg, who had just been liberated, like Meiser, received enthusiastic support from a people whose convictions were confirmed by their ancestral traditions of 'enlightened Pietism'.

The bold stand of Meiser and Wurm brought allies. From distant Silesia, Bishop Zänker brought the good news that eight hundred and fifty out of his nine hundred clergy were the active allies of the Confessing Church and the Lutheran Bishops. He joined with Meiser, Wurm, and Marahrens in sending a message to the *Reichsbischof*, whose resignation was obviously

[29] Between autumn 1933 and 1936 the number of German Christian clerics had sunk from 2,500 to 2,000, while the 'Confessing' pastors had increased from 2,500 to 6,000. As there are about 20,000 Protestant clergy in Germany, it will be seen that the majority were neutral.

[30] The Roman Catholic Church was able to put up a consistent defence against the Nazis all along the line, while Protestantism was weakened by numerous gaps inviting penetration.

the only solution. Hitler, tired of the ecclesiastical conflict, was ready to let things drift awhile. Müller lost heart and gradually faded out; he became (in the Victorian phrase) 'an ornamental bishop' and eventually resigned. His resignation, however, did not lead to the appointment of Bishop Marahrens, a moderate who (at that time) would have satisfied men of varying views.

The year 1935 witnessed a decline in the Christian front. Old-fashioned Lutherans were yearning to make terms with the State on almost any conditions that were plausible (some of their leaders had 'booked a season ticket on the line of least resistance'). Not even the black record of totalitarianism could erase their hereditary respect for the divinely-ordered authority of the State. The Synod of Augsburg (July 1935) revealed a line of cleavage. A Lutheran Congress was called later in the month and appointed an executive committee. This *Lutherisches Rat* was willing to go some way with the Confessing Church, but reserved the right to make its own arrangements with the State as expediency indicated.

A fresh phase of the conflict opened with the invention of a new instrument of coercion, a *Reich* Ministry for Church Affairs (19th July 1935). Herr Kerrl, a Nazi of ten years standing and formerly an obscure official in the law courts at Kiel, was appointed. This *Reichskirchlichenregiment* was definitely a *Reichkerrlichenregiment*. It was established by a decree signed by Hitler whereby Kerrl was given full authority to settle the Church crisis 'in complete freedom and peace'. The method of coercion was a series of State-appointed Church Committees; they did the dirty work, while respectable ecclesiastics like Superintendent Zöllner acted as figureheads to give an appearance of legality. It was not long before Kerrl showed his hand. He used a weapon that, strangely enough, had not yet been consistently applied—financial pressure. He began by confiscating the trustees funds of the Confessing Church on 28th November. It was not so easy to cut off supplies at source, as regards the regular *Landeskirchen*.[31] Hitler boasted of his liberality in continuing to pay an annual sum of RM. 20,000,000; this

---

[31] The income of the *Reichskirche* was derived as follows:

Annual interest on past loans to the State .	RM.20,000,000
Church tax on members	RM.200,000,000
Free gifts from Church people . . .	RM.25,000,000
State grant	RM.50,000,000
Total—RM.295,000,000	

(*World Dominion*, Wartime Survey, No. 6)

was the interest due by the State to the Church on account of accumulated loans; it had been met by the Weimar Republic during the deflation period. Fully ten thousand of the older parishes still possessed endowments derived from Church lands, in addition to the sources in income already noted in tabulated form. Salaries and pensions continued to be paid even to pastors who refused to take the oath prescribed by the State. Kerrl tightened the screw as far as possible, and forced a good many pastors to conform, by the threat of reducing their families to indigence. So miscellaneous, however, were the Church's sources of income that coercive measures could not be applied wholesale; a certain amount of revenue trickled through local sources that were sometimes friendly to the Church.

The beginning of 1936 saw the Confessing Church once more on the defensive; relations with the Lutheran Bishops of the regional Churches still 'intact' were now less close. Censorship had been imposed on books and even typed communications. The right of public meeting was severely restricted, while the 'German Christians' were given every facility for propaganda. For instance, as early as 26th April 1935 no less than fifteen thousand people (mostly young) assembled at the *Sportpalast*, Berlin (an auditorium which neither Catholics nor orthodox Protestants were allowed to use). They were harangued by Count Reventlow and Professor Hauer, who waxed eloquent on such congenial themes as 'The Voice of the Divine in the Blood', 'The Vitality of Pure Race', and 'The Sacred Rhythm of German Nationality'; it was made clear that 'the God whom we worship would not exist if it were not for our soul and blood'. Early in 1936 Heinz Weidemann, Bishop of Bremen since 1934, 'cashed in' on anti-Semitic feeling by demanding a revision of the Bible palatable to National Socialism. Good Nazis could no longer tolerate Moses or 'Rabbi Paul'; Jesus was a 'Galilean', well represented by John as engaged in long arguments with the Jews. Anti-Semitic feeling broke out against certain of the clergy. Dr. Jacobi needed a guard of fifty Confessing Pastors when he preached to four thousand supporters in the Kaiser Wilhelm Memorial Church, Berlin (16th February). A large number of German Evangelicals denounced the 'German Christians' as heretics, but only a minority were unequivocal in declaring the persecution of the Jews un-Christian; fewer still protested against the 'Aryan clause' excluding Jewish Christians from the Church.

Step by step German Youth was handed over to Hitler. The *Evangelische Jugend Deutschlands*, which had a membership of 700,000, had been confined to 'spiritual' activities as early as July 1933, and was linked to the Hitler Youth by 21st December of the same year. The new heathenism left little time for Christian instruction on Sunday, while it gained an effective hold on the day-school.[32] In the autumn of 1936 all Youth organizations were finally merged with the Hitler Youth. Early in 1937 the theological college, established by the Confessing Church at Elberfeld, was closed by the authorities. The new religious nurture was defined by Himmler: 'To train and lead Germans from the cradle to the grave and prepare them for the holy fire which burns for Germany.'

It was now the declared policy of the Nazi State to eradicate from the Church all leaders and potential leaders. 'The Church Ministry remains in my hands,' said Kerrl to the assembled heads of the official *Reichskirche* (13th February 1937). . . . 'I will recognize no authority except those authorized by myself.' Karl Barth was dismissed from his Chair at Bonn, and had to continue his ministry of counsel and inspiration from Basel in his native Switzerland, much as Calvin encouraged the persecuted remnant from his international watch-tower at Geneva.[33]

The *Reichsminister* found it 'intolerable' that Pastor Niemöller should be allowed to declare from the pulpit: 'Our Führer is the golden calf around which the people dance.' The fact that the prophet of Dahlem had served as a U-Boat Commander in the First World War and was definitely a Nazi in politics only secured him immunity for a time. From his influential pulpit in a fashionable Berlin suburb he proclaimed the Church's right to insist on pure doctrine and the integrity of its constitution.[34] On 27th June 1937 he preached with great power and fervour on the relevance of Gamaliel's plea for fairness. A few days later he was arrested and kept in prison without trial. On 7th February 1938 he was brought before a Special Court at the Moabit prison—one of the great trials of history.[35] He was charged with misuse of the pulpit, under a

[32] Even before 1933 Lutheran Sunday-schools existed in twelve thousand parishes, of which only one third had adopted modern methods of graded teaching. Attendance was decreasing, and soon after the Nazi Revolution fell to about one tenth of the Protestant children.
[33] Barth, *Trouble and Promise in the Struggle of the Church in Germany* (Oxford, 1938).
[34] See his autobiography, *From U-Boat to Pulpit* (London, 1939).
[35] See Duncan-Jones, op. cit., Chapter 6; Appendix A, Dr. Niemöller's Sermon.

law dating from Bismarck's *Kulturkampf* revived by the Nazis. His imprisonment without trial was taken into account and the verdict amounted to a virtual acquittal. Niemöller stepped out of the dock a free man—only to be seized by the secret police and sent to a concentration camp 'by the direct order of Hitler'. No attention was paid to a telegram from the Archbishops of Canterbury, Uppsala, Thyateira, etc. No miscarriage of justice since the Dreyfus case aroused such indignation. Niemöller's treatment was not exceptional. One thousand three hundred pastors were arrested between 1934 and 1938, about one fifteenth of the total number.

The outbreak of war in 1939 made the position of the Confessing Church much more difficult. It was the first war that the German State Religion has not blessed. No chaplains were appointed for the *Luftwaffe* and the *Waffen S.S.* By 1944 one thousand divinity students and over six thousand clergy were mobilized. Candidates of the 'Confessing Church' were excluded from the four theological faculties that were still functioning in the universities; they had no hope of being appointed to parishes. The Ministry of Church Affairs worked out a rigorous system of financial control for the raising and spending of ecclesiastical funds. In Württemberg the State refused to collect Church taxes. Throughout Germany, no coal was usually available for heating places of worship. No more religious papers, Bibles, and hymnaries could be printed.[36] Thousands of pastors were victimized, but the witness of faith survived, as Dr. Rieger has related in his *Silent Church*. Like the persecuted Christians of remote centuries, the faithful worshipped in houses, barns, and forests.

In June 1941 Marahrens and certain other 'Evangelical' Bishops sent a message to Hitler's headquarters: 'May Almighty God assist you . . . so that all Europe may expect a New Order under your guidance!'[37] Even in the Confessing Church there was a widespread tendency to accept Nazi ideals and methods, provided the Church itself were left alone. However, a staunch

---

[36] See Herman, op. cit., Part III, 'The Impact of War'; Adolf Keller, *Christian Europe Today* (London, 1942).

[37] In 1834 Heine predicted: 'Christianity . . . has occasionally calmed the brutal German lust for battle, but it cannot destroy that savage joy. And when once that restraining talisman, the Cross, is broken . . . the old stone gods will rise from unremembered ruins and Thor will leap to life at last and bring down his gigantic hammer on the Gothic cathedrals. . . . This is no mere fantasy. . . . The thought always precedes the act as the lightning the thunder. . . . Never doubt it; the hour will come.'

remnant survived, the 'seven thousand who have not bowed the knee unto Baal'. After the Allies had overrun Germany in the spring of 1945 Bishop Wurm of Württemberg summoned a Church Assembly, which met at Treysa in the British zone at the end of August. Of the eighty-eight delegates present, about half had suffered prison for conscience' sake. Among the leaders were Dr. Dibelius, Bishop Meiser of Bavaria, Herr Lilje, the Student Christian Movement leader from Hanover, and Karl Barth. 'We should all go on our knees and thank God that the war ended in the way it did. Had there been a German victory, we should none of us have been here today. There would have been no Christianity in Germany.'

An executive council of twelve pastors and laymen was appointed with Wurm as president, and Niemöller as vice-president. Their task was indeed formidable and prospects grim; but a handclasp from without broke down their sense of isolation. To the first meeting of this council at Stuttgart, on 18th October, came a deputation from the World Council of Churches, which included representatives from Britain, America, France, Holland, and Norway. After a dramatic reading of Jeremiah 14[19ff.], by Niemöller, the Germans made the following declaration: 'We are all the more grateful for this visit. . . . With great pain do we say: Through us had endless suffering been brought to many peoples and countries. What we have often borne witness to before our congregations, that we declare in the name of the whole Church.' After the Germans had been invited to join the World Council of Churches (which they did), Pastor Maury of France replied: 'We cannot take away your misery; but we can see that Germany has a proper place in a new beginning for the world.'

In the allied countries there was some doubt whether this confession of guilt on the part of the German Church leaders held good of the rank and file; they disowned Hitler, now that he had failed—did they also disown the aggressive nationalism of Bismarck? Critics in the British Press pointed out that even Niemöller had welcomed the advent of Hitler from the pulpit in 1933, as 'the fulfilment of cherished hopes'.[38] The Bishop of Chichester and Dr. Nathaniel Micklem explained that Niemöller's background must be understood; he was brought up as a Lutheran of the traditional type, drilled to leave politics to the *Obrigkeit*, 'the powers that be'. Later, Niemöller himself pub-

[38] cf. correspondence in *The Spectator* (June 1945).

licly confessed that he had learnt his error by sad experience. He now understood that the Church should be 'the conscience of the State' and not its subservient tool; but, he added, the Germans would not find this an easy lesson—'We shall have to wait until the old politicians die.' Meanwhile, the Church's task was 'to enter the schools, rebuild youth organizations, influence the universities . . . and accept broad responsibilities in political and economic life.'

It still remains to be seen whether the large 'neutral block' of Lutherans will voluntarily purge themselves from the subservient tradition of the past; men like Bishop Marahrens compromised themselves hopelessly with National Socialism. While negotiations for the reconstitution of the German Evangelical Church were going on in 1947, this section demanded a considerable degree of autonomy, which Niemöller and other leaders considered retrograde.[39] The Confessing Church made a gesture of conciliation by voluntary surrender of their administration, improvised during the anti-Nazi struggle, retaining only the right to advance the spiritual principles of the Barmen Declaration. The threat to war-forged unity was averted by a *via media* between a loose confederation and complete fusion. Concessions had to be made to meet the opinions of a tenacious though not numerically large Lutheran group, mostly in Bavaria, who, prevented from attaining their ideal of an all-Lutheran *Reichskirche*, did their best to make the connexion with the Reformed as tenuous as possible, stopping short of inter-communion. These 'spikes' [reminiscent of Anglo-Catholics] must be treated with kindness as weaker brethren, said Bishop Wurm, but on any other grounds would be resisted.

In 1848, 'Germany's shipwreck year', the Frankfurt Parliament announced the formation of a *Reichskirche*.[40] During the summer of 1948 the leaders of German Protestantism assembled at historic Eisenach (in the 'Russian zone'). They accepted the decisions of the Barmen Synod confirming the Church's spiritual independence and loyalty to Christian fundamentals. They constituted the various groups of Evangelicals into a *Bund* (league or federation). Three 'Confessions'

---

[39] Uncompromising Lutheranism has been forcibly expressed by Hans Sasse's *Was heisst Lütherisch?* (2nd ed., Munich, 1936). He is dead against any union of Lutheran and Reformed though willing to contemplate a purely external alliance of the two Churches. His reply should be compared to the parallel answer of Niessel to *Was heisst reformiert?*

[40] See p. 209f., *supra*.

(Lutheran, Reformed, and 'United Evangelical') were recognized as autonomous units sharing a wider fellowship. That did not imply inter-communion unless it was genuinely desired by the regional Churches. It was agreed, however, that visitors from another communion should be welcomed at the Lord's table, 'not as a matter of right, but by pastoral goodwill'. It remains to be seen whether the new *Bund* will overcome the difficulties that beset the Prussian United Church during the nineteenth century. Fellowship between the Reformed and the vital Lutherans, forged by the struggle against the Nazi State is a bond likely to last, and may hold the balance against High-and-dry Lutheran attempts at loosening the federation unduly. It would appear, however, that the *'evangelische Kirche in Deutschland'* (known as the E.K.I.D.) contains too many 'erratic blocks' to facilitate fusion. It remains to be seen whether this new union will fulfil its destiny; at all events Unity is now sought from a spiritual rather than a semi-political motive. There is more hope for the *Reichskirche* of 1948 than for that of 1848.

How far will the reorganized body of Evangelicals constitute a National Church in the main stream of German life? It is remarkable that over ninety per cent. of the German people retain formal Church membership in spite of the anti-Christian bias of the Third *Reich*. Only one and a half per cent of the population openly deny that they have any religion. In 1939 it became possible to register as *Gottgläubig*, without adhering to any Confession; but only three and a half per cent took advantage of this loophole of leaving the Church without stigma, free from any obligation to pay taxes toward its support —and yet able to claim the name of 'God-believer'! In 1941 Count Keyserling predicted that 'the majority of Germans . . . will in the final analysis always profess some kind of theology because they cannot tolerate not receiving definite, precise, and conclusive answers to all questions'.

Does this amorphous mass of nominal adherents not offer a unique field for conversion? Critics there are who consider that the past of German Protestantism damns its future; 'history, unlike chemical action, is not a reversible process'. Whatever may be said of this *dictum* on the human side, the supernatural fact of Conversion cannot be denied. Churches, like individuals, can be born again.[41] They can transcend dogmatism,

41 Stewart Herman, *The Rebirth of the German Church* (S.C.M., 1946)

pietism, and rationalism by the grace of God. Protestant and Catholics, taught by Nazi persecutors to form a Christian front, can face together the common foes of materialism, communism, and despair. Professor Einstein, writing as an exile, testified:

> Being a lover of freedom, when the [Nazi] revolution came, I looked to the universities to defend it, knowing that they had always boasted of their devotion to the cause of truth; but no, the universities were immediately silenced. Then I looked to the great Editors of the newspapers, whose flaming editorials in days gone by had proclaimed their love of freedom; but they, like the universities, were silenced in a few short weeks. . . .
>
> Only the Church stood squarely across the path of Hitler's campaign for suppressing the truth. I never had any special interest in the Church before, but now I feel a great affection and admiration for it because the Church alone has had the courage and persistence to stand for intellectual and moral freedom. I am forced to confess that what I once despised I now praise unreservedly.[42]

Making full allowance for the bleak prospects of Germany, the poisoning of the national mind by the Nazis, and the disillusionment of the people with ideals and loyalties, we may claim that the Confessing Church[43] has given a fresh start to Evangelical Christianity in the land of Luther. Wordsworth's noble lines may be appropriately applied to this *demonstratio evangelica:*

> Thou hast left behind . . .
> Powers that will work for thee.
> . . . Thou hast great allies;
> Thy friends are exultations, agonies,
> And love, and man's unconquerable mind.

[42] *New York Times* (31st December 1940).
[43] See Wilhelm Niemöller's *Kampf u. Zeugnis der Bekennenden Kirche* (1949). Dedicated 'To my dear brother Martin'. An adequate moving account of the battle and witness of the Confessing Church. No E.T. as yet.

INDEX